Cases and Materials
in Land Law

Cases and Materials
in Land Law

Second edition

Hilary Lim LLB, MA, PhD

Kate Green LLB, PhD

PITMAN PUBLISHING
128 Long Acre, London WC2E 9AN

A Division of Pearson Professional Limited

First published in Great Britain 1992
Second edition 1995

© Pearson Professional Limited 1995

ISBN 0 273 61425 8

British Library Cataloguing in Publication Data
A CIP catalogue record for this book is available from the British Library

10 9 8 7 6 5 4 3 2 1

Typeset by Land and Unwin (Data Sciences) Ltd
Printed and bound in Great Britain by Bell & Bain, Glasgow

The Publishers' policy is to use paper manufactured from sustainable forests.

'The most beautiful thing to own in the world is land.'
'Why?'
'So you can walk on it, idiot!'

(Gerard Dépardieu, 1991)

Contents

Preface

One of our aims in compiling these cases and materials on land law was to provide, within a book of convenient size, the key legal sources for land law students. No one will need a shopping trolley to transport this case book. In compiling the second edition we have sought to limit additions. While there has been a large number of case law developments, particularly arising out of the recession, parliamentary legislation has been scant. Our choice of statutes and cases continues to be determined by what we find most illuminating, thought-provoking or simply entertaining.

A further aim is to stimulate students' thinking around the subject, to question assumptions about the law and its workings. We seek to challenge the 'conceptual formalism' of the orthodox land law course and to expand its texts. The second edition further widens the horizon of the subject.

Therefore, we have drawn upon a variety of materials, such as Law Commission reports, other jurisdictions, novels and oral history. These are approached critically, and the reader should be able to place the English land law system as one amongst many. This variety serves to unsettle the standard framework of land law, with its fixed questions and 'rational order'.

Excluded from this book are future interests and perpetuities, as well as detail of the law concerning strict settlements. The law of leases is inevitably skeletal, as on most land law courses. In this edition coverage of the lease/licence debate has been reduced markedly owing to the effect of the Housing Act 1988.

These materials are organised and divided along familiar lines. However, active reading is encouraged through the footnotes, questions, cross-referencing, and further reading suggestions.

This arrangement will, we hope, maximise the potential for diverse readings of the extracts. Thus, it should serve the reader who simply wishes to explore a particular area as well as provide students with an arresting view of land law, involving them as participants in, rather than passive receptacles of, our conversation with the land.

We have endeavoured to state the law as it stood on 2 October 1994.

Hilary Lim
Kate Green
October 1994

Acknowledgements

We would like to express our thanks to the following copyright owners who willingly gave permission for the publishing of extracts:

Blackwell Publishers
Cambridge University Press
Canada Law Books Inc.
Central Statistical Office
Cornell University
Croom Helm
Fred B. Rothman & Co.
Harper Collins Publishers
Her Majesty's Stationery Office
The Incorporated Council of Law Reporting for England & Wales
Jonathan Cape
Jordan & Sons Ltd
The Law Journal
The Law Society of England and Wales
Legal Action Group
Methuen & Co.
The Mitchie Company
Oxford University Press
Robert Hale Ltd
Routledge
Sheenagh Pugh
University of New South Wales
Unwin Hyman
The Yale Law Journal Co.

Table of Cases

Table of Statutes

1 Property and possession

INTRODUCTION

Land law is a part of a wider law 'of property'. It is therefore important to be aware of the debates around the traditional western ('liberal') concept of property. Of course, a selection of important writings on property could fill a dozen books; those extracted here illustrate various starting points as the beginning of a broader understanding.

MEANINGS AND FUNCTIONS OF PROPERTY

Explanations of the meaning of property inevitably become entangled with the author's own view of the function of, and justification for, property. The writers extracted here have in common that they emerge directly from the liberal tradition (see pp. 8–11), which is linked to a particular conception of the 'nature of man'.[1]

Whatever ideology is adopted in a given society, certain issues, it would seem, have to be resolved:

R.A. Epstein 'Possession as the Root of Title' 13 *Georgia L Rev* (1979) 1221

A beautiful sea shell is washed ashore after a storm. A man picks it up and puts it in his pocket. A second man comes along and takes it away from him by force. The first man sues to recover the shell, and is met with the argument that he never owned it at all. How does the legal system respond to this claim. How should it respond?

The same man finds the same shell, only now the state, through its public processes, comes along and insists that the shell belongs to the common fund. It offers the man nothing for it, claiming that the shell was found by luck and

---

1 Often women are excluded – see p. 16 below and C. Pateman *The Sexual Contract*, Polity Press, 1988.

coincidence and not by planned and systematic labor. How does the legal system respond to this claim? How should it respond?

The questions just put can recur in a thousand different forms in any organized legal system. The system itself presupposes that there are rights over given things that are vested in certain individuals within that system. And the system knows full well that these property rights in things are defined not against the thing, but over the thing and against the rest of the world; that property rights normally entail (roughly) exclusive possession and use of one thing in question and the right to transfer it voluntarily to another. The exact contours of these rights, however important to basic theory, are not central to the main concern here. The more insistent question is: What principles decide *which* individuals have ownership rights (whatever they precisely entail) over *what* things?[2]

The question must be distinguished from the related issue which simply asks what are the social or public functions of the institution of ownership. It could be decided that ownership is necessary to create effective incentives for the development and improvement of property or to reduce or eliminate conflicts between private persons. Yet even if these points are true, such broad justifications for ownership do not solve the more particular question of how given bits of property are matched with given individuals.

Property can thus be said to mean 'exclusive possession' and 'transferability'.

Felix Cohen wrote his famous 'Dialogue' in the 1950s; it is an extended, imaginary seminar in the 'Socratic form' used by American law professors, in which various students are tested to destruction. Here, F is forced to consider his assumptions about the nature of property:

F.S. Cohen 'Dialogue on Private Property' IX *Rutgers L Rev* 2 (1954) 357

The Case of the Montana Mule

C. Mr F., there's a big cottonwood tree at the southeast corner of Wright Hagerty's ranch, about 30 miles north of Browning, Montana, and under that tree this morning a mule was born. Who owns the mule?

F. I don't know.

C. Do you own the mule?

F. No.

C. How do you know you don't own the mule? You just said you didn't know who owns the mule. Might it not be you?

F. Well, I suppose that it is possible that I might own a mule I never saw, but I don't think I do.

C. You don't plan to declare this mule on your personal property tax returns?

F. No.

C. Why not, if you really don't know whether you own it? Or do you know?

F. Well, I never had any relation to any mules in Montana.

---

2 For recent cases which raise this question, see Chapters 9, pp. 256–71, and 10, pp. 289–307.

C. Suppose you did have a relation to this mule. Suppose it turns out this mule's father was your jackass. Would that make you the owner of the mule?

F. I don't think it would.

C. Suppose you owned the land on which the mule was born. Would that make you the owner of the mule?

F. No.

C. Suppose you owned a piece of unfenced prairie in Montana and the mule's mother during her pregnancy ate some of your grass. Would that make you the owner of the mule?

F. No, I don't think it would.

C. Well, then you seem to know more about the ownership of this Montana mule than you admitted a few moments ago. Now tell us who really owns the mule.

F. I suppose the owner of the mare owns the mule.

C. Exactly. But tell us how you came to that conclusion.

F. Well, I think that is the law of Montana.

C. Yes, and of all other states and countries, as far as I know. For example, the Laws of Manu, which are supposed to be the oldest legal system in the world, declare:

> 50. Should a bull beget a hundred calves on cows not owned by his master, those calves belong solely to the proprietors of the cows; and the strength of the bull was wasted.

Now, how does it happen do you suppose, that the law of Montana in the twentieth century corresponds to the law of India of 4000 years ago?...

F. Well, it does seem to be in accordance with the laws of nature that the progeny of the mother should belong to the owner of the mother.

C. Wouldn't it be just as much in accordance with the laws of nature to say that the progeny of the father belong to the owner of the father?

F. I suppose that might be so, as a matter of simple biology, but as a practical matter it might be pretty hard to determine just which jackass was the mule's father.

C. Then, as a practical matter we are dealing with something more than biology. We are dealing with the human need for certainty in property distribution...

Then whether we call our rule of property in livestock an example of natural law or not, its naturalness has some relation to the social need for certainty, which seems to exist in 48 different states and 48 different centuries. Do you think that property law reflects some such human demand for certainty?

F. I think it does in the cases we have been discussing.

C. Couldn't we have some other equally certain and definite rule, say that the mule belongs to the owner of the land where it was born?

F. It might be a hard thing to do to locate the mule's birthplace, but the young mule will show us its own mother when it's hungry.

C. Suppose we decided that the mule should belong to the first roper. Wouldn't that be a simple and definite rule?

F. Yes, but it wouldn't be fair to the owner of the mare who was responsible for its care during pregnancy if a perfect stranger could come along and pick up the offspring.

C. Now, you are assuming that something more than certainty is involved in rules of property law, and that somehow such rules have something to do with ideas of fairness, and you could make out a good case for that proposition in this case. But suppose you are trying to explain this to a cowboy who has just roped this mule and doesn't see the fairness of this rule that makes it the property of the mare owner. Are there any more objective standards that you could point to in support of this rule? What would be the economic consequences of a rule that made the mule the property of the first roper instead of the mare's owner?

F. I think that livestock owners wouldn't be so likely to breed their mares or cows if anybody else could come along and take title to the offspring.

C. But, tell me, is there any reason to suppose that the owner of the mare will be able to raise the mule more economically than, say, the first roper or the owner of the ground on which the mule was born?

F. Well, so long as the mule depends upon its mother's milk, it will be less expensive to raise it if the owner of the mother owns the offspring. And presumably the owner of the mother has physical control over his animals, and no extra effort is involved in his controlling the offspring as long as they are dependent upon their mother.

C. So, in effect, the rule we are talking about takes advantage of the natural dependency of the offspring on the mother animal. By enlisting the force of habit or inertia, this rule economises on the human efforts that might otherwise be expended in establishing control over the new animal. The owner of the mare has achieved the object of all military strategy – he has gotten there 'fustest with the mostest'. We don't need to pay a troop of Texas Rangers to seize the mule and deliver it to the owner of the jackass father who may be many miles away. But why should we have a simple definite rule in all these cases? Wouldn't it be better to have a more flexible standard so that we might consider in each case what the owner of the mare contributed, what the owner of the jackass contributed, what was contributed by the grass owner who paid for the mare's dinners, and then on the basis of all the facts we might reach a result that would do justice to all the circumstances of the individual case?

F. The trouble with that is that the expense of holding such investigations might exceed the value of the mule.

C. And would it be easier or harder to borrow from the bank to run a livestock business if the owner of a mare or a cow didn't know in advance that it would own the offspring?

F. If I were a banker I'd certainly hesitate to make a livestock loan to a herd owner without such a simple definite rule.

C. Could we sum up this situation, then, by saying that this particular rule of property law that the owner of the mare owns the offspring has appealed to many different societies across hundreds of generations because this rule contributes to the economy by attaching a reward to planned production; is simple, certain and economical to administer; fits in with existing human and animal habits and forces; and appeals to the sense of fairness of human beings in many places and generations?

F. I think that summarises the relevant factors.

C. And would you expect that similar social considerations might lead to the development of other rules of property law, and that where these various considerations of productivity, certainty, enforceability, and fairness point in divergent directions instead of converging on a single solution, we might find more controversial problems of private ownership?

    F. That would seem to be a reasonable reference...

    C. Suppose we say, that is property to which the following label can be attached:

To the world
Keep off X unless you have my permission, which I may grant or withhold,
Signed: Private Citizen
Endorsed: The State

Felix Cohen focuses on property as a means of satisfying what he describes as the human need for rewards for useful work, for simplicity and certainty, and for 'fairness'. To this may be added Smith's stress on the need for security in the ownership of scarce resources:

J.C. Smith, 'The Concept of Native Title' *Univ of Tor L Jo* 24 (1974) 1

Property is a social institution whereby people regulate the acquisition and use of the resources of our environment according to a system of rules. If we lived in an environment where there was an inexhaustible supply of resources which could be appropriated and used without labour, there would be absolutely no need for any society to have an institution of property. If everyone could have all the food, clothing, shelter, etc. that he wished without in any way affecting the supply available to others, and without effort on anyone's part, there would be no need for regulating the acquisition of resources, nor any need even to have a concept such as 'theft'. Where, for instance, land has been in abundance, and the use of the land has not required the expending of labour, land will generally be considered to be open to inclusive enjoyment. Thus, nomadic tribes in an area of abundant land used only for grazing purposes generally don't recognise property in land, nor have such a concept as 'trespass'. Scarcity of labour can thus be said to be the foundation of the institution of property.[3]

Every society, without exception, has institutions of property because no society exists in an environment where there are not at least some resources which are scarce, and some which require labour to appropriate or be usable. Man is, by the structure of his brain, a rule-making animal, and it is in the best long-term interests of all to regulate the acquisition of resources by rules, and to give community protection to the fruits of one's labour, rather than to let a man's relation to the resources of his environment be determined solely in terms of naked power.[4]

In order to have an institution of property, there must, at least, be the following:

(1) a community,
(2) a quantity of limited or scarce resources,

---

3 What assumptions are being made here about the nature of 'property'? Compare Chapter 2, pp. 27–8.
4 For 'property and power', see p. 15 below.

(3) a set of rules regulating the acquisition of rights to, and use of, those resources. This set of rules will be made up of at least the following sub-sets –
    (A) a set of rules which provides the manner in which the property relation is created,
    (B) a set of rules which provides for the transfer of this relation from one member of the community to another,
    (C) a set of rules which determines how and when the property relation is terminated so that the resources are open to acquisition by others,
(4) a set of possessive pronouns such as 'mine', 'yours', 'his', 'hers', 'theirs', etc. whereby this relation can be expressed,
(5) a set of rules protecting the property relation by, for instance, providing sanctions when it is wrongfully interfered with.[5]

There are many points in the above extract with which it is possible to argue. Smith's assumptions about human nature and human society are particularly closely linked with ideas first widely published in seventeenth-century England, in the time of Hobbes and Locke (below, p. 8) when the liberal concept of property developed alongside modern capitalist methods of production. Our ideas of property are inextricably linked with our understanding of the economic and social system.

G. Trasler 'The Psychology of Ownership and Possessiveness' 32 in P. Hollowell (ed.) *Property and Social Relations* (Heinemann: 1982)

This brief and incomplete review has illustrated something of the complexity of the relations between men and women and their possessions, and in doing so it has pointed to the daunting difficulties of constructing an adequate psychology of ownership and possessiveness. We can, however, essay one conclusion with some confidence: it is not possible to explain the vast structure of institutions to which we assign the name 'property' as the expression, the means of satisfaction, of man's desire for physical objects . Even the earliest possessions, as we have seen, have meanings for the individual which are social, that have to do with his relationships with others and his standing among his fellows. It would be redundant here to try to enumerate the many kinds of social meanings with which possessions are invested; we have already considered the ways in which children and adults depend upon their possessions for security (in several senses of the term), for reassurance, as a means of expressing love and acknowledging loveworthiness, and as the means of exerting power over others and defending oneself against intrusions upon autonomy. There is much more to be said about the significance of personal property in contemporary society – and indeed a great deal has been written, with characteristic succinctness and clarity, by T.H. Marshall [*Brit Jo of Medical Psychology* 15, 1935, especially p. 80]. The child clutching his 'cuddly', the young business executive purchasing his 'customised' motor car, the

---

5 See Chapter 2, pp. 51–4, regarding acquisition, Chapter 7 regarding use, and Chapter 3, pp. 60–75, regarding abandonment.

Soviet citizen protecting the property of his collective, the warrior engaged in the strange destructive world of the potlatch,[6] and even the adolescent housebreaker, are performing actions which can only be described in terms which reflect the particular meanings which possessions have in the societies of which they are members...

V.G. Kiernan 'Private Property in History' 361 in J. Goody, J. Thirsk and E.P. Thompson *Family and Inheritance* (C.U.P.: 1976)

Much of the history of property can be sought for in the fossil record of language. The word itself is from the Latin *proprius*, probably derived from *pro privo*, private or personal, which gave thirteenth century English its word 'proper'. This evolved towards its modern self-complacent meaning – whatever is ours must be *right* – and the idea of 'propriety'; also towards the word 'property', meaning ownership, usually private, and from the fifteenth century, but more generally from the seventeenth, things owned. 'Wealth' is related to 'well', and in the thirteenth century meant both riches and welfare. About the same time the plural *goods* came into circulation, a parallel to the Latin *bona*, French *biens*, and a Norse equivalent: the 'goodness' of things consists in their belonging to men. On the other hand, an Elizabethan 'miser' might be either an avaricious person, or as in Latin a pitiful wretch. It is good to possess, but not to possess too many goods, or too selfishly...

Old property

---

6 A tribal feast at which an aspirant chief gives presents (Native Americans of the Pacific coast).

JUSTIFICATIONS OF, AND CHALLENGES TO, THE LIBERAL CONCEPT OF PROPERTY[7]

As already mentioned, our assumptions about the nature of property originate largely in the seventeenth century. John Locke's writing is often taken as the foundation for this. He wrote a reply to the claim of the divine right of kings, and suggested how individual rights of property might come into being, and, therefore, why the king should not interfere with them. When he wrote, much of England was still common land, and the recently discovered Americas appeared to offer unlimited common lands for further exploitation.

John Locke *Second Treatise on Government* (1690) (Cambridge Univ Press: 1964)

Whether we consider natural Reason, which tells us, that Men, once being born, have a right to their Preservation, and consequently to Meat and Drink, and such other things, as Nature affords for their Subsistence; Or Revelation, which gives us an account of those Grants God made of the World to *Adam*, and to *Noah*, and his sons: 'Tis very clear, that God, as King *David* says *has given the Earth to the Children of Men*, given it to Mankind in common. But this being supposed, it seems to some a very great difficulty how any one should ever come to have a Property in any thing... But I shall endeavour to show, how Men might come to have a property in several[8] parts of that which God gave to Mankind in common, and that without any express Compact of all the Commoners.

26. God, who hath given the World to Men in common, hath also given them reason to make use of it to the best advantage of life, and convenience. The Earth, and all that is therein, is given to Men for the Support and Comfort of their being. And though all the Fruits it naturally produces, and Beasts it feeds, belong to Mankind in common, as they are produced by the spontaneous Hand of Nature; and no Body has originally a private Dominium, exclusive of the rest of Mankind, in any of them, as they are thus in their natural state; yet being given for the use of Men, there must of necessity be a means to appropriate them some way or other before they can be of any use, or at all beneficial to any particular Man. The Fruit, or Venison, which nourishes the wild *Indian* who knows no Inclosure,[9] and is still a Tenant in common, must be his, and so his, ie. a part of him, that another can no longer have any right to it, before it can do him any good for the support of his Life.

27. Though the Earth, and all inferior Creatures be common to all Men, yet every Man has a *Property* in his own Person. This no Body has any Right to but himself. The *Labour* of his Body, and the Work of his Hands, we may say, are properly his. Whatsoever then he removes out of the State that Nature hath provided, and left it

---

7 See also A. Ryan *Property and Political Theory*, Blackwell, 1984.
8 'Separated'.
9 Compare the Native American concept of property, Chapter 2, p. 27–28.

in, he hath mixed his Labour with it, and joyned to it something that is his own, and thereby makes it his Property. It being removed from the common state Nature placed it in, it hath by this Labour something annexed to it, that excludes the common right of other Men. For this *Labour* being the unquestionable Property of the Labourer, no Man but he can have a right to what that is once joyned to, at least where there is enough, and as good left in common for others.

28. He that is nourished by the Acorns he picked up Under an Oak, or the Apples he gathered from the Trees in the Wood, has certainly appropriated them to himself. No Body can deny but the nourishment is his. I ask then when did they begin to be his? When he digested? Or when he eat? Or when he boiled? Or when he brought them home? Or when he picked them up? And 'tis plain, if the first gathering made them not his, nothing else could.[10] That Labour put a distinction between them and common. That added something to them more than Nature, the common Mother of all, had done, and so they became his private Right. And will any say he had no right to those Acorns or Apples he thus appropriated, because he had not the consent of all Mankind to make them his? Was it a Robbery thus to assume to himself what belonged to all in Common? If such a consent as that was necessary, Man had starved, not withstanding the Plenty God hath given him. We see in Commons, which remain so by Compact, that 'tis the taking any part of what is common, and removing it out of the state Nature leaves it in, which begins the Property; without which the Common is of no use...

39. And thus, without supposing any private Dominium, and Property in *Adam*, over the World, exclusive of all other Men, which can no way be proved, nor any one's Property be made out from it; but supposing the World given as it was to the Children of Men in common, we see how Labour could make Men distinct Titles to several parcels of it, for their private uses; wherein there could be no doubt of Right, no room for quarrel.

40. Nor is it so strange as perhaps before consideration of it may appear, that the Property of Labour should be able to overbalance the Community of Land. For 'tis Labour indeed that puts the difference of value on every thing; and let any one consider, what the difference is between an Acre of Land planted with Tobacco, or Sugar, sown with Wheat or Barley; and an Acre of the same Land lying in common, without any Husbandry on it; and he will find, that the improvement of labour makes the far greater part of the value...

45. Thus Labour, in the Beginning, gave a Right of Property, wherever any one was pleased to employ it, upon what was common, which remained, a long while, the far greater part, and is yet more than Mankind makes use of. Men, at first, for the most part, contented themselves with what unassisted Nature offered to their Necessities; and though afterwards, in some parts of the World, where the Increase of People and Stock, with the Use of Money, had made Land scarce, and so of some value, the several Communities settled the Bounds of their distinct Territories, and by laws within themselves, regulated the Properties of the private Men of their Society, and so, by Compact and Agreement, settled the Property which Labour and Industry began...

---

10 As Nozick (see Ryan, note 7 above) asked, why does not the apple tree become his?

Hegel, in 1821, presented a more subtle view than John Locke of the meaning and importance of property in human lives:

G.W.F. Hegel *Philosophy of Right* (trans. Knox; quoted in M.R. Cohen & F.S. Cohen, *Readings in Jurisprudence and Legal Philosophy* (Little Brown & Co: 1975))

A person has the right to direct his will upon any object, as his real and positive end. The object thus becomes his. As it has no end in itself, it receives its meaning and soul from his will. Mankind has the absolute right of appropriation over all things...

A man may own anything because he is a free will, and is therefore self-contained and self-dependent. But the mere object is of an opposite nature... As the thing is in its nature external it has no purpose of its own... Only the will is the unlimited and absolute, while all other things in contrast with the will are merely relative... When the living thing becomes my property I give to it another soul than it had. I give it my will...

Since property makes objective my personal individual will, it is rightly described as a private possession. On the other hand, common property, which may be possessed by a number of separate individuals, is the mark of a loosely joined company, in which a man may or may not be allowed his share to remain at his choice...

In property my will is personal. But the person, it must be observed, is this particular individual, and, thus, property is the embodiment of this particular will. Since property gives visible existence to my will, it must be regarded as 'this' and hence as 'mine'...

As Knowles concluded, 'Property is thus an essential element of [human] self-consciousness... Men must have property if they are to be, and see themselves, as free agents' (R. D. Knowles 'Hegel on Property and Personality' 33 *The Phil Quarterly* (1983) 130 45).

The nineteenth century saw an acceleration of a process begun at least a hundred years earlier, the development of new kinds of property. In the years after Locke wrote, the common lands of England were subjected to a continuous and relentless privatisation by the Enclosure Acts, and the rural poor found themselves in a new and desperate situation. Parallel to these enclosures came the criminalisation of what had been customary rights, and the bloody penal code which was designed by, and in order to protect, men of property who used Locke as their justification.

D. Hay 'Property, Authority and the Criminal Law' 17 in D. Hay, E. P. Thompson and P. Linebaugh (eds) *Albion's Fatal Tree* (Allen Lane: 1975)[11]

[T]he number of capital statutes grew from about 50 to over 200 between the years 1688 and 1820. Almost all of them concerned offences against property.

This flood of legislation is one of the great facts of the eighteenth century, and it occurred in the period when peers and gentry held power with least hindrance from Crown or people. The Glorious Revolution of 1688 established the freedom not of men, but of men of property. Its apologist, John Locke, distorted the oldest arguments of natural law to justify the liberation of wealth from all political or moral controls; he concluded that the unfettered accumulation of money, goods and land was sanctioned by Nature and, implicitly, by God[12]... William Blackstone, the most famous eighteenth-century writer on the law and constitution, declared it self-evident that 'there is nothing which so generally strikes the imagination, and engages the affections of mankind, as the right of property; or that sole and despotic dominion which one man claims and exercises over the external things of the world, in total exclusion of the right of any other individual in the universe'... [13]

Once property had been officially deified, it became the measure of all things... Again and again the voices of money and power declared the sacredness of property in terms hitherto reserved for human life. Banks were credited with souls, and the circulation of gold likened to that of blood. Forgers, for example, were almost invariably hanged, and gentlemen knew why: 'Forgery is a stab to commerce, and only to be tolerated in a commercial nation when the foul crime of murder is pardoned'...

As the industrial revolution accelerated, the alienating and dehumanising effect of the factory system as the catalyst for new kinds of property became clear. Socialists began to criticise the received justifications of private property. The most famous of these was Karl Marx.

K. Marx *Communist Manifesto* (1848) (quoted by C.B. Macpherson (ed.) below)

The distinguishing feature of Communism is not the abolition of property generally, but the abolition of bourgeois property. But modern bourgeois property is the final and most complete expression of the system of producing and appropriating products, that is based on class antagonism, on the exploitation of the many by the few.

In this sense, the theory of the Communists may be summed up in the single sentence: Abolition of private property.

We Communists have been reproached with the desire of abolishing the right of personally acquiring property as the fruit of a man's labour, which property is alleged to be the ground of all personal freedom, activity and independence...

You are horrified at our intending to do away with private property. But in your

---

11 See also E.P. Thompson *Whigs and Hunters* (Penguin: 1975).
12 Is this what Locke wrote, or what the ruling class read from him?
13 See too Blackstone's view of married women, p. 16 below.

existing society, private property is already done away with for nine-tenths of the population; its existence for the few is solely due to its non-existence in the hands of those nine-tenths. You reproach us, therefore, with intending to do away with a form of property, the necessary condition for whose existence is, the non-existence of any property for the immense majority of society.

In one word, you reproach us with intending to do away with your property. Precisely so; that is just what we intend...

Communism deprives no man of the power to appropriate the products of society: all that it does is to deprive him of the power to subjugate the labour of others by means of such appropriation.

C.B. Macpherson, in the twentieth century, sought to reconcile the 'possessive individualism' of liberal theory with democratic ideas of a fair society.

C.B. Macpherson (ed.) *Property: Mainstream and Critical Positions* (University of Toronto Press: 1978)

The central problem of liberal-democratic theory may be stated as the difficulty of reconciling the liberal property right with that equal effective right of all individuals to use and develop their capacities which is the essential ethical principle of liberalism. The difficulty is great. For when the liberal property right is written into law as an individual right to the exclusive use and disposal of the resources provided by nature and of parcels of the capital by past work on them, and when it is combined with the liberal system of market incentives and rights of free contract, it leads to and supports a concentration of ownership and a system of power relations between individuals and classes which negates the ethical goal of free and independent individual development. Thus there appears to be an insoluble difficulty within the liberal-democratic theory. If, as liberal theory asserts, an individual property right is required by the very necessities of man's nature and condition, it ought not to be infringed or denied. But unless it is seriously infringed or denied, it leads to an effective denial of the equal possibility of individual human fulfilment...

Liberal-democratic theory has not yet found a way out of this difficulty... [It] could be traced to the deep-rootedness of what I [have] called the possessive individualism of the liberal theory, a set of assumptions about man and society which proved incompatible with democratic aspirations but which could not be given up as long as society was to rely on market incentives and institutions. Alternatively ... the difficulty could be stated as an incompatibility between two concepts of the human essence both of which are present within liberal-democratic theory – a concept of man as a consumer, desirer, maximizer of utilities, and a concept of man as doer, as exerter and developer of his uniquely human attributes...

[T]he individual property right which liberal theory has inferred from the nature of man is ... too narrow.[14] What is needed is to broaden it. When this is seen, the old difficulty disappears...

14 See also Gray at p. 23–24 below, and compare Bowles and Gintis in Chapter 11, p. 323.

[P]roperty, although it will always be an individual right, need not be confined, as liberal theory has confined it, to a right to exclude others from the use or benefit of some thing, but may equally be an individual right not to be excluded by others from the use or benefit of some thing. When property is so understood, the problem of liberal-democratic theory is no longer a problem of putting limits on the property right, but of supplementing the individual right to exclude others by the individual right not to be excluded by others. The latter right may be held to be the one that is most required by the liberal-democratic ethic, and most implied in a liberal concept of the human essence. The right not to be excluded by others may provisionally be stated as the individual right to equal access to the means of labour and/or the means of life...

The concept of property, like all concepts, has been shaped by theorists. Political concepts are generally shaped by theorists who are not simply grammarians or logicians but who are seeking to justify something. The most solid basis on which to justify any institution or a right is to derive it from the supposed essential nature and needs of man – to show that the human being, to be fully human, requires that institution or that right. The [liberal] theorists who have shaped the concept of property have generally done this. And no matter how much they might insist that man was a social animal, in the end they had to come down to the individual human being. So the concept of property had to be based on the individual: property could only be seen as a right of an individual, a right derivable from his human essence, a right to some use or benefit of something without the use or benefit of which he could not be fully human. The very idea of property, therefore, is the idea of an individual right.

A second general proposition, which would scarcely have to be stated here were it not for the fact that current common usage appears to contradict it, is that property is a right, not a thing. It is an enforceable claim to some use or benefit of something (and sometimes, but not always, to its disposal): it is not the thing itself.

A third proposition may also be asserted. Inasmuch as the concept of property is the concept of an enforceable claim – an individual claim that will be enforced by society – property is the creation of society. Property is, as Bentham said, entirely the work of law.

These three propositions are, I think, all that can be asserted of property as such. Property is a right, not a thing. It is an individual right. It is an enforceable claim created by the state.

But, whatever our views about ourselves and our property, our imagination can always challenge us. If there were another species, who lived off 'our' property...

M. Norton *The Borrowers* (Dent: 1952)

Arietty, a Borrower, has met a human boy:

The boy sat thoughtfully on his haunches, chewing a blade of grass. 'Borrowing,' he said after a while. 'Is that what you call it?'

'What else would you call it?' asked Arietty.

'I'd call it stealing.'

Arietty laughed. She really laughed. 'But we *are* Borrowers,' she explained, 'like you're a – a Human Bean or whatever it's called. We're part of the house. You might as well say that the fire-grate steals the coal from the coal-skuttle.'

'What is stealing?'

Arietty looked grave. 'Supposing my Uncle Hendreary borrowed an emerald watch from Her dressing-table and my father took it and hung it up on our wall. That's stealing.'

'An emerald watch!' exclaimed the boy.

'Well, I just said that because we have one on the wall at home, but my father borrowed it himself. It needn't be a watch. It could be anything. A lump of sugar even. But Borrowers don't steal.'

'Except from human beans,' said the boy.

Arietty burst out laughing; she laughed so much she had to hide her face in the primrose. 'O dear,' she gasped with tears in her eyes, 'you are funny!' She stared upwards at his puzzled face. 'Human Beans are *for* Borrowers – like bread's for butter!'

The protection of human property by the criminal law[15] is an important part of the concept. Borrowing is not – usually – theft, but:

DPP v *Lavender* (1993) The Independent, June 4 (QBD) Tuckey J

Lavender, a local authority tenant, 'borrowed' doors from an empty house owned by the authority because it refused to repair his doors (claiming he had damaged them himself). He was charged with theft of the doors under s. 1, Theft Act 1968. The issue was whether he intended 'permanently to deprive' the owner.

Tuckey J:

The question was, did the respondent intend to treat the doors as his own in dealing with the council, regardless of their rights? The answer must be 'yes'.

The council's rights included the right not to have the doors at No.25 removed and to require the tenant at No.37 to replace or pay for the damaged doors. In dealing with the doors regardless of those rights, the respondent manifested an intention to treat them as his own.

He was therefore guilty of theft of the doors.

---

15 See also *R* v *Velumyl* [1989] Crim LR 299, and generally J.C. Smith, *The Law of Theft* 7th edn (Butterworths: 1993), pp. 66–75. For doors as a part of land see 'fixtures' in Chapter 2 at pp. 44–7 and for 'stealing land' compare adverse possession in Chapter 3.

PROPERTY AND POWER

Rights of property can amount to direct power over other human beings:

H.A. Jacobs *Incidents in the Life of a Slave Girl* (1861) J.F. Yellin (ed.) (Harvard University Press: 1987)[16]

I was born a slave; but I never knew it till six years of happy childhood had passed away. My father was a carpenter, and considered so intelligent and skilful in his trade, that, when buildings out of the common line were to be erected, he was sent for from long distances, to be head workman. On condition of paying his mistress 200 dollars a year, and supporting himself, he was allowed to work at his trade, and manage his own affairs. His strongest wish was to purchase his own children; but, though he several times offered his hard-won earnings for that purpose, he never succeeded. In complexion my parents were a light shade of brownish yellow, and were termed mulattoes. They lived together in a comfortable home; and, though we were all slaves, I was so fondly shielded that I never dreamed I was a piece of merchandise, trusted to them for safe keeping, and liable to be demanded of them at any moment. I had one brother, William, who was two years younger than myself – a bright, affectionate child. I had also a great treasure in my maternal grandmother who was a remarkable woman in many respects. She was the daughter of a planter in South Carolina, who, at his death, left her mother and his three children free, with money to go to St Augustine, where they had relatives. It was during the revolutionary War; and they were captured on their passage, carried back, and sold to different purchasers. Such was the story my grandmother used to tell me; but I do not remember all the particulars. She was a little girl when she was captured and sold to the keeper of a large hotel. I have often heard her tell how hard she fared during childhood. But as she grew older she evinced so much intelligence, and was so faithful, that her master and mistress could not help seeing it was for their interest to take care of such a valuable piece of property...

Her master died and the property was divided among his heirs. The widow had her dower in the hotel, which she continued to keep open. My grandmother remained in her service as a slave; but her children were divided among her master's [four] children. As she had five, Benjamin, the youngest one, was sold, in order that each heir might have an equal portion of dollars and cents... Though only ten years old, seven hundred and twenty dollars were paid for him. His sale was a terrible blow to my grandmother; but she was naturally hopeful, and she went to work with renewed energy, trusting in time to be able to purchase some of her children. She had laid up three hundred dollars, which her mistress one day begged as a loan, promising to pay her soon. The reader probably knows that no promise or writing given to a slave is legally binding; for, according to Southern laws, a slave, being *property,* can *hold* no property...

Such were the unusually fortunate circumstances of my early childhood.

---

16 See also P. Williams, 'On Being the Object of Property' 13 *Signs* (1988) 5.

The ownership of property within the family also indicates the way in which 'property equals power'. In the 1804 Napoleonic Code it was stated: 'The woman is the property of the man, as the fruit tree is the property of the gardener.'

A.H. Manchester 'The Family and the Law' in *Modern Legal History* (Butterworths: 1979)

Blackstone summarised the essence of the wife's position at common law as follows:

> 'By marriage the husband and wife are one person in law; that is the very being or legal existence of the woman is suspended during the marriage, or at least is incorporated and consolidated into that of the husband: under whose wing, protection, and cover, she performs everything:[17] and is therefore called in or law-french a *feme covert* ... and her condition during her marriage is called her coverture.'

In law, therefore, husband and wife were one. Yet, as the wags put it, it was the husband who was that one...

All freeholds of which the wife was seised at the time of the marriage, or afterwards, were by law vested in the husband and wife, during the coverture in right of the wife...

The husband became entitled to leaseholds of which his wife had been possessed at the time of the marriage or which accrued to her during coverture...

The personal chattels of the wife, whether they belonged to her at the time of the marriage, or accrued to her during coverture, became in general the absolute property of the husband...

In return, the wife received an imperfectly enforced right to maintenance...

Equity mitigated some of the rigours of the common law doctrine by the doctrine of the separate use. Equity recognised any trust created in favour of the wife...[18]

The early equitable glosses upon the common law position of the wife may have been due in part to a paternalistic desire to protect the wife who all too frequently, as Lord Chancellor Thurlow put it, was 'kicked or kissed out of her money'. Yet the common law doctrine had become increasingly unacceptable as the leasehold grew in importance as a form of investment property and fortunes were made in money rather than through the ownership of land. Such valuable monies must be protected from the rapacious husband. Primarily, therefore, equity acted not so much to protect the married woman and certainly not to advance any concept of equality between husband and wife but rather to enable married women as individuals to take an active part in business. The purpose of equity was to keep the family (kinship) property intact... The nineteenth century legislation can also be seen as a response to a revolution in production.

---

17 Now see husbands and wives and banks in Chapter 5 at pp. 138–41.
18 For the history of the trust see Chapter 2 at p. 37–41, for modern trusts of land see Chapter 9.

L. Holcombe *Wives and Property* (Martin Robertson: 1983)

A few years after this [1869], Millicent Garrett Fawcett had her purse snatched by a young thief in London. When she appeared in court to testify against him, she heard the youth charged with 'stealing from the person of Millicent Fawcett a purse containing £1 18s. 6d., the property of Henry Fawcett.' ...

It was not the fact of being female but the status of wife that entailed severe legal disabilities. Legally deprived of property, married women were also deprived both of power and of the civil rights of other citizens...

Feminists had won a major victory with passage of the Married Women's Property Act of 1882. For twenty-seven years they had fought the good fight to win for wives the same property rights that were enjoyed by men and unmarried women. They had struggled to end the 'virtual slavery of marriage' imposed upon women, particularly those of the lower classes, by the common law, and also to abolish the special, privileged status that wealthy women enjoyed under the provisions of equity...

L. Davidoff and C. Hall *Family Fortunes* (Routledge: 1987)

Patterns of ownership were closely related to patterns of control. It was primarily women who were the beneficiaries of 'passive' property yielding income only: trusts, annuities, subscriptions and insurance. Under the terms of a trust, the needs and wishes of the beneficiary were supposed to be fulfilled but interpretations could vary. Dr Dixon of Witham being called to act as a trustee noted in his diary that 'Miss Cox's present views are of entire indifference to me'. The situation was particularly serious for an Essex woman who wanted to separate from her husband who had already borrowed money against her marriage settlement ... The problem was that trustees were overwhelmingly male kin or friends of the family ... In fact one of the most commonly named trustees was a son-in-law, in other words the husband of the women whose property was in a trust.

English law no longer recognises the right to keep slaves[19] and wives no longer live as enforced dependants. Nevertheless, as Marx wrote, property rights can indirectly amount to rights to control other people. This was taken up by Morris Cohen whose famous article provided legal justification for the New Deal legislation in the United States during the depression.

M.R. Cohen 'Property and Sovereignty' 13 *Cornell LQ* (1927–8) 8[20]

Property and sovereignty, as every student knows, belong to entirely different branches of the law. Sovereignty is a concept of political or public law and property belongs to civil or private law...

The character of property as sovereign power compelling service and obedience

---

19 *Somerset* v *Stewart* 12 Geo 3, (1772) KB.
20 © 1927–8 by Cornell University. All rights reserved. See also R. Cotterell, Chapter 9, p. 232.

may be obscured from us in a commercial economy by the fiction of the so-called labor contract as a free bargain and by the frequency with which service is rendered indirectly through a money payment. But not only is there actually little freedom to bargain on the part of the steel worker or miner who needs a job, but in some cases the medieval subject had as much power to bargain when he accepted the sovereignty of his lord. Today I do not directly serve my landlord if I wish to live in the city with a roof over my head, but I must work for others to pay him rent with which he obtains the personal service of others. The money needed for purchasing things must for the vast majority be acquired by hard labor and disagreeable service to those to whom the law has accorded dominion over the things necessary for subsistence.

To a philosopher this is of course not at all an argument against private property. It may well be that compulsion in the economic as well as the political realm is necessary for civilized life. But we must not overlook the actual fact that dominion over things is also *imperium* (command) over our fellow human beings.

The extent of the power over the life of others which the legal order confers on those called owners is not fully appreciated by those who think of the law as merely protecting men in their possession. Property law does more. It determines what men shall acquire. Thus, protecting the property rights of a landlord means giving him the right to collect rent, protecting the property of a railroad or a public service corporation means giving it the right to make certain charges. Hence the ownership of land and machinery, with the rights of drawing rent, interest, etc., determines the future distribution of goods that will come into being – determines what share of such goods various individuals shall acquire...

[N]ot only medieval landlords but the owners of all revenue-producing property are in fact granted by the law certain powers to tax the future social product. When to this power of taxation there is added the power to command the services of large numbers who are not economically independent, we have the essence of what historically has constituted political sovereignty...

Let me conclude. There can be no doubt that our property laws do confer sovereign power on our captains of industry and even more so on our captains of finance.

Now it would be unworthy of a philosopher to shy at government by captains of industry and finance. Humanity has been ruled by priests, soldiers, hereditary landlords and even antiquarian scholars. The results are not such as to make us view with alarm a new type of ruler. But if we are entering a new era involving a new set of rulers, it is well to recognize it and reflect on what is involved...

THE LEGAL CONCEPTS OF OWNERSHIP AND POSSESSION

Lawyers categorise property in various ways, but the most traditional view is that 'property' means rights which 'bind the whole world'.

P.J. Fitzgerald *Salmond on Jurisprudence* (Sweet & Maxwell: 1966)

108. *Meanings of the term property*

The substantive civil law is divisible into three great departments, namely: the law of property, the law of obligations, and the law of status. The first deals with rights *in rem*,[21] the second with proprietary rights *in personam*,[22] and the third with personal or non-proprietary rights, whether *in rem* or *in personam*...

The term property, which we here use as meaning proprietary rights *in rem*, possesses a singular variety of different applications having differrent degrees of generality. These are the following:

1. *All legal rights.* In its widest sense, property includes all a person's legal rights, of whatever description. A man's property is all that is his in law...

2. *Proprietary rights* ... In a second and narrower sense, property includes not all a person's rights, but only his proprietary as opposed to his personal rights. The former constitute his estate or property, while the latter constitute his status or personal condition. In this sense a man's land, chattels, shares and the debts due to him are his property; but not his life or liberty or reputation...

3. *Proprietary rights in rem* ... In a third application, which is that adopted in this chapter, the term includes not even all proprietary rights, but only those which are both proprietary and *in rem*. The law of property is the law of proprietary rights *in rem*...

4. *Corporeal property* ... Finally, in the narrowest use of the term, it includes nothing more than corporeal property – that is to say, the right of ownership in a material object, or that object itself...

109. *Kinds of property*

All property is, as we have already seen, either corporeal or incorporeal. Corporeal property is the right of ownership in material things; incorporeal property is any other proprietary right *in rem*. Incorporeal property is itself of two kinds, namely (1) *jura in re aliena* (rights over another's land, such as easements and profits) or encumbrances, whether over material or immaterial things (for example, leases, mortgages and servitudes , and (2) *jura in re propria* (rights over one's own things) over immaterial things (for example, patents, copyrights, and trade-marks)...

Writers on property in the English legal tradition have attempted to identify the common attributes of ownership and possession in different legal orders. Such analyses may be helpful in that they require readers to reflect on their own understanding of the importance, or otherwise, of these terms in legal argument. These writings are also useful for an understanding of property today because they indicate the extent to which legal philosophers are as imbued with ideology as the more overtly political authors.

The word 'ownership' first appeared in England in the fifteenth century. The idea of ownership grew out of the concept of 'seisin'.

---

21 'Against the world'.
22 'Against individuals'.

A.M. Honore 'Ownership' 107 in A.G. Guest (ed.) *Oxford Essays in Jurisprudence* (Oxford University Press: 1961)[23]

(1) The Liberal Concept of Ownership

If ownership is provisionally defined as the *greatest possible interest in a thing which a mature system of law recognizes,* then it follows that, since all mature systems admit the existence of 'interests' in things, all mature systems have, in a sense, a concept of ownership. Indeed, even primitive systems, like that of the Trobriand islanders, have rules by which certain persons, such as the 'owners' of canoes, have greater interests in certain things than anyone else.

For mature legal systems it is possible to make a larger claim. In them certain important legal incidents are found, which are common to different systems. If it were not so, 'He owns that umbrella', said in a purely English context, would mean something different from 'He owns that umbrella', proffered as a translation of 'Ce parapluie est à lui'. Yet, as we know, they mean the same. There is indeed, a substantial similarity in the position of one who 'owns' an umbrella in England, France, Russia, China and any other modern country one may care to mention. Everywhere the 'owner' can, in the simple uncomplicated case, in which no other person has an interest in the thing, use it, stop others using it, lend it, sell it or leave it by will. Nowhere may he use it to poke his neighbour in the ribs or to knock over his vase. Ownership, *dominium, proprieté, eigentum* and similar words stand not merely for the greatest interest in things in particular systems but for a type of interest with common features transcending particular systems. It must surely be important to know what these common features are?

Honore disclaims any idea that the modern notion of ownership is inevitable or universal and then goes on to list its common features:

(1) the right to possess;
(2) the right to use;
(3) the right to manage;
(4) the right to the income;
(5) the right to the capital;
(6) the right to security;
(7) the incident of transmissibility [to pass it on by will];
(8) the incident of absence of term [that it will last for ever];
(9) the prohibition of harmful use;
(10) the liability to execution [to be taken to pay debts];
(11) residuary character [that lesser rights vest back into the owner]...

It is interesting to compare common law ownership with the civil law ('Romanic') concept which was consciously adopted by many European legal systems in the eighteenth and nineteenth centuries. This is particularly so, in that the more formal, civil concept of ownership may become significant in English land law as the system of registered title expands, for the 'statutory title' of the registered

---

23 See also A. Ross 'Tu-Tu' 70 Harv LR (1957) 812; J. Waldron, Oxf Jo L S 5 (1985) 313; J.F. Garner (1986) Jo Pl L 404.

proprietor resembles the civil law rather than the common law tradition. (See Chapter 10, p. 281, 289.)

J.H. Merryman 'Ownership and Estate' 48 *Tulane L Rev* (1974) 916[24]

What we are really facing is this: the Romanic concept of ownership is a product of the age of reason applied to Roman legal materials and has been worked out with the kind of legal precision that is typical of the period in European history that saw the introduction of decimal currency and the adoption of the metric system of weights and measures...[25]

The contrast with English theory is remarkable. In England, ownership resided in the king, and the distribution and retention of lands throughout the kingdom was carried out according to the theory of tenure...[26]

This basic difference between Romanic ownership and the Anglo-American 'estate' or 'interest' in land can be illustrated by a simple metaphor. Romanic ownership can be thought of as a box, with the word 'ownership' written on it. Whoever has the box is the owner ... as long as he keeps the box, he still has the ownership, even if the box is empty. The contrast with the Anglo-American law of property is simple. There is no box. There are merely various sets of legal interests...

The concept of possession in English law is no less vague.

D.R. Harris 'The Concept of Possession in English Law' 69 in A. G. Guest (ed.) *Oxford Essays in Jurisprudence* (Oxford University Press: 1961)

The concept of Possession has always had a strange fascination for lawyers. Many writers have attempted to analyse the concept whether in Roman law, in a modern system, such as German law, or in English law... English judges have been rightly suspicious of a uniform rigid 'theory' of possession in the common law: for instance, Earl Jowitt has said – 'in truth, the English law has never worked out a completely logical and exhaustive definition of "possession" '.

It is the thesis of this essay that the English decisions preclude us from laying down any conditions, such as physical control or a certain kind of intention, as absolutely essential for a judicial ruling that a man possesses something...

[The] rules, all employing the word 'possession', deal with such different situations that it is not in the least surprising that English judges have not adopted any consistent approach to the meaning of possession.[27] They have used 'possession' in the various rules of law as a functional and relative concept, which gives them some discretion in applying an abstract rule to a concrete set of facts ... according to the dictates of justice and social policy.

---

24 See also O. Kahn-Freund *Introduction to Renner, The Institutions of Private Law and Their Social Functions* (Routledge, Kegan Paul, 1949).
25 English money was then counted in 12s and 20s.
26 See Chapter 2, pp. 38.
27 For examples of possenssion of land, see Chapter 3.

Under English law, the owner of a thing is normally entitled to possess it. However, the law also recognises possession as a root of title: 'the taking possession of unowned things is the only possible way to acquire ownership of them' (see Epstein, p. 1).

C.M. Rose 'Possession as the Origin of Property' 52 *U Chic L Rev* (1985) 73

How do things come to be owned? This is a fundamental puzzle for anyone who thinks about property. One buys things from other owners to be sure, but how did the other owners get those things? A chain of ownership or title must have a first link. Someone had to do something to anchor that link. The law tells us what steps we must follow and why these steps should do the job...

For the common law, *possession* or 'occupancy' is the origin of property. This notion runs through a number of fascinating old cases with which teachers of property law love to challenge their students.[28] Such inquiries into the acquisition of title to wild animals and abandoned treasure may seem purely academic; how often, after all, do we expect to get into disputes about the ownership of wild pigs or long-buried pieces of eight? These cases are not entirely silly though. People do still find treasure-laden vessels, and statesmen do have to consider whether someone's acts might support a claim to own the moon, for example, or the mineral nodes at the bottom of the sea. Moreover, analogies to the capture of wild animals show up time and again when courts have to deal on a non-statutory basis with some 'fugitive' resource that is being reduced to property for the first time, such as oil, gas, groundwater, or space on the spectrum of radio frequencies.

With these more serious claims in mind then, I turn to the maxim of the common law: first possession is the root of title. Merely to state the proposition is to raise two critical questions: what counts as possession, and why is it the basis for a claim to title? In exploring the quaint old cases' answers to these questions we hit on some fundamental views about the nature and purposes of a property regime.

Consider *Pierson* v *Post* [3 Cai. R 175 (NY Sup Ct) 1805] , a classic wild animal case from the early nineteenth century. Post was hunting a fox one day on an abandoned beach and almost had the beast in his gunsight when an interloper appeared, killed the fox and ran off with the carcass. The indignant Post sued the interloper for the value of the fox on the theory that his pursuit of the fox had established his property right to it.

The court disagreed. It cited a long list of learned authorities to the effect that 'occupancy' or 'possession' went to the one who killed the animal, or who at least wounded it mortally or caught it in a net. These acts brought the animal within the 'certain control' that gives rise to possession and hence a claim to ownership.

Possession thus means a clear act, whereby all the world understands that the pursuer has 'an unequivocal intention of appropriating the animal to his individual use'. A clear rule of this sort would be applied, said the court, because it prevents confusion and quarrelling among hunters (and coincidentally makes the judges'

---

28 It is a modern question too: see Chapter 3; see also the law of outer space and the law of the sea.

task easier when hunters do get into quarrels)...

Possession as the basis of property ownership, then, seems to amount to something like yelling loudly enough to all who may be interested. The first to say, 'This is mine', in a way that the public understands, gets the prize, and the law will help him keep it against someone else who says, 'No, it is mine'. But if the original communicator dallies too long and allows the public to believe the interloper, he will find that the interloper has stepped into his shoes and has become the owner.

Similar ideas of the importance of communication, or as it is more commonly called, 'notice', are implicit in our recording statutes and in a variety of other devices that force a property claimant to make a public record of her claims on pain of losing them altogether.[29] Indeed, notice plays a part in the most mundane property-like claims to things that the law does not even recognize as capable of being reduced to ownership. 'Would you please save my place?' one says to one's neighbour in the movie line, in order to ensure that others in line know that one is coming back and not relinquishing one's claim. In my home town of Chicago, one may choose to shovel snow from a parking place on the street, but in order to establish a claim to it one must put a chair or some other object in the cleared space. The useful act of shovelling snow does not speak as unambiguously as the presence of an object that blocks entry.

Why, then, is it so important that property owners make and keep their communications clear? Economists have an answer: clear titles facilitate trade and minimize resource-wasting conflict...

We may enjoy nature and enjoy wildness, but those sentiments find little resonance in the doctrine of first possession. Its texts are those of cultivation, manufacture, and development. We cannot have our fish both loose and fast ... and the common law of first possession makes a choice. The common law gives preference to those who convince the world that they have caught the fish and hold it fast. This may be a reward to useful labor, but it is more precisely the articulation of a specific vocabulary within a structure of symbols approved and understood by a commercial people. It is this commonly understood and shared set of symbols that gives significance and form to what might seem the quintessentially individualistic act: the claim that one has, by possession, separated for oneself property from the great commons of unowned things.

THE SUBSTANCE OF PROPERTY

This brief explanation of 'property' ends with three contrasting views of what property might mean to different people in different places.

K. Gray 'Property in Thin Air' 50 *Cam L Jo* (1991) 252

Proudhon got it all wrong. Property is not theft – it is fraud. Few other legal notions

---

29 For examples, see Chapter 10, pp. 310, and Appendix 1, pp. 336–45.

operate such gross or systematic deception. Before long I will have sold you a piece of thin air and you will have called it property. But the ultimate fact about property is that it does not exist: it is mere illusion. It is a vacant concept – oddly enough rather like thin air.

Gray goes on to investigate property rights in airspace, and concludes that behind decisions about, for example, nuisance law, lies a 'primordial principle': that resources which are not susceptible to exclusive use ('non-excludable') cannot be property.

[T]he criterion of 'excludability' gets us much closer to the core of 'property' than does the conventional legal emphasis on the assignability or enforceability of benefits. For 'property' resides not in consumption of benefits but in control over benefits. 'Property' is not about *enjoyment of access* but about *control over access...*

'Property', he continues, is therefore a concept which can change over time and which has inherent moral limits. At the same time, this means that it is a concept open to new argument:

[P]roperty terminology is merely talk without substance – a filling of empty space with empty words. When subjected to close analysis the concept of 'property' vanishes ... Claims of *meum* and *tuum* [30]do not protect rights of any sacrosanct or *a priori* nature, but merely purport with varying degrees of sophistication to add moral legitimacy to the assertion of self-interest in the beneficial control of valued resources. In the end the 'property' notion, in all its conceptual fragility, is but a shadow of the individual and collective human response to a world of limited resources and attenuated altruism.[31]

Helene Cixous 'The Author in Truth' in *Coming to Writing* (Harvard University Press: 1991)

Knowing How to Have What One Has

A series of [Clarice Lispector's] texts work on the question of having, of knowing how to have what one has. This is one of the most difficult things in the world. Poor humans that we are, no sooner do we have than we no longer have ... Having what we have is the key to happiness. We have, we have a great deal, but because we have, and as soon as we have, we no longer know that we have.

What can we do to have what we have? There is a secret to it: it is 'Clandestine Felicity' – a story about childhood, a little prophetic book just a few pages long. There are two little girls. One is little Clarice. The other is a little redheaded friend whose father owns a bookstore, and so she is surely in paradise. She has the

---

30 'Mine' and 'yours'.
31 See also Chapter 11.

father and the books. But by chance (life is like this), the redheaded girl from the bookstore is a little pest. A bad witch. She tells Clarice she is going to lend her an enormous and extraordinary book. She keeps her walking, running, for weeks, telling her, 'Come over to my house and I'll give it to you'. Clarice goes across town in a state of absolute happiness. Under the footsteps of the enchanted one, the world turns to sea. The entire world is pleasuring. She gets there, the horrid little redhead opens the door and tells her each time, 'I don't have it, come back next week.'... Without fail, Clarice returns to the door, until the day when the mother of the horrid little girl happens to be on the scene and discovers the mechanism of hate that has been put into operation. The mother is devastated by the discovery of her daughter's wickedness, but, mother of all the little girls in the world, she immediately makes amends. The book must be lent! And furthermore, Clarice adds, the mother says, 'You may keep it as long as you wish'. The mother gives the desiring one the endlessness of the book. Misfortune of joy! From the moment Clarice can dispose of this book endlessly, what will become of the race across town, the desire, the twisted and tortured joy? Will everything escape her because she has everything, forever? But there is a limit: the book has not been given to her, it has been given to her to keep for as long as she wants. And this is the moral of the story: it is yours for as long as you have the strength to want it. So Clarice invents the marvellous, magical means, the positive sorcery, the art of remaining on the brink ... happiness is its own secret, one can really have only if one knows how to have in a way that does not destroy, does not possess.

The secret: remembering at every instant the grace of having.

Keeping in this having the breathless lightness of hoping to have. Barely having after not having had. Always keeping to oneself the emotion of almost not having had. For to have is always a miracle.

On the other hand:

M. Ondaatje *The English Patient* (Pan Books: 1993)

...Not seeing each other for months. Just the Bedouin and us, criss-crossing the Forty Days Road. There were rivers of desert tribes, the most beautiful humans I've met in my life. We were German, English, Hungarian, African – all of us insignificant to them. Gradually we became nationless. I came to hate nations. We are deformed by nation-states. ...

The desert could not be claimed or owned – it was a piece of cloth carried by winds, never held down by stones, and given a hundred shifting names long before Canterbury existed, long before battles and treaties quilted Europe and the East. Its caravans, those strange rambling feasts and cultures, left nothing behind, not an ember. All of us, even those with European homes and children in the distance, wished to remove the clothing of our countries. It was a place of faith. We disappeared into landscape. Fire and sand. We left the harbours of oasis. The places water came to and touched ... Ain, Bir, Wadi, Foggara, Khottara, Shaduf. I didn't want my name against such beautiful names. Erase the family name! Erase nations! I was taught such things by the desert.

Still, some wanted their mark there. On that dry water course, on this shingled knoll. Small vanities in this plot of land north-west of the Sudan, south of Cyrenaica. Fenelon-Barnes wanted the fossil trees he discovered to bear his name. He even wanted a tribe to take his name, and spent a year on the negotiations. Then Bauchan outdid him, having a type of sand dune named after him. But I wanted to erase my name and the place I had come from.

2 Land as property

LAND AS A KIND OF PROPERTY

Sheenagh Pugh

GEOGRAPHY 2

The land wrote itself before any
came to chart it: continents broke
and reassembled; two masses crashed
and threw a mountain range, a border
waiting for customs posts; glaciers cut
narrow valleys, close and separate,
each shuttered cautiously from its neighbour.
A coast curved itself into a haven
for shipping; a hill kept watch
on the landscape till the fort was built
A river spread rich gentle living
over these fields; elsewhere, the want
of water made the contours stand out
like starved bones.

And when it was all ready
they came, at last, to be masters
of it all; to take up the lives
mapped out for them.

The Native American relationship to land

Within the Western world the notion that land can be conceived of as property is
so deeply embedded an ideology as to have become 'self-evident'. However, as
shown in the following extracts, many cultures regard land as incapable of
ownership by human beings, or award them a form of tenure quite at variance with
the Western tradition. These different visions of land have often come into
conflict, most strikingly shown 'in the white man's inability to comprehend the
indian's reverence for the land' (Donald W. Large, 'This Land is Whose Land:
Changing Concepts of Land as Property' (1973) 4 *Wisc. LR* 1039, 1042).
T. McLuhan in *Touch the Earth* (Abacus: 1972) (54) quotes a chief from one of

the principal bands of the northern Blackfeet upon being asked to sign a Land Treaty by white men in his region:

Our land is more valuable than your money. It will last forever. It will not even perish by the flames of fire. As long as the sun shines and the waters flow, this land will be here to give life to men and animals. We cannot sell the lives of men and animals: therefore we cannot sell this land. It was put here for us by the Great Spirit and we cannot sell it because it does not belong to us. You can count your money and burn it within the nod of a buffalo's head, but only the Great Spirit can count the grains of sand and the blades of grass of these plains. As a present to you, we will give you anything we have that you can take with you; but the land, never.

Aboriginal songlines

The Native Americans are not alone in perceiving an intimate and religious connection between human life and the land.

B. Chatwin *The Songlines* (Picador: 1987)

White men, he began, made the common mistake of assuming that, because the Aboriginals were wanderers, they could have no system of land tenure. This was nonsense. Aboriginals, it was true, could not imagine territory as a block of land hemmed in by frontiers: but rather as an interlocking network of 'lines' or 'ways through'.

'All our words for "country" ', he said, 'are the same as the words for "line" '. For this there was one simple explanation. Most of Outback Australia was arid scrub or desert where rainfall was always patchy and where one year of plenty might be followed by seven years of lean. To move in such landscape was survival: to stay in the same place suicide. The definition of 'a man's own country' was 'the place in which I do not have to ask'. Yet to feel 'at home' in that country depended on being able to leave it. Everyone hoped to have at least four 'ways out', along which he could travel in a crisis. Every tribe – like it or not – had to cultivate relations with its neighbour...

'The trade route is the Songline,' said Flynn. 'Because songs, not things, are the principal medium of exchange. Trading in "things" is the secondary consequence of trading in song.'

Before the whites came, he went on, no one in Australia was landless, since everyone inherited, as his or her private property, a stretch of the Ancestor's song and the stretch of country over which the song passed. A man's verses were his title deeds to territory. He could lend them to others. He could borrow other verses in return. The one thing he couldn't do was sell or get rid of them.

Supposing the Elders of a Carpet Snake clan decided it was time to sing their song cycle from beginning to end? Messages would be sent out, up and down the track, summoning song-owners to assemble at the Big Place. One after the other, each 'owner' would then sing his stretch of the Ancestor's footprints. Always in the correct sequence!

'To sing a verse out of order', Flynn said sombrely, 'was a crime. Usually meant the death penalty.'

'I can see that,' I said. 'It'd be the musical equivalent of an earthquake.'

'Worse,' he scowled. 'It would be to un-create the Creation.'

Islamic ownership of land versus the Torrens system in Malaysia

The resounding clash between two different cultures and legal systems can be seen in modern Malaysia, where the Torrens system – a relic of British colonial rule (see Chapter 10, p. 273) – exists in a country where Islam is the national religion. The Islamic concept of ownership over land is at variance with a system that confers an indefeasible title upon the registered owner. The Qur'an does recognise a right to private property but it is subject to important limitation, as indicated in the next extract.

C.G. Weeramantry *Islamic Jurisprudence – An International Perspective* (Macmillan: 1988)

Since all property belongs to God, its holders are only trustees. They must not use it selfishly without regard to the social purposes which it should serve. Thus, while legal ownership was permitted and protected by the law, it was subject to an overall social orientation. A landowner who neglected to cultivate his land for an inordinate period of time might lose his right to retain his property and his neighbours might acquire the right to purchase and cultivate it.[1]

Such concerns become important particularly in the modern age, with its emphasis on environmental concerns. The planet was inherited not by any one generation but by mankind and all its posterity from generation to generation. 'Do you not see that God has subjected to your use all things in the heavens and on earth and has made his bounties flow to you in exceeding measure, both seen and unseen?' (Qur'an, xxxi:20.) Each generation is only the trustee. No one generation has the right to pollute the planet or to consume all its natural resources in a manner that leaves for posterity only a polluted planet or one seriously denuded of its resources.

Therefore some Malaysian lawyers are concerned to examine the prospects for Islamisation of this field of law:

Haji Salleh Haji Buang *Malaysian Torrens System* (Percetekan Dewan Bahasa dan Pustaka: 1989)

It is generally believed that the law of real property in Malaysia is totally devoid of Islamic content...

An in-depth study of our early land law reveal(s) the existence of a substantial body of Islamic legal principles, a historical fact which contemporary scholars find

---

1 Compare Chapter 3, pp. 60–75.

themselves in difficulty to accept, having been so engrossed with the civil law system introduced in these shores after the arrival of the English administrators towards the close of the eighteenth century. This important point needs to be reemphasised if we are to consider seriously the possibility of re-introducing Islamic precepts into the law of property in Malaysia...

As stated earlier, indefeasibility of title has no place in Islam. In the Quran, Allah says that everything in this universe vests absolutely in Allah (Sura al-Maidah, ayat 17) and that the State is but a mere Trustee. The State has powers to alienate the rights of possessions to such 'deserving grantees' (the deserving grantees, according to Islamic law, are the landless, the warriors and others who serve the State, those who can actually cultivate the land, and those who have just embraced Islam) who are able to put the land to productive use and to be of benefit to the society at large. Although such possessory rights are capable of being disposed *inter vivos* and can devolve to one's heirs upon death, the cardinal rule in Islam is that the State can at any time repossess the land if such land is required for the public good. Historical precedents abound in Islam...

ENGLISH AND WELSH LAND

The influence of climate upon the landscape

Climate has had a dramatic effect upon the landscape, the kinds of cultivation and the uses of land for industrial and domestic purposes.

G. Manley *Climate and the British Scenery* (Collins: 1952)

The climate of the British Isles is such that the inhabitants enjoy, but are not subordinate to, the power of the sun. It has accordingly been stigmatised by Latin Europe. Tacitus left a renowned note on the subject: 'The climate is objectionable with frequent rains and mists, but there is no extreme cold'. Dumas gave vent to the views of the romantic Sturm-and(sic)-Drang period, 'L'Angleterre est un pays ou le soleil rasemble à la lune'.[2]

By contrast, more discriminating observers have often found room for praise; and Englishmen themselves, especially those who have not dwelt for long elsewhere, or have resisted the seductions of lands nearer the equator, are evidently very proud of their climate. As a Venetian Ambassador said in 1497, 'The English are great lovers of themselves and of everything belonging to them'... Charles [I] said that the English climate is the best in the world. A man can enjoy outdoor exercise on all but five days in a year' [and this] has been echoed by most energetic Englishmen...

In the British Isles, structure goes far to mould the diversities of our climate. Yet in its turn climate goes far to set limits to the use that can be made of the physical features of the country in which we live. There are large areas in which the normal agricultural yield is thoroughly adequate for the maintenance and accumulation of

---

2 'England is a country where the sun looks like the moon.'

energy, a fact well shown not only by doubling of our population in the eighteenth century, but also by the evidence of energy to spare for the graces of life whether in the form of meteorological recording, tours to the Lake District, walnut furniture or epistolary accomplishment.

But there are large areas in which practically no material yield is obtainable at all. Thirty-five percent of Great Britain is mountain and moorland. Practically all the land above 1,500 feet falls into this category and a great deal of it is so poorly drained that only the sourest peaty soils are found. Elsewhere on the steeper slopes leaching removes enough mineral content from the thin poor soils to render them infertile and incapable of supporting more than a poor vegetation carrying very little stock.

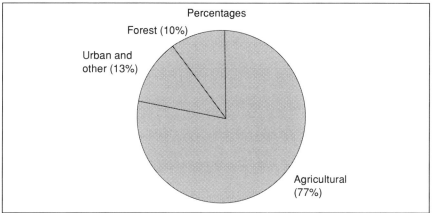

United Kingdom

Fig. 2:1 Land Use, 1991
More than three-quarters of the land area in the United
Kingdom is still used for agriculture; a further 10 per
cent is covered by forest and woodland
(*Source: Social Trends (1994) No. 24*, Department of the
Environment)

Origins of the landscape

A.E. Trueman *Geology and Scenery in England and Wales* (Pelican: 1971)

In England and Wales we are singularly placed to appreciate the relationship of scenery and structure, for few other parts of the earth's surface show in a similar small area so great a diversity of rock types and of landscape features: 'Britain is a world by itself'; its mountains are not high, nor its rivers long, but within a few hundred miles of travel from east to west one may see more varieties of scenery than are to be found in many bigger countries.

There are hill-forms of every type; smooth contoured chalk downs in a great belt encircling the London basin, the long line of the Cotswold edge, even-topped plateaux in Wales and Devon, bleak granite moorlands and craggy volcanic cliffs. All these types reflect their underlying structure and their origin is apparent in their shape.

In many of these different regions the native stone has given character and fitness to the buildings; the wide variety of stones, together with the frequent use of wood and brick and thatch, especially in the stoneless areas, has added charm to English villages and towns, and has made the dwellings, particularly the smaller cottages (for stones for churches and large houses were carried for many miles even in early times), ideally suited to their surroundings. With the improvement of transport during the nineteenth century, building materials were more frequently carried over greater distances, and soon after the opening of railways houses began to lose that harmony with the countryside so characteristic of the older cottages. The towns which thus sprung up at some railway centres are examples of the way in which individuality was lost, and lately the housing estate has spread a new uniformity even more widely over the country.

The combination of nature, human ingenuity and climate has indeed wrought a landscape which changes at nearly every turn. Small pockets of 'English countryside', as depicted by Wordsworth and Constable, do exist. The rural idyll is, however, the privilege of the minority. Many rural dwellers are agricultural workers, most of whom are harnessed to jobs through their housing, under the system of tied cottages. Moreover, tensions exist between the 'real' rural population and town dwellers who buy second homes in the more accessible areas of the countryside.

For most inhabitants of England and Wales, from the nineteenth century onwards, it is the town and not the field which represents home.

D. Thomson *England in the Nineteenth Century* (Penguin: 1978)

It was during the generation after Waterloo that the balance of English economic and social life changed from being predominantly agricultural to being predominantly industrial; and with this change ... came the growth of urbanization, the development of the mine and factory as the unit of production, and the transformation of the 'average' Englishman into a townsman rather than a countryman. The normal community in England was no longer a village, but an industrial town. The horizon of Englishmen in their daily life and work was not the open fields but the sky-line of rooftops and chimney-stacks. The home was not for most a country house or a cottage, but a town villa or tenement.

The rapid building of cheap, poor quality housing was to provide a later generation with serious problems.

P. Malpass *The Housing Crisis* (Croom Helm: 1986)

The early development of Britain as an urban industrial society bequeathed to the twentieth century a huge stock of dwellings which were old, small, densely packed together, often poorly built originally and badly maintained subsequently. Apart from problems of structural instability and dampness, lack of heating, hot water and modern sanitation made many of these dwellings unfit for human habitation.[3] The poor quality of nineteenth century working class housing, particularly that occupied by lower paid workers, reflected the significant gap between the cost of decent accommodation and the price that many workers could afford to pay.

The ravages of two World Wars upon the environment led the new breed of town planners in the period from 1945 to the late 1950s to build on blitzed sites and green fields outside the cities. Thus, began the construction of so-called 'new towns'. However, with the political parties vying in their promises to build more new houses – in 1951 Harold Macmillan, then Minister of Housing, promised to build 300,000 in one year – it became necessary to begin to clear the old slum housing built in the Victorian era.

A.E.B. Leaper *Health, Wealth and Housing* (Basil Blackwell: 1980)

[F]rom the early 1960s the bulldozers began to bite into the inner cities: slum clearance in Britain rose from less than 35,000 houses a year in 1955 to a steady 70,000 a year from 1960. In that year 135,000 houses were improved with the help of government grants: in 1955 there had been too little improvement to record in official statistics. City centre redevelopment, the boom in office building, the expansion of universities, polytechnics and hospitals, and the urban motorways that carved through Glasgow, Birmingham and other great cities posed problems.

The dispersal of people to increasingly distant suburbs and the growing concentrations of service industries in city centres were bound to lead to a re-invasion by young professionals and executives of inner areas long abandoned to the working class...

'Gentrification', a term coined by Ruth Glass for this process, entered the vocabulary of planning debate... The long established working class were rehoused on a massive scale, but many were stacked in tower blocks: the numbers of Council flats in England and Wales built fifteen or more storeys from the ground rose from 8 in 1955 to 17,351 in 1965. There began to take shape a social division between middle-class people living in houses and workers living in flats – 'people silos' as they were called in Sweden. Even before one of them collapsed in a gas explosion at Ronan Point in London, the tower block became a focus of special hatred.

B. Campbell *Wigan Pier Revisited* (Virago:1984)

Tower blocks have become the symbol of our disaffection, monumental mistakes

---

3 See also Chapter 4, pp. 97–103.

for which we can all justifiably blame the politicians and professionals.[4] But the pressure was on, with state housing subsidies inciting the architects, builders and local councils to build ever upward and experiment with barely tested materials, to cram the maximum population onto the minimum land mass, so that during the twenty-year tower block boom nearly half a million high-rise homes were built.

All over England there are relics of this reckless eldorado. One block in the middle of the Northeast garden city, Washington New Town, now stands completely empty. These flats, the size of a Victorian mill, were evacuated only fifteen years after being built. People just won't live there ... What was once a landscape of banks of back-to-backs has become an asymmetrical mess of flats and maisonettes. There's the notorious lowrise Noble Court stranded beside a highway overlooking the Tyne with 'Get us out of this hell' written on the wall. The very complexion of some of our cities has changed. The regional shades of red brick and yellow stone which once coloured the cityscape have disappeared, replaced by the grey monotone of concrete. On the edge of Sheffield town centre the eye confronts some long walls the colour of a storm, so forbidding that not even the kids have made their mark. This is another monstrosity celebrated as a brilliant piece of architectural engineering. It looks like a bunker.

Who owns the land?

R. Norton-Taylor and K. Cahill 'Keep out: this land is their land', *The Guardian*, 13 August 1994

We know, or can discover through published records, who owns the largest companies which trade in Britain: the stockmarket is relatively transparent. It is also straightforward to identify the owner of a house or an office block. But try to discover who owns a field, a hedgerow or a wood and you will be greeted with ignorance and defensive hostility...

Who are the biggest landowners? The Government won't tell you, and the official Land Registry is only partially complete. A detailed investigation by the Guardian suggests that the biggest 10 landowners own over 1.5 million acres between them (see Table 2.1).

The figures, obtained over several months from searches through county records, company reports, local archives, official registries and published interviews and investigations, represent what we believe to be held by landowners directly and via their trusts and corporations ... we cannot be certain that every acre is included. But the information is as complete as it can be from sources within the public domain...

Fortunately, another government, some 120 years ago, was far more open. It published a detailed document with which we can compare the 1994 figures: *Return of Owners of Land*. (See Table 2.2 on page 35). Issued in July 1875, this resembles a Victorian *Domesday Book*, and includes the names of every landowner in England, Wales, Scotland and Ireland, the quantity of land they

---

4 For the court's response to the challenges posed by tower blocks, see *Liverpool CC* v *Irwin* (1977), Chapter 6, p.172–3.

Table 2.1

	Top 10 Individual owners, 1994[1]	Acres
1	The Duke of Buccleuch/Buccleuch Estates Co.	277,000
2	The Duke of Westminster/Grosvenor Estates	190,000
3	The Earl of Seafield	185,000
4	The Prince of Wales/Duchy of Cornwall	141,000
5	Duke of Atholl	130,000
6	Countess of Sutherland	126,000
7	Cptn A A Farquharson	119,000
8	The Earl of Stair	110,000
9	Sir Donald Cameron of Lochiel	98,000
10	The Duke of Northumberland	95,000

[1] *Individual ownership is almost always held in some form of trust or corporation*

owned, and the approximate value. All of which can be compared to the modern figures to reveal the remarkable conservatism of the landowning classes: as the tables show, traditional owners have been extremely successful at holding on to their estates.

Many of the same names were there in the Victorian top 10. The size of total landholdings have changed ... But in a century when whole new classes have gained economic power, when universal suffrage has shifted political power, and when population growth and immigration have redefined the demographic landscape, landownership has remained relatively untouched. The club has not bothered to welcome too many newcomers...

Today's top 10 are among the 1 per cent of the population estimated to own more than 50 per cent of the land. The estimate was made by the Royal Commission on the Distribution of Income and Wealth before it was wound up by Mrs Thatcher's Government in 1981. It noted: 'The paucity of up to date information on land ownership is remarkable'...

This lack of openness might not matter within our culture of closed government,

Table 2.2

	Top 10 Landowners, 1875	Acres	Gross est. rent
1	Duke of Sutherland	1,358,546	£141,679
2	Duke of Buccleuch	459,108	£215,593
3	Earl of Breadalbane	438,358	£58,292
4	Sir Charles Ross	356,500	£17,264
5	Earl of Seafield	305,930	£78,227
6	Duke of Richmond	286,411	£79,683
7	Duke of Fife	249,220	£71,312
8	Alexander Matheson	220,663	£26,461
9	Duke of Atholl	201,640	£42,030
10	Duke of Devonshire	198,493	£180,795

(*Source: Return of Owners of Land in England and Wales, Scotland and Ireland, Local Government Board, July 1875; excludes London*)

but for one expensive factor of late 20th-century life: the Common Agricultural Policy. As European Union farm policy takes growing numbers of British fields out of use, farmers are claiming increasing amounts of subsidy, provided by taxpayers. Yet if the subsidy brings particular benefits to a small number of big landowners, shouldn't the taxpayers know why?...

The Government has already begun a big survey to help farmers claim payments from the EU ... Pressure has come from the set-aside scheme, by which farmers are paid about £130 per acre *not* to grow crops. The ministry [of Agriculture] demanded that farmers submit OS maps, with their fields marked, along with their claim forms. The result has been the most detailed survey of land use in recent years. The work has cost the Government £120 million, according to Peter Gilbert of the Royal Institution of Chartered Surveyors.

Yet the information unearthed by the survey remains an official secret. The ministry says that British farmers are paid more than £1.1 billion a year for taking land out of use, out of a total set-aside subsidy of £3 billion, but it will not say who is receiving this money or how many acres each claim represents. What we do know, from a written Parliamentary answer, is that money goes to 33,000 farmers to leave some of their fields empty. And, according to a ministry spokesperson, this year seven farmers will receive over £500,000.

[Last month] ... Captain Mark Phillips, former husband of the Princess Royal, who manages her Gatcombe Park estate in Gloucestershire ... said that 90 per cent of his profits came from set-aside: 'The presence of a set-aside scheme is crazy. There is no sense in it, although financially we are doing well out of it'.

THE LEGAL FRAMEWORK

Introduction

The subject-matter of traditional land law is not concerned with the whole landscape of England and Wales. Its focus is the abstract categories of ownership, occupation and use. The common law does not regard land as capable of being owned. Only 'estates and interests' in land are property, and carry with them the rights to exclusive use of the land and to transfer it.

Further, as Norman Ginsburg in *Class, Capital and Social Policy* (Macmillan: 1979) suggests, the role of land law is primarily 'to facilitate the process of realisation of surplus value for the builder and the process of exchange for the consumer'. The state provides 'the legal framework within which this all takes place, but is not otherwise concerned in the regulation ... aspects of the private housing market' (p. 129). Great questions such as the way in which buildings may be rehabilitated, or private, council and housing association landlords forced to meet basic standards of health and safety within their properties, have been largely pushed into the field of what has been designated 'Housing Law'. The latter is less concerned with providing a framework for exchange than a means for intervening on behalf of the more vulnerable members in society.

Common law and equity

The framework of real property is a combination of rules derived from common law, equity and statute. The origins of this system lie in English legal history. (See also Chapters 8 and 9 below.)

P. Todd *Textbook on Trusts* (Blackstone: 1991)

The legal system divides into common law and equity: two different systems and until recently[5] two separate jurisdictions. Equity and trusts are found exclusively in England and in other non-Roman legal systems, and neither has any place, for example, on the Continent. That a legal system should develop two separate concepts of ownership, both of which can apply simultaneously to the same property, and effectively two separate legal systems, is by no means self-evident. The reason lies in historical differences between England and Continental countries, dating from the feudal era, and in particular the Norman Conquest...

The rigidity of many legal systems is mitigated by discretionary executive power. In England and Wales today, for example, there is a great deal of executive discretion in both prosecution and sentencing under a criminal law which, if rigidly enforced, could be very burdensome, even for relatively law-abiding individuals. The medieval Chancellor (who was usually an ecclesiastic) performed an analogous function in relation to the rigidity of the common law at the time; he had the power to issue the royal writs, and this function came to be exercised in a discretionary manner, based on notions of conscience and justice. He also had powers to act against individuals, and to enforce those orders against them by imprisonment. This discretionary use of power was the foundation of equity. Eventually, probably during the 15th century, the Chancellor's office took on many of the features of a court, and the Court of Chancery was born.

The story is taken up in the next extract with particular reference to the history of uses:

B. McCutcheon and P.C. Soares *Euro-Trusts – The New European Dimension for Trusts* (Legal Studies Publishing Ltd: 1993)

The use mechanism involved a transfer of real property from A to B for certain purposes, requiring A to rely on B to carry out those purposes. If A wished C to have the benefit of the use of the property, A would enfeoff B, whereby B would agree to hold the property for the use, i.e. the benefit of, C. A was referred to as the '*feoffor to uses*' ...; B, the '*feoffee to uses*' ...; and C, the '*cestui que use*'...

According to legal scholars, uses were in operation by at least the thirteenth century. For approximately the first two centuries of the existence of the use mechanism in England it had no legal significance; that is, in the above example, B's agreement to hold the land for the benefit of C was unenforceable at law. By the fifteenth century the developing common law of England became increasingly

---

5 What other profession regards 1873 as recent?

inflexible and complex and the courts of law continued to refuse to recognise the use. Therefore, the use was merely a moral obligation which depended on B's trustworthiness for its effectiveness. Nevertheless, the use functioned well enough to become widely employed, even without the intervention of any court. It is probable that the Chancellor began to enforce the use sometime in the fifteenth century.

The use mechanism became popular because it permitted a person to avoid the consequences of legal ownership, while enjoying the benefits of ownership ... [T]he Chancellor's willingness to require *feofees* to fulfil their duties and responsibilities to the *cestuis* significantly increased the effectiveness and popularity of the use mechanism. Subsequently, the enjoyment of the rights to use property no longer depended solely on the honesty of the *feoffees*. Even though the *cestui* was protected in Chancery and had an equitable interest in the use of the property, the law courts continued to refuse to recognise his interest. Therefore, the escape from the disadvantages of legal ownership continued to be effective. In this manner, the dual system of law and equity enabled the unique situation to exist in which one person, in reality only a nominee, was recognised in the law courts as the sole owner of the property with all the legal consequences that the traditional doctrines of common law had attached to such ownership, while the beneficiary enjoyed protection in Chancery free of those consequences...

[P]erhaps the most important and influential [reason for the employment of uses] was the desire to provide for the testamentary disposition of real property. From the 1200s until 1540, no disposition of real property could be made by will. During this period, many people wished to avoid the doctrine of primogeniture, by which the eldest son received all his father's real property at a time when real property was the principal form of wealth. In the absence of a will, it was impossible for a father to provide adequately for his daughters and younger sons or to devote part of his real property to charitable uses.

Another important factor in the development of uses was the wish to escape the onerous feudal incidents that were payable on the occurrence of various events and, most important, on the death intestate of the owner of land...

The use mechanism became so popular that it is said that during the War of the Roses, or by the year 1500, almost all the land in England was held to uses.

Although most of England was favourably disposed to the development of the use, the King was not. Landowners other than the King, as feudal lords, would lose by the evasion of feudal incidents, but they would also gain as feudal tenants. By the fifteenth century the feudal regime was waning, and it had become a system of unpopular taxes. The King, at the top of the feudal landholding structure, would always lose and never gain with respect to uses, because he was feudal lord over all and tenant to none.

In Tudor times Henry VIII made a valiant attempt to collect some of the revenue lost to him by the employment of the use. He forced a reluctant Parliament to pass the Statute of Uses 1535 which was intended to abolish the system of dual ownership so that the legal estate vested in the *cestui que use*. The latter would then be liable for feudal taxes. However, the Statute of Uses was not effective against all use mechanisms and by the seventeenth century the use revived in the form of the trust. This re-emergence put a further strain upon an already difficult relationship between the jurisdictions of common law and equity.

R.J. Walker and M.G. Walker, *The English Legal System* (Butterworths: 1985, 6th edn)

By the very nature of the jurisdiction it exercised the Court of Chancery was bound to come into conflict with the courts of common law. Equity both supplemented the common law and corrected its deficiencies. Where equity supplemented the common law, as by the recognition of uses and the grant of equitable remedies for the infringement of legal rights, it was not particularly repugnant to common lawyers because it did not countermand their authority. However, this was not the case where equity corrected the common law. In these instances there was a direct conflict between the common law courts and the Chancellor. Thus the Chancellor would rescind a contract or rectify a deed where the common law courts would enforce it in accordance with its original terms. Equity would allow a mortgagor to redeem where the common law would recognise no fetter on the mortgagee's legal estate. In such a case equity would have to prevail or be of no effect. Consequently, in order to assert its prevalence, the Court of Chancery began to issue common injunctions which, although directed at the litigant personally rather than the common law courts, had the effect of limiting common law jurisdiction.[6]... The conflict ... came ... with the appointment of Coke as Chief Justice of the Common Pleas in 1606. Coke, a bitter opponent of prerogative power, attacked vigorously the jurisdiction of all the courts exercising this jurisdiction. In 1613 he was transferred to the King's Bench in which court he held in a case in 1615 (*Courtney v Glanvil* [1615] Cro. Jac. 343) that where a common law court had decided a case the Court of Chancery had no power to intervene between the parties ... Lord Ellesmere, the Lord Chancellor, brought the dispute to a head in the same year by declaring, in the *Earl of Oxford's case* ((1615) 1 Rep. Ch. 11) the power of the Chancery to set aside common law judgments 'not for any error or defect in the judgment, but for the hard conscience of the party'. The dispute was referred to the King, James I. James I decided in favour of the Court of Chancery and upheld the validity of the common injunction. The supremacy of equity was established though in the next eighty years this supremacy was by no means unchallenged.

In 1873 Gladstone's government passed the Judicature Act (succeeded by further statutes over the following two years). No longer, therefore, would common law and equity be administered in different courts but in one High Court, albeit subdivided into a variety of divisions. In case of conflict between the rules of equity and the common law it was provided by s. 25 of the 1973 Act, now s. 49, Supreme Court Act 1981, that the rules of equity would prevail.

The Court of Chancery had become a byword for administrative delay (for example, *Walsh* v *Lonsdale* (1882) – see Chapter 4, p. 87), as famously depicted

---

6 For examples of discretion in equitable remedies, see for example, *Shaw* v *Applegate* [1977] Chapter 7 at p. 211.

by Dickens. (For a case involving a real 'Bleak House', see *Flegg*, Chapter 10, p. 293.)

Charles Dickens *Bleak House* (1853) New York, (Signet Classics: 1964)

This is the Court of Chancery: which has its decaying houses and its blighted lands in every shire; which has its worn-out lunatic in every madhouse, and its dead in every churchyard; which has its ruined suitor, with his slipshod heels and threadbare dress, borrowing and begging through the round of every man's acquaintance; which gives to monied might, the means abundantly of wearying out the right; which so exhausts finances, patience, courage, hope: so overthrows the brain and breaks the heart; that there is not an honourable man among its practitioners who would not give – who does not often give – the warning, 'Suffer any wrong that can be done you, rather than come here'.

Thus the main motivating force behind the Judicature Acts was to rid the Court of Chancery of its ability to prolong cases for many years. There has been much debate since the Judicature Acts as to whether they did something more than fuse the two systems at a procedural level, namely to change the substantive law.

This debate has received fresh impetus from judicial statements, particularly within the New Zealand jurisdiction, that the 'two confluent streams are thoroughly intermixed' (Lord Simon of Glaisdale, *United Scientific Holdings Ltd* v *Burnley Borough Council* [1975] AC 945). An indication of the strong views which the subject of 'fusion' produces may be gained from the following extracts:

A. Mason 'The Place of Equity and Equitable Remedies in the Contemporary Common Law World' (1994) 110 *LQR* 238

It is remarkable that the common law has remained for so long impervious to the beguiling charms of equity. More than 100 years elapsed after the introduction of the original Judicature Act before lawyers became receptive to the notion, still regarded as heretical by some Australian commentators, that equity and common law are capable of constituting a single body of law rather than two separate bodies of law adminstered together ...

Concentration on the effect of the Judicature Acts to the exclusion of other considerations is likely to result in overemphasis on the state of equitable doctrine as it existed immediately before the original Judicature Act was introduced ... For my part, I agree with the comment of Somers J in *Elders Pastoral Ltd* v *Bank of New Zealand* [1989] 2 NZLR 180 at 193:

'Neither law nor equity is now stifled by its origin and the fact that both are administered by one Court has inevitably meant that each has borrowed from the other in furthering the harmonious development of the law as a whole.'

J. Martin 'Fusion, Fallacy and Confusion; A Comparative Study' (1994) *Conv* 13

The 'fusion fallacy' is the view that the Judicature Act somehow codified law and equity into one subject-matter and severed the roots of the conceptual distinctions between them. This has led to decisions which cannot be explained on the basis of either law or equity, but only on the basis that the Act changed the substantive law ...

None would advocate that our common law and equitable doctrines should be inflexible or unable to develop. The view that such flexibility and capacity for development is best achieved by disregarding the legal or equitable origins of causes of action, remedies or defences is misconceived ...

To deny that the Judicature Acts fused law and equity is not to suggest that law and equity became incapable of future development in 1873. One effect of a fused administration of law and equity must be to encourage the coherent development of legal and equitable doctrines, with each branch being beneficially influenced by the proximity of the other. The ability to 'take wisdom where we find it' does not depend on the notion that law and equity are fused.

The 1925 legislation

After 1875, the next important date in real property chronology is 1925 which saw the enactment of the Law of Property Act, the Settled Land Act, the Trustee Act, the Administration of Estates Act, the Land Registration Act and the Land Charges Act (the latter amended and re-enacted in 1972). There has been much debate about the real underlying purposes of this legislation which has been generally vaunted, especially in the major textbooks, as designed to ease the buying and selling of land (see Chapter 10). However, the next extract raises questions about the particular vision of history inherent in the popular interpretation of 1925.

S. Anderson 'Land Law Texts and the Explanation of 1925' *Current Legal Problems* (1984) 63[7]

The principles which are used to explain the legislation are political and economic, derived from a reading of the nineteenth century land reform movement, and in particular from its hostility to the strict settlement. But only those parts of the movement concerning the modern, artificial construct called 'land law' are studied, and only those parts which were successful. There is no attempt to understand the movement in its context, to appreciate the purposes of those whose words are used, to consider either the views of their antagonists or those of later researchers ... by omitting these a distorted view of what was wrong with 'the land laws' has been fostered. The standard land lawyer's view of the nineteenth century heritage ... is portrayed as one whose lands were fettered by the strict settlement,[8] whose

---

7 See also A. Offer (1986) 40 MLR 505.
8 See Chapter 8.

buildings were falling into ruin and whose agriculture was stagnant. The evidence for this comes not from historians but, usually, from a lawyer, Underhill, or from the Liberal Party propagandists...

The structure of Liberal argument, both at the time and as it has come down to us in modern land law texts, is thus built upon two suppositions. The first is that there was a significant correlation between the legal form of land-holding and the form and extent of commercial development of the land. All modern research denies this. The second supposition is ideological, that ownership ought to be individual. But ... this was an argument that was applied with the greatest selectivity; it was essentially a stick to beat the aristocracy ... The second theme to the philosophy of 1925 is to do with improving methods of conveyancing...

For those who argue that the 1925 legislation represents a series of reforms in order to facilitate conveyancing, the foundation of the legislation lies in s. 1, Law of Property Act, where Parliament reduced the number of estates and interests recognisable by the law, but did not alter equitable rules concerning land ownership:

Law of Property Act 1925

Legal estates and equitable interests

1. (1) The only estates in land which are capable of subsisting or of being conveyed or created at law are –
   (a) An estate in fee simple absolute in possession;
   (b) A term of years absolute.
   (2) The only interests or charges in or over land which are capable of subsisting or of being conveyed or created at law are –
   (a) An easement, right or privilege in or over land for an interest equivalent to an estate in fee simple absolute in possession or a term of years absolute;
   (b) A rentcharge in possession issuing out of or charged on land being either perpetual or for a term of years absolute;
   (c) A charge by way of legal mortgage;
   (d) ... any other similar charge on land which is not created by an instrument;
   (e) Rights of entry exercisable over or in respect of a legal term of years absolute, or annexed, for any purpose, to a legal rentcharge.
   (3) All other estates, interests, and charges in or over land take effect as equitable interests;
   (4) The estates, interests, and charges which under this section are authorised to subsist or be conveyed or created at law are (when subsisting or conveyed or created at law) in this Act referred to as 'legal estates,' and have the same incidents as legal estates subsisting at the commencement of this Act; and the owner of a legal estate is referred to as 'an estate owner' and his legal estate is referred to as his estate.
   (5) A legal estate may subsist concurrently with or subject to any other legal estate in the same land in like manner as it could have done before the commencement of this Act.

(6) A legal estate is not capable of subsisting or of being created in an undivided share in land or of being held by an infant.[9]
(8) Estates, interests and charges in or over land which are not legal estates are in this Act referred to as 'equitable interests,' and powers which by this Act are to operate only in equity are in this Act referred to as 'equitable powers'.

Much more recently the Lord Chancellor's Department has produced a consultation paper proposing a new estate in land – commonhold.[10] This recommendation was made in response to concern about long leaseholds, including high levels of service charges and poor management by landlords. However, the government has met such criticisms with the introduction of a system of enfranchisement rather than any new estate in land. The resulting legislation seems to have pleased very few.

S. Bright 'Enfranchisement – A Fair Deal For All Or For None' (1994) *Conv* 211

The Leasehold Reform, Housing and Urban Development Act 1993 ('the 1993 Act') was heralded as fulfilling the Conservative Party's manifesto commitments to furthering home ownership. In its passage through Parliament it made good friends and fierce enemies – the friends believing that it was giving tenants their due and the enemies regarding it as an unjustifiable expropriation of property. On its face it appears to give long leaseholders of flats the collective right to purchase the freehold of their block of flats or, alternatively, to extend their leases. In practice, there are real fears that the complexity of the Act and the cost of enfranchising will render it a little-used provision...

It already seems that there is no great rush by tenants to seek collective enfranchisement. Perhaps some who have considered the option have realised the problems arising from the fact that the right is *collective*. Agreement among a disparate group of tenants is not going to be easy. Disputes about valuations of their own flats which may 'enjoy' different features can easily be imagined; some will be less committed to the venture than others. Almost inevitably, an agreement between the participating tenants will be needed to cover the contributions each is to make to the price, costs, setting up a management company as nominee purchaser, and so forth. In the face of significant disagreement on the issues, a solicitor appointed to act for all the tenants may feel there is a potential conflict of interest and be unable to advise on the resolution of the terms of acquisition in dispute between individual tenants. For all these reasons, the right to a new lease looks attractive.[11]

---

9 See Chapter 9.
10 'Commonhold – A Consultation Paper' (Lord Chancellors Dept, HMSO: 1990). See also M. McKeone (1990) Law Soc Gaz No. 44, 8; Working Group 137 NLJ (1987) 715: C. Owen 142 NLJ (1992) 765.
11 Generally on this reform see J. South (ed) 'Leasehold – the Case for Reform' (Collected Papers of the Leasehold Enfranchisement Association: 1993) and P. Matthews and D. Millichap, *A Guide to the Leasehold Reform, Housing and Urban Development Act* (Butterworths: 1993).

To have a legal estate, whether freehold or leasehold, is to enjoy quite a considerable degree of individual freedom, within the private space accorded to you by the law.

J.W. Harris 'Ownership of Land in English Law' in N. MacCormick and P. Birks (eds) *The Legal Mind: Essays for Tony Honore* (Clarendon Press: 1986)

A legal estate is the right to possess land for a determinate or an indefinite period of time. Granted that one has that right, what rights, privileges, powers, and immunities relating to land does one have? Keep out the world and live as a recluse; admit what visitors one wishes; create tenancies or sub-tenancies; grow mushrooms in the cellar; sing bawdy songs in the bath; paint the front door a luminous green; sunbathe in the nude – no-one could list them all. Their open-endedness is and can only be captured by a conception whose imprecision makes it uncongenial to real property lawyers, though it plays as important a part in legal doctrine as does the traditional tally of technical terms. If one has the legal estate, one is empowered and privileged to do anything in relation to the land which the culture of the time, as represented and interpreted by the judiciary, accords to an 'owner of land'.

Contrary to Harris's statement, the definition section of the Law of Property Act 1925 legal framework does provides some indication of the 'rights, privileges, powers and immunities' which the owner of the legal estate, or indeed any other estate or interest in or over land, may enjoy:

Law of Property Act 1925

205. (1) (ix) Land includes ... land of any tenure, and mines and minerals, whether or not held apart from the surface, buildings or parts of buildings (whether the division is horizontal, vertical or made in any other way) and other corporeal hereditaments; also a manor, an advowson,[12] and a rent and other incorporeal hereditament, and an easement, right, privilege, or benefit in, over, or derived from land; but not an undivided share in land; and 'mines and minerals' include any strata or seam of minerals or substances in or under any land, and powers of working and getting the same but not an undivided share thereof; and 'manor' includes a lordship, and reputed manor or lordship; and 'hereditament' means any real property which on an intestacy occurring before the commencement of this Act might have devolved upon an heir...

Fixtures and fittings

The owner of the freehold will also be entitled to enjoy any 'fixtures', that is anything which would generally be classified as personalty but which, by virtue of

---

12 'The right to appoint a parson'.

its attachment to the land, becomes a part of the land and is therefore treated as realty. The distinction between fixtures and fittings is crucial whenever a freehold or leasehold estate is sold to another, for the incoming purchaser will want to know what she is entitled to use as her own and the outgoing seller will want to know what she can remove.[13] The next case provides some useful guidance on distinguishing between fixtures and fittings.

Berkley v *Poulett* (1976) 241 *Estates Gazette* 911 (CA) Stamp, Scarman and Goff LJJ

The court had to determine whether a number of pictures, fixed by screws into the recesses of a panelled dining room in a mansion house, a white marble statue of a Greek athlete and a sundial in the garden, comprised part of the conveyance to the purchaser of the estate.

Scarman LJ:

The answer today to the question whether objects which were originally chattels have become fixtures, that is to say part of the freehold, depends upon the application of two tests: (1) the method and degree of annexation; (2) the object and purpose of the annexation. The early law attached great importance to the first test. It proved harsh and unjust both to limited owners who had affixed valuable chattels of their own to settled land and to tenants for years. The second test was evolved to take care primarily of the limited owner, for example a tenant for life. In *Leigh* v *Taylor* [1902] AC 157 the House of Lords invoked it to protect the interest of the tenant for life who had affixed large and valuable tapestries to the walls of the house for the purpose of adornment and enjoyment of them as tapestries. As I read that decision, it was held that she had not made them fixtures. 'They remained chattels from first to last,' said Lord Lindley at p. 164 of the report ... The governing relationship with which this case is concerned is that of a beneficial owner of the legal estate selling the freehold to a purchaser. Such a seller can sell as much or as little of his property as he chooses. Lord Poulett excluded certain named objects from the sale, but the contract was silent as to the objects claimed by the plaintiff...

Since *Leigh* v *Taylor* the question is really one of fact. The two tests were explained in that case by the Lord Chancellor ... who commented that not the law but our mode of life has changed over the years; that what has changed is 'the degree in which certain things have seemed susceptible of being put up as mere ornaments whereas at our earlier period the mere construction rendered it impossible sometimes to sever the thing which was put up from the realty.' In other words, a degree of annexation which in earlier times the law would have treated as conclusive may now prove nothing. If the purpose of the annexation be for the better enjoyment of the object itself, it may remain a chattel, notwithstanding a high degree of physical annexation. Clearly, however, it remains significant to discover the extent of physical disturbance of the building or the land involved in the removal of the object. If an object cannot be removed without serious damage to, or

---

13 Removing fixtures may be theft; see *DPP* v *Lavender* (1993) at p.14 above.

destruction of, some part of the realty, the case for its having become a fixture is a strong one. The relationship of the two tests to each other requires consideration. If there is no physical annexation there is no fixture ... Nevertheless an object, resting on the ground by its own weight alone, can be a fixture, if it be so heavy that there is no need to tie it into a foundation, and if it were put in place to improve the realty ... Conversely, an object affixed to realty but capable of being removed without much difficulty may yet be a fixture, if, for example, the purpose of its affixing be that 'of creating a beautiful room as a whole' (Neville J *In Re Whaley* [1908] 1 Ch 615, 619)...

The 7th Earl decided in the early part of the twentieth century to install in the two rooms the panelling and so designed it that there were recesses for pictures. It is this feature which lends plausibility to the suggestion that the pictures, fitted into the recesses left for them, were not to be enjoyed as objects for themselves but as part of the grand architectural design of the two rooms. The Vice Chancellor rejected this view. So do I ... The panelling was Victorian, the pictures a heterogeneous collection. According to Sotheby's expert they were of different dates ... of different styles, by different hands, the sort of set anyone could put together at any time...

The statue and sundial give rise in my judgment to no difficulty. Neither was at the time of the sale physically attached to the realty. The sundial was a small object and, once the Earl had detached it (as he did many years earlier) from its pedestal, it ceased to be part of the realty. The statue was heavy. It weighed 10 cwt and stood 5 ft 7 in high on its plinth. There is an issue as to whether it was cemented into the plinth ... The question is not decisive, for, even if was attached by a cement bond, it was (as events proved) easily removable ... The best argument for the statue being a fixture was its careful siting in the West Lawn so as to form an integral part of the architectural design of the west elevation of the house. The design point is a good one so far as it goes ... But what was put on the plinth was very much a matter for the taste of the occupier of the house for the time being ... Being, as I think, unattached, the statue was, prima facie, not a fixture, but even if it were attached, the application of the second test would lead to the same conclusion.

The increasing marketability of 'architectural antiques' such as fireplaces and panelling poses problems for those who wish buildings of historic interest to be conserved. Fixtures in listed buildings may not be removed (Planning (Listed Buildings and Conservation Areas) Act 1990). For example:

Conveyancers Notebook (1994) *Conv* 1

Leighton Hall, Powys, Wales

This romantic turreted 'Tudorbethan Gothic' property was built between 1850 and 1856 and has now fallen into a dilapidated condition. The grounds contained a statue of Icarus plunging head-first into an ornamental lake which was a focal part of the garden design. It was damaged by a falling tree and the owner removed it for repair but did not reinstate it as he said that it was in danger from theft. He pleaded guilty to a charge under s. 9 of the 1990 Act. He has now sold three of the chandeliers from the Great Hall and a unique carillon clock. The panelling and the cornice work of the room in which the clock stands and in the room below were designed so as to accommodate its wires and pulleys. There is now a disagreement between the consultant employed by the owner (who considers that the chandeliers and clock are not covered by the listing) and the local authority which says that listing building consent is needed for their removal.

BUYING AND SELLING LAND

Introduction

Land has always been a precious kind of property. Thus there have been – and still are – particular rules about transferring ownership of it. Originally the rules linked the old and new owners with the land itself by the 'delivery of seisin', the handing over of a clod of earth on site. But, as paper evidence became more significant, special documents were used – deeds – to demonstrate the importance of the transfer.[14]

It is usual for there to be a contract for the sale of land before ownership is to be transferred. Initially, the making of the contract was not subject to any particular rules. However, in the late seventeenth century, perjury was perceived as a problem, so writing was required by the Statute of Frauds 1677 to prevent the wrongful enforcement of alleged oral agreements for the sale of land (as well as for certain other contracts).[15] Where it seemed that this would cause injustice, equity stepped in with the doctrine of 'part performance': if the contract were partly performed, equity would not allow a statute to be used 'as an engine of fraud'.

Most recently, the Law of Property (Miscellaneous Provisions) Act 1989 updated the definition of a deed and also strengthened the rules concerning writing. This latter reform can be seen as more paternalistic, to protect people from accidentally becoming bound by contract.[16]

The agreement

Law of Property (Miscellaneous Provisions) Act 1989

Contracts for sale etc. or land to be made by signed writing[17]

2. (1) A contract for the sale or other disposition of an interest in land can only be made in writing and only by incorporating all the terms which the parties have expressly agreed in one document or, where contracts are exchanged, in each.

---

14 See Pottage, Chapter 10 at pp. 274–5.

15 See also A.W.B. Simpson, *History of the Common Law of Contract* (Clarendon: 1975), Chapter 8.

16 See Law Commission No. 164 para. 1.11. (1987).

17 See also P.H. Pettit 54 Conv (1990) 431; C. Hill 106 LQR (1990) 396; P.M.J. Dickens 87 Law Soc Gaz (1990) 17; Law Commission No. 163 'Deeds and Escrows' (1987).

(2) The terms may be incorporated in a document either by being set out in it or by reference to some other document.

(3) The document incorporating the terms or, where contracts are exchanged, one of the documents incorporating them (but not necessarily the same one) must be signed by or on behalf of each party to the contract.

(4) Where a contract for the sale or other disposition of an interest in land satisfies the conditions of this section by reason only of the rectification of one or more documents in pursuance of an order of the court, the contract shall come into being, or be deemed to have come into being, at such time as may be specified in the order.

(5) This section does not apply in relation to –
(a) a contract to grant such lease as is mentioned in section 54(2)[18] of the Law of Property Act 1925 (short leases);
(b) a contract made in the course of a public auction; or
(c) a contract regulated under the Financial Services Act 1986;
and nothing in this section affects the creation or operation of resulting, implied or constructive trusts.

(6) In this section –
'disposition' has the same meaning as in the Law of Property Act 1925;
'interest in land' means any estate, interest or charge in or over land or in or over the proceeds of sale of land.

(7) Nothing in this section shall apply in relation to contracts made before this section comes into force.

(8) Section 40 of the Law of Property Act 1925 (which is superseded by this section) shall cease to have effect.

This section affects all land contracts made on or after 27 September 1989. Contracts made earlier are subject to the old rules about writing and part performance contained in s. 40 Law of Property Act 1925. It seems unlikely that many cases will occur now in relation to the old law, and therefore it is omitted from this book. However, full details can be found in E.H. Burn *Cheshire and Burn's Modern Law of Real Property* (Butterworths: 1994, 15th edn, 111–121).

Once there is a contract in writing to satisfy s. 2, equity will provide the remedy of specific performance, that is the court will order the contract to be performed. (Other remedies may also be available, such as rectification or damages.) A contract for the sale of land is called an 'estate contract' and is itself an equitable interest in land because 'equity looks on that as done which ought to be done'.

---

18 See also Chapter 4, p. 81.

In *Spiro* v *Glencrown Properties Ltd* [1991] 2 WLR 931,[19] the first case decided on the section, it was held that s. 2 does not apply to a notice that the option is being exercised, so this 'unilateral act' need not be signed by both parties.

Record v *Bell* [1991] 1 WLR 853[20]

The agreement here was for the sale of a London house for £1.3 million, plus furniture for a further £200,000. The contracts satisfied s. 2, but then there was a difficulty getting proof of title from the Land Registry, so, in order to encourage the buyer to exchange contracts, the seller made an extra promise (a 'collateral warranty') to the effect that *he* would guarantee the title. This extra promise was not signed by both parties.

Then the buyer lost money because of the Gulf crisis, and the price of land began to fall, so he decided not to go through with the contract. The seller sued for specific performance and the buyer responded with s. 2. The seller replied that either (1) the later promise was incorporated into the original contract or (2) it was a collateral contract which was not for 'the sale of land' and thus did not need to fulfil s. 2.

Judge Paul Baker:

The particular area [of the Act] I am concerned with is where a contract in two parts has been duly signed by the respective parties and is awaiting exchange. Then some term is orally agreed immediately prior to exchange and confirmed by the exchange of letters. Is the statute satisfied? That, as I see it, is a very common situation especially where there is some pressure to get contracts exchanged, as there frequently is, and one often finds that at exchange not all the loose ends are tidied up and it is necessary to have some last minute adjustment of the contract which takes the form of side letters...

I start with the defendant's [the buyer's] first two points, that is to say, if there are to be side letters they have to be incorporated into the main agreement, and these were not incorporated. If there has to be a last minute addition to the contract after the document has been prepared and is awaiting exchange, it could be written into the draft contract before exchange, or some reference to it could be added to the contract so long as all that was done with the authority of the parties who signed it. I would see no difficulty in adjusting the contract before exchange in that way. But it could not in my judgment, be done simply by a document which itself refers to the contract...

On the issue of a collateral warranty:

[M]y conclusion on this is unhesitating. This was in my judgment, an offer of a warranty ... as to the state of the title, and it was done to induce him to exchange. That offer was accepted by exchanging contracts. It would be unfortunate if

---

19 See also A.J. Oakley (1991) CLJ 237.
20 See also M. Harwood Conv (1991) 471; R.J. Smith 108 LQR (1992) 217. For another case on two separate contracts (though not 'collateral' contracts) see *Tootal Clothing Ltd* v *Guinea Properties Management Ltd* [1992] 41 EG 117 and Luther (1993) Conv 90.

common transactions of this nature should nevertheless cause the contracts to be avoided. It may of course lead to a greater use of the concept of collateral warranties than has hitherto been necessary.[21]

Thus, the seller won, and the buyer had to complete the contract at the original price. (The contracts for the furniture were not, of course, the subject of s. 2.)

Not everyone is a fan of s. 2.

V. Gersten 'Nightmare on Main Street' (1993) *Law Soc Gaz* (September 1) 2

Section 2 is a nightmare. The Statute of Frauds was enacted in 1677 and the courts worked out ways of getting round it for the next 200 years. If s. 2 remains in force it may take the courts another 200 years to get back to the sensible situation which obtained before the section came into force. It should be repealed and the old law restored.

Section 2, in its insistence on the formality of writing for a contract for land, enables the continuation of 'gazumping': typically, the seller secretly 'accepts' several offers, and finally chooses to enter a contract with the best one – and the other would-be buyers, who may have spent £100s in expenses, have no recourse. (In a falling market, buyers may play an equivalent game – 'gazundering'.) A Mr Pitt has entered legal history as having avoided being gazumped by creating a 'lock-out' agreement, and the Court of Appeal also took the opportunity to share the pains of the property-owning classes:

Pitt v *PHH Asset Management Ltd* [1993] 4 All ER 961 (CA)
Sir Thomas Bingham MR, Peter Gibson and Mann LJJ[22]

Sir Thomas Bingham MR:
For very many people, their first and closest contact with the law is when they come to buy or sell a house. They frequently find it a profoundly depressing and frustrating experience. The vendor puts his house on the market. He receives an offer which is probably less than his asking price. He agonises over whether to accept or hold out for more. He decides to accept, perhaps after negotiating some increase. A deal is struck. Hands are shaken. The vendor celebrates, relaxes, makes plans for his own move and takes his house off the market. Then he hears that the purchaser who was formerly pleading with him to accept his offer has decided not to proceed. No explanation is given, no apology made. The vendor has to embark on the whole dreary process of putting his house on the market all over again.

For the purchaser the process is, if anything, worse. After a series of futile visits to unsuitable houses he eventually finds the house of his dreams. He makes an offer, perhaps at the asking price, perhaps at what the agent tells him the vendor is likely to accept. The offer is accepted. A deal is done. The purchaser instructs

---

21 As predicted by the Law Commission No, 164, (paras 20–22), which led to the 1989 Act.
22 See also M. Halliwell (1994) Conv 58.

solicitors to act. He perhaps commissions an architect to plan alterations. He makes arrangements to borrow money. He puts his own house on the market. He makes arrangements to move. He then learns that the vendor has decided to sell to someone else, perhaps for the price already offered and accepted for an increased price achieved by a covert, unofficial auction. Again, no explanation, no apology. The vendor is able to indulge his self-interest, even his whims, without exposing himself to any legal penalty...

For the purchaser there is, however, one means of protection: to make an independent agreement by which the vendor agrees for a clear specified period not to deal with anyone other than the purchaser. The effect is to give that purchaser a clear run for the period in question. The vendor does not agree to sell to that purchaser – such an agreement would be covered by s. 2 of the 1989 Act – but he does give a negative undertaking that he will not for the given period deal with anyone else. That, I am quite satisfied, is what happened here, as the judge rightly held. The vendor and the prospective purchaser made what has come to be called a 'lock-out' agreement. That was a contract binding on them both. The vendor broke it. He is liable to the prospective purchaser for damages which remain to be assessed.

New technology

Lawyers are used to relying on paper as evidence of legal transactions but new technology may come to challenge that reliance. For some years now, conveyancers have 'exchanged contracts' by telephone and the law of contract has had to come to terms with electronic mail in the form of faxes. (For another example of the law's response to new technology, see Chapter 6, p. 172.) Computers are now able to 'talk' to one another without human control, and computer memories can be altered without trace. The very flexibility which makes these machines attractive provides a danger to a profession which relies on unalterable evidence.

C. Reed 'Authenticating Electronic Mail Messages and Some Evidential Problems' 52 *MLR* (1989) 649

Although electronic messages potentially offer a convenient way of negotiating and establishing contractual or other rights, their use for these purposes is evidentially hazardous. Electronically stored documents are admissible in court, but because computer technology permits documents stored on such to be edited without leaving any trace, there is the danger that if the identity of the sender of the content of the document is disputed it will be impossible to prove to the court's satisfaction that the message is authentic. Methods of authentication such as the use of trusted third parties can be effective, and highly specialised services such as SEADOCS have advantages in certain transactions. However, the practical implementation of these specialised services is too cumbersome for regular use outside these fields of activity, and more general services such as Telecom Gold, whilst offering the possibility of adequate authentication, can prove expensive (and thus unattractive) if used for that purpose. What is required is some way of authenticating these matters which does not impinge too greatly on the ease of use of electronic messaging, and the best method of authentication is undoubtedly some form of digital signature. Digital signatures are possible using presently available technology, in particular the RSA cipher, and in spite of the technical complexity will provide sufficient information to permit proof that the document is indeed authentic.[23]

Transferring legal ownership

A contract for the sale of land or an interest in land is completed when the deed is delivered and the buyer pays the price. The buyer only becomes the legal owner of registered land when the transfer is received by the Land Registry (see Chapter 10). Where land is not yet registered, and for the creation or sale of interests which are not registrable (for example, leases of between three and twenty years), a deed is used. Without a deed, there can be *no* change in the legal ownership of the land. (Appendix 2 gives an example of a deed.)

Law of Property Act 1925

Conveyances to be by deed

52. (1) All conveyances of land or of any interest therein are void for the purpose of conveying or creating a legal estate unless made by deed.

(2) This section does not apply to –
(a) assents by a personal representative;
(b) disclaimers made in accordance with section 54 of the Bankruptcy Act 1914 or not required to be evidenced in writing;
(c) surrenders by operation of law, including surrenders which may, by law, be effected without writing;
(d) leases or tenancies or other assurances not required by law to be made in writing;[24]
(e) receipts not required by law to be under seal;
(f) vesting orders of the court or other competent authority;
(g) conveyances taking effect by operation of law.

Law of Property (Miscellaneous Provisions) Act 1989

Deeds and their execution

1. (1) Any rule of law which –
(a) restricts the substances on which a deed may be written;
(b) requires a seal for the valid execution of an instrument as a deed by an individual; or
(c) requires authority by one person to another to deliver an instrument as a deed on his behalf to be given by deed, is abolished.

---

23 For ideas as to how technology changes the concept of property, see Pottage, Chapter 10 at p. 274.
24 See Chapter 4, p. 81.

(2) An instrument shall not be a deed unless –
(a) it makes it clear on its face that it is intended to be a deed by the person making it, or, as the case may be, by the parties to it (whether by describing itself as a deed or expressing itself to be executed or signed as a deed or otherwise); and
(b) it is validly executed as a deed by that person or, as the case may be, one or more of those parties.

(3) An instrument is validly executed as a deed by an individual if, and only if –
(a) it is signed –
(i) by him in the presence of a witness who attests the signature; or
(ii) at his direction and in his presence and the presence of two witnesses who each attest the signature; and
(b) it is delivered as a deed by him or a person authorised to do so on his behalf.

(4) In subsection (2) and (3) above 'sign', in relation to an instrument, includes making one's mark on the instrument and 'signature' is to be construed accordingly.

(5) Where a solicitor or licensed conveyancer, or an agent or employee of a solicitor or licensed conveyancer, in the course of or in connection with a transaction involving the disposition or creation of an interest in land, purports to deliver an instrument as a deed on behalf of a party to the instrument, it shall be conclusively presumed in favour of a purchaser that he is authorised so to deliver the instrument.

(6) In subsection (5) above –
'disposition' and 'purchaser' have the same meanings as in the Law of Property Act 1925; and
'interest in land' means any estate, interest or charge in or over land or in or over the proceeds of sale of land.

(7) Where an instrument under seal that constitutes a deed is required for the purposes of an Act passed before this section comes into force, this section shall have effect as to signing, sealing or delivery of an instrument by an individual in place of any provision of that Act as to signing, sealing or delivery.

(9) Nothing in subsection (1)(b), (2), (3), (7) or (8) above applies in relation to deeds required or authorised to be made under –
(a) the seal of the county palatine of Lancaster;
(b) the seal of the Duchy of Lancaster; or
(c) the seal of the Duchy of Cornwall.

(10) The references in this section to the execution of a deed by an individual do not include execution by a corporation sole and the reference in subsection (7) above to signing, sealing or delivery by an individual does not include signing, sealing or delivery by such a corporation.

(11) Nothing in this section applies in relation to instruments delivered as deeds before this section comes into force.[25]

EQUITABLE INTERVENTIONS

Although part performance has been abolished there may, as demonstrated by the recent decision of *Morritt* v *Wonham* [1993] NPC 2, still be life in the old doctrine with respect to the gradually diminishing number of contracts made prior to 26 September 1989.[26]

A continuing role for the doctrine of proprietary estoppel

Notwithstanding s. 2, the courts may, of course, intervene and exercise their discretion to do justice between particular parties. The primary vehicle for their intervention is the doctrine of proprietary estoppel, [27] as in the following case:

Walton v *Walton and Others* (1994) (Lexis: Transcript John Larking) (CA) Glidewell, Kennedy and Hoffmann LJJ

Mrs Walton was left a small farm by her husband in 1962. The plaintiff, her son Alfred, had worked on that farm since leaving school in 1960 at the age of 15. When he married he built a bungalow there where he lived with his wife and two children. Until 1970 he worked up to 70 hours a week, for which his mother paid him a wage considerably lower than a hired agricultural worker. In 1977 she was persuaded to hand the day-to-day management of the farm business over to him and he used the profits from the farm to invest in new buildings and make improvements.

Relations between them gradually deteriorated: in 1988 she contracted to sell the farm to a neighbouring landowner. Before completion could take place her son went to court to stop it. The old lady subsequently died, leaving money to her niece and her grandchildren. Payment of these legacies would require the sale of the farm, so her son argued that his mother had repeatedly promised that the farm would eventually be his.

Hoffmann LJ:
The plaintiff's claim is based upon equitable estoppel. That sounds very technical but the principle is quite simple. Ordinarily the law does not enforce promises

---

25 The section came into force on 31 July 1990.

26 This is particularly significant in relation to equitable leases and options.

27 See also *In Re Basham Deceased* [1986] 1 WLR 1498 and *Lim Teng Huan* v *Ang Swee Chuan* [1992] 1 WLR 113 (PC). A further means of avoiding formality rules lies in the doctrine of *donatio mortis causa* ('a gift in contemplation of death. See *Sen* v *Hedley* [1991] 2 All ER 636 (CA).

unless they have been made formally under seal or as part of a contract. Mrs Walton's promise was not, of course, made under seal and ... I do not think it was part of a contract. So if there was nothing more than the promise, she would have been free to change her mind. It would have been a matter for her conscience and not the law. But the position is different if the person who has been promised some interest in property has, in reliance upon it, incurred expense or made sacrifices which he would not otherwise have made. In such a case the law will provide a remedy ... The choice of the remedy is flexible. The principle on which the remedy is given is equitable estoppel. As Oliver J put it in *Taylors Fashions Ltd* v *Liverpool Trustees Co Ltd* [1982] 1 QB 133, 151 ... the question is:

> 'whether, in particular individual circumstances, it would be unconscionable for a party to be permitted to deny that which, knowingly or unknowingly, he has allowed or encouraged another to assume to his detriment.'

The plaintiff says that this is the case here. His mother encouraged him to believe that one day the farm would be his. She repeatedly told him so. In reliance on that belief, he worked for years for low wages and put work and money into improving the land and buildings. These acts were irrevocable. He cannot have his life over again. If he does not get the farm, he will have to start again at the age of nearly 50, whereas if Mrs Walton had never promised him the farm, he might by now have established himself in some other way. So it would be unjust, or, in the language of equity, 'unconscionable' for the plaintiff now to be turned off the land.

The judge found against the plaintiff. He asked himself the question: 'Would it be unconscionable for Mrs Walton to deny the plaintiff the right to have the farm on her death?' and gave a negative answer. He said that the plaintiff had been 'hard done by' but there was nothing unconscionable about his not getting the farm. For my part, I find this a startling conclusion. It is hard to believe that the law can produce such an unjust result. I must therefore examine the judge's reasoning with care.

For this purpose, one can divide up the case into four parts. First, was there a promise? Secondly, did the plaintiff rely on the promise? Thirdly, did his reliance involve a detriment, ie some expense or sacrifice on his part? And fourthly, if the answers to the first three questions are yes, what remedy should be given.

1 The promise
The promise must be unambiguous and must appear to have been intended to be taken seriously. Taken in its context, it must have been a promise which one might reasonably expect to be relied upon by the person to whom it was made. The judge said he had no doubt that the promises of which the plaintiff spoke were made. On this point he accepted the evidence of the plaintiff himself and several other witnesses. What the judge said was:

> 'Such promises were, as I say, made but when I use the word promises I use it very loosely. When such words were used I take them to mean a statement of the probable expectations of a young man in the plaintiff's position at the time. I have no doubt that such words were spoken from time to time by Mrs Minnie Walton ... They were never ... words that were intended to create a legal

obligation ... Words such as these get spoken in families ... They were not sufficient to create an equity.'

There are a number of strands here which need to be disentangled. ...what did the judge mean when he said that the promises were not 'intended to create a legal obligation'? Intention to create legal relations is a familiar concept in the law of contract ... But none of this reasoning applies to equitable estoppel ... it looks backwards from the moment when the promise falls due to be performed and asks whether, in the circumstances which have actually happened, it would be unconscionable for the promise not to be kept ... So if the judge meant that the claim must fail because neither party thought that Mrs Walton was intending to enter into a legally binding contract, then in my view he was wrong in law. But Mr Caswell [counsel for the defendants] says ... he ... should be interpreted as saying that the promise could not reasonably have been taken seriously and that the plaintiff did not himself so regard it.

Hoffmann LJ then reviewed the statements of the plaintiff and his witnesses, who included a retired fertiliser salesman who had regularly called at the farm, a deputy headmaster of a school and the manager of a children's clothing shop in a town nearby. All of these witnesses testified to hearing Mrs Walton make statements indicating that the farm was promised to her son. He concluded:

There is nothing in any of these witnesses to suggest that the promise was not seriously meant. They all seemed to think that it was. ...The evidence on the other side was that of the late Mrs Walton, in an affidavit ... and of Mrs Daphne Walton and the plaintiff's daughter Amanda ... Like Mrs Walton, Mrs Daphne Walton did not say that the promise had been made but without intention that it should be taken seriously. She said: 'There was never any promise of the farm'. To find any trace of support for the judge's finding one must go to the evidence of Miss Amanda Walton ... She gave evidence on what her grandmother had said would happen to the farm:

'Q: Did she say who she wanted the farm to go to?

A. I think it used to be whoever was the favourite at the time, really...'

The judge made no comment on Miss Walton's credibility but I do not think that she can be regarded as a reliable witness. Her dislike of her father emerges too strongly. In any case, the question is not whether Mrs Walton promised the farm to others, but whether a person in the position of the plaintiff would reasonably have regarded the promises which the judge found to have been made as serious statements upon which he could rely. There was nothing to show that the plaintiff knew (if such was the case) that promises had been made to others ... Accordingly there was in my view nothing to suggest to him that the statements repeatedly made by his mother could not be taken at face value.

Mr Caswell said that the fact that the promise was made in a family context and related to what would happen many years later was itself enough to show that it could not be taken seriously. I do not see why this should be so. Many of the cases on proprietary estoppel concern promises made in a family or other intimate relationship. Even within a family it may not be unreasonable to expect that promises will be kept.

2 Reliance

Did the plaintiff rely upon the promise? The passage from his evidence in which he says that if he had known that the promise would not be kept he would have left and made his own way in the world, seems to show that he did. The recent decision of this court in *Wayling* v *Jones* (21 July 1993, unreported) shows that when a promise has been made, one does not test reliance by asking what the plaintiff would have done if it had never been made. One asks what he would have done if, the promise having been made, he had been told it would not be kept...

It seems to me clear that the plaintiff's conduct in working for low wages for the period until 1977 and thereafter in making improvements to the land, was of such a nature that it could be inferred that it was induced by the promise having been made and his not having been told that it would not be kept. There is no evidence that his conduct was attributable to any other reason and consequently in my judgement the element of reliance is made out.

3 Detriment

The plaintiff made both sacrifices and expenditure in reliance on the promise. He made sacrifices in low wages ... And he incurred expenditure after 1977 by making improvements with his own labour and money which would otherwise have been profits which he could draw from the business. All these acts were to his detriment.

4 Satisfying the equity

How should the equity be satisfied? ... In my judgment ... the only way to satisfy the equity in the plaintiff's favour is to order a transfer to him of the farm subject to the mortgage.

FRENCH LAW OF CONVEYANCING

It is interesting to contrast these rules regarding contracts for the sale of land with those operating in France:

H. Dyson French Real Property and Succession Law (Robert Hale: 1988)

There is no requirement in French law that a binding contract for the sale of land should be in or evidenced by writing. A verbal agreement to sell, provided it embodies such essential elements as a correct description of the property and the price, is enforceable in France, though there are obvious difficulties of proof. A letter of instruction, for example, by one of the parties to his Notary[28] to prepare the conveyance will be considered good evidence of the existence of such verbal contract.

---

28 'A public, specially trained, legal official'.

Quite apart from the obvious undesirability of verbal agreements for the sale or purchase of land, no transfer of land can be validly achieved in France other than by an *acte de vente*,[29] which is a notarial document prepared by a Notary and signed by all parties or their Attorneys before him...

From the practical point of view, it seems that the majority of land transactions ... are based on the bilateral *compromis de vente*. The vast majority of contracts are prepared in standard form by the local Estate Agent...

Such a contract comes within the provisions of Article 1589 of the Code Civil, which states that, where there is agreement as to subject matter and price, a promise to sell is equivalent to a sale. Whilst the sale itself can be effected only by *acte notarie*, it is worth remembering that many of the contracts drawn by sellers' Agents are prepared without a sight of the title deeds. It is, therefore, important to ensure that the contract contains all that it should...

The contract will normally include a date for completion. The normal period between contract and completion is a little over a month, but the Lois Scrivener rules must be taken into account in fixing a date, as ... considerable delays ... can occur in obtaining replies to Land Registry searches. Completion dates tend to be on an 'on or before' rather than a fixed date and frequently pass by without completion taking place ... It will be appreciated that something less than the sanctity which attaches to completion in England exists in France ... to resort to the courts to enforce a contract would be a rare and tediously long process and is hardly considered in textbooks as a remedy.

---

29 'Act of sale'.

3 Adverse possession

INTRODUCTION

The area of land law in this chapter provides a focus on the way in which land is capable of being possessed, and what amounts to possession in English law. Possession has traditionally been a basis of title: in English land law, the concept of 'seisin' (settled possession) lies behind more modern ideas of ownership or possession.

E.H. Burn *Cheshire and Burn's Modern Law of Real Property* (Butterworths: 15th edn, 1994)

It may be said at once that the doctrine of tenure[1], as developed in England, made it difficult, if not impossible to regard either [the tenant] or his lord as the owner of the land itself. The land could not be owned by the tenant, since it was recoverable by the lord if the tenurial services were not faithfully performed; it could not be owned by the lord, since he had no claim to it as long as the tenant fulfilled his duties.

Quite apart from this practical difficulty, however, the truth is that English law has never applied the conception of ownership to land. 'Ownership' is a word of many meanings, but in the present context we can take it to signify a title to a subject matter ... English law ... has directed its attention not to ownership, but to possession, or, as it is called in the case of land, *seisin*. Seisin is a root of title, and it may be said without undue exaggeration that so far as land is concerned there is in England no law of ownership, but only a law of possession.[2]

A.W.B. Simpson *An Introduction to the History of English Land Law* (Clarendon:1961)

Seisin is the concept which connects the person ... with the land itself... Titles are better or worse according to the age of the seisin upon which they are based, and even a very recent (and perhaps transparently wrongful) seisin is to some extent

---

1 i.e., of holding land from a lord in exchange for performing feudal services – see Chapter 1, pp. 19–23; Chapter 2, pp. 37–39.

2 R. Plucknett *Concise History of the Common Law* (5th edn) 358.

protected. Thus any person who is seised of land has a protected interest in that land, good against all but those who have a title based on an older seisin. From this it is deduced that one who is seised must have an estate, and unless he claims through some gift which cuts down the estate[3] then it will be a fee simple...

As already seen in Chapter 1, possession and ownership in English law are normally 'exclusive', that is, they involve 'Keep off!' actions and attitudes towards the property and towards other people. A landowner, therefore, has the right to keep people off the land, and can sue any trespassers.[4] In adverse possession, the claimant must show not only actual possession for twelve years (normally) together with an intention to possess the land, but also that the possession was 'adverse', which normally means 'designed to keep out the real ("paper") owner'. The question is, 'Did that person possess the land in fact, while intending to use the land and to keep out the whole world?'

In addition, courts' decisions on adverse possession must be seen in the context of an ideological battle waged between government and 'squatters', those who do not espouse the territorial idolatry of the establishment. Cases on adverse possession today are part of a larger war; the debates over the Criminal Justice and Public Order Act 1994 (below) are another aspect of this war. The Bill has been viewed with fear by many who are forced or choose to live on society's margins, including 'travellers', but has also been opposed by organisations like the Ramblers' Association. Adverse possession, therefore, demonstrates clearly the tensions within modern ideas about law, property and social life.

JUSTIFICATIONS OF ADVERSE POSSESSION

Adverse possession is not new to English law, although the period used to be much longer than twelve years.

D. Hardy and C. Ward, *Arcadia For All* (Mansell: 1984)

Squatting dates back as long as the process of land settlement itself, and most cultures have a traditional belief in 'squatters' rights' whether these are recognised by statute or not. Not only throughout Britain, but in many parts of Europe and in the New World, it was widely accepted that if a person succeeded in erecting a dwelling on common or waste land between sunset and sunrise and lighting a fire in it he could not lawfully be dispossessed. There are innumerable variants on this formula and on the definition of the amount of land that might be enclosed...

---

3 For example, if a widow is left a life interest in land in a will.
4 See K. Gray *Elements of Land Law* 2nd edn (Butterworths: 1993) 307–11. Another area of land law where possession is tested by 'keep out' is in the lease–licence distinction: see Chapter 4 p. 78–80.

An Act was passed in the reign of Elizabeth I 'against the erecting and maintaining of cottages' with the aim of 'avoiding the great inconveniences which are found to grow by the creating ... of great numbers and multitudes of cottages'...

In 1662, after the restoration of the monarchy, a further law, the Act of Settlement, restricted the movement of those who were not freeholders or who could not afford a rent of £10 per year. Between these two pieces of legislation directed against 'cottagers' and 'paupers' – in other words against squatters – there occurred the most famous of what we would now call 'ideologically-inspired' squats, that of Winstanley and the Diggers at Walton-on-Thames in Surrey in 1649.

> '[Mrs Kit Nash], year by year, extended the boundaries of her plot by trimming the bramble hedges always from the inside, allowing them to spread and flourish on the outside... She had only a squatter's title to the land, but after her death this was legally registered in her name by the local authority, and it was sold so that they could recover the money which she owed them.' [K. Lloyd, *Country Life*, 11 October 1973]

The leader of the Digger movement had written:

G. Winstanley *The New Law of Righteousness* (1649), quoted in H. Girardet (ed.) *For the People* (Crescent: 1976)

In the beginning of time, the Great Creator Reason, made the earth to be common treasure ... The work we are going about is this, to dig up George's Hill and the wasteland thereabouts, and to sow corn, and to eat our bread together by the sweat of our brows, and to lay the foundations of making the earth a common treasury for all, both rich and poor ... Not enclosing any part into a particular hand, but all as one man, working together and feeding together as sons of one father, members of one family ... For though you and your ancestors got your property by murder and theft, and you keep it by the same power from us that have an equal right to the land with you by the righteous law of creation, yet we shall have no occasion of quarrelling ... For the earth with all her fruits of corn, cattle and such like, was made to be a common storehouse of livelihood to all mankind, friend and foe, without exception.

Winstanley's ideas still have many adherents:

Who Owns the Park?, unattributed, quoted in G. Lefcoe *An Introduction to American Property Law* (Bobbs Merrill: 1974)

Someday a petty official will appear with a piece of paper, called a land title, which states that the University of California owns the land of the People's Park. Where did that piece of paper come from? What is it worth?

A long time ago the Costanoan Indians lived in the area now called Berkeley. They had no concept of land ownership. They believed that the land was under the care and guardianship of the people who used it and lived on it.

Catholic missionaries took the land away from the Indians. No agreements were made. No papers were signed. They ripped it off in the name of God.

The Mexican Government took the land away from the Church. The Mexican Government had guns and an army. God's word was not as strong.

The Mexican Government wanted to pretend that it was not the army that guaranteed them the land. They drew up some papers which said they legally owned it. No Indians signed those papers.

The Americans were not fooled by the papers. They had a stronger army than the Mexicans. They beat them in a war and took the land. Then they wrote some papers of their own and forced the Mexicans to sign them.

The American Government sold the land to some white settlers. The Government gave the settlers a piece of paper called a land title in exchange for some money. All this time there were still some Indians around who claimed the land. The American army killed most of them.

The piece of paper saying who owned the land was passed around among rich white men. Sometimes the white men were interested in taking care of the land. Usually they were just interested in making money. Finally some rich men, who run the University of California, bought the land.

Immediately these men destroyed the houses that had been built on the land. The land went the way of so much other land in America – it became a parking lot.

We are building a park on the land. We will take care of it and guard it, in the spirit of the Costanoan Indians. When the University comes with its land title we will tell them: 'Your land title is covered with blood. We won't touch it. Your people ripped off the land from the Indians a long time ago. If you want it back now, you will have to fight for it again.'

[By July 1972 the People's Park had become a dusty, informal campsite for wayfarers (*Los Angeles Times*, 30 July 1972).]

The significance of paper title is challenged also by more established voices:

Ruoff and Roper *On the Law and Practice of Registered Conveyancing* 4th edn (Stevens: 1979)[5]

Misunderstandings have sometimes arisen from an unwarrantable belief that title deeds are sacrosanct documents, whereas the truth is that neither a conveyance nor a land certificate retains its value if the landowner is so indifferent as to lose physical control of his land.

However, justifications for adverse possession go beyond 'property is theft' and 'stale claims'. People who use land and invest their labour in it are benefiting society more than those real owners who neglect it to the extent of ignoring it for twelve years or more. And the law, it is suggested, should value the attachment that comes from working on land:

Oliver Wendell Holmes

I can say that truth, friendship and the statute of limitations have a common root in

5 See also A.R. Mellows (1962) 26 Conv & Prop Law 269.

time. The true explanation of title by [adverse possession] ... seems to me to be that man, like a tree in a cleft rock, gradually shapes his roots to his surroundings, and when the roots have grown to a certain size, can't be displaced without cutting at his life. The law used to look with disfavor on the statute of limitations, but I have been in the habit of saying that it is one of the most sacred and indubitable principles that we have...

As mentioned at the start of this section, the common law is not the only legal system in which rights to land are lost by abandonment:

N. Smith *Maori Land Law* (A.H. & A.W. Reed: 1960)[6]

If a Maori left his tribe and went to live in another district, either through marriage or otherwise, and he and his descendants remained away for three generations, they would forfeit all rights to the land so abandoned; their claims would become *ahimataotao*. The meaning of this term is cold or extinguished fire and as applied to the instance just given would signify that the rights of the claimants had gone cold and their claims extinguished. The same rule applied to voluntary migrations of a whole family group or *hapu*. They may have allied themselves with some enemy and been forced to leave. If, however, the claimants who had voluntarily abandoned the land sent some of their children back at intervals to occupy the lands, or to exercise some right of ownership, and there was no objection from the tribe, that would be sufficient to relight the flame and so keep their fires burning, and their rights alive. In the example just given, if the Maoris remained away without exercising their rights continuously for one generation, their claims would not be materially affected, but absence for two generations would seriously weaken the claims and render them subject to some recognition by the tribe; they would not entirely cease until after an absence of three generations...

'With regard to the Native custom affecting cases of this kind, there is possibly no definite rule that can be made applicable to all cases and to all districts, but this rule appears to be applicable everywhere, that when a woman of one tribe or *hapu* marries into another tribe or *hapu*, her rights become extinguished, unless some act of ownership is exercised either by herself or her immediate descendants. It is said that she leaves her *ahi-ka* (burning fire) and becomes an *ahi-tere* (unstable fire). If she or her children return before the ashes become cold, it becomes again an *ahi-ka*, but there is a difference of opinion whether the grandchildren can recover their rights in that way, but there is no doubt that the great grandchildren cannot do so unless they are expressly invited and welcomed by the tribe.' [Nap. Appellate Court Minute Book, 48/78]

The modern British context

Against such traditional and widespread justifications for adverse possession may

---

6 See also L. Caldecott & S. Leland, *Reclaim the Earth* (The Women's Press: 1983) Ch 17; for a Nigerian view, see M.G. Yakubu, *Land Law in Nigeria* (Macmillan: 1985), 102–3.

be compared some modern views against squatters. For example, there was press outrage in the 1970s:

The Daily Telegraph 16 July 1975

Squatting Conspiracy

Of the many strange and frightening features of contemporary British life, none carries a more obvious and direct threat than the growing phenomenon of squatting. Innumerable houses up and down the country are now in illegal occupation by organised gangs of thugs, layabouts and revolutionary fanatics. Costly and irrecoverable damage is continually being done to private property from sheer malice ... In reality the motive for most of this squatting is either political – a settled purpose of subverting public order – or simple greed and aggression.[7]

The campaign resulted in the invention of new civil procedures against people on others' land, and five crimes of squatting ('criminal trespass') in ss. 6–10, Criminal Law Act 1977. With increasing homelessness and marginalisation due to unemployment during the 1980s, the Government continued to seek new ways to criminalise squatters. The latest legislation is the Criminal Justice and Public Order Act 1994, clauses 72–76, which amend existing laws and make new provisions designed to outlaw many variants of squatting. These sections are found in Part V of the Act, which also contains Draconian measures to curtail the activities of 'new age travellers', 'ravers', hunt saboteurs, protesters against road development and gypsies. As R. Sandiland points out ((1994) 44 NLJ 750) this part of the bill is headed 'Public Order: Collective Trespass and Nuisance on Land', providing the clearest of signs of the government's intention to collapse the distinctions between the various target groups: they are, simply, one 'Collective Nuisance'.

At the same time, the large number of reported cases in respect of claims by landowners seeking to absorb strips of their neighbours' land during the last 15 or so years indicate that not all squatters are to be collectively criminalised.

THE RULES

P.J. Dalton Land Law 3rd edn (Pitman: 1982) 126[8]

There is a social need for certainty of title to land. For centuries therefore, statute has placed a limit on the time after which a claimant to an interest in land may bring an action to establish it in the face of the possession of another person holding under a later title ... The general effect of the [Limitation] Act is not to

---

7 Quoted by P. Vincent-Jones 13 Jo Law and Soc (1986) 343.
8 See also M.J. Goodman (1970) 33 MLR 281; M. Dockray (1985) Conv 272.

confirm any particular claim to land but merely to extinguish stale titles to it...[9] A man of ninety suddenly finds himself the oldest man in the village not necessarily because he is ninety but because a man of ninety-one died yesterday. The scythe of time creates superiority of title as it does seniority of age. Title is never extinguished because of its age of course. Quite the contrary. It is only extinguished or 'barred' because the claim it gives to land has been allowed to remain unpressed for a long time in face of a rival title ... the effect of the Act is to eliminate.

The rules today are contained in the Limitation Act 1980.

Limitation Act 1980

Time limit for actions to recover land

15 (1) No action shall be brought by any person to recover any land after the expiration of twelve years from the date on which the right of action accrued to him or, if it first accrued to some person through whom he claims, to that person.[10]

Time limit for actions to recover rent

19 No action shall be brought, or distress made, to recover arrears of rent, or damages in respect of arrears of rent, after the expiration of six years from the date on which the arrears became due.

Fresh accrual of action on acknowledgment or part payment

29 (2) If the person in possession of the land ... acknowledges the title of the person to whom the right of action has accrued –
    (a) the right shall be treated as having accrued on and not before the date of the acknowledgment...[11]

Postponement of limitation period in case of fraud, concealment or mistake

32 (1) Subject to subsection (3) below, where in the case of any action for which a period of limitation is prescribed by this Act, either –
    (a) the action is based upon the fraud of the defendant; or
    (b) any fact relevant to the plaintiff's right of action has been deliberately concealed from him by the defendant; or
    (c) the action is for relief from the consequences of a mistake;
the period of limitation shall not begin to run until the plaintiff has discovered the fraud, concealment or mistake (as the case may be) or could with reasonable diligence have discovered it...
    (3) Nothing in this section shall enable any action –
    (a) to recover, or recover the value of, any property; or

---

9 Compare the role of the registrar when land is registered – Chapter 10.
10 For examples, see *Miller* (1991) and *Moran* (1989) below.
11 For example, see *Miller* (1991) below.

(b) to enforce any charge against, or set aside any transaction affecting, any property;

to be brought against the purchaser of the property or any person claiming through him in any case where the property has been purchased for valuable consideration by an innocent third party since the fraud or concealment of (as the case may be) the transaction in which the mistake was made took place...

Equitable jurisdiction and remedies

36 (2) Nothing in this Act shall affect any equitable jurisdiction to refuse relief on the ground of acquiescence or otherwise.

Schedule 1

Accrual of right of action in case of present interests in land

1 Where the person bringing an action to recover land, or some person through whom he claims, has been in possession of the land, and has while entitled to the land been dispossessed or discontinued his possession, the right of action shall be treated as having accrued on the date of the dispossession or discontinuance.

Right of action not to accrue or continue unless there is adverse possession

8 (1) No right of action to recover land shall be treated as accruing unless the land is in the possession of some person in whose favour the period of limitation can run (referred to below in this paragraph as 'adverse possession'); and where under the preceding provisions ... any such right of action is treated as accruing on a certain date and no person is in adverse possession on that date, the right of action shall not be treated as accruing unless and until adverse possession is taken of the land.

(2) Where a right of action to recover land has accrued and after its accrual, before the right is barred, the land ceases to be in adverse possession, the right of action shall no longer be treated as having accrued and no fresh right of action shall be treated as accruing unless and until the land is again taken into adverse possession...

(4) For the purpose of determining whether a person occupying any land is in adverse possession of the land it shall not be assumed by implication of law that his occupation is by permission of the person entitled to the land merely by virtue of the fact that his occupation is not inconsistent with the latter's present or future enjoyment of the land.[12]

This provision shall not be taken as prejudicing a finding to the effect that a person's occupation of any land is by implied permission of the person entitled to the land in any case where such a finding is justified on the actual facts of the case ...

There are special rules in relation to future interests (s. 15(2) and Schedule 1), the Crown or spiritual corporations (30 years, Schedule 1) and children or people of

---

12 Interpreted in *Moran* (1989) below.

unsound mind (six years from the end of the disability to a maximum of 30 years: s. 28).

Where land is registered, rights gained by adverse possession amount to an overriding interest, and defeat a purchaser even if not on the register.

Land Registration Act 1925

Acquisition of title by possession

75 (1) The Limitation Acts shall apply to registered land in the same manner and to the same extent as those Acts apply to land not registered, except that where, if the land were not registered, the estate of the person registered as proprietor would be extinguished, such estate shall not be extinguished but shall be deemed to be held by the proprietor for the time being in trust[13] for the person who, by virtue of the said Acts, has acquired title against any proprietor, but without prejudice to the estates and interests of any other person interested in the land whose estate or interest is not extinguished by those Acts.

(2) Any person claiming to have acquired a title under the Limitation Acts to a registered estate in the land may apply to be registered as proprietor thereof.[14]

(3) The registrar shall, on being satisfied as to the applicant's title, enter the applicant as proprietor either with absolute, good leasehold, qualified, or possessory title as the case may require...[15]

Cases

In order to succeed against paper owners who seek possession, squatters must prove that, for the required period, they have *actually* possessed the land, and have done so *intentionally* (*animus possidendi*)[16] and *adversely*. These requirements are difficult to disentangle and the cases here demonstrate the complex relationship between them. The starting point in the majority of the recent decisions – of which there are many – is the Court of Appeal's judgment in the following case:

Buckingham County Council v *Moran* [1989] 2 All ER 225 (CA) Slade, Nourse and Butler-Sloss LJJ

From 1971 (following his predecessor in title, probably since 1967) Moran occupied as a part of his garden a patch of land adjoining the end of his garden. The paper owner, the local council, had bought it for eventual use as a road, but

---

13 Presumably on constructive trust – see Chapter 9, p. 258 *et seq.*

14 For example, see *Boosey* v *Davis* (1988) 55 P&CR 83.

15 See Chapter 10, p. 281.

16 See M. Dockray (1982) 46 Conv 256 and 345; *Hughes* v *Cork* (1994) (Lexis: transcript John Laing).

An Englishman's home

had no immediate use for it. In 1985, they 'woke up' and sued for possession but failed at first instance.

This case is the most recent in a long line of cases involving the question whether, if the paper owner has no present use for the land, there can be any possession 'adverse' to his rights.

Slade LJ:

If the law is to attribute possession of land to a person who can establish no paper title to possession, he must be shown to have both factual possession and the requisite intention to possess (*animus possidendi*). A person claiming to have dispossessed another must similarly fulfil both these requirements. However, a further requirement which the alleged dispossessor claiming the benefit of the 1980 Act must satisfy is to show that his possession has been adverse within the meaning of the Act ....

Possession is never 'adverse' ... if it is enjoyed under a lawful title. If, therefore, a person occupies or uses land by licence of the owner with the paper title and his licence has not been duly determined, he cannot be treated as having been in 'adverse possession'...[17]

Before the passing of the 1980 Act certain decisions of this court, in particular *Wallis' Cayton Bay Holiday Camp Ltd* v *Shellmex and BP Ltd* [1974] 3 All ER 575

---

17 In *BP Properties Ltd* v *Buckler* (1988) 55 P & CR 337, the paper owner's letter to a squatter was deemed to grant a licence which prevented adverse possession succeeding; see also H. Wallace (1994) Conv 196 for a discussion of the wider implications.

and *Gray* v *Wykeham-Martin* [1977] CA Transcript 10A were thought to have established a general doctrine that in one special type of case there would be implied in favour of the would-be adverse possessor, *without any specific factual basis for such implication*, a licence permitting him to commit the acts of possession on which he sought to rely; the effect of implying such a licence would, of course, be to prevent the squatter's possession from being 'adverse'. That special type of case was broadly one where the acts of an intruder, however continuous and far-reaching, did not substantially interfere with any plans which the owners might have for the future use of undeveloped land...

On any footing, it must, in my judgment, be too broad a proposition to suggest that an owner who retains a piece of land with a view to its utilisation for a specific purpose in the future can never be treated as dispossessed, however firm and obvious the intention and however drastic the act of dispossession of the person seeking to dispossess him may be. Furthermore, while it may well be correct to say that the implied licence doctrine (so long as it survived) itself involved the 'adaptation' of the literal application of the statutory provisions 'to meet one special type of case', I do not think it correct that the [old] decisions ... authorise or justify an application of the statutory provisions otherwise than in accordance with their ordinary and natural meaning...

If in any given case the land in dispute is unbuilt land and the squatter is aware that the owner, while having no present use for it, has a purpose in mind for its use in the future, the court is likely to require very clear evidence before it can be satisfied that the squatter who claims a possessory title has not only established factual possession of the land, but also the requisite intention to exclude the world at large, including the owner with the paper title, so far as is reasonably practicable and so far as the processes of the law will allow. In the absence of clear evidence of this nature, the court is likely to infer that the squatter neither had had nor had claimed any intention of asserting a right to the possession of the land...

In the present case, the defendant was well aware that the council had acquired the plot in order to construct a road on it at some time in the future and meantime had no present use for the land. This factor ... should make the court the more cautious before holding that the defendant had had both a factual possession and *animus possidendi* sufficient to confer on him a possessory title... [E]very ... type of case such as this must involve questions of fact and degree.

First ... did the defendant have factual possession of the plot? I venture to repeat what I said in *Powell* v *McFarlane* (1977) 38 P & CR 452 at 470–1:

'Factual possession signifies an appropriate degree of physical control. It must be a single and [exclusive] possession... Thus an owner of land and a person intruding on that land without his consent cannot both be in possession of the land at the same time. The question what acts constitute a sufficient degree of exclusive control must depend on the circumstances, in particular the nature of the land and the manner in which land of that nature is commonly used or enjoyed.'[18]

18 See for further discussion on this point *Treloar* v *Nute* [1976] 1 WLR 1295 and *Boosey* v *Davis* (1988) 55 P & CR 83.

On evidence it would appear that by 28 October 1973 [twelve years before the writ] the defendant had acquired complete and exclusive physical control of the plot...

However, the more difficult question is whether the defendant had the necessary *animus possidendi*. As to this, counsel for the council accepted the correctness of the following statement (so far as it went) which I made in *Powell* v *McFarlane* (at 471–2):

'... the *animus possidendi* involves the intention, in one's own name and on one's own behalf to exclude the world at large, including the owner with the paper title if he be not himself the possessor, so far as is reasonably practicable and so far as the processes of the law will allow.'...

In my judgment ... the placing of the new lock and chain and gate did amount to a final unequivocal demonstration of the defendant's intention to possess the land. I agree with the judge in his saying:

'... I do not think that if the council, on making an inspection, had found the gate newly padlocked, they could have come to any conclusion other than that [the defendant] was intending to exclude everyone, including themselves, from the land.'...

I agree with the judge that 'What is required for this purpose is not an intention to own or even an intention to acquire ownership but an intention to possess,' that is to say, an intention *for the time being* to possess the land to the exclusion of all other persons, including the owner with the paper title. No authorities cited to us establish the contrary position...

I have already accepted that the court should be slow to make a finding of adverse possession in a case such as the present...

However, the council lost their case and their land. A good comparison is seen in the next extract where the Court of Appeal decided that the squatter failed:

Pulleyn v *Hall Aggregates (Thames Valley) Ltd* (1992) 65 P & CR 276 (CA) Dillon and Russell LJJ

The defendants were registered proprietors of flooded gravel pits which were used by members of sailing clubs under informal arrangements, and a strip of land, 'the yellow land', used by the sailing clubs for parking cars and boats. The yellow land bordered the gravel pits and Searl Farm, which had been sold by their predecessors in title to Mr Dixon. He was the predecessor in title of the plaintiff, Pulleyn, and believed himself the owner also of the yellow land – a mistake shared by the defendants' predecessors.

Dillon LJ:
Although not himself a sailing man, Mr Dixon was on friendly terms with the successive clubs. He allowed the members to park cars and boats whenever they liked on the yellow land and also, though not at first, on the land just over the

northern boundary of the yellow land and within the boundaries of his own registered title...

In addition Mr Dixon, when walking his dog, kept an eye open for any sign of vandalism of the club's boats. On occasions he supplied the current club with materials for works the club wanted to carry out on the yellow land and on occasions he himself lent a hand with physical work being carried out by the members. In return he received from successive clubs what was referred to at times as a peppercorn or nominal rent – a bottle or bottles of whisky and a box of chocolates at Christmas, the cost of which was entered in the club accounts as rent. He and his wife were also invited to the club's annual dinner dance...

The first question is ... in my judgement, to consider whether the true owners, Hyde Crete [the former paper owners] and Hall Aggregates ever were dispossessed by Mr Dixon.

The judge seems to have had it in mind, though he reached no decision, that if Mr Dixon and Hyde Crete shared a common mistaken belief that the yellow land had been conveyed to Mr Dixon and Mr Dixon had therefore had no intention to take possession of land which was not his, there could never have been adverse possession on Mr Dixon's part because he never intended to dispossess anyone. That would not be a correct approach in law, if the acts of possession by Mr Dixon on the yellow land were unequivocally sufficient to dispossess the true owner...

The real difficulty here is that all that Mr Dixon ever did in respect of the yellow land was to let the successive clubs park cars and boats on it, and that, on the evidence, was precisely the same as Hyde Crete and Hall Aggregates wanted to do with the yellow land; they wanted a thriving sailing club to have its base on the land to the south of the yellow land and they wanted that club to have on the yellow land the parking it needed.

What has to be shown to establish dispossession of the true owner of the land is discussed in the judgement of this court in *Buckinghamshire County Council* v *Moran*. The practical task in the present case is to apply the law there stated to the facts of the present case...

Dillon LJ then quoted extensively from Slade LJ's judgment in *Moran* and continued:

The plaintiff's case is not helped by the fact that the extension of the parking over the yellow land was gradual. Mr Dixon ... states that when he moved into Searl's Farm the sailing club was nowhere near the size it is now. He attributes the expansion of the club to the activities of Mr Clive Flemming ... But Mr Flemming in his witness statement says that when he joined the AWRE sailing club in 1971 only approximately half the yellow land ... was being used by the club.

Looking at the facts as a whole, my conclusion is that the true owner was never dispossessed by Mr Dixon because Mr Dixon never had, for the necessary twelve years before his sale to the plaintiff in 1983, the requisite factual possession and *animus possidendi* of the yellow land.

The extracts above illustrate the most common type of adverse possession case where an existing landowner gradually adds a bit on to their own land, often a garden. The decision in the *Pulleyn* case indicates that it is no easy task to succeed with such a claim where the land is 'empty'. However, examination of another group of cases (below) suggests that the task is more onerous where the land in question is all or part of an urban dwelling. The legal rules do not distinguish between these two different types of squatting, but it should be remembered that these decisions are made in the context of a contemporary 'moral panic' about urban squatting.

East Sussex County Council v *Miller* 26 April 1991 (CA) Farquharson, Beldam LJJ (LEXIS)

The council bought a shop and the flat above in 1975 with a view, eventually, to demolishing it in order to extend Brighton Polytechnic. A Mr Carey (with his girlfriend) began squatting there a few months later, and offered to pay rent which amounted to an acknowledgement of title, but this was refused. Meanwhile, the council allowed the squatted flat to be rated (taxed) separately from the shop below, and the squatters paid the rates. Miller moved into the flat in 1979 and remained there until the writ for possession in July 1989, more than once offering to pay rent. The trial judge granted the possession order, holding that, although the premises had been occupied for the requisite period, there was no adverse possession here because there was an implied licence.

Farquharson LJ:

In my judgment there was evidence upon which the learned judge could conclude that Mr Carey and Miss Burrow were living in the premises with leave of the respondent and that during the period of his occupation Mr Carey was not in adverse possession. In those circumstances it must follow, for the reasons already given, that the appellant cannot establish his defence to the present claim.

The final matter considered by the judge was whether the appellant had established the necessary *animus possidendi* in relation to the premises. Inasmuch as the appellant is not able to establish the necessary twelve years adverse possession, a decision on this question is strictly *obiter*, but as the judge has dealt with the point and counsel have argued it before us I will not conclude without making some reference to it. To succeed in a claim based on adverse possession the appellant would have to show a continuing intention to exclude the whole world from the premises including the legal owner...

By way of establishing the necessary *animus* Mr Watkinson on behalf of the appellant pointed out that both Mr Carey and the appellant had changed the locks of the premises and carried out works of repair and maintenance inside. Furthermore, they paid rates throughout their occupation and discharged the electricity bills in their own names. It is true that in the case of *Buckinghamshire County Council* v *Moran* Slade LJ attached considerable significance to the fact that the land there in question had been fenced off and the gate locked, but the position it seems to me is quite different in a metropolitan context such as one finds in Brighton. There the changing of the locks is easily to be explained by the needs of security; and the fact that they paid the rates and settled the electricity bill and tried to improve the premises really takes the matter no further. Each of those payments would have been made even if they were not lawfully in possession...

[In discussions, at] no stage did the appellant attempt to assert a title or to exclude the representatives of the respondent from the premises...

I do not have to decide this point (that is, the question of the existence of the necessary *animus*) but I think I would have just decided that there was not quite sufficient *animus possidendi* bearing in mind all the circumstances of this case.

Thus, the squatter lost – and would have lost even had he been there for the twelve years.

In one recent case an urban squatter did succeed in the Court of Appeal – although it must be noted that the trial judge had been ready to accept a particularly arcane argument in order to prevent the squatter winning the land:

Pollard v *Jackson* (1994) 67 P & CR 327 (CA) Dillon, Stuart-Smith and Evans LJJ

In 1971, a Mr Bennett died. He had let the downstairs part of his house to a weekly tenant, Mr Jackson, who from then on paid no rent and, indeed, took over the whole house. Mr Bennett's heir was his daughter, the plaintiff, who had emigrated to Canada nearly 20 years before. The rest of the facts appear from the judgment:

Dillon LJ:
On the evidence ... Mr Bennett's condition at the latter part of his life was pretty squalid ... [After the death] Mr Jackson tried to get various public agencies interested in the squalid state of the upper part of the property, but the Environmental Health Department took no action, so Mr Jackson burnt the clothes ... The judge commented: 'If his description is right – and I have no reason to doubt it – that was the most sensible thing he could have done'. Having done that, he cleaned the upper part of the property, and he and his family moved into it.

Shortly afterwards Mr Jackson found a box of documents in the loft which were Mr Bennett's personal papers ... These Mr Jackson took to his mother's house for safety.

Time passed, and in about December 1983, more than 12 years having elapsed since Mr Bennett's death, Mr Jackson consulted solicitors about his claim to the ownership of the property by adverse possession ... The solicitors caused a caution to be entered on the register of the title to the property[19] and advised the Treasury Solicitor of the circumstances in case of any claim that the property was *bona vacantia*. The Treasury Solicitor carried out investigations. The upshot was that in October 1984 he traced Mr Bennett's former wife and Mrs Pollard, who were living in Canada. Mrs Pollard took out letters of administration to the estate of Mr Bennett in September 1986 and thereafter she was registered as the proprietor of the

---

19 See Chapter 10 at p. 310.

property. Mr Jackson remained in occupation, claiming to have a title to the property...

The judge decided the case in favour of Mrs Pollard on this basis. He said that this was property comprised in the estate of Mr Bennett to which no grant of representation had been obtained. Therefore, Mr Jackson, in taking possession of the property, constituted himself an executor *de son tort*.[20] Therefore, he was a constructive trustee of the property for whoever was beneficially interested[21] in the estate of Mr Bennett, and time could not run in his favour under the Limitation Act once Mr Bennett was dead because time cannot run in favour of a trustee, against his beneficiary. The judge said that mere knowledge of the death of Mr Bennett was enough in the circumstances to satisfy the requirement for a constructive trust.

I find this a very strange conclusion that the judge has reached because the case of a person in adverse possession has never hitherto, so far as I am aware, been regarded as a case of executorship *de son tort* ... Mr Jackson's ... claim is adverse to the estate, and there is no question whatever that an adverse title to a landowner's property can be acquired under the Limitation Act free from the landowner's liabilities ... Mr Jackson did not at any stage do anything which might have been regarded as characteristic of an executor. The burning of unpleasant clothing and so forth ... is not to be regarded as constituting him executor of the estate; it was a clearance of rubbish which could have become a health hazard...

I cannot see that by continuing in possession of the ground floor without paying the rent due from him, or by taking wrongful possession of the upper floor as a squatter, Mr Jackson can be said to have received or held any real estate of a deceased's person. So I do not see that Mr Jackson exposed himself to liability as an executor *de son tort* in respect of this property...

Then it is said that he became a constructive trustee. Again I find that very strange. Mr Jennings [counsel for the plaintiff] shrinks from saying that any person who occupies land as a squatter is a constructive trustee for the true owner, or is under a duty to notify the true owner of his occupation of the land. But he says that it is different where the land is trust property and the squatter has grounds for suspecting that it is trust property. This would mean that nobody could acquire a title by limitation to land, the true owner of which was known to have died, when there was a delay before anyone came forward to obtain a grant and assert title to the land...

I find that wholly out of kilter with the clearly stated and long-understood law in the Limitation Act as to the acquisition of title by adverse possession. Similarly, it would mean that it would not be possible for a squatter to acquire title to land which he knew or reasonably believed to be land held on trust...

I do not see that Mr Jackson was under any duty to try and search out Mrs Pollard, or whoever else might be entitled to succeed to Mr Bennett's estate, wherever she might be. I do not believe that he was under a duty to take steps to cause some other public authority to trace Mrs Pollard or whoever else might be entitled. He was entitled to remain in adverse possession until someone else turned up in sufficient time to make a claim against him. But that did not happen. On the facts [had it not been for the trusteeship] the judge found that Mr Jackson was in adverse possession of the whole house for more than 12 years ...

---

20 'Self-appointed executor'.
21 For constructive trusts, see Chapter 9 at p. 258 *et seq.*

Accordingly, I would allow the appeal, set aside the order of the judge and, subject to argument, I would declare ... that Mr Jackson is entitled to the property absolutely for an estate in fee simple. I would make the order which is sought for rectification of the title at HM Land Registry.[22]

CONCLUSION

The tests of adverse possession – actual and intended exclusive occupation of land – enables the courts to distinguish between the mere trespasser and the successful adverse possessor. It is clear from legislation and case law that not all squatters are the same: those engaged in temporary trespass resulting either from housing need or political strategy have a different relationship to the law than those who succeed under the Limitation Act. In most of the cases reported recently, the successful adverse possessor is already a landowner (even Mr Jackson was a legal tenant) who thus increases her estate. Meanwhile, the 'unworthy' squatters, especially the homeless, are increasingly excluded from land by both civil and criminal provisions.

In some senses however, all adverse possession is on the margins of land law which, traditionally, focuses on the marketplace. In addition, adverse possession relies on the ancient significance of possession as the basis of property rights, as opposed to the modern reliance on documentation as the proof of title.[23] Nevertheless, despite – or, perhaps, in the long run, because of – government policy, the reliance of would-be adverse possessors and other unlawful occupants of land on access and occupation may go hand in hand with visions of a new property (see Chapter 11).

---

22 For rectification of registered title, see chapter 10 at pp. 314–18.
23 See also the analysis of A. Pottage on documentation and land law, Chapter 10 at pp. 274–5.

4 Leases

INTRODUCTION

A brief history

In order to understand the legal rules governing leases, it is important to appreciate the history of the landlord–tenant relationship:

W.T. Murphy and S. Roberts *Understanding Property Law* (Fontana: 1987)

In this century, a substantial body of functionally differentiated statute law has grown up around the landlord–tenant relationship, such that today the nineteenth-century rules have limited – though still very important – practical application. But to get the subject as a whole into perspective, it is necessary to look back to the past ... The principal contextual difference is between the rural and urban sectors, or, slightly differently as we shall see, between agricultural land – farms – and housing.

The rural context: farms

The 'broad acres' of a landed estate were in fact composed of a number of farms, each yielding a rent paid by the tenant farmer who worked the farm. Until changes which came in the wake of the First World War, in which the scions of landed families fell alongside the sons of tenant farmers in the trenches by the Somme, such tenancies, to judge from the evidence, commonly remained in one farming family over several generations. But such tenancies were very often extremely informal, as those devoted to the cause of improving the state of agriculture in England emphasised with growing intensity from the middle of the nineteenth century. Why?

People of the time called these farming tenancies 'tenancies at will', as do today's historians. Strictly, lawyers call them yearly periodic tenancies.[1] But the same thing is meant by both, for a simple reason: the legal conceptualisation of these relationships was largely a matter of clothing fact with right. The landowner could terminate the tenancy at his pleasure, but, given the nature of farming, at pleasure would normally mean giving notice on certain days of the year, and

---

1 See, for example, *Javad* v *Aquil* [1991] 1 All ER 243; S. Bridge (1991) CLJ 232.

allowing the tenant six months, principally in order to gather such crops as he may have planted. At one level this meant that the exiguous legal structure of this relationship afforded much social power to the landowner, whose ability to terminate the tenancy at pleasure might hang like a sword of Damocles over the heads of his tenant farmers. But the legal relationship was for the most part enveloped in a broader normative framework ... The landowner, in many cases, was principally interested in his rental income. In a time of severe agricultural depression, for example, the landlord might do better to allow his tenant farmers to go into arrears rather than exercise his legal rights, in the hope that over time things would balance out.

The modern regulatory scheme springs principally from the problems of Ireland. It is interesting to note that legislation was required, because, as said above, mid-nineteenth-century reformers thought that most of what was needed could be achieved by formalising the relationship by means of a lease. Let us return to why they thought this to be so...

People interested in agricultural improvement in the nineteenth century – in improving farming methods, in increasing the potential yield of land and in methods of improving the manner of storage of its produce – saw the formal lease as a mechanism for spelling out in advance precisely who was responsible for what, and for enshrining in legal terms how the land was to be utilised. Those who advocated the adoption of leases hoped, by formalising all this, to focus the minds of the parties at the time of entering into the transaction. The traditional tenancy, because of its informal character, was seen as an obstacle to improvement in these respects ... what incentive was there for the tenant farmer to engage in agricultural improvement? Why should he build barns, drain land, clear wasteland and so on, if his landlord could turn him out at any time and reap the benefit of the improvement himself? These questions, which were posed with most intensity in the Irish context, because, on the whole, absentee landlords behaved that much worse, shaped the form taken by legislative interventions...

The urban context: housing

It is even harder to generalise with any accuracy about the legal forms through which the occupation of houses was arranged ... Whatever the position in remoter times, when most people lived in the country, the urbanisation of England in the nineteenth century meant, among other things, that farmland adjacent to what were once small towns became the target of urban development.[2] People who owned such land at the time that pressure for development came upon it – whether industrial or residential; indeed obviously, the two went together – were faced with two choices. They could sell their land to a developer. But such a course of action would involve the problem of alternative safe places for the proceeds of sale. So the course which was widely adopted was not to sell up entirely but to grant leases of land wanted for development. Such leases would draw upon all the expertise of lawyers, and contain detailed plans for how the land let to the builder should be built upon. Lawyers called these leases 'building leases', which were typically of sixty or ninety years' duration. Under such leases, the builder/developer would be

---

2 See Chapter 2, p. 32.

responsible for erecting a building or a number of buildings upon a particular site, and detailed provision might be made for the manner of their construction and continuing maintenance, even down to the type of subsequent letting of the buildings which was to be permitted. The lease would reserve a 'ground rent' for the landowner...

The speculative, 'capitalist' builder was faced with a choice of his own. He could sell on the term (as lawyers say, 'assign' it). Or he could rent out the property ... So in the urban context we encounter two rental incomes generated from the same physical entity: the ground rent and the house or occupancy rent...

The complexity of tenancies and sub-tenancies relating to just one house or building in the urban context, together with a flavour of the experiences of working class tenants at the turn of the century, can be gained from the following extract. This originally appeared as part of a Fabian Women's Group report based upon research from 1909–13 into the daily lives of families living in Lambeth.

M.P. Reeves *Round About A Pound A Week* (Virago: 1979)

The kind of dwelling to be had for 7s or 8s a week varies in several ways. If it be light, dry and free from bugs, if it be central in position, and if it contain three rooms, it will be eagerly sought for and hard to find. Such places exist in some blocks of workmen's dwellings, and applications for them are waiting long before a vacancy occurs, provided, of course, that they are in a convenient district. Perhaps the next best bargain after such rooms in blocks of workmen's dwellings is a portion of a small house. These small houses are let at rents varying from 10s to 15s, according to size, condition and position. They are let to a tenant who is responsible to the landlord for the whole rent, and who sublets such rooms as she can do without in order to get enough money for the rent-collector. She is often a woman with five or six children, who would not, on account of her large family, be an acceptable sub-tenant. If she is a good woman of business, it is sometimes possible for her to let her rooms advantageously ... But there is always a serious risk attached to the taking of a whole house – the risk of not being able to sub-let, or, if there are tenants, of being unable to make them pay...

The question of vermin is a very pressing one in all the small houses. No woman, however clean, can cope with it. Before their confinements some women go to the trouble of having the room they are to lie in fumigated. In spite of such precautions, bugs have dropped on to the pillow of the sick woman before the visitor's eyes[3] ... The fault is not entirely that of the sanitary authorities or of the immediate landlords ... The sanitary standard is ... deplorably low. That is simply because it has to be that low if some of these houses are to be considered habitable at all, and if others are to be inhabited by two, or often by three, families at the same time.

Exclusive possession and rent

It is the very essence of a lease that a tenant should be given the right to 'exclusive possession' – the right to exclude all other persons, including the

---

3 See also *Smith* v *Marrable* (1843) below, p. 98.

landlord, from the premises. However, this concept is more than a description of a right accruing to all tenants. It has become, since the 1985 House of Lords decision in *Street* v *Mountford* [1985] AC 809, the means of distinguishing between leases and licences, the latter being the means by which lawyers sought to find a way around statutory controls regarding the levels of rent and security for the tenant.

Legislation in the 1960s and 1970s had singled out tenants for protection regarding rent levels and security, but mere licensees were excluded from this. Inevitably, property owners, seeking ways to avoid Parliament's intervention, consulted their lawyers, who devised the 'non-exclusive occupation licence agreement'. 'These agreements usually obliged the "licensees", as they were called in the agreements, to share occupation with other persons the landlord might from time to time nominate, each to bear responsibility for part of the rent' (R. Cranston *Legal Foundations of the Welfare State* (Weidenfeld & Nicholson: 1985)). As one of the main features of a tenancy was exclusive occupation these 'licence agreements' sought to exclude it.

The courts, of course, were asked on a number of occasions to determine whether such agreements created licences or leases. In *Street* v *Mountford* the House of Lords made clear that the status of such agreements was not a question of the parties' intentions:

Street v *Mountford* [1985] AC 809

Lord Templeman:

In the present case, the agreement ... professed an intention by both parties to create a licence and their belief that they had in fact created a licence ... Both parties enjoyed freedom to contract or not to contract and both parties exercised that freedom by contracting on the terms set forth in the written agreement and on no other terms. But the consequences in law of the agreement, once concluded, can only be determined by consideration of the effect of the agreement. If the agreement satisfied all the requirements of a tenancy, then the agreement produced a tenancy and the parties cannot alter the effect of the agreement by insisting that they only created a licence. The manufacture of a five-pronged manual implement for manual digging results in a fork even if the manufacturer, unfamiliar with the English language, insists that he intended to make and has made a spade...

My Lords, the only intention which is relevant is the intention demonstrated by the agreement to grant exclusive possession for a term at a rent.

Neither Lord Templeman's statements above, nor the later decision of the House of Lords in *AG Securities* v *Vaughan; Antoniades* v *Villiers* [1988] 3 WLR 1205, achieved a clear distinction between leases and licences. The Court of Appeal has continued to make decisions, over a wide variety of factual situations, according to a fine and technical discourse.[4] However, the number of cases is reducing as

---

4 See, for example, *Skipton Building Society* v *Clayton and others* [1993] below at p. 84–6.

legislation has once again swung in the favour of landlords. Changes in the Housing Act 1988 introduced new kinds of tenancies which strengthened the position of residential landlords. Licence agreements are no longer necessary for the cautious landlord seeking to acquire an income from their properties. Nevertheless, deregulation only applies to occupation agreements made after 15 January 1989, and there are still potential cases in the pipeline. Moreover, the Housing Act 1988 applies only to residential occupation and has no effect upon lease-licence cases with respect to business or office premises.

The payment of rent, in terms of money or money's worth, would seem to be the very crux of the relationship around which all the other secondary promises by tenant and landlord are built. Indeed, in *Street* v *Mountford* [1985] AC 809, Lord Templeman stated that '(t)o constitute a tenancy the occupier must be granted exclusive possession for a fixed or periodic term certain in consideration of a premium or fixed periodical payments' (p. 818). This could be interpreted to mean that rent is an integral part of a lease. However, there have always been leases without rent (for example, mortgages) and the statutory definition of a term of years absolute is clear on this point:

Law of Property Act 1925

General definitions

205(1)   (xxvii) 'Term of years absolute' means a term of years (taking effect either in possession or in reversion whether or not at a rent) with or without impeachment for waste, subject or not to another legal estate, and either certain or liable to determination by notice, re-entry, operation of law, or by a provision for cesser on redemption, or in any other event (other than the dropping of a life, or the determination of a determinable life interest); but does not include any term of years determinable with life or lives or with the cesser of a determinable life interest, nor, if created after the commencement of this Act, a term of years which is not expressed to take effect in possession within twenty-one years after the creation thereof where required by this Act to take effect within that period; and in this definition the expression 'term of years' includes a term for less than a year, or for a year or years and a fraction of a year or from year to year...

However, the Court of Appeal has held that there certainly may be a lease without rent: *Ashburn Anstalt* v *Arnold* (1988) 2 WLR 706.[5]

---

5 Although there must be some doubt thrown over the force of this statement (see *Prudential Assurance Co Ltd* v *London Residuary Body* (1992), below p. 81). But see *Canadian Imperial Bank of Commerce* v *Bello, etc.* (1992) 24 HLR 155: contrast with *Bostock (Exec)* v *Bryant and Another* (1991) 61 P & CR 23.

THE 1925 RATIONALISATION

Legal leases

Since 1925 a lease cannot be a legal estate unless it is made by a deed. This is a consequence of s. 52(1), Law of Property Act 1925 (Chapter 2). However, there is a statutory exception:

Law of Property Act 1925

Creation of interests in land by parol

54 (2) Nothing in the foregoing provisions of this Part of this Act shall affect the creation by parol of leases taking effect in possession for a term not exceeding three years (whether or not the lessee is given power to extend the term) at the best rent which can be reasonably obtained without taking a fine.[6]

Thus, a lease for less than three years may be validly created on an informal basis, provided that it is for a market, as opposed to a 'peppercorn', rent. Periodic tenancies, although they may ultimately exceed three years, are also covered by this section and may take effect orally: *Kushner* v *Law Society* [1952] 1 KB 264.

In order to be legal a lease must also be for a *term of years absolute*, according to s. 1(1)(b), Law of Property Act 1925. As made clear in s. 205(1)(xxvii) (above) this means that a valid legal lease must be for a fixed and certain period of time.

Prudential Assurance Co Ltd v *London Residuary Body* [1992] 2 AC 386 (HL), Griffiths, Browne-Wilkinson, Mustill, Templeman and Goff LJJ

In 1930 a lease of land, which fronted onto Walworth Road, had been created by the London County Council with a Mr Samuel Nathan (tenant). The council was a highway authority and envisaged widening the road in the future. The lease contained a provision (clause 6) that it would continue until the landlord required the land to implement the road-widening scheme, at which time the council would give the tenant two months' notice of the date on which the land was required. The case arose when the London Residuary Body – in which the reversion had vested – served a notice upon the Prudential Assurance Co Ltd, successor in title to the tenant. The validity of the notice rested on whether the original agreement had created a periodic tenancy or a tenancy for a fixed term. Millet J held that the parties had made a periodic yearly tenancy. The Court of Appeal interpreted the agreement as a tenancy for a term of uncertain duration:

Lord Templeman:
...When the agreement in the present case was made, it failed to grant an estate in

---

6 See also Law of Property (Miscellaneous Provisions) Act 1989, S. 2(5), in Chapter 2.

land. The tenant however entered into possession and paid the yearly rent of £30 reserved by the agreement. The tenant entering under a void lease became by virtue of possession and the payment of a yearly rent, a yearly tenant holding on the terms of the agreement so far as those terms were consistent with a yearly tenancy. A yearly tenancy is determinable by the landlord or the tenant at the end of the first or any subsequent year of the tenancy by six months' notice unless the agreement between the parties provides otherwise...

Now it is said that when in the present case the tenant entered pursuant to the agreement and paid a yearly rent he became a tenant from year to year on the terms of the agreement, including clause 6 which prevents the landlord from giving notice to quit until the land is required for road widening. This submission would make nonsense of the rule that a grant for an uncertain term does not create a lease and would make nonsense of the concept of a tenancy from year to year because it is of the essence of a tenancy from year to year that both the landlord and the tenant shall be entitled to give notice determining the tenancy...

The landlord has ... served such a notice. The Court of Appeal have, however, concluded that the notice was ineffective and that the landlord cannot give a valid notice until the land is required 'for the purposes of the widening of Walworth Road' in conformity with clause 6 of the agreement.

The notion of a tenancy from year to year, the landlord binding himself not to give notice to quit ... was ... revived and applied by the Court of Appeal in *In re Midland Railway Co's Agreement* [1971] Ch 725. In that case a lease for a period of six months from 10 June 1920 was expressed to continue from half year to half year until determined. The agreement provided for the determination of the agreement ... given by either party to the other subject to a proviso that the landlords should not exercise that right unless they required the premises for their undertaking. The successors to the landlords served a six months' written notice ... although they did not require the premises for the undertaking. The Court of Appeal ... declared the notice to quit was invalid and of no effect [and] ... held that the decision in *Lace* v *Chantler* [1944] KB 368 did not apply to a periodic tenancy...

My Lords, I consider that the principle in *Lace* v *Chantler* ... reaffirming 500 years of judicial acceptance of the requirement that a term must be certain applies to all leases and tenancy agreements. A tenancy from year to year is saved from being uncertain because each party has power by notice to determine at the end of any year. The term continues until determined as if both parties made a new agreement at the end of each year for a new term for the ensuing year. A power for nobody to determine or for one party only to be able to determine is inconsistent with the concept of a term from year to year: see *Warner* v *Browne* 8 East 165 and *Cheshire Lines Committee* v *Lewis & Co* 50 LJQB 121. In *Re Midland Railway Co's Agreement* ... there was no 'clearly expressed bargain' that the term should continue until the crack of doom if the demised land was not required for the landlord's undertaking or if the undertaking ceased to exist. In the present case there was no 'clearly expressed bargain' that the tenant shall be entitled to enjoy his 'temporary structures' in perpetuity if Walworth Road is never widened. In any event principle and precedent dictate that it is beyond the power of the landlord and the tenant to create a term which is uncertain.

A lease can be made for five years subject to the tenant's right to determine if the war ends before the expiry of five years. A lease can be made from year to year subject to a fetter on the right of the landlord to determine the lease before the expiry of five years unless the war ends. Both leases are valid because they create a determinable certain term of five years. A lease may purport to be made for the duration of the war subject to the tenant's right to determine before the end of the war. A lease may be made from year to year subject to a fetter on the right of the landlord to determine the lease before the war ends. Both leases would be invalid because each purported to create an uncertain term. A term must either be certain or uncertain. It cannot be partly certain because the tenant can determine it at any time and partly uncertain because the landlord cannot determine it for an uncertain period. If the landlord does not grant and the tenant does not take a certain term the grant does not create a lease.

The decision of the Court of Appeal in *Re Midland Railway Co's Agreement* ... was taken a little further in *Ashburn Anstalt* v *Arnold* [1989] Ch 1. That case, if it was correct, would make it unnecessary for a lease to be of a certain duration. In an agreement for the sale of land the vendor reserved the right to remain at the property after completion as licensee and to trade therefrom without payment of rent

> 'save that it can be required by Matlodge [the purchaser] to give possession on not less than one-quarter's notice in writing upon Matlodge certifying that it is ready at the expiration of such notice forthwith to proceed with the development of the property and the neighbouring property involving, *inter alia*, the demolition of the property.'

The Court of Appeal held that this reservation created a tenancy. The tenancy was not from year to year but for a term which would continue until Matlodge certified that it was ready to proceed with the development of the property. The Court of Appeal held that the term was not uncertain because the vendor could either give a quarter's notice or vacate the property without giving notice. But of course the same could be said of the situation in *Lace* v *Chantler* ... The cumulative result of the two Court of Appeal authorities in *Re Midland Railway Co's Agreement* ... and *Ashburn's* case ... would therefore destroy the need for any term to be certain.

In the present case the Court of Appeal were bound by the [above] decisions .... In my opinion both these cases were wrongly decided. A grant for an uncertain term does not create a lease. A grant for an uncertain term which takes the form of a yearly tenancy which cannot be determined by the landlord does not create a lease. I would allow the appeal. The trial judge, Millet J, reached the conclusion that the six months' notice served by the London Residuary Body was a good notice. He was, of course, bound by the Court of Appeal decisions but managed to construe the memorandum of agreement so as to render clause 6 ineffective in fettering the right of the landlord to serve a notice to quit after the landlord had ceased to be a road-widening authority. In the circumstances this question of construction need not be considered. For the reasons which I have given the order made by Millet J must be restored...

Lord Browne-Wilkinson:
My Lords, I agree with the speech of my noble and learned friend, Lord Templeman, that this appeal must be allowed for the reasons he gives. However, I reach that conclusion with no satisfaction.

...The agreement made in 1930 was part of a sale and leaseback arrangement whereby a part of Mr Nathan's land ('the strip') was sold to the LCC for road widening. Mr Nathan retained the freehold of the remainder ... Up until today, the remainder ... together with the strip has been let and occupied as one single set of retail shop premises with a frontage to the Walworth Road. As a result of our decision Mr Nathan's successor in title will be left with the freehold of the remainder ... which, though retail premises, will have no frontage to a shopping street: the LCC's successors in title will have the freehold to [the strip] ... with a road frontage but probably incapable of being used save in conjunction with the land from which it was severed in 1930...

It is difficult to think of a more unsatisfactory outcome or one further away from what the parties to the 1930 agreement can ever have contemplated...

This bizarre outcome results from the application of an ancient and technical rule of law which requires the maximum duration of a term of years to be ascertainable from the outset. No one has produced any satisfactory rationale for the genesis of this rule. No one has been able to point to any useful purpose that it serves at the present day ... But for this House to depart from a rule relating to land law which has been established for many centuries might upset long-established titles. I must, therefore, confine myself to expressing the hope that the Law Commission might look at the subject to see whether there is in fact any good reason now for maintaining a rule which operates to defeat contractually agreed arrangements ... and which is capable of producing such an extraordinary result as that in the present case.[7]

The concept of 'certainty of duration' also means that a lease granted for the period of someone's life is incapable of being legal, as stated in s. 205(1)(xxvii) above. The 1925 legislation made special provision for such leases. Statute further ensured that reversionary leases (i.e. leases to take effect in the future), although capable of being legal, must take effect not more than 21 years from the date of their creation. This legislation, together with the issues of certainty and exclusive possession, are discussed in the next extract:

Skipton Building Society v *Clayton* (1993) 66 P & CR 223 (CA) Nourse and Butler-Sloss LJJ and Sir Christopher Slade

Mr Browne who was in arrears with his mortgage entered into a 'sale and leaseback arrangement' by which he transferred his flat to Mr Clayton and Mr Thomas who were duly entered as the registered proprietors. They paid £26,000 (less than one-third of the flat's market value) which enabled Mr Browne to pay off his arrears. Under a 'licence' agreement Mr Browne was allowed to remain, with his family, in occupation of the flat. Mr Clayton and Mr Thomas later granted a mortgage on the property to the Skipton Building Society but did not keep up the mortgage instalments. The Society obtained an order for possession

---

7 For a critique of the House of Lords' decision see Sparkes (1993) 109 LQR 93; Wilde (1994) 57 MLR 117. For further discussion of the certainty issue see *Skipton Building Society* v *Clayton*, below.

and the Brownes applied to have it set aside. Hull J held that the Browne's licence agreement was in fact a tenancy binding upon the Society under s. 70(1)(g) of the Land Registration Act 1925.[8] The Society appealed:

Sir Christopher Slade:
At the date of the grant of the mortgage to the society, were Mr and Mrs Browne mere licensees, as opposed to tenants, of the property?

The decision of the House of Lords in *Street* v *Mountford* clearly establishes, that whether the label which the parties choose to attach to their arrangement be a tenancy or a licence, an arrangement under which exclusive possession of residential property is granted for a term at a rent will normally be regarded by the law as the grant of a tenancy ... as Lord Templeman recognised the same legal result will ensue if the occupier is granted exclusive possession for a fixed or periodic term certain in consideration for a premium.

Mr Behrens [counsel for the Society] accepted that it is possible to have a tenancy without any provision for the payment of rent ... In his submission, however, the absence of any provision for the payment of rent by Mr and Mrs Browne is at least one factor which points to the absence of any tenancy in the present case.

In general terms he reminded us that both sides to the arrangements had had legal advice, that the 1989 agreement called itself a licence and, according to its wording, granted no more than a licence ... In regard to the crucial question of exclusive possession he naturally attached particular weight to clause 5(b), which purported to reserve management, possession and control of the property to the so-called licensor and specifically not to give exclusive possession to the so-called licensees...

In this context the judge's findings of fact were clear and unequivocal. He found...

'The first defendants were dishonest ... The licence agreement, which was drafted by their solicitors, is artfully contrived in an endeavour to avoid the consequences of *Street* v *Mountford* ... The provision that the first defendants were to have possession, management and control of the flat was a sham. The first defendants had not the slightest intention of sharing the flat with the Brownes or exercising any of the supposed rights of shared possession and occupation ... The intentions of the parties and the reality of the situation were that the Brownes were to have exclusive use, occupation and possession of the flat for the rest of their lives, having parted with Mr Brownes ownership for a very much reduced sum...'

We must ... proceed on the basis that the 1989 agreement, notwithstanding its misleading provisions, did operate to grant exclusive possession of the property to Mr and Mrs Browne.

The next important question is whether the term of years granted to them by that agreement was of sufficiently certain duration to give rise to a tenancy, as opposed to a licence. The recent decision of the House of Lords in *Prudential Assurance Company Limited* v *London Residuary Body* has reaffirmed that it is a requirement

---

8 See Chapter 10 at p. 290.

of all leases and tenancy agreements ... that the maximum duration of the term shall be ascertainable from the outset.

Mr Behrens submitted that the only way in which the term granted to Mr and Mrs Browne by the 1989 agreement could satisfy this requirement would be through the applicaton of s. 149(6) of the Law of Property Act 1925, which in his submission does not in fact apply. This subsection, omitting immaterial words, reads:

> 'Any lease ... at a rent, or in consideration of a fine, for life or lives ... shall take effect as a lease ... for a term of ninety years determinable after the death ... of the survivor of the original lessees, by at least one month's notice in writing...'

Section 205(1)(xxiii) of that Act states that 'fine' includes 'a premium or foregift and any payment, consideration, or benefit in the nature of a fine, premium or foregift'.

The 1989 agreement provided for no payment of rent; nor, in Mr Behren's submission, can it be said to have been entered into by the first defendants in consideration of a 'fine' within the statutory definition ... since no monetary payment was made by Mr and Mrs Browne for the rights granted to them...

However, to consider the validity or otherwise of Mr Behren's submissions in this context, it is necessary to look at the judge's findings as to the consideration given by Mr and Mrs Browne to the first defendants...:

> 'In my judgment, the true view of the licence agreement when its sham provision for shared occupation and possession and its misleading title are ignored, is that it was the grant of a term of years by the first defendants to Mr and Mrs Browne for their joint lives and the life of the survivor. The premium for this grant is the discount of more than two-thirds of the value of the flat for which it was sold to the first defendants.'

This analysis of the facts is, in my judgment, unassailable ... in return for the rights granted by the 1989 agreement the first defendants received a 'benefit in the nature of a ... premium' ... It follows that ... Mr and Mrs Browne have at all material times been entitled to a tenancy of the property by virtue of the 1989 agreement, a tenancy to which s. 149(6) of the Law of Property Act 1925 applies.

Equitable leases

Equitable leases may be created in four different ways:

1. Expressly – when a settlor declares a trust in favour of beneficiaries of a property in which the settlor owns a legal term of years. The beneficiaries will acquire an equitable interest and, therefore, an equitable lease.
2. Impliedly – when a leasehold property is conveyed into the name of one party, but purchased with the funds of two. This will give rise to a resulting trust in favour of both in equity with the same result as in (1). (See Chapter 9.)
3. It is a legal rule that no one can transfer a better title than the one which they own. This means that the owner of an equitable lease can only grant an equitable sub-lease, not a legal lease, irrespective of the mode of the sub-tenancy's creation.

4. Even if there is no deed, as necessary under s. 52, LPA 1925 above, provided the requirements of s. 2, Law of Property (Miscellaneous Provisions) Act 1989, have been fulfilled there may be a specifically enforceable contract to create a lease. This will take effect in equity.

This fourth method for the creation of an equitable lease, prima facie, presents a problem. If, for instance, X enters into Y's property with Y's consent, X becomes a tenant at will. If X starts to pay a regular sum of money to Y, X may become a periodic tenant. This periodic tenancy could also be a legal tenancy if X and Y's rental relationship complies with the three conditions for informal legal leases (see s. 54(2), LPA 1925 above).

However, equity may also recognise X's rights on the basis of the agreement with Y if there is sufficient writing as required by s. 2 of the 1989 Act. Thus, in theory, X could, simultaneously, have both a legal and an equitable lease. In practice, however, this problem is resolved by what is known as the doctrine in *Walsh* v *Lonsdale*.

Walsh v *Lonsdale* (1882) Ch 9 (CA) Sir George Jessell MR, Cotton and Lindley LJJ

The case involved a lease on a mill which was capable, on the facts, of taking effect as an equitable seven year lease, subject to specific express covenants, or a legal periodic tenancy, without any such terms.

Jessell MR:

There is an agreement for a lease under which possession was given. Now since the Judicature Acts the possession is held under the agreement. There are not two estates as there were formerly, one estate at common law by reason of the payment of the rent from year to year, and an estate in equity under the agreement. There is only one Court and the equity rules prevail in it.[9] The tenant holds under an agreement for a lease. He holds, therefore, under the same terms in equity as if a lease has been granted...

Assignment of leases

The assignment of a legal lease must be in the form of a deed to be effective: s. 52(1), Law of Property Act 1925. Thus as was reaffirmed recently in *Crago* v *Julian* [1992] 1 WLR 373 CA leases for a term of less than three years, although they may be created orally, can only be assigned by deed. However, it is possible to have an equitable assignment of a legal lease, provided that the terms of s. 2 of the 1989 Act for the creation of an enforceable contract are complied with by the parties. A lease originally created in equity must be assigned in writing:

---

9 See Chapter 2 at p. 39.

Law of Property Act 1925

Instruments required to be in writing

53(1) (c) [A] disposition of an equitable interest or trust subsisting at the time of the disposition, must be in writing signed by the person disposing of the same, or by his agent thereunto lawfully authorised in writing or by will.[10]

COVENANTS IN LEASES

A regime of private law

Leases are contracts and both parties, landlord and tenant, will be bound by any express terms in that agreement. These terms involve promises either to do, or refrain from doing something, made by either party. They are known as covenants because these promises are generally made in the form of a deed. A deed was traditionally a contract under seal or covenant.

These covenants may be carefully drawn up by lawyers seeking to create a system which will match the requirements of the particular landlord/tenant relationship. Unlike many other contracts, the courts have not exercised a strong influence over the framework of this relationship and the common law only imposes a few terms upon leasehold parties.

However, the small number of implied covenants have a part to play in contributing towards the comfort of tenants and some have attracted the attention of Parliament. Those terms which are commonly found in leases, both express and implied, are detailed below.

Covenant for quiet enjoyment

Kenny v *Preen* [1963] 1 QB 499 (CA) Ormrod, Donovan and Pearson LJJ

Pearson LJ:

The implied covenant for quiet enjoyment is not an absolute covenant protecting a tenant against eviction or interference by anybody, but is a qualified covenant protecting the tenant against interference with the tenant's quiet and peaceful possession and enjoyment of the premises by the landlord or persons claiming through or under the landlord. The basis of it is that the landlord, by letting the premises, confers on the tenant the right of possession during the term and impliedly promises not to interfere with the tenant's exercise and use of the right of possession during the term. I think the word 'enjoy' used in this connection is a

---

10 This section is currently under review by the Law Commission.

translation of the Latin word '*fruor*' and refers to the exercise and use of the right and having the full benefit of it, rather than to deriving pleasure from it...

I would decide on two grounds in favour of the tenant's contention that there was, in this case, a breach of covenant for quiet enjoyment. First, there was a deliberate and persistent attempt by the landlord to drive the tenant out of her possession of the premises by persecution and intimidation, and intimidation included threats of physical eviction of the tenant and removal of her belongings. In my view that course of conduct by the landlord seriously interfered with the tenant's proper freedom of action in exercising her right of possession, and tended to deprive her of the full benefit of it, and was an invasion of her rights as tenant to remain in possession undisturbed, and so would in itself constitute a breach of covenant, even if there were no direct physical interference with the tenant's possession and enjoyment. No case of this kind has ever been considered by the courts before, and I do not think the *dicta* in the previous cases should be read as excluding a case of this kind where a landlord seeks, by a course of intimidation, to 'annul his own deed', to contradict his own demise, by ousting the tenant from possession which the landlord has conferred upon her.

Secondly, if direct physical interference is a necessary element in the breach of covenant that element can be found in this case to a substantial extent...

A breach of a covenant of quiet enjoyment *may* also amount to a criminal offence.

Protection from Eviction Act 1977 (as amended by s. 29, Housing Act 1988)

Unlawful eviction and harassment of occupier

1 (1) In this section 'residential occupier', in relation to any premises, means a person occupying the premises as a residence, whether under a contract or by virtue of any enactment or rule of law giving him the right to remain in occupation or restricting the right of any other person to recover possession of the premises.

(2) If any person unlawfully deprives the residential occupier of any premises of his occupation of the premises or any part thereof, or attempts to do so, he shall be guilty of an offence unless he proves that he believed, and had reasonable cause to believe, that the residential occupier had ceased to reside in the premises.

(3) If any person with intent to cause the residential occupier of any premises –
    (a) to give up the occupation of the premises or any part thereof; or
    (b) to refrain from exercising any right or pursuing any remedy in respect of the premises or part thereof;
does acts likely to interfere with the peace or comfort of the residential occupier or members of his household, or persistently withdraws or withholds services reasonably required for the occupation of the premises as a residence, he shall be guilty of an offence.

(3A) Subject to subsection 3B (below) the landlord of a residential occupier or an agent of the landlord shall be guilty of an offence if –
(a) he does acts likely to interfere with the peace or comfort of the residential occupier or members of his household, or
(b) he persistently withdraws or withholds services reasonably required for the occupation of the premises in question as a residence, and (in either case) he knows, or has reasonable cause to believe, that the conduct is likely to cause the residential occupier to give up the occupation of the whole or part of the premises or to refrain from exercising any right or pursuing any remedy in respect of the whole or part of the premises.

(3B) A person shall not be guilty of an offence under subsection (3A) above if he proves that he had reasonable grounds for doing the acts or withdrawing or withholding the services in question.

(3C) In subsection 3A (above) 'landlord', in relation to a residential occupier of any premises, means the person who, but for –
(a) the residential occupier's right to remain in occupation of the premises, or
(b) a restriction on the person's right to recover possession of the premises,
would be entitled to occupation of the premises and any superior landlord under whom that person derives title.

(4) A person guilty of an offence under this section shall be liable –
(a) on summary conviction, to a fine not exceeding £1,000 or to imprisonment for a term not exceeding 6 months or to both;
(b) on conviction on indictment, to a fine or to imprisonment for a term not exceeding 2 years or to both.

(5) Nothing in this section shall be taken to prejudice any liability or remedy to which a person guilty of an offence thereunder may be subject in civil proceedings.

(6) Where an offence under this section committed by a body corporate is proved to have been committed with the consent or connivance of, or to be attributable to any neglect on the part of, any director, manager or secretary or other similar officer of the body corporate or any person who was purporting to act in any such capacity, he as well as the body corporate shall be guilty of that offence and shall be liable to be proceeded against and punished accordingly.

Historically, successful convictions under the 1977 Act were rare, largely because it was necessary to prove that the landlord subjectively intended, through his or her actions, to force the 'residential occupier' to leave the property in question. As a disincentive to landlords wishing to rid themselves of 'sitting tenants', Parliament inserted into the Housing Act 1988 a strengthening of harassment remedies. Section 1, Protection From Eviction Act 1977, was amended to enable more prosecutions and at the same time introduced a new criminal offence.[11]

---

11 For a recent case demonstrating the continuing difficulties in sustaining a conviction against a landlord, see *R* v *Mitchell* (1994) 26 HLR 394. The civil action in this case may be found in *Sampson and Another* v *Wilson and Others* (1994) 26 HLR 486.

The provisions of the Protection from Eviction Act 1977 and the purpose of the changes made in 1988 are discussed in the following case:

Cardiff City Council v Destrick (1994) QBD (Unreported: Lexis: John Larking) (Staughton, McCullough LJJ)

Staughton LJ:

This is an appeal by case stated from a decision of the South Glamorgan Justices. The facts are that Mr Destrick, the respondent, is the owner of a house which is divided into a number of flats. He lets them out and he makes a charge for electricity. ...Two of his tenants in a flat were Mr McMorrow and Miss Wright. He says that they did not pay the electricity charge, that they were abusive, that they kept the flat in disorder and mocked him. There was a dispute about that, but it is at least possible that the Justices accepted his version of the events. So, on 26 June 1992, he served the tenants with a notice seeking possession. That, of course, would still require him to go to court, which takes time and costs money.

Early in August, he visited the premises and warned these two tenants that he would disconnect the electricity. On 13 August, he visited the premises and did disconnect the gas and the electricity. The same day a police constable came round and reconnected the gas ... On the following day, Mr McMorrow, Miss Wright and their small baby left the premises and were rehoused by the Cardiff City Council.

The Council then laid two charges against Mr Destrick. The first was of an offence against s. 1(3) of the Protection from Eviction Act 1977 ... On that charge Mr Destrick was acquitted by the Justices, and the case stated does not deal with that matter. It is accepted...

The second charge was laid under s. 1(3A), that he did an act likely to interfere with the peace or comfort of a residential occupier, and knew or had reasonable cause to believe that his conduct was likely to cause the residential occupier to give up occupation. It would be a defence to that charge, as provided in s. 1(3B), if Mr Destrick proved that he had reasonable grounds for doing the acts, or withdrawing or withholding the services in question.

The Justices in their case made two critical findings. First...

'The Respondent did not intend that his act of disconnecting the electricity supply would make the tenants leave, nor could he reasonably expect that such an act (in the summer months) would cause them to leave.'

If that finding ... stands, then an essential element of the charge in s. 1(3A) is not made out and Mr Destrick is not guilty.

Secondly, the Justices said ... as follows:

'We are of the opinion ... that it was not the intention of the Respondent to make Mr McMorrow and Miss Wright leave the flat by means of cutting the electricity supply. We are of the opinion that he did so in order to mitigate any loss he could foresee as a result of their refusal to pay the service charge ... the Respondent was entitled to infer ... that there was no real prospect of receiving payment for the electricity and consequently he had behaved reasonably when he disconnected the supply...'

Staughton LJ said that he was required to consider whether the the first of these two findings was one which any reasonable Bench of Justices could make.

...No doubt it is a hardship to live in a flat with no electricity, particularly if you have a small child, but I believe that quite a number of people do. The natural inference that I would draw from Mr Destrick's conduct was that the tenant would be persuaded to pay up and to reach an agreement with the landlord rather than promptly moving out...

That conclusion means that, in any event, Mr Destrick must be acquitted for this charge. However, Miss McGrath [for the Council] invited us to go on to consider the other point, that is the defence under s. 1(3B). She says that in law the Justices were wrong to find that it was established in this case.

Miss McGrath sought to use *Hansard* in support of her position and, although in Staughton LJ's view the necessary requirements of *Pepper* v *Hart* [1993] AC 593 were not met,[12] the material she relied on was discussed:

On 9 November 1988, in column 392, in dealing with the Housing Act 1988 the Minister said:

> 'The whole thrust of clauses 27 and 29 is against harassment. The clauses introduce a new criminal penalty and swingeing civil penalties. The conduct of a tenant will have to be very bad indeed for a court to decide that it is reasonable to mitigate damages that are clearly designed as a penalty for committing an illegal act.'

Then further down the same column:

> 'Misconduct by the tenant which provoked him to a particular act might or might not be considered by the courts to be reasonable grounds for that act. The courts will of course always be aware that illegal eviction and the withholding or withdrawing of services can be criminal offences, and that the proper way in which to obtain possession is through the courts, and will have that in mind in assessing any situation.'

That material is valuable, to my mind, if only to confirm that which I would derive from the law in any event. The general rule is, if a landlord wants to get his tenant out he must go to court. He is not entitled to rely on self-help and eviction. He is not entitled to indulge in harassment. The fact that it takes money to go to court, and that the courts are very often booked up for months ahead, is just too bad. The landlord must suffer those ills. But there is this defence against a charge of harassment where the acts of the tenants are said to be reasonable grounds. The harassment must, as Miss McGrath submits, in that event be proportionate; and it would be quite wrong to say that a wholly disproportionate response by the landlord to mild misbehaviour by the tenants would be justified. But subject to that, it is up to the Justices to determine what were reasonable grounds...

I cannot say that their findings were so irrational that no reasonable Bench of

---

12 Reference can be made to *Hansard* where (1) the legislation is ambiguous or obscure, or leads to absurdity; (2) the material consists of statements by a Minister or other promoter of the Bill; and (3) the statements relied on are clear. Staughton LJ said that the first of these requirements was not made out in this case.

Justices could make them.

As indicated above the Housing Act 1988 also introduced a new statutory tort providing tenants with civil compensation for unlawful eviction:

Housing Act 1988

Damages for unlawful eviction

27 (1) This section applies if, at any time after 9th June l988, a landlord (in this section referred to as 'the landlord in default') or any person acting on behalf of the landlord in default unlawfully deprives the residential occupier of any premises of his occupation of the whole or part of the premises.

(2) This section also applies if, at any time after 9th June 1988, a landlord (in this section referred to as 'the landlord in default') or any person acting on behalf of the landlord in default –
    (a) attempts unlawfully to deprive the residential occupier of any premises of his occupation of the whole or part of the premises, or
    (b) knowing or having reasonable cause to believe that the conduct is likely to cause the residential occupier of any premises –
        (i) to give up his occupation of the premises or any part thereof, or
        (ii) to refrain from exercising any right or pursuing any remedy in respect of the premises or any part thereof,
does acts likely to interfere with the peace or comfort of the residential occupier or members of his household, or persistently withdraws or withholds services reasonably required for the occupation of the premises as a residence, and, as a result, the residential occupier gives up his occupation of the premises as a residence.

(3) Subject to the following provisions of this section, where this section applies, the landlord in default shall, by virtue of this section, be liable to pay to the former residential occupier, in respect of his loss of the right to occupy the premises in question as his residence, damages assessed on the basis set out in section 28 below.

(6) No liability shall arise by virtue of subsection (3) above if –
    (a) before the date on which proceedings to enforce the liability are finally disposed of, the former residential occupier is reinstated in the premises in question in such circumstances that he becomes again the residential occupier of them; or
    (b) at the request of the former residential occupier, a court makes an order (whether in the nature of an injunction or otherwise) as a result of which he is reinstated as mentioned in paragraph (a) above...

(8) In proceedings to enforce a liability arising by virtue of subsection (3) above, it shall be a defence for the defendant to prove that he believed, and had reasonable cause to believe –

(a) that the residential occupier had ceased to reside in the premises in question at the time when he was deprived of occupation as mentioned in subsection (1) above or, as the case may be, when the attempt was made or the acts were done as a result of which he gave up his occupation of those premises; or

(b) that, where the liability would otherwise arise by virtue only of the doing of acts or the withdrawal or withholding of services, he had reasonable grounds for doing the acts or withdrawing or withholding the services in question.

The measure of damages

28 (1) The basis for the assessment of damages referred to in section 27(3) is the difference in value, determined as at the time immediately before the residential occupier ceased to occupy the premises in question as his residence, between –

(a) the value of the interest if the landlord in default determined on the assumption that the residential occupier continues to have the same right to occupy the premises as before that time; and

(b) the value of that interest determined on the assumption that the residential occupier has ceased to have that right.

(3) For the purposes of the valuation referred to in subsection (1) above, it shall be assumed –

(a) that the landlord in default is selling his interest on the open market to a willing buyer;

(b) that neither the residential occupier nor any member of his family wishes to buy; and

(c) that it is unlawful to carry out any substantial development of any of the land in which the landlord's interest subsists or to demolish the whole or part of any building on that land.

One of the first decisions with respect to this new statutory tort was *Tagro* v *Cafane* [1991] 2 All ER 235 which is reviewed in the next extract:

C. Rodgers 'Unlawful Evictions – Testing the Water' *Conv* (1991) 297:

Tagro v *Cafane* gave the Court of Appeal its first opportunity to examine the scope of liability under the 1988 Act, and to resolve some perceived difficulties in the new provisions.

The landlord in *Tagro* v *Cafane* had adopted the time-honoured tactic of changing the locks to the plaintiff's bedsit in order to effect an eviction. Finding herself unable to gain entry the plaintiff obtained an ex parte injunction to readmit her to the premises. The landlord then relented in part and gave her back the keys to the bedsit. On seeking readmittance, however, she found that the front door had been smashed and that the flat had been ransacked. Many of her clothes and personal belongings had been stolen. Faced with this scenario, the plaintiff gave evidence that she was too frightened to sleep at the premises and had not done so since her initial eviction. For this conduct, the landlord was, on November 24, 1989, ordered to pay £31,000 damages by Lambeth County Court. The landlord appealed on the ground that he had reinstated the tenant in the flat, thus affording himself a defence under the 1988 Act, and that the award was too high. This raised two issues for consideration in the Court of Appeal.

(i) Scope of liability and defences ...

Tagro v *Cafane* gives valuable guidance on the scope of the 'reinstatement' defences ... Both defences depend upon reinstatement being offered or obtained. What does 'reinstatement' require, as a matter of law? Regrettably, no definition is offered by the 1988 Act itself, and this makes the Court of Appeal's observations in *Tagro* the more valuable. It was here held that giving the tenant the keys, and readmitting her to the premises, did not suffice. There was, according to Lord Donaldson MR 'no suggestion that the room was put in proper order, the locks repaired or any offer made to Miss Tagro to allow her to resume occupation in any realistic sense of the word' (241). Any suggestion that reinstatement consists in merely handing the tenant the key to a lock which does not work, and inviting her to resume occupation of a room which has been completely wrecked 'is an argument which simply does not run' (239). The facts here being admittedly extreme, the Court of Appeal could dismiss this suggestion without difficulty. Regrettably, however, having given clear guidance as to what is not reinstatement, no help is to be found in *Tagro* as to what will suffice for this purpose...

(ii) *Quantum* of damages ...

The general tenor of Lord Donaldson's observations in *Tagro* indicates that the courts will be loath to lay down strict requirements as to how th[e] valuation should be conducted, preferring instead to leave valuation matters to the skill and expertise of qualified surveyors employed by the parties.[13] Two points were, however, resolved in the Court of Appeal. The relevant date for valuation purposes is the time immediately before the occupier ceases to be in residence, with the inevitable consequence that changes in market conditions between that date and the hearing are inadmissible. Secondly, the valuer is directed to make his valuation on the assumption that the landlord in default is selling his interest on the open market to a willing buyer. According to the Court of Appeal in *Tagro* v *Cafane* this requires the valuer to assume that he can sell it on the open market to a willing buyer, and in so doing to ignore any covenant against assignment which restricts alienation of the landlord's interest.

Non-derogation from grant

The nature of this covenant, implied into every lease, together with an appreciation of the narrow judicial interpretation placed upon it, can be understood from the following extract.

Browne v *Flower* [1911] 1 Ch 219

The tenant of a first-floor flat, having subdivided the apartment with the lessor's

---

13 For example, *Brooks and Arden* v *Woodcock* (1989) *Legal Action* Sept 1989. p. 25 – damages = £17,000; *Canlin* v *Berkshire Holdings* (1990) *Legal Action* Sept 1990. p. 10 – damages = £35,000; *Nwokorie* v *Mason* (1994) 26 HLR 60 – £4,500.

consent, erected an external staircase which provided access to one part of the first floor. The staircase stood in a garden overlooked by both the first floor and a ground-floor flat let to the plaintiffs. It ran up between the windows of two rooms used as bedrooms by the plaintiffs, thus allowing anyone using the staircase to see directly into the ground-floor flat. In the plaintiffs' opinion this seriously affected their privacy and thus breached the covenant of 'non-derogation from grant', since the ground-floor had been let as a dwelling house.

Parker J:

The plaintiffs ... relied on the maxim that no one can be allowed to derogate from his own grant. This maxim is generally quoted as explaining certain implications which may arise from the fact that, or the circumstances under which, an owner of land grants or demises part of it, retaining the remainder in his own hands. The real difficulty is in each case to ascertain how far such implications extend. It is well settled that such a grant or demise will ... impliedly confer on the grantee or lessee ... easements over the land retained[14] corresponding to the continuous or apparent quasi-easements enjoyed at the time of the grant or demise by the property granted or demised over the property retained ... But the implications usually explained by the maxim ... do not stop short with easements ... Thus, if the grant or demise be made for a particular purpose, the grantor or lessor comes under an obligation not to use the land retained by him in such a way as to render the land granted or demised unfit or materially less fit for the particular purpose for which the grant or demise was made...

It is quite reasonable for a purchaser to assume that a vendor who sells land for a particular purpose will not do anything to prevent its being used for that purpose, but it would be utterly unreasonable to assume that the vendor was undertaking restrictive obligations which would prevent his using land retained by him for any lawful purpose whatsoever ... Under these circumstances the question is whether the existence of this staircase renders the plaintiff's premises unfit or materially less fit to be used for the purposes for which they were demised, that is, for the purpose of a residential flat. In my opinion it does not. The two rooms in question can be and are still in fact used for the same purpose for which they were used prior to the erection of the staircase. It is only the comfort of the persons so using the rooms that is interfered with by what has been done ... Much as I sympathise with the plaintiffs, it would, in my opinion, be extending the implications based on the maxim ... to an unreasonable extent if it were held that what has been done in this case was a breach of an implied obligation.[15]

Covenants to repair

Covenants connected with the repair and upkeep of buildings are obviously, given the British climate, amongst the most important contained in leases. (See Chapter 2, p. 30.) Disrepair, as indicated by the following extract, is a key problem within the private rented sector.

---

14 See also Chapter 6, p. 184.
15 See also D.W. Elliot (1964) 80 LQR 244; M.A. Peel (1965) 81 LQR 28.

J. Luba *Repairs: Tenant's Rights* 2nd edn (LAG: 1991)

The latest survey of national housing conditions was undertaken in 1985/86. It embraced all housing tenures by sample but focused mainly on older housing rather than new-build. The results ... confirm a dire state of disrepair in the housing stock with virtually no improvement achieved since the earlier survey conducted in 1982 ... The figures reveal:

(a)   5% of the total housing stock is unfit for human habitation;
(b)   a further 2.4 million dwellings are in poor repair;
(c)   15% of the total housing stock is in poor condition; and
(d)   543,000 dwellings lack basic amenities.

The scale of disrepair disclosed by the survey affects all tenure sectors although, as usual, the condition in the private rented sector is worse than elsewhere; for example, one in six dwellings in the private sector was found to be unfit for human habitation...

In London, figures collected by the London Research Centre with the help of the London boroughs revealed not only the rapid decay of inner city housing as suggested by the national survey, but also the extent to which chronic disrepair is now prevalent even in suburban areas. In London as a whole, 370,000 houses are seriously unsatisfactory (many of them 'unfit'). In outer London 200,000 homes required repairs costing more than £4,200 in each case...

Converting this sort of projection into figures for the amount of necessary new-build and rehabilitation is not an exact science. However, it has been suggested that on the present basis it would take 46 years to clear the backlog in housing disrepair...

Given the importance of repairs it is perhaps surprising that English law in this area is an uncoordinated, disorganised confusion of common law, statute and express terms.

Paradise Row, Agar Town, London

At common law, if a house is let furnished, there is an implied term that the premises are at the commencement of the tenancy fit for human habitation. The courts have found breaches of this covenant in situations where homes were in such a poor condition when let that they represented a serious danger to health or safety. Examples include premises infested with bugs – *Smith* v *Marrable* (1843) 11 M & W 52 – and one having a defective sewerage system – *Harrison* v *Malet* (1886) 3 TLR 58. Most of the decisions on this covenant are rather old, due to the restrictive interpretation placed on it by the courts.

Collins v *Hopkins* [1923] 2 KB 617

McCardie J:

This case before me definitely raises the question of the contractual duty of a person who lets a furnished house lately occupied by one suffering from an infectious disease. It is not, of course, enough for the landlord to say that he honestly believes that the house is fit and proper for safe habitation. It must in fact be fit and safe ... Nor on the other hand, can a tenant renounce his contract because of a mere apprehension of risk or through mere dislike of the premises through the fact e.g. that a person has died upon the premises of smallpox ... In my view the question in such a case ... is this: Was there any actual and appreciable risk to the tenant, his family or household, by entering and occupying the house ... If the risk be serious, no one, I think could doubt that the tenant may renounce. But in dealing with bacilli which may mean illness and death, I think further that an appreciable measure of actual risk justifies the tenant in throwing up his contract ... Amongst the matters to be considered are the nature of the disease; the degree and persistence of its infectivity; the date when the sufferer resided in the house; the steps taken to prevent risk of infection and the like.

On the particular facts McCardie J found that the house and its contents were not free of tuberculosis bacilli and it was not fit for human habitation.

There are also statutory covenants requiring landlords, of properties let at a low rent, to ensure that they are both fit for human habitation at the start of the tenancy and are kept fit for habitation throughout the lease:

Landlord and Tenant Act 1985

Implied terms as to fitness for human habitation

8 (1) In a contract to which this section applies for the letting of a house for human habitation there is implied, notwithstanding any stipulation to the contrary –
   (a) a condition that the house is fit for human habitation at the commencement of the tenancy, and
   (b) an undertaking that the house will be kept by the landlord fit for human habitation during the tenancy.

(3) This section applies to a contract if –
(a) the rent does not exceed the figure applicable in accordance with subsection (4),[16] and
(b) the letting is not on such terms as to the tenant's responsibility as are mentioned in subsection (5)...

(5) This section does not apply where a house[17] is let for a term of three years or more (the lease not being determinable at the option of either party before the expiration of three years) upon terms that the tenant puts the premises into a condition reasonably fit for human habitation.

Fitness for human habitation

10 In determining for the purposes of this Act whether a house is unfit for human habitation, regard shall be had to its condition in respect of the following matters –

repair,
stability,
freedom from damp,
internal arrangement,
natural lighting,
ventilation,
water supply,
drainage and sanitary conveniences,
facilities for preparation and cooking of food and for the disposal of waste water;

and the house shall be regarded as unfit for human habitation if, and only if, it is so far defective in one or more of those matters that it is not reasonably suitable for occupation in that condition.

Further, there is an obligation upon landlords, of premises let for a term of less than seven years, to maintain in a state of repair the basic structure and services of the property:

Landlord and Tenant Act 1985

Repairing obligations in short leases

11 (1) In a lease to which this section applies (as to which, see sections 13 and 14[18]) there is implied a covenant by the lessor –
(a) to keep in repair the structure and exterior of the dwelling-house (including drains, gutters and external pipes),[19]
(b) to keep in repair and proper working order the installations in the

---

16 Before 1957 for London and elsewhere = £40. After 1957 London = £80, elsewhere = £52.
17 A house includes part of a house + yard + outbuildings + garden.
18 Section 14 lists the exceptions to s. 11, including certain agricultural leases.
19 For an interesting discussion on the standard of repair required by s. 11 see *Trustees of the Dame Margaret Hungerford Charity* v *Beazley* (1993) *The Times,* May 17.

dwelling-house for the supply of water, gas and electricity and for sanitation (including basins, sinks, baths and sanitary conveniences, but not other fixtures, fittings and appliances for making use of the supply of water, gas or electricity), and

(c) to keep in repair and proper working order the installations in the dwelling-house for space heating and heating water...

(2) The covenant implied by subsection (1) ('the lessor's repairing covenant') shall not be construed as requiring the lessor –

(a) to carry out works or repairs for which the lessee is liable by virtue of his duty to use the premises in a tenant-like manner [below], or would be so liable but for an express covenant on his part,

(b) to rebuild or reinstate the premises in the case of destruction or damage by fire, or by tempest, flood or other inevitable accident, or

(c) to keep in repair or maintain anything which the lessee is entitled to remove from the dwelling-house.

(3) In determining the standard of repair required by the lessor's repairing covenant, regard shall be had to the age, character and prospective life of the dwelling-house and the locality in which it is situated...

(4) A covenant by the lessee for the repair of the premises is of no effect so far as it relates to the matters mentioned in subsection (l)(a) to (c), except so far as it imposes on the lessee any of the requirements mentioned in subsection (2)(a) or (c).

Leases to which s. 11 applies: general rule

13 (1) Section 11 (repairing obligations) applies to a lease of a dwelling house granted on or after 24th October 1961 for a term of less than seven years.

(2) In determining whether a lease is one to which section 11 applies –

(b) a lease which is determinable at the option of the lessor before the expiration of seven years from the commencement of the term shall be treated as a lease for a term of less than seven years, and

(c) a lease (other than a lease to which paragraph (b) applies) shall not be treated as a lease for a term of less than seven years if it confers on the lessee an option for renewal for a term which, together with the original term, amounts to seven years or more.

The niceties of judicial pronouncements concerning the interpretation of these sections are clearly apparent from a decision in the Court of Appeal on s. 32(1), Housing Act 1961, which was the predecessor to s. 11(1), Landlord and Tenant Act 1985.

Hopwood v *Cannock Chase District Council* (1975) 1 WLR 373 (CA) Cairns, Stephenson LJJ and Brightman J

Cairns LJ:

At the [material] time the plaintiff had come from the back door of the house and had walked diagonally across the first concrete area; she was intending to go and have a chat with her neighbour at the next house. But when she came to one edge of the paving slabs ... she tripped and fell; and it was common ground that there was a difference in height between the concrete and the paving slab of an inch and a half ... The judge found that the defendants, by their servants, well knew of this condition.

The judge had however to consider whether there was any obligation on the defendants to keep this part of the premises in repair. He held that there was no such obligation ... In reaching his decision he founded himself on the only reported case as far as we know that has been decided under this provision; it is the decision of the Court of Appeal in *Brown* v *Liverpool Corporation* [1969] 3 AER 1345. That was a case in which the house had a path running to the steps which went up to the road, the house being at a lower level than the road, and the plaintiff met with an accident on those steps ... Danckwerts LJ, giving the first judgment, first easily reached the conclusion that they did not form part of the structure and then went on...

'In the end, however, I have come to the conclusion that the learned county court judge adopted the right approach and did treat this question as one of degree and fact. He referred specifically to the point that this concrete path was only "seven feet long", and it seems to me that on the evidence he was entitled to come to the conclusion which he reached on the question of fact, i.e. that in all the circumstances the steps formed part of the building.'

One matter on which all three members of the court founded their judgments was that in that case the path and steps formed an essential part of the means of access to the house, in that it was the only way in. In this case that certainly was not so; the ordinary means of access to the house was from the front of the house and to my mind it is very doubtful whether this yard could be regarded as a means of access to the house at all ... in my view the section cannot be extended beyond what was held in *Brown's* case so as to include a yard of this kind.

In two cases, *Smith* v *Bradford MC* (1982) 4 HLR 86 and *McCauley* v *Bristol City Council* [1991] 3 WLR 968, it has been held in similar circumstances that a landlord was liable in tort under s. 4, Defective Premises Act 1972.

There is also an implied covenant imposed upon the landlords of high rise blocks to keep the lifts, stairs and corridors reasonably fit and safe for use: *Liverpool City Council* v *Irwin* [1976] AC 39 (see Chapter 6, pp. 172–3).

Obligations concerned with the day-to-day upkeep of leasehold property have also been placed upon tenants, although this implied covenant 'to act in a tenant-like manner', does not amount to a requirement to make repairs.

Warren v Kean (1954) 1 QB 15 (CA) Somervell, Denning and Romer LJJ

Lord Denning:

Apart from express contract, a tenant owes no duty to the landlord to keep the premises in repair. The only duty of the tenant is to use the premises in a husbandlike, or what is the same thing, a tenantlike manner ... It can, I think, best be shown by some illustrations. The tenant must take proper care of the place. He must, if he is going away for the winter, turn off the water and empty the boiler. He must clean the chimneys, when necessary, and also the windows. He must mend the electric light when it fuses. He must unstop the sink when it is blocked by his waste. In short, he must do the little jobs about the place which a reasonable tenant would do. In addition, he must, of course, not damage the house, wilfully or negligently; and he must see that his family and guests do not damage it: and if they do, he must repair it. But apart from such things, if the house falls into disrepair through fair wear and tear or lapse of time, or for any reason not caused by him, then the tenant is not liable to repair it...

Further, tenancy agreements frequently contain express contractual covenants to repair imposing considerable obligations upon tenants. Perhaps because of the often unequal bargaining positions of landlord and tenant, at least with respect to residential leases, it is rare to find an express covenant to repair placing the duty to repair upon the landlord.[20] Landlords are, however, subject to the Unfair Contract Terms Act 1977 and cannot include unreasonable covenants in leases which seek to relieve them of their own common law or statutory obligations. Moreover, it has long been accepted that repairing covenants do not require the covenantor to renew the whole property or modernise an elderly and decaying building.

Following a series of proposals in earlier Reports relating to repairs, which have largely not been implemented, the Law Commission has again raised the issue for discussion. The following extract indicates their suggested new approach to this area.

Law Commission (1992) Consultation Paper No. 123 *Landlord and Tenant: Responsibility for State and Condition of Property*

5.5   An alternative approach to the present rules could place emphasis on the purpose for which property was let ... The attraction of duty linked to the use is that it treats the grant of the lease as an integrated transaction, recognising that the physical state of the property can determine whether the tenant is able to obtain the intended benefit. Such a use-based approach would clearly be a radical change for English law, and it therefore requires detailed examination.

---

20 At common law, there may be leases where no repairing obligation is imposed, either expressly or impliedly, on either party to the lease. See *Demetriou* v *Robert Andrews (Estate Agencies) Ltd* (1991) 62 P & CR 537.

5.7   ... The duty – which for the convenience we shall refer to below as the 'duty to maintain' – would include making good all defects whether original or developed later ... – as appropriate repair, replacement, improvement or renewal. The standard required would be such as was appropriate in putting those premises to that use; that will allow the necessary flexibility to recognise the age of a building.

5.17 If the general obligation for maintenance of the fabric of the property was linked to the use to which it was put, there would be a case for ceasing to have separate statutory provision relating to fitness for human habitation. However ... [l]andlords could have a duty to maintain, and [a] statutory standard of fitness for human habitation could be expressly adopted as a minimum standard for compliance with the general duty.

5.18 Whatever the extent of the duty to work on the premises, it is also necessary to determine on whom the duty is to be placed. Without statutory provisions, it is not uncommon ... for no obligation to be imposed in relation to some ... premises. This is unsatisfactory. As a fall-back statute should imply duties to do all the work needed on the state and condition of the property let ...

5.22 Our provisional conclusion is that primary responsibility should be placed on the landlard ... [whose] responsibility could by agreement be freely transferred to the tenant, except in specified exceptional cases.

5.34 Many statutes at present refer to obligations. Clearly, if the fundamental obligation of the parties to leases became a duty to maintain, many of these provisions would need amending. We ... suggest ... that the approach might be as follows:
(a) Provisions imposing a duty to repair should become a duty to maintain,
(b) Provisions regulating the consequences of breaches of a repairing duty should be extended to apply to the consequences of breaches of duty to maintain.

5.60 It is perhaps in the enforcement of repairing duties that the view taken of underlying purposes of these obligations is most important. The emphasis of the law until now has been on the economic view of leases: damages are payable for loss of value to the party with the benefit of the covenant, rather than for the cost of work not done ... This seems to us inconsistent with an approach which places the emphasis on ensuring that the necessary work be done and alternatives based on that view should be considered.

Covenants not to assign or sublet

Leases frequently include express covenants restricting the right of the tenant to assign or sublet the property. These covenants may be: (a) absolute – where the tenant agrees not to assign or sublet at all; or (b) qualified – where the tenant may only assign or sublet with the consent of the landlord; or (c) fully qualified – as in

(b) but the landlord may not withhold consent unreasonably. A further requirement governing consent has been imposed by statute.

Landlord and Tenant Act 1927

Provisions as to covenants not to assign, etc., without licence or consent

19 (1) In all leases whether made before or after the commencement of this Act containing a covenant condition or agreement against assigning, under-letting, charging or party with the possession of a demised premises or any part thereof without licence or consent, such covenant condition or agreement shall, notwithstanding any express provision to the contrary, be deemed to be subject –

    (a) to a proviso to the effect that such licence or consent is not to be unreasonably withheld, but this proviso does not preclude the right of the landlord to require payment of a reasonable sum in respect of any legal or other expenses incurred in connection with such licence or consent;...

The Law Commission Report (1985) on Covenants Restricting Dispositions, Alterations and Change of User No. 141 made a number of recommendations with respect to covenants in leases which place restrictions upon a tenant's ability to assign or sublet. These included the abolition of absolute covenants by translating them into fully qualified covenants; the elimination of qualified covenants such that they would take effect as a fully qualified covenant; and the placing of the burden of proof for proving 'reasonableness' where consent has been withheld, together with a restriction upon landlords seeking to delay their decisions regarding consent. Some of their suggestions, albeit relatively minor in nature, were implemented by Parliament:[21]

Landlord and Tenant Act 1988

Qualified duty to consent to assigning, underletting etc. of premises

1 (1) This section applies in any case where –

    (a) a tenancy includes a covenant on the part of the tenant not to enter into one or more of the following transactions, that is –

        (i) assigning,

        (ii) underletting,

        (iii) charging, or

        (iv) parting with the possession of,

    the premises comprised in the tenancy or any part of the premises without the consent of the landlord or some other person, but

    (b) the covenant is subject to the qualification that the consent is not to be unreasonably withheld (whether or not it is also subject to any other qualification).

---

21 For a critique of the Law Commission's Report see P.F. Smith (1994) Conv 186.

(3) Where there is served on the person who may consent to a proposed transaction a written application by the tenant for consent to the transaction, he owes a duty to the tenant within a reasonable time –

(a) to give consent, except in a case where it is reasonable not to give consent,

(b) to serve on the tenant written notice of his decision whether or not to give consent specifying in addition –

(i) if the consent is given subject to conditions, the conditions,

(ii) if the consent is withheld, the reasons for withholding it.

(6) It is for the person who owed any duty under subsection (3) above –

(a) if he gave consent and the question arises whether he gave it within a reasonable time, to show that he did,

(b) if he gave consent subject to any condition and the question arises whether the condition was a reasonable condition, to show that it was,

(c) if he did not give consent and the question arises whether it was reasonable for him not to do so, to show that it was reasonable,

and, if the question arises whether he served notice under that subsection within a reasonable time, to show that he did.

However, there remains much confusion in this area about the means by which the courts test whether the refusal of an individual landlord is reasonable or unreasonable and the issue has been the subject of recent judicial decisions.

Olympia and York Canary Wharf Ltd and another v *Oil Property Investments Ltd* [1994] 29 EG 121 (CA) Sir Donald Nicholls VC, Leggatt, Henry LJJ[22]

Sir Donald Nicholls VC:

By a lease dated 4 April 1985 Electricity Supply Nominees Ltd granted a lease of office property ... to a company known as ICI Petroleum Ltd, but now known as Enterprise Petroleum Ltd. The lease was for a term of 25 years from 8 March 1985. The lease contained in clause 3(14) a common form provision prohibiting assignment without the lessor's consent, such consent not to be unreasonably withheld. The lease also contained a tenant's break clause, clause 5(13) which enabled the lease to be determined at the end of the 10th year of the term ... The only exceptional feature of the clause was that the right conferred was exerciseable only by Enterprise, the original lessee ... notice has to be given by early March 1994 and, if the option is duly exercised, the lease will end in March 1995.

It is this provision which has given rise to the present dispute. The lessor is now Oil Property Investment Ltd (OPIL), which acquired the freehold in March 1991. The lease itself is presently held by Olympia and York Canary Wharf Ltd (O&Y) in whose favour Enterprise assigned the lease in October 1987.

Nearly two years ago, in May 1992, O&Y became insolvent and an administration order was made. The insolvency of O&Y, an assignee from the

---

22 See also *CIN Properties Ltd* v *Gill* (1994) 67 P & CR 288 and *Worth* v *Beale*; *Worth* v *Reynolds* (CA) (Lexis: 1994) (Transcript: John Larking) and L. Crabb (1994) Conv 316.

original lessee, did not mean that the lessor would thenceforth have to whistle for its money. Enterprise, the original lessee, was liable on its covenant to pay the rent for the whole term of the lease and it remained liable despite the assignment to O&Y. Since May 1992 OPIL has been looking to Enterprise for the rent and, perforce, Enterprise has been paying up.

What has happened now is that O&Y does not itself wish to retain the lease or occupy the property, but the lease is not saleable at present. The rent payable under the lease is far in excess of the current open market rent of the property ... Further, the property would be likely to stand un-let for some time. Either that or, which comes to the same, the tenant would have to be offered a substantial rent-free period of perhaps a year to 18 months. In those circumstances, if a buyer for this lease could be found at all, he would need to be paid a reverse premium of not less than £4m to persuade him to take on this lease...

It is in these circumstances that O&Y wishes now to assign the lease to Enterprise, the original lessee. Enterprise for its part is willing, indeed anxious to accept a reassignment, because this would enable Enterprise to exercise its right under clause 5(13) and thereby put an end to its continuing rent liability as original lessee. This liability, from March 1995 onwards, has a current capitalised value of some £7–8 million. So this course is hugely attractive to Enterprise. This course is also attractive to O&Y because it would enable that company to get shot of this expensive and unwanted lease...

...this course is correspondingly unattractive to the lessor. I have mentioned the disparity between the rent payable under the lease and the rent obtainable if the property were to be re-let on the open market. Given this disparity, if the lessor were not forced to accept the determination of the lease, it would suffer a rent loss of the order of £3.6 million, and the value of its reversion would be reduced at once by about £6 million ... So it came about that when the administrators of O&Y sought OPIL's consent for assignment of the lease to Enterprise on 10 December 1992, OPIL refused ... on 8 July 1993 Harman J refused to make declarations that OPIL was unreasonably withholding its consent and ... granted an injunction restraining O&Y from assigning the lease to Enterprise until after March 1995. Enterprise and O&Y have appealed against those orders...

Over the years there have been many cases in which, in widely differing factual contexts, the court has considered whether a lessor's withholding of consent to an assignment is unreasonable. The particular facet of the principles which is relevant in the present case is that, as a general rule, it would be unreasonable for a lessor to refuse consent to an assignment by taking objection to some consequential happening when the lease itself envisaged that happening as unobjectionable ... in *Deverall* v *Wyndham* (1989) 58 P & CR 12 ... Judge Paul Baker QC ... held that a refusal to permit underlettings was unreasonable even though that might result in the landlord suffering heavy financial loss at the end of the term because, among other reasons, the lease expressly contemplated and required multiple occupation of the property. Thus to refuse consent would be to deprive the tenant of an important part of the benefit of the lease. In such cases ... it was not within the reasonable contemplation of the parties to the lease that consent would be refused on the grounds set out by the respective landlords...

In my view, the key to the present case lies in keeping in mind one fact which is incontrovertible, namely that clause 5(13) was not intended by the parties to confer any right on an assignee from Enterprise ... Clause 5(13) did confer a right on Enterprise, but in these proceedings Enterprise is not asserting a right against OPIL. Enterprise is very much interested in the outcome of the dispute between O&Y and OPIL, but that is what this dispute is: a dispute between the present tenant and its landlord. Enterprise itself has no right to compel OPIL to permit an assignment in its favour...

This analysis is open to criticism that it is legalistic. But its underlying basic soundness is confirmed if one raises one's eyes and looks at the matter more widely. The consequence of Enterprise's argument is, in effect, that an assignee such as O&Y has an unqualified right to assign the lease to Enterprise for the purpose of enabling Enterprise to exercise a right which was personal to it. Thus O&Y is seeking to compel the lessor to accept a proposal which will enable O&Y to achieve indirectly what it cannot achieve directly...

Against that background, I do not see how OPIL's unwillingness to permit an assignment to Enterprise for the purpose of enabling it to exercise its right under clause 5(13) can be regarded as unreasonable ... I have very much in mind that Enterprise is in an unfortunate position. So are many original lessees at the present time. It is Enterprise's unhappy lot that its assignee O&Y, part of a once great worldwide property group, suffered such a massively adverse turn of the wheel of fortune. That is Enterprise's misfortune ... I agree with the judge. I would dismiss the appeals.

Landlords cannot refuse their consent on grounds of either race or sex – Race Relations Act 1976, s. 21(1)(b), s. 21(3); Sex Discrimination Act 1975, s. 30(1)(b), s. 30(3).

Usual covenants

A lease may be granted subject to the 'usual covenants'. These include in addition to the above: (a) a covenant by the tenant to keep the premises in repair; (b) an implied covenant giving a right of re-entry to the landlord where there is non-payment of rent, and (c) an undertaking by the tenant to pay rent. In the absence of any express agreement to the contrary, the 'usual covenants' are implied into every equitable lease.

ENFORCEABILITY OF COVENANTS

Introduction

A covenant in a lease is, prima facie, a contract binding only on the lessor and lessee. On the basis of the strict principles of privity of contract, therefore, only the original parties to the lease would be able to enforce those covenants. However, many landlords and tenants possess very valuable transmissible interests. Indeed, the value of those interests may depend to a large degree upon

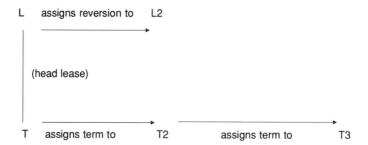

Fig. 4.1

the obligations that each has assumed in the lease. Thus, even medieval land law, although conscious of the principle that third parties to a contract cannot sue or be sued upon it, recognised that the covenants in leases might have a wider operation than in ordinary contracts. It is therefore necessary to ask the question: in what circumstances can persons, other than the original landlord or landlady (L) and the original tenant (T), sue or be sued upon the covenants in the lease? Or, to put it another way, when will the covenants contained in a lease *run with the land*?

Covenants touching and concerning the land

Only those leasehold covenants which 'touch and concern the land' or, in its statutory form (see ss. 141 and 142, Law of Property Act 1925, below, p. 112), which have 'reference to the subject matter' of that lease, may be enforced by, or against, assignees of either the lease (T2) or of the reversion (L2). The meaning of the phrase 'touch and concern the land', which derives from a decision in *Spencer's Case* (1583) 5 Co Rep 15a, has been the subject of much academic and judicial debate.[23] In 1948 Scott LJ attempted to elucidate a modern formula for ascertaining whether a covenant was capable of running with the land:

Breams Property Investment Co Ltd v *Stroulger* (1948) 2 KB 1 (CA)
Bucknell and Scott LJJ

Scott LJ:
The phrase 'subject-matter of the lease' was, as we know, substituted for the ancient expression 'touching and concerning the land.' Professor Cheshire's elucidation of its meaning on pp. 214–15 of the 5th edn of his book on *Modern Real Property,* in my respectful opinion, supplies the true test. 'If a simple test ... is desired for ascertaining into which category a covenant falls, it is suggested that the proper inquiry should be whether the covenant affects either the landlord *qua*

---

23 See also Chapter 7, p. 193.

landlord or the tenant *qua* tenant. A covenant may very well have reference to the land, but, unless it is reasonably incidental to the relation of landlord and tenant, it cannot be said to touch and concern the land so as to be capable of running therewith or with the reversion. Tested by this principle the following covenants have been held to touch and concern the land.' Of the covenants by the tenant running with the land that 'to pay rent or taxes' and 'not to assign or underlet,' and by the landlord running with the reversion, 'to renew the lease' are the most apposite of the instances which he quotes from decided cases. Although the case of a limitation upon, or condition precedent to a right to serve a notice to quit, does not appear to have been the subject of judicial decision, his principle that, if a covenant affects a landlord *qua* landlord, it must necessarily run with the reversion, appears to me a sound criterion...

In spite of Scott LJ's efforts the prevalent view of textbook writers is that 'It can be said that any covenant which affects the landlord *qua* landlord or the tenant *qua* tenant will probably be with the class of covenants which [run], but this is not very helpful, and it is better to note examples from decided cases' (P.F. Smith, *Evans: The Law of Landlord and Tenant* (Butterworths: 1985) 75).

In addition to those covenants mentioned by Scott LJ above examples of those which have been deemed to touch and concern the land include: a covenant for quiet enjoyment; a covenant by the landlord agreeing to supply a housekeeper to clean a block of flats; a covenant in which a landlord agreed not to open a public house within half a mile of the tenanted premises; a covenant placing an obligation on the tenant to repair; and a covenant in which the tenant agreed not to carry on a particular trade at the premises.[24]

There are particular difficulties on the question of whether a covenant is purely personal or runs with the land where the obligation in question, whether on the part of the lessor, lessee, or third party guarantor, involves the payment of money other than rent. A direct challenge to the orthodox test arose in two cases decided in 1987.

Hua Chiao Commercial Bank Ltd v *Chiaphua Industries Ltd* [1987] 1 AC 99 (PC) Lord Bridge of Harwich, Lord Brandon of Oakbrook, Lord Oliver of Aylmerton, Lord Goff of Chievely and Sir Ivor Richardson

This case involved an appeal to the Privy Council from Hong Kong. A lease was granted for a period of five years in which the tenant agreed to pay the landlord a sum equivalent to two months rent as a security deposit. The landlord agreed that, provided there were no breaches by the tenant of any of the terms in the agreement, the deposit would be returned to the tenant at the end of the five years. The tenant paid the deposit and moved in. Subsequently, the landlord entered into a mortgage agreement in which it assigned the reversion to Hua Chiao Bank, with

---

24 Lists of examples of decided cases can be found in E.H. Burn *Cheshire & Burn's Modern Law of Real Property* (Butterworths: 1994), pp. 446–8.

provision for reassignment upon redemption. When the landlord defaulted the bank went into possession. The tenant had committed no breach of any term in the lease and, since the original lessor was now in liquidation, instituted proceedings for 'return' of the deposit from the bank. The Court of Appeal of Hong Kong held that the bank was under an obligation to return the deposit and the bank appealed:

Lord Oliver:

There is, of course, no doubt that the mere fact that a covenant, whether on the part of the landlord or of a tenant, involves an obligation to pay a liquidated sum of money does not of itself demonstrate that the covenant is not one which touches and concerns the land ... The tenant argues ... that, inasmuch as the tenant's obligation to pay over the deposit on the execution of the lease was an obligation to secure the performance of covenants which touched and concerned the land, it was an obligation inextricably associated with covenants whose benefit and burden would pass with the reversion in the lease respectively. The landlord's obligation to repay if those covenants are observed is, it is argued, inseparable from that associated obligation and must therefore possess the same characteristics as the covenants whose performance is secured by the associated obligation. ...

To say that the obligation to 'return' the amount of the deposit is 'inextricably bound up with' covenants which touch and concern the land ... does not, in their Lordships' view answer the critical question of whether it itself touches and concerns the land. It certainly does not *per se* affect the nature, quality or value of the land either during or at the end of the term. It does not *per se* affect the mode of using or enjoying that which is demised.[25] And to ask whether it affects the landlord *qua* landlord or the tenant *qua* tenant is an exercise which begs the question. ... Whilst it is true that the deposit is paid to the original payee because it is security for the performance of contractual obligations assumed throughout the term by the payer and because the payee is the party to whom the contract is entered into, it is, in their Lordships' view, more realistic to regard the obligation as one entered into with the landlord *qua* payee rather than *qua* landlord ... The nature of the obligation is simply that of an obligation to repay money which has been received and it is neither necessary nor logical, simply because the conditions of repayment relate to the performance of covenants in a lease, that the transfer of the reversion should create in the transferee an additional and co-extensive obligation to pay money which he has never received and in which he never had any interest or that the assignment of the term should vest in the assignee the right to receive a sum which he has never paid...

Kumar v Dunning [1987] 2 All ER 801 (CA) Sir Nicolas Browne-Wilkinson VC, Croom-Johnson and Neill LJJ

This case raised the question of whether an assignee of a reversion on a lease could enforce the payment of rent against someone who had entered into surety covenants as a guarantee of the tenant's obligations in the lease.

---

25 Compare *Breams* v *Stroulger* above.

Sir Nicholas Browne-Wilkinson VC:

I will first state how the matter strikes me as a matter of impression. The surety covenant is given as a support or buttress to covenants given by a tenant to a landlord. The covenants by the tenant relate not only to the payment of rent, but also to repair, insurance and user of the premises. All such covenants by a tenant in favour of the landlord touch and concern the land, i.e. the reversion of the landlord ... As it seems to me, in principle a covenant by a third party guaranteeing the performance by the tenant of his obligations should touch and concern the reversion as much as do the tenants' covenants themselves.

Yet in all save one of the cases decided at first instance, the court has held that the surety covenant does not touch and concern the land ... From these authorities I collect two things. Firstly, that the acid test whether or not benefit is collateral is that laid down by Best J, namely 'Is the covenant beneficial to the owner for the time being of the covenantee's land, and to no one else?' Secondly, a covenant simply to pay a sum of money, whether by way of insurance premium, compensation or damages, is a covenant capable of touching and concerning the land provided that the existence of the covenant, and the right to payment thereunder, affects the value of the land in whomsoever it is vested for the time being...

Applying the test laid down by Best J, a covenant by a surety securing the performance of a tenant's covenants in a lease satisfies it. The surety covenant increases the value of the reversion in that the landlord can look not only to the tenant but also to the sureties for the payment of a sum equal to the rent and for damages for failure to comply with the other tenant's covenants. Such surety covenant is of value to no one other than the owner for the time being of the reversion ... Counsel for the second defendant ... relied on *Hua Chiao Commercial Bank Ltd* v *Chiaphua Industries Ltd* ... The liability to repay the deposit at the end of the term remained throughout on the original landlord and was an obligation to repay to the original tenant. So viewed, the decision is entirely consistent with the test laid down by Best J. The benefit of the covenant to repay could not touch and concern the land because someone other than the owner for the time being of the term could take the benefit of it...

A year later the House of Lords approved the statements of the Vice-Chancellor in *Kumar* v *Dunning* with a brief addition of its own.

Swift Investments v *C.E.S.G. plc* [1988] 3 WLR 311 (HL) Lord Keith of Kinkel, Lord Roskill, Lord Templeman, Lord Ackner, Lord Oliver of Aylmerton

Lord Oliver:

Formulations of definitive tests are always dangerous, but it seems to me that, without claiming to expound an exhaustive guide, the following provides a satisfactory working test for whether, in any given case, a covenant touches and concerns the land: (1) the covenant benefits only the reversioner for the time being, and if separated from the reversion ceases to be of benefit to the covenantee; (2)

the covenant affects the nature, quality, mode of user or value of the land of the reversioner; (3) the covenant is not expressed to be personal (that is to say neither being given only to a specific reversioner nor in respect of the obligations only of a specific tenant); (4) the fact that a covenant is to pay a sum of money will not prevent it from touching and concerning the land so long as the three foregoing conditions are satisfied and the covenant is connected with something to be done on, or to in relation to the land.

Enforcement following assignment of the reversion

Liability of T towards L2 and vice-versa rests upon a statutory basis.

Law of Property Act 1925

Rent and benefit of lessee's covenants to run with the reversion [see Law Commission No. 174 below]

141 (1) Rent reserved by a lease, and the benefit of every covenant or provision therein contained, having reference to the subject-matter thereof, and on the lessee's part to be observed or performed, and every condition of re-entry and other condition therein contained, shall be annexed and incident to and shall go with the reversionary estate in the land, or in any part thereof, immediately expectant on the term granted by the lease, notwithstanding severance of that reversionary estate, and without prejudice to any liability affecting a covenantor or his estate.

Obligation of lessor's covenants to run with the reversion

142 (2) The obligation under a condition or of a covenant entered into by a lessor with reference to the subject-matter of the lease shall, if and as far as the lessor has power to bind the reversionary estate immediately expectant on the term granted by the lease, be annexed and incident to and shall go with that reversionary estate, or the several parts thereof, notwithstanding severance of that reversionary estate, and may be taken advantage of and enforced by the person in whom the term is from time to time vested by conveyance, devolution in law, or otherwise; and, if and as far as the lessor has power to bind the person from time to time entitled to that reversionary estate, the obligation aforesaid may be taken advantage of and enforced against any person so entitled.

Enforcement following assignment of the lease

Once one goes beyond the relationships which are governed by privity of contract and its statutory extension, the rules governing the enforceability of leasehold obligations are simply stated:

1. Only those leasehold covenants which touch and concern the land are capable of enforcement; and

2. No covenant can be enforced unless 'privity of estate' exists between the plaintiff and defendant.

The meaning of 'privity of estate' has been described in the following way:

Sir Robert Megarry and H.W.R. Wade *The Law of Real Property* (Stevens: 1984)

Privity of estate means that there is tenure between the parties, i.e. that the relationship of landlord and tenant exists between them; cases in this category are thus confined to leases and tenancies. If L grants a lease to T and then T assigns it to A, there is no privity of contract between L and A since there has been no direct transaction between them; but there is privity of estate, for A has become L's tenant by acquiring the estate which L created and which is held of L as the immediate landlord. Similarly, if L assigns his reversion to X, there is privity of estate between X and A. In such cases any covenants in the lease which 'touch and concern' the land, e.g. repairing covenants, are enforceable both at law and in equity.

Can covenants in a head lease be enforced by, or against, a subtenant?

As shown in Fig. 4.2, it is quite clear that there is no privity of estate between S and either L or L2. Thus, even those covenants which 'touch and concern the land' are incapable of enforcement by direct action between L or L2 and S. However, there are two possible ways around this difficulty:

1. Under the general law in *Tulk* v *Moxhay* (1848) 2 PH 774 (see Chapter 7);
2. An express proviso for re-entry contained in the head lease.

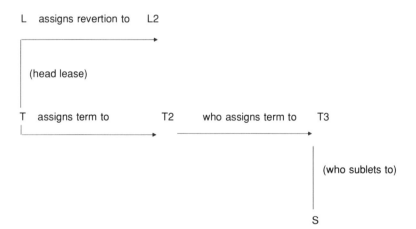

Fig. 4.2

The right of re-entry in a legal lease is one of the legal interests listed in s. 1(2), Law of Property Act 1925, and therefore binds the whole world. This enables the landlord to seek forfeiture against any occupier of the leased premises. A right of re-entry may therefore be exercised by L or L2 against S.

Enforceability by, or against, other strangers to the lease

Note the provisions of s. 56 and s. 78(1), Law of Property Act 1925, discussed in Chapter 7.

Continuing liability of the original landlord and tenant after assignment

L and T have promised to keep to their obligations, the covenants, for the whole period of their lease – which may of course be for the next thousand years. They or their heirs can enforce this contract against one another for the whole period. However, traditionally, it was generally believed that, as a consequence of the wording of ss. 141 and 142, once landlords assigned their reversionary interest they could only sue or be sued by the original tenant. There is some doubt upon this point, as indicated in the following hypothetical discussion.

D. Gordon, The Burden and Benefit of the Rules of Assignment *Conv* (1987) 103

This case is based on an example considered by Scott J in *Celsteel* v *Alton House Holdings Ltd (No. 2)* (1986) 1 WLR 666 at 672 to 673. L1 demised Sevenoaks Farm to B and Greenland to C. L1 granted B a right of way over Greenland, and C was entitled to the benefit of a covenant granted by L1 for the quiet enjoyment of Greenland. L1 then assigned the reversion to L2, and C assigned Greenland to D. There were no express terms limiting the assignment of the benefit of the covenant for quiet enjoyment, or the liability of L1 or L2.

Scott J concluded that if D's enjoyment of Greenland was interrupted by B exercising a right of way over Greenland, D could enforce the covenant for quiet enjoyment against L1, even though there was neither privity of contract nor privity of estate between D and L1.

> 'The language of section 142(1) of the Law of Property Act 1925 seems to me wide enough to enable an action to be brought by [D] against [L]. [It may be] ... that the purpose of section 142 and its statutory predecessors was to cause the burden of the lessor's covenants to run with the reversion ... But I do not see why its language should not be taken advantage of by an assignee of the lease who desires to sue the original lessor on his covenants in the lease.'

Thus, Scott J concluded that not only does an original landlord remain liable to an original tenant throughout the lease, but he remains liable to a later assignee of the lease, despite the absence of any privity, thus achieving mutuality between the liability of an original landlord and that of an original tenant ... Scott J did not hint at the reason for such a conclusion, leaving one to speculate as to whether the continued liability of L1 derives from the fact that he is an original party to the lease and therefore subject to the continued liability imposed by the doctrine of privity of contract, or if the important fact is that it was L1 who granted the right of way (to B) the exercise of which amounted to a breach of covenant.

Scott J further concluded that in the above example, D could sue L2 as well as L1. L2 held the reversion at the time of the breach and therefore was liable, under section 142, for any breach of the landlord's covenant occurring at that time. It appears to be of no importance that the covenant is broken by the exercise of a right granted by L2's predecessor in title...

The Law Commission,[26] commenting on Scott J's interpretation of section 142, concluded that, if correct, it would be a considerable extension of liability under the privity of contract principle as it has been generally understood.

The original tenant of a lease carries even greater burdens:

S. Bridge 'First Tenant's Liability in the Lords' (1994) *Cambridge Law Journal* 28:

The lot of a tenant to whom a lease is granted (as opposed to one who obtains his interest by assignment) is not a happy one. The present law enables the enforcement of leasehold covenants against the so-called original tenant even though he assigned the lease many years ago, and the rent has been substantially increased on review...: see *Centrovincial Estates plc* v *Bulk Storage Ltd* (1983) 46 P & CR 393 ... The liability of the original tenant being 'primary', he cannot complain that the landlord has failed to exhaust his remedies against the tenant currently in possession, or that he should have refused consent to assign to that tenant (*Baynton* v *Morgan* (1888) 22 QBD 74; *Norwich Union Life Insurance Ltd* v *Low Profile Fashions Ltd* [1992] 1 EG 86). The defences of the original tenant are few: that the covenants have been performed, either by the tenant or an assignee, or that some operation such as a surrender has been conducted on the lease which has put an end to liability under the covenants ... And although the original tenant may have rights of indemnity against the defaulting assignee, either on established restitutionary principles, or under the statutorily implied covenants for title ...[27] he must be ready to accept that the motivation for the landlord's pursuit of the original tenant derives from the insolvency of that assignee.[28]

In the important decision of *City of London Corporation* v *Fell* [1993] 3 WLR 1164, the House of Lords has at last thrown a meagre crumb of comfort to the unfortunate original tenant. It has decided that, in the absence of a covenant indicating a contrary intention, the original tenant will not be liable for breaches of

---

26 Working Paper No. 95 (1986).

27 Section 77, Law of Property Act 1925 implies an indemnity between the parties to an assignment for value made after 1925.

28 See, for example, *Estate Gazette Ltd* v *Benjamin Restaurants Ltd and another* [1994] 1 WLR 1528 (CA).

covenant, including unpaid rent, occurring during the statutory continuation of a business tenancy pursuant to Part II of the Landlord and Tenant Act 1954 ... There is no doubt that the decision will be greeted with relief by original tenants everywhere, and that it accords commendably with the purpose ... of the 1954 Act, which, as Lord Templeman observed, was clearly 'intended and expressed to protect occupying tenants against their landlords, not to impose liability on former tenants who cease to have any interest in the property before or after the 1954 Act'.

It should be recognised, however, that each covenant which is sought to be enforced must be carefully examined, for the question remains one of construction. In *Fell*, the covenant was to pay the rent 'during the term'. However, in *Herbert Duncan Ltd* v *Cluttons* [[1992] 1 EG 101], a superficially similar covenant was qualified by a definition clause stating that 'term' included 'not only the term hereby granted but also the period of any holding over or of any extension thereof whether by statute or common law'. This was sufficient to impose liability on the original tenant for rent due during the continuation tenancy under the 1954 Act.[29]

Law Commission Working Paper *Landlord and Tenant: Privity of Contract and Estate* No. 174 1988)

4.1 Our proposals for reform recognise the importance of two principles:

First, a landlord or a tenant of property should not continue to enjoy rights nor be under any obligation arising from a lease once he has parted with all interest in the property.

Secondly, all the terms of the lease should be regarded as a single bargain for letting the property. When the interest of one of the parties changes hands the successor should fully take his predecessor's place as landlord or tenant, without distinguishing between different categories of covenant.

4.3 We propose a general rule that the liability of the original tenant, and his entitlement to benefits under the lease, should not survive an assignment of the lease. For this purpose, we propose that all the covenants in a lease should be treated in the same way, whether or not at present they touch and concern the land. Nevertheless, it would be possible for the landlord, when granting consent to the assignment, to impose a condition that the tenant will be liable to guarantee the performance of some or all of the lease covenants by his immediate successor.

4.5 For landlords, we propose a rule that when they part with their interest in the property let by a lease they will escape further responsibility for the lease obligations if, but only if, they comply with prescribed conditions. These will involve their giving notice to the tenant and his being able to withhold consent if it is reasonable for him to do so. Again, the benefits of being landlord, so far as they can enure to an owner who has parted with the property, would only continue for a former landlord who had continuing liability.

The Lord Chancellor announced on March 31, 1993 that changes in the law will be made. He did not accept the Commission's recommendations in their entirety and there is, as yet, no draft legislation.

---

29 For further discussion of *City of London* v *Fell*, see M. Haley (1994) Conv 247.

Enforceability of covenants in equitable leases

As between L and T, and indeed L2 and T, there is no difference on questions of enforceability between equitable leases and legal leases. The terms of ss. 141 and 142 are applicable to equitable leases. The differences between the two different estates and the limitations over the running of covenants in equitable leases are revealed, as indicated below, once T assigns his interest to T2:

R.J. Smith 'The Running of Covenants in Equitable Leases and Equitable Assignments of Legal Leases' CLJ (1978) 98

The traditional view is that privity of estate requires a legal lease. This limits the running of covenants in equitable leases ... The principle that an equitable lease does not give rise to privity of estate has several important exceptions. Before these are considered, however, it is expedient to examine the general principle.

In recent years the principle has come under attack. The source of the attack emanates from the celebrated dicta of Jessel MR in *Walsh* v *Lonsdale*[30] describing the effect of the Judicature Act 1873 ... The only case to apply this approach to the running of covenants is *Boyer* v *Warbey* [1953] 1 QB 234, in which Denning LJ stated:

'I know that before the Judicature Act 1873, it was said that the doctrine of covenants running with the land only applied to covenants under seal and not to agreements under hand ... But since the fusion of law and equity, the position is different. The distinction between agreements under hand and covenants under seal has been largely obliterated. There is no valid reason nowadays why the doctrine of covenants running with the land – or with the reversion – should not apply equally to agreements under hand as to covenants under seal.'

In the light of these *dicta*, it appears that the traditional view referred to above has been overthrown. However, before one can reach this conclusion – one that is refreshingly straightforward and easy to apply – it is necessary to consider the material in rather more detail...

The fourth and most convincing case is *Purchase* v *Lichfield Brewery Co* (1915) 1 KB 184. The facts were quite straightforward. The plaintiff agreed to lease a property to Lunnis, who assigned this equitable lease by way of mortgage. It was quite clear under the earlier law that the assignee of a legal lease by way of mortgage was just as liable as any other assignee. But was an assignee of an equitable lease liable? Counsel urged that, following *Walsh* v *Lonsdale*, the situation was as if there were a legal lease. In the Divisional Court, Horridge J rejected this argument on the basis that an assignee who had neither taken possession nor attorned tenant could not claim specific performance in his own right ... Lush J took a more accurate approach, it is submitted, in stressing that specific performance would not be granted 'against mere mortgagees who only took an assignment by way of security' and that 'It is impossible that specific performance of a contract can be decreed against a person with whom there is

---

30 See p. 87.

neither privity of contract nor privity of estate.' Thus the action failed and the case is authority for the immunity of an assignee of an equitable lease from liability on the covenants. It is not, however, conclusive authority...

It may be conceded that these cases do not put the point beyond argument, although they clearly point towards non-liability in the assignee. Further, in the context of equitable assignments of legal leases ... it has been held that covenants cannot run under privity of estate. The firm refusal of the courts to equate legal and equitable assignments is strong authority in favour of distinguishing assignments of legal and equitable leases.

LEASES AND REMEDIES

When a covenant in a lease is breached the general contractual remedies – injunction, specific performance and damages – are available to whichever party suffers as a consequence. However, there are also remedies specific to leases.

The rights of the lessor: distress and re-entry

In addition to the general remedies, the lessor may use either:

1. distress (for non-payment of rent); or
2. forfeiture (a 'right of re-entry' – i.e. ending the lease).

Distress

Distress is an anachronistic remedy surviving from the earliest days in the history of the lease. It allows the landlord, where a tenant has fallen into arrears with rent, to enter the premises and take possession of sufficient of the tenant's belongings up to the value of the rent owed. After five days, if the tenant does not pay the rent, the goods may be sold. Over the past two hundred years a degree of protection has been accorded to the tenant against the distraining landlord. However, in the words of the Law Commission[31] it is 'difficult and distasteful' and 'at least questionable in an age when self-help remedies generally are not regarded with favour'. Nevertheless, L. Wise recently stated (Solicitors Journal, 18 November 1994, 1186) that 'it is surprising that more landlords do not exercise a right they have had for over 800 years. I think if more accountants and solicitors thought to remind their client of their ancient right there would be less grumbling, fewer solicitors' letters, fewer bad debts and a great deal more (primitive) satisfaction' (1187).

---

31 See Working Paper No. 97 1986 *Distress for Rent.*

Forfeiture

Forfeiture, that is the right to end a lease before it determines naturally, is the landlord's security over the property. Indeed, it is one of the interests capable of being legal under s. 1(2)(e), Law of Property Act 1925. Such a right of re-entry, which is an express proviso in most legal leases and is implied into all equitable leases, gives the landlord the right literally to take possession of the land. Any covenant called a condition automatically gives right of forfeiture. If the landlady accepts rent knowing of a breach, she waives her right to forfeit the lease. However, under the terms of the Protection from Eviction Act 1977 the landlord must enter peacefully upon the land and may not use the right of re-entry at all if the premises are used for residential purposes. The inherent difficulties in taking possession away from a tenant, who may in any event be inclined to resist, are displayed in the following extract:

Ashton v *Sobelman* [1987] 1 WLR 177

The plaintiffs were tenants of a lock-up shop which they had sublet. Unfortunately, the plaintiffs fell into arrears with their rent and the landlords – 'Twogates' – wanted to forfeit the lease. However, the landlords sought to come to an arrangement with the sub-tenant, a Mr Clayton, under which they would peaceably re-enter the premises and change the locks. The sub-tenant agreed and when the locks were changed, on 19 October 1984, his wife was given keys, together with a letter requesting that, in future, he should pay rent directly to 'Twogates'. The latter then sold the reversion to the defendant at an auction. The plaintiffs, upon discovering the sale, offered the defendants the arrears of rent. The money was not accepted and the plaintiffs brought an action for a declaration that the lease had not been forfeited.

John Chadwick QC:

In the present case, it appears to me apt to describe the changing of the lock at 195, Burnt Oak Broadway as 'an idle ceremony.' This is, I think, illustrated by the fact that, when told by Mr Clayton that the new lock was unsatisfactory, Twogates through their solicitors were content that the lock should be replaced by Mr Clayton himself. There was never any intention on the part of the landlords to exclude the subtenant from possession. There is, to my mind, no doubt that Mr Bloch and his locksmith would not have been permitted by Mr Clayton to interfere with the existing lock if Mr Clayton had been told that that act was intended in any way to interfere with his rights under his existing sub-lease. Mr Clayton was not told this. On the contrary he was assured, by Mr Bloch in person and by the first of the letters dated 19 October 1984 that Twogates were not in any way challenging his right to remain in occupation of the premises ... under the provisions of his existing underlease. If there was a re-entry in the present case, it was not effected by the changing of the lock.

The real question on this part of the case, as it appears to me, is whether the landlords effected a re-entry, constructively, by obtaining Mr Clayton's consent to their actions upon the terms of the first letter of 19 October 1984. In my judgment even if it could be said that Mr Clayton attorned tenant to Twogates by tacitly accepting the terms of that letter, such an attornment[32] would not be evidence of an unequivocal intention on the part of the landlords to re-enter under the provisions of the ... lease ... In these circumstances, it is, in my judgment, impossible to regard the arrangements which Twogates made on 19 October 1984 as amounting to a re-entry under the ... lease.[33]

However, in *Billson* v *Residential Apartments Ltd* [1991] 3 WLR 264 the Court of Appeal[34] accepted peaceable re-entry had taken place although factual possession lasted only a few hours. The landlords' agents went into the leased premises at 6 a.m., when it was vacant, and changed the locks. At 10 a.m. of the same day workmen, employed by the tenants, retook factual possession and started work. Nevertheless, there can be no peaceable re-entry where the tenant is a company subject to an Administration Order – s. 11(3)(c), Insolvency Act 1986, as interpreted in *Exchange Agency Ltd (In Administration)* v *Triton Property Trust plc* [1991] LSG 27 March, 33.

A more likely recourse for a landlord seeking to re-enter premises is through a court order for possession, which if necessary will be enforced by a bailiff. Forfeiture for non-payment of rent follows a different procedure from that of forfeiture for breach of any other covenant in the lease.

Rights of the lessor: forfeiture for non-payment of rent

In theory the first step in the procedure is a formal application for payment of arrears by either the landlord or someone acting as an agent. In practice, many leases expressly exclude this requirement on the part of the landlord and statute dispenses with this part of the procedure in many cases:

Common Law Procedure Act 1852

Proceedings in ejectment by landlord for non-payment of rent

210   In all cases between landlord and tenant, as often as it shall happen that one half year's rent shall be in arrear, and the landlord or lessor, to whom the same is due, hath right by law to re-enter for the non-payment thereof, such landlord or lessor shall and may, without any formal demand or re-entry, serve a writ in ejectment for the recovery of the demised premises, which service shall stand in the place and stead of a demand and re-entry; and in case of judgment against the defendant for non-appearance, if it shall be made appear to the court where the said action is depending, by affidavit, or be proved upon the trial in case the defendant appears, that half a year's rent

---

32 'Transferring loyalty to a new landlord (from feudal times)'.

33 See also the comments of Staughton LJ in *Cardiff City Council* v *Destrick*, above p. 91.

34 This part of the decision was accepted by the House of Lords in *Billson* v *Residential Apartments Ltd* [1992] 2 WLR 15.

was due before the said writ was served, and that no sufficient distress was to be found on the demised premises, countervailing the arrears then due, and that the lessor had power to re-enter, then and in every such case the lessor shall recover judgment and execution, in the same manner as if the rent in arrear had been legally demanded, and a re-entry made; and in case the lessee or his assignee, or other person claiming or deriving under the said lease, shall permit and suffer judgment to be had and recovered on such trial in ejectment, and execution to be executed thereon, without paying the rent and arrears, together with full costs, and without proceeding for relief in equity within six months after such execution executed, then and in such case the said lessee, his assignee, and all other persons claiming and deriving under the said lease, shall be barred and foreclosed from all relief or remedy in law or equity, other than by bringing error for reversal of such judgment, in case the same shall be erroneous, and the said landlord or lessor shall from thenceforth hold the said demised premises discharged from such lease; provided that nothing herein contained shall extend to bar the right of any mortgagee of such lease, or any part thereof, who shall not be in possession, so as such mortgagee shall and do, within six months after such judgment obtained and execution executed pay all rent in arrear, and all costs and damages sustained by such lessor or person entitled to the remainder or reversion as aforesaid, and perform all the covenants and agreements which, on the part and behalf of the first lessee, are and ought to be performed.

The next step is for the lessor to make a court application to obtain an order for possession. At this stage, however, the tenant can also apply for relief from forfeiture. Proceedings may be brought by the landlord in the County Court or the High Court and the rules on relief within each court vary slightly. The rights of the tenant in the High Court are governed by the same Act:

Common Law Procedure Act 1852

Tenant paying all rent with costs, proceedings to cease

212   If the tenant or his assignee do or shall, at any time before the trial in such ejectment, pay or tender to the lessor or landlord, his executors or administrators, or his or their attorney in that cause, or pay into the court where the same cause is depending, all the rent and arrears, together with the costs, then and in such case all further proceedings on the said ejectment shall cease and be discontinued; and if such lessee, his executors, administrators, or assigns, shall, upon such proceedings as aforesaid, be relieved in equity, he and they shall have, hold, and enjoy the demised lands, according to the lease thereof made, without any new lease.

The framework for relief from forfeiture in the county court is provided by the County Courts Act 1984.

County Courts Act 1984

Provisions as to forfeiture for non-payment of rent

138 (1) This section has effect where a lessor is proceeding by action in a county court to enforce against a lessee a right of re-entry or forfeiture in respect of any land for non-payment of rent.

(2) If the lessee pays into court not less than 5 clear days before the return day all the rent in arrear and the costs of the action, the action shall cease, and the lessee shall hold the land according to the lease without any new lease.

(3) If –
   (a) the action does not cease under subsection (2); and
   (b) the court at the trial is satisfied that the lessor is entitled to enforce the right of re-entry or forfeiture,
the court shall order possession of the land to be given to the lessor at the expiration of such period, not being less than 4 weeks from the date of the order, as the court thinks fit, unless within that period the lessee pays into court all the rent in arrear and the costs of the action.

(4) The court may extend the period specified under subsection (3) at any time before possession of the land is recovered in pursuance of the order under that subsection...[35]

Rights of the lessor: forfeiture for breach of other covenants

The Law of Property Act 1925 provides the basis for forfeiture actions and for relief against forfeiture for both tenants and sub-tenants where the breach is for other than non-payment of rent:

Law of Property Act 1925

Restrictions on and relief against forfeiture of leases and under-leases

146 (1) A right of re-entry or forfeiture under any proviso or stipulation in a lease for a breach of any covenant or condition in the lease shall not be enforceable, by action or otherwise, unless and until the lessor serves on the lessee a notice –
   (a) specifying the particular breach complained of; and
   (b) if the breach is capable of remedy, requiring the lessee to remedy the breach; and
   (c) in any case, requiring the lessee to make compensation in money for the breach;
and the lessee fails, within a reasonable time thereafter, to remedy the breach, if it is capable of remedy, and to make reasonable compensation in

---

35 For a detailed discussion of relief against forfeiture for non-payment of rent see *United Dominions Trust Ltd* v *Shellpoint Trustees Ltd* [1993] 4 All ER 310.

money, to the satisfaction of the lessor, for the breach.

(2) Where a lessor is proceeding, by action or otherwise, to enforce such a right of re-entry or forfeiture, the lessee may, in the lessor's action, if any, or in any action brought by himself, apply to the court for relief, and the court may grant or refuse relief, as the court, having regard to the proceedings and conduct of the parties under the foregoing provisions of this section, and to all the other circumstances, thinks fit; and in case of relief may grant it on such terms, if any, as to costs, expenses, damages, compensation, penalty, or otherwise, including the granting of an injunction to restrain any like breach in the future, as the court, in the circumstances of each case, thinks fit.

(4) Where a lessor is proceeding by action or otherwise to enforce a right of re-entry or forfeiture under any covenant, proviso, or stipulation in a lease, or for non-payment of rent, the court may, on application by any person claiming as an under-lessee any estate or interest in the property comprised in the lease or any part thereof, either in the lessor's action (if any) or in any action brought by such person for that purpose, make an order vesting, for the whole term of the lease or any less term, the property comprised in the lease, or any part thereof in any person entitled as under-lessee to any estate or interest in such property upon such conditions as to execution of any deed or other document, payment of rent, costs, expenses, damages, compensation, giving security, or otherwise, as the court in the circumstances of each case may think fit, but in no case shall any such under-lessee be entitled to require a lease to be granted to him for any longer term than he had his original sub-lease.

Section 146 distinguishes between remediable and irremediable breaches of covenant. In the case of the former, the tenant may avoid forfeiture by compliance with the covenant and payment of any financial compensation, if requested by the landlord.[36]

In the case of an irremediable breach the landlord need only give notice of the nature of that breach and then proceed to forfeiture. It is vital therefore to distinguish between the two kinds of breach of covenant.

Decisions in the first half of this century concentrated upon the tenants' use of property in a manner which could cast a stigma upon 'the address'.

Rugby School (Governors) v *Tannahill* (1935) 1 KB 87 (CA) Greer, Maugham and Roche LJJ

Greer LJ:

The material facts are that, some time before the notice was served, the defendant had been knowingly and actively permitting the house to be used as a brothel ... The covenant, the breach of which is complained of, expressly forbids the tenant to permit the premises to be used for such a purpose ... In those circumstances the

---

36 But only if he wants it: *Lock* v *Pearce* [1893] 2 Ch 271.

plaintiffs were entitled to obtain possession of the premises unless they failed to comply with the terms of s.146 of the Law of Property Act 1925. It is conceded that in the notice given by the plaintiffs the defendant was not required to remedy the breach, nor was she required to make compensation in money in respect thereof. [Counsel for the defendant] ... contends that in view of these omissions the proceedings to recover possession fail *ab initio*.

The first point is, whether this particular breach is capable of remedy ... This particular breach ... conducting the premises, or permitting them to be conducted, as a house of ill-fame ... is one which in my judgment was not remedied by merely stopping the user. I cannot conceive how a breach of this kind can be remedied. The result of committing the breach would be known all over the neighbourhood and seriously affect the value of the premises. Even a money payment together with cessation of the improper use of the house could not be a remedy. Taking the view as I do that this breach was incapable of remedy, it was unnecessary to require in the notice that the defendant should remedy the breach.

The further question is whether the absence of any statement in the notice requiring compensation in money in respect of the breach is fatal to the validity of the notice ... the statute requires notice to be given specifying the breach complained of, as the first thing, and, if the breach is capable of remedy, requiring the lessee to remedy it, and 'in any case requiring the lessee to make compensation in money for the breach.' Supposing the lessor does not want compensation, is the notice to be held bad because he does not ask for it? There is no sense in that...

More recently, it has been made clear that breach of a covenant not to assign or sublet is similarly irremediable.

Scala House & District Property Co Ltd v *Forbes* [1974] 1 QB 575 (CA) Russell, James LJJ and Plowman J

Russell LJ:

I stress again that where there has been unlawful subletting which has determined (and which has not been waived) there has been a breach which at common law entitles the lessor to re-enter: nothing can be done to remedy that breach: the expiry of the subterm has not been annulled or remedied the breach: in such a case the lessor plainly need not, in his section 146 notice, call upon the lessee to remedy the breach which is not capable of remedy, and is free to issue his writ for possession, the possibility of relief remaining. Can it possibly be that, while there is the situation in such a case, it is otherwise if the lessee has failed to get rid of the subterm until after a notice is served? Is the lessee then in a stronger position and the lessor in a weaker position? In my judgment not so. These problems and questions arise only if such a breach is capable of remedy, which in my judgment it is not.

As a consequence of the above cases, it had often been implied that breach of any restrictive covenant would be irremediable. However, this argument was rejected by the Court of Appeal.

Expert Clothing Service & Sales Ltd v *Hillgate House Ltd* [1985] 3 WLR 359 (CA) O'Connor, Slade LJJ, Bristow J

The tenants had breached covenants requiring them to reconstruct the premises by a certain date and to notify the landlords of any changes related to the premises.

Slade LJ:

In a case where the breach is 'capable of remedy' within the meaning of the section, the principal object of the notice procedure provided for by section 146(1), as I read it, is to afford the lessee two opportunities before the lessor actually proceeds to enforce his right of re-entry, namely (1) the opportunity to remedy the breach within a reasonable time after service of the notice, and (2) the opportunity to apply to the court for relief from forfeiture. In a case where the breach is not 'capable of remedy', there is clearly no point in affording the first of these two opportunities; the object of the notice procedure is thus simply to give the lessee the opportunity to apply for relief.

Unfortunately the authorities give only limited guidance as to what breaches are 'capable of remedy'...

Slade LJ continued by pointing out that, although the breach of a positive covenant is not always capable of remedy:

Nevertheless, I would, for my part, accept ... submission that the breach of a positive covenant (whether it be a continuing breach or a once and for all breach) will ordinarily be capable of remedy ... the concept of capability of remedy for the purpose of section 146 must surely be directed to the question whether the harm that has been done to the landlord by the relevant breach is for practicable purposes capable of being retrieved. In the ordinary case, the breach of a promise to do something by a certain time can for practical purposes be remedied by the thing being done, even out of time...

However, this did not mean that negative covenants are always irremediable covenants. He continued:

[T]he ultimate question for the court was this: if the section 146 notice had required the lessee to remedy the breach and the lessors had then allowed a reasonable time to elapse to enable the lessee fully to comply with the relevant covenant, would such compliance, coupled with the payment of any appropriate monetary compensation, have effectively remedied the harm which the lessors had suffered or were likely to suffer from the breach? If, but only if, the answer to this question was 'No,' would the failure of the section 146 notice to require remedy of the breach have been justifiable ... In the present case, however ... I think the answer to it must have been 'Yes.'

My conclusion, therefore, is that the breach of the covenant to reconstruct, no less than the breach of the covenant to give notice of charges, was 'capable of remedy'.

If a breach is remediable the landlord must allow the tenant reasonable time in which to remedy the breach, after the service of a s. 146 notice. Relief may be granted by the court, subject to the court imposing whatever conditions it may think fit – s. 146(2) (see above). Sub-tenants may, of course, suffer if a head lease is forfeited for a breach of covenant by the tenant, however, they may apply for relief under s. 146(4) (see above). There may also be circumstances where there may be a 'lawful excuse' for non-performance of a covenant which provides a defence to forfeiture. (See for example *John Lewis Properties plc* v *Viscount Chelsea* (CA) (1994) 67 P & CR 120.)

The House of Lords has recently answered some outstanding questions regarded relief from forfeiture.

Billson & Others v *Residential Apartments Ltd* [1992] 2 WLR 15
Lord Keith of Kinkel, Lord Templeman, Lord Oliver of Aylmerton, Lord Goff of Chievely and Lord Hauncey of Tullichettle

Residential Apartments had been the tenants of the relevant premises since May 1989 when the lease, dated 17 July 1964 and due to expire in 1997, had been duly assigned to them. Their landlords were trustees who owned the freehold reversion. The lease included a covenant by the tenants not to make alterations/additions to the premises without the written consent of the landlords. Further the lease contained a right of re-entry for non-payment of rent or breach of any covenant by the tenant. When the tenants began extensive alterations at the property the landlords served a s. 146 notice dated 4 July 1989, however, the tenants did not remedy their breach of covenant within a reasonable time. On 18 July 1989 at 6 a.m. the landlords' agents peaceably re-entered the premises and changed the locks. Within four hours workmen engaged by the tenant had regained possession of the premises. The landlords then brought an action claiming possession and the tenants claimed relief against forfeiture. Both the trial judge and the Court of Appeal held that they could not grant relief under s. 146(2), Law of Property Act 1925 since the tenants had not applied for relief prior to the landlords' re-entry on 18 July 1989. The tenants appealed.

Lord Templeman:
I accept that it is now settled law that a tenant cannot apply for relief after the landlord has recovered judgement for possession and has re-entered in reliance on that judgement. But I do not accept that any court has deprived or is entitled to deprive a tenant of any right to apply for relief if the landlord proceeds to forfeit otherwise than by an action instituted for that purpose...

The result of section 146 and the authorities are as follows. A tenant may apply for appropriate declarations and for relief from forfeiture under section 146(2) after the issue of a section 146 notice but he is not prejudiced if he does not do so. A tenant cannot apply for relief after a landlord has forfeited a lease by issuing and serving a writ, has recovered judgement and has entered into possession pursuant to that judgement. If the judgement is set aside or successfully appealed the tenant will be able to apply for relief in the landlord's action but the court in deciding whether to grant relief will take into account any consequences of the original order and repossession and the delay of the tenant. A tenant may apply for a relief after a landlord has forfeited a re-entry without first obtaining a court order for that purpose but the court in deciding whether to grant relief will take into account all the circumstances, including delay, on the part of the tenant. Any past judicial observations which might suggest that a tenant is debarred from applying for relief after the landlord has re-entered without first obtaining a court order for that purpose are not to be so construed.

Thus their Lordships allowed the appeal showing a reluctance to refuse the right to relief from forfeiture. Commenting upon a post-*Billson* decision – *Fuller and Another* v *Judy Properties Ltd* (CA) [1992] 14 EG 106 – a contributor to the *New Law Journal* ((1992) 142 NLJ 609) remarked that the courts are also unlikely to deny relief itself 'where the current tenant has paid a significant premium, even where there has been a deliberate breach and a new lease has been granted' (609).

Rights of the lessee

Most textbooks do not have a heading 'Rights of Tenants', because tenants do not have many special (non-contractual), rights against their landlords. Tenants do not have rights of distress or forfeiture. A tenant who has, for example, a problem in enforcing a covenant for repairs undertaken by the landlord will have to search to find the appropriate means to encourage the landlord to fulfil their promises. Methods include the following:

Ordinary contractual remedies

The following extract represents a succinct judicial explanation of the application of general contract law to breaches of leasehold covenants to repair.

Calabar Properties Ltd v *Stritcher* (1984) 1 WLR 287 (CA)
Stephenson, Griffiths and May LJJ

Griffiths LJ:

The object of awarding damages against a landlord for breach of his covenant to repair is not to punish the landlord but, so far as money can, to restore the tenant to the position he would have been in had there been no breach. This object will not be achieved by applying one set of rules to all cases regardless of the particular circumstances of the case. The facts of each case must be looked at carefully to see what damage the tenant has suffered and how he may be fairly compensated by a monetary award.

In this case on the findings of the judge the plaintiff landlords, after notice of the defect, neglected their obligation to repair for such a length of time that the flat eventually became uninhabitable. It was also clear that unless ordered to do so by an order of the court, the plaintiffs had no intention of carrying out the repairs. In these circumstances the defendant had two options that were reasonably open to her: either of selling the flat and moving elsewhere, or alternatively of moving into temporary accommodation and bringing an action against the plaintiffs to force them to carry out the repairs, and then returning to the flat after the repairs were done. If the defendant had chosen the first option then the measure of damages would indeed have been the difference in the price she received for the flat in its damaged condition and that which it would have fetched in the open market if the plaintiffs had observed their repairing covenant. If, however, the defendant did not wish to sell the flat but to continue to live in it after the plaintiffs had carried out the necessary structural repairs it was wholly artificial to award her damages on the basis of loss in market value, because once the plaintiffs had carried out the repairs and any consequential redecoration of the interior was completed there would be no loss in market value. The defendant should be awarded the cost to which she was put in taking alternative accommodation, the cost of redecorating, and some award for all the unpleasantness of living in the flat as it deteriorated until it became uninhabitable. These three heads of damage will, so far as money can, compensate the defendant for the plaintiff's breach...

Set-off against rent

The tenant may do the repairs and set off the cost against the rent, if the landlord refuses or neglects to make repairs of which notice has been given. Express covenants in leases may exclude the right of set-off and these are not covered by the Unfair Contract Terms Act 1977.[37] However, in the recent case of *Connaught Restaurants Ltd* v *Indoor Leisure Ltd* [1993] 1 WLR 501 it was emphasised that clear unambiguous words were needed to preclude this right.[38]

Action in tort for statutory nuisance or negligence

The framework for such actions is to be found in the Environmental Protection Act 1990, particularly, ss. 79–82. A statutory nuisance will arise where premises are in such a state of disrepair as to be 'prejudicial to health', which phrase is defined in s. 79(7) to mean 'injurious or likely to cause injury, to health'. There are also provisions in the same Act for local authorities to take action once satisfied of the existence of a statutory nuisance. Local authorities are further required by the Housing Act 1985 to take action to tackle individual properties which are unfit for human habitation.

Proposals for reform

The Law Commission in their 1985 Report 'Forfeiture of Tenancies' (No. 142)

---

37 See *Electricity Supply Nominees Ltd* v *IAF Group Ltd* (1994) 67 P & CR 28.
38 For an interesting discussion concerning the tenant's entitlement to set off and the landlord's right to distrain, see *Eller* v *Grovecrest Investments Ltd* [1994] A All ER 845.

made proposals for large-scale reforms to the law of forfeiture. In 1993 the Commission published a draft 'Termination of Tenancies Bill' which would implement many of the proposals in the earlier Report. The main provisions in the Bill, together with a critique of the proposed new termination scheme, are set out in the next extract:

H.W. Wilkinson 'The Rush to Simplification' (1994) *Conv* 177:

The Law Commission seems to have taken an objection to all that beautiful and involved learning which has for so long been a delight to the industrious student. Once more it has produced proposals for 'simplifying' the law, heedless of the wise maxim derived from our transatlantic cousins, 'if it ain't real broke, don't fix it'.

For example, if a tenant is in breach of a covenant or condition in a lease, all that the landlord has to do is to enter into a stately minuet whose moves are clearly choreographed...

He then details the statutory provisions governing forfeiture for breach of covenants and continues:

The practical defects of these statutory provisions were many and they are thoroughly discussed and commented upon in the Law Commission's Report 'Forfeiture of Tenancies'. Following representations and further discussions the Law Commission has produced a modified scheme and draft Bill.

The House of Lords decision in *Billson* v *Residential Apartments Ltd*[39] which confirmed the effectiveness of peaceable re-entry as a means of forfeiture was described by Lord Templeman in the case as a 'dubious and dangerous method of determining the lease', prompted reconsideration of the 1985 Report. It also led the Law Commission to comment that, 'The backlog of unimplemented law reform reports emphasises the need to give priority to the most urgent measures'. In their own words from the 1985 Report:

> 'The law of forfeiture is obviously defective: it is more complicated than it needs to be to carry into effect the main substance and purpose of the existing law. The needless complications add to the costs incurred by the people caught up in the working of the law.'

The Law Commission considered back in 1985 that 'forfeiture of tenancies is an area of law in daily use, affecting a large number of people, which urgently needs reform'. In the first Report it had considered both a landlord's termination order scheme and a tenant's termination order scheme but found in their responses that there was no consensus over the latter, so it has been left aside for the present.

Outline of the scheme
The Law Commission outlines its proposed new scheme as follows. A landlord will no longer be able to forfeit a lease for breach of covenant or insolvency, or for failure to fulfill a condition. He will instead have the right to bring termination order

---

39 See above p. 126.

proceedings to end the lease. A proviso for re-entry or other such provision would not be needed in the lease, but the right to bring termination proceedings could be excluded [or presumably restricted] by an express term. The tenancy will continue until a court orders that it should end. The court order could be of two types, the first that it will end on a stated day, the other that it will end if the tenant has not taken specified remedial action within a stated period. Any derivative interest will come to an end unless the landlord or the owner of the derivative interest makes an appropriate application to the court and an order in his favour is made. A Termination of Tenancies Bill is included in the Report...

By clauses 13 and 14 there are three cases in which the court will have a duty to make an absolute termination order. The first is where it is satisfied that a termination event of a serious character has occurred whilst the tenant has held the tenancy or that terminating events have been frequent during that time ... and in addition it appears to the court that the tenant is therefore such an unsatisfactory tenant that he ought not to remain a tenant. The purpose of this is to deal with the 'stigma' cases[40] but to decide each on its own merits. The second case is where the tenancy has been assigned to forestall the risk of an absolute order under the first provision and where, in addition, it appears to the court that there is a substantial risk of the continuance of the termination events (this is to prevent profitable continued misuse of the property). The third case is where there has been an assignment in breach of the tenant's obligations or an insolvency event ... has occurred and the court is satisfied that a remedial order will not provide an adequate remedy.

The timetable

We have mentioned the requirement for due process under s. 146 of the Law of Property Act 1925 and the need to follow the common law as amended. The new regime too will have its stately minuet. By clause 10 the landlord is under a time limit. He must commence proceedings for a termination order within six months of the date the termination event 'first came to his knowledge' ... The landlord may choose to give the tenant an opportunity to correct the breach, in which case he will serve, within the six months' period, a 'termination order event notice'. This notice will specify the event and particularise it, specifying the action needed to set things right and requiring that action to be taken. A time limit for compliance can be imposed. Service of the notice will suspend the landlord's right to take proceedings ... After the end of the suspension period the landlord will have three months to start proceedings ... It will be a relevant factor that any action specified in the suspension notice was or was not reasonable and that the time for compliance was or was not reasonable where the court is deciding between a remedial order and an absolute order. Clearly the need for a well-maintained diary so that steps and limits are not missed will be as important as it ever was...

Ah well, those who think that the law of forfeiture produces 'needless complication' may yet have their way. Next they will wish to simplify the rules of chess.

---

40 See p. 123.

5 Mortgages

INTRODUCTION

The aim of this chapter is to provide brief material on the history and modern context of mortgages. The focus is on mortgages and the family home.

The concept of a mortgage

A mortgage is, in effect, an invisible label on a piece of land (either freehold or leasehold) which states that, unless a sum of money is repaid on or by a certain day (or, often, by monthly instalments), the land itself will be sold to repay the loan. The mortgage is a charge (burden) imposed on land as security for debt. There may be several mortgages on one piece of land.

Traditionally, land has been regarded as especially good security for a loan of money because of its permanence, identifiability and value. However, unlike a pawn or a pledge arrangement, where for example a diamond ring is handed to the moneylender, the land itself cannot be handed over. The Land Certificate (or title deeds) represent the land (normally the Certificate is held in the Registry during the mortgage).

Although there are many commercial mortgages, the most common modern understanding of a mortgage is a building society or bank (the mortgagee) loaning money for home-buying. The borrower (the mortgagor) is warned that if the money is not repaid, the borrower's home may be sold.

Mortgages and home buying

It has been recognised that we now live in a 'real-property-owning', particularly a 'real-property-mortgaged-to-a-building-society-owning democracy' (Lord Diplock in *Pettit* v *Pettit* [1970] AC 777 at 824).

E.F. Cousins and S. Ross *The Law of Mortgages* (Sweet & Maxwell: 1989)[1]

The original purposes of building societies, as stated in the preamble to the Building Societies Act 1836, was to enable persons of moderate means to buy small properties. In the early societies, funds were derived from subscriptions, but societies also raised funds by the issue of shares and by receiving deposits or loans...

Building society mortgages are governed by the general law of mortgages. The main difference between building society mortgages and other mortgages is the incorporation of the society's rules into the mortgage. The mortgage usually provides that the mortgagor shall be bound by an alteration of the rules, and, while a society has extensive powers to alter its rules, such alteration must be one which could reasonably be considered as within the contemplation of the members of the society when the contract of membership was made.

Social Trends No. 24 (HMSO: 1994)

Housing Supply

There were almost 24 million dwellings in the United Kingdom at December 1992, and more than twice as many dwellings were owner occupied compared with 1961.

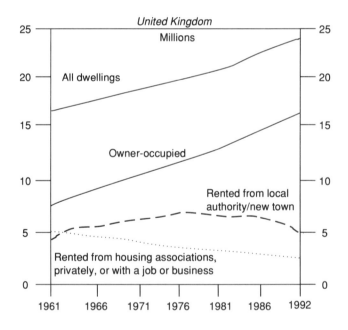

Fig. 5.1 Stock of dwellings: by tenure
Source: Department of the Environment

---

1 See also M. Boleat, *The Building Society Industry* (Allen & Unwin: 2nd edn 1986).

Tax relief is available on a loan to purchase a property in the United Kingdom providing that the house is used as the borrower's main residence. In 1992–3 tax relief, at 25 per cent, was available on the interest paid on the first £30,000 of a mortgage loan. This tax relief will be restricted to 15 per cent from April 1995. By 1990–91 the cost of this to the government in real terms increased tenfold to reach £8.3 billion.

It is also of note that building societies pay a lower rate of corporate tax than other commercial concerns.

There are important political implications to the expansion of home ownership and – the other side of the coin – the growth of the financial institutions whose growth is fuelled by this expansion. There is a building society on the street corner of most people's lives.

S. Merrett and F. Grey *Owner Occupation in Britain* (Routledge & Kegan Paul: 1982)

The core of home ownership today consists in the very extensive control it gives over the use of the dwelling to the possessing household and, even more important, the right to alienate the rights in that property, that is the right to sell...

In opposition to the philosophy of property of John Locke[2] ... I propose that the evident desire of very substantial numbers of British working people to own their home rests entirely on an unmistakable foundation ... owner-occupation, for households on average of higher than average wages and salaries, in general gives access to dwellings that are ranked higher in terms of their use-value and which are perceived to offer greater housing mobility and long-term financial advantages...

Since the 1930s government policy-makers and politicians, partly at least because of an assumed electoral advantage, have often argued the central place of owner-occupation in the well-being of individual, family and society. During the interwar period one of the key parliamentary figures, Neville Chamberlain, saw home-ownership as 'a revolution which of necessity enlisted all those who were affected by it on the side of law and order and enrolled them in a great army of good citizens'...

This philosophy culminated in the statement of Michael Heseltine in 1980:

'There is in this country a deeply ingrained desire for home ownership. The Government believe that this spirit should be fostered. It reflects the wishes of the people, ensures the wide spread of wealth through society, encourages a personal desire to improve and modernise one's home, enables people to accrue wealth for their children, and stimulates the attitudes of independence and self-reliance that are the bedrock of a free society.'

Increasingly, then, the view that owner-occupation propagates individual and societal well-being has been accepted by both Labour and Conservative governments. In turn, this has been related to the relegation of council housing as

---

2 See also chapter 1, pp. 8–10.

a second-best welfare tenure for those unable or unwilling to accept the challenge of owner-occupation. It has gone hand-in-hand with financial and other policies favouring owner-occupation ... and with, for example, the more recent Conservative drive towards council house sales. Turning to housing institutions and agencies, a similar picture emerges of owner-occupation being seen as a positive influence on social relations ... Harold Bellman, one of the central figures of the building society movement during the interwar years, was ... amongst the most vocal concerning the benefits of home-ownership:

> 'The man who has something to protect and improve – a stake of some sort in the country – naturally turns his thoughts in the direction of sane, ordered and perforce economical government. The thrifty man is seldom or never an extremist agitator. To him revolution is anathema; and, as in the earliest days Building Societies acted as a stabilising force, so today they stand, in the words of The Rt. Hon. G.N. Barnes, as a "bulwark against Bolshevism and all that Bolshevism stands for.'

However, comparative studies show that the development and nature of home-ownership varies widely from country to country, bearing no clear relationship to per capita GNP, and not showing a general tendency to increase over time. For example, although one might suppose the 'desire' and 'need' for owner-occupation to be more easily fulfilled the greater the wealth of the nation, West Germany, Switzerland and Sweden (all economically more successful than Britain) have lower levels of owner-occupation.[3] Similarly, at times during the post-war period, home-ownership has actually fallen in countries such as Canada, Australia and Switzerland. The 'ingrained', 'natural' and 'basic' 'desire' and 'need' may, on this basis, correctly be exposed as a myth ... [which] 'functions by projecting on to individuals the characteristics of the particular socio-economic system in which they are located – a system largely founded on private ownership of property'...[4]

Owner-occupation can perhaps best be seen as a property form that can combine with a range of social relations. Sometimes these relationships may support the existing social order, but at other times owner-occupation may be an arena for housing and wider political struggle. Similarly individual families may be either advantaged or disadvantaged in living in the tenure. They may be able to lead a 'full and freer life' either, depending on one's political stance, as an individual integrated into capitalist society, or as someone who has partially withdrawn from that system. Equally, owner-occupation may act to reinforce an individual's poverty and general class position in society. Under these circumstances, home-owners with similar interests may unite together in a common housing struggle; or people may remain as alienated, isolated and exploited individuals.

Longer-term economic change, the roller-coaster of the capitalist economic system, has also affected the role of owner-occupation in determining social relations. During periods of prosperity shared by the majority of the population many people have had a better material life, and a freer range of social relationships through home-ownerships, particularly in contrast to tenants of state

---

3 Portugal, Greece and Ireland, however, have the highest owner-occupation rate in Europe.
4 R. Boddy *The Building Societies* (Macmillan: 1980), p. 25.

housing as it presently exists in Britain. The reverse is also true. Economic crisis increasingly impinges on the ability of the tenure to provide people with satisfactory housing or to produce a stable social structure.[5] Under these conditions the potential grows for housing or wider political struggle by home-owners. Yet, in turn, this potential may only be realised through political awareness and activity arising through wider class-consciousness.

Sexual politics are also relevant here:

C. Glendinning and J. Millar *Women and Poverty in Britain in the 1990s* (Harvester Wheatsheaf: 1992)

To talk of 'households', of course, disguises the reality of where the burden of indebtedness lies. By virtue of the position they hold within two-partner households, many women carry responsibility for budgeting and, thereby, for making ends meet in times of financial crisis. Further, by virtue of the position they hold in society, women, though apparently equal users of credit with men, are likely to have unequal access to certain types of low-cost credit, including mortgages. As is so often the case, a legislative framework which appears to enshrine equality ... is unable to redress those structural inequalities which actually determine access to resources. Finally, if the dissolution of marriage or a partnership brings with it a reduced income, women may be particularly susceptible to debt in their own right, including housing arrears, with the threat of losing their homes. They may also be left to carry responsibility for arrears and debts which were jointly incurred before the ending of the relationship.

THE LEGAL RELATIONSHIP BETWEEN BORROWER AND LENDER

The forms of mortgages

Before 1925, a standard mortgage arrangement was (briefly) as follows: H lent K £10,000 to be repaid in one year's time, and in exchange K conveyed her fee simple to H as security for the loan. In the conveyance there was a promise that when the money was repaid, H would re-convey the land to K. H, as legal owner of the land, could treat it as her own and would be entitled to move in but normally would not take the trouble to do so.

E.H. Burn *Cheshire and Burn's Modern Law of Real Property* 15th edn (Butterworths: 1994)

The prevailing practice by which the legal fee simple [or long lease] was conveyed to a mortgagee, presented a difficult problem to the draftsmen of the 1925

---

5 The 1990–2 crisis in housing prices illustrates this.

legislation. How were they to bring it into line with the principles that they intended to introduce?

The cornerstone of their policy was that the legal fee simple should always be vested in its true owner and that he should be able to convey it free from equitable interests. In the eyes of the law the true owner is the mortgagor.[6] Yet, all that he held before 1926 was an equitable interest, and unless some alteration were made there could be no question of his ability to convey any kind of legal estate during the continuance of the mortgage...

The solution contained in the Law of Property Act 1925 is to revert to the old fifteenth-century method of effecting mortgages by means of a lease for a term of years.

Mortgages by which the legal fee simple [or long lease] is vested in the mortgagee are prohibited, and a mortgagee who requires a legal estate instead of a mere equitable interest is compelled to take either a long term of years or a newly invented interest called a '*charge by deed expressed to be by way of legal mortgage*'. Thus in the first case both parties have legal estates: the mortgagee has a legal term of years absolute, and the mortgagor has a reversionary and legal fee simple, subject to the mortgagee's term. In the case of a charge by way of legal mortgage, however, the mortgagee has the same protection, powers and remedies as if he had taken a legal term of years.

In this way, the principle that the legal fee simple should always remain vested in the true owner has been maintained.

Law of Property Act 1925

Mode of mortgaging freeholds

85 (1) A mortgage of an estate in fee simple shall only be capable of being effected at law either by a demise for a term of years absolute, subject to a provision for cesser on redemption, or by a charge by deed expressed to be by way of legal mortgage: Provided that a first mortgagee shall have the same right to the possession of documents as if his security included the fee simple.

(2) Any purported conveyance of an estate in fee simple by way of mortgage made after the commencement of this Act shall (to the extent of the estate of the mortgagor) operate as a demise of the land to the mortgagee for a term of years absolute, without impeachment for waste, but subject to cesser on redemption, in manner following, namely:
   (a) A first or only mortgage shall take a term of three thousand years from the date of the mortgage;
   (b) A second or subsequent mortgagee shall take a term (commencing from the date of the mortgage) one day longer than the term vested in the first or other mortgagee whose security ranks immediately before that of such second or subsequent mortgagee:
and, in this subsection, any such purported conveyance as aforesaid includes an absolute conveyance with a deed of defeasance and any other assurance which, but for this subsection, would operate in effect to vest the fee simple in a mortgage subject to redemption.

---

6 Compare the view of Lord Oliver in *Cann's* case, Chapter 10, p. 299.

Mode of mortgaging leaseholds

86 (1) A mortgage of a term of years absolute shall only be capable of being effective at law either by a subdemise for a term of years absolute, less by one day at least than the term vested in the mortgagor, and subject to a provision for cesser on redemption, or by a charge by deed expressed to be by way of legal mortgage; and where a licence to subdemise by way of mortgage is required, such licence shall not be unreasonably refused:

Provided that a first mortgagee shall have the same right to the possession of documents as if his security had been effected by assignment.

(2) Any purported assignment of a term of years absolute by way of mortgage made after the commencement of this Act shall (to the extent of the estate of the mortgagor) operate as a subdemise of the leasehold land to the mortgagee for a term of years absolute but subject to cesser on redemption, in manner following, namely:

(a) The term to be taken by a first or only mortgagee shall be 10 days less than the term expressed to be assigned;

(b) The term to be taken by a second or subsequent mortgagee shall be one day longer than the term vested in the first or other mortgagee whose security ranks immediately before that of the second or subsequent mortgage, if the length of the last mentioned term permits, and in any case for a term less than the term expressed to be assigned;

and in this subsection, any such purported assignment as aforesaid includes an absolute assignment with a deed of defeasance and any other assurance which, but for this subsection, would operate in effect to vest the term of the mortgagor in a mortgagee subject to redemption.

Charges by way of legal mortgage

87 (1) Where a legal mortgage of land is created by a charge by deed expressed to be by way of legal mortgage, the mortgagee shall have the same protection, powers and remedies (including the right to take proceedings to obtain possession from the occupiers and the persons in receipt of rents and profits, or any of them) as if –

(a) where the mortgage is a mortgage of an estate in fee simple, a mortgage term for three thousand years without impeachment of waste had been thereby created in favour of the mortgagee; and

(b) where the mortgage is a mortgage of a term of years absolute, a sub-term less by one day than the term vested in the mortgagor had been thereby created in favour of the mortgagee.

Thus, the lender has an interest (lease or charge) in the borrower's land. The borrower retains legal ownership. The borrower also has rights created over the centuries by the courts of equity; this set of rights is called the 'equity of redemption'. Legal mortgages of registered land rank according to the date of their registration (s. 29, Land Registration Act 1925).

Legal and equitable mortgages

Like many other interests in land, mortgages may be either legal or equitable (see Fig. 5.2). It is important to be able to distinguish between them because of priority over other interests in the land, and also because an equitable mortgagee may have different remedies from a legal mortgagee.

Special duties of lenders

The rise in owner-occupation and the increasing co-ownership of family homes, together with the recession, have led to a number of cases of 'sexually transmitted

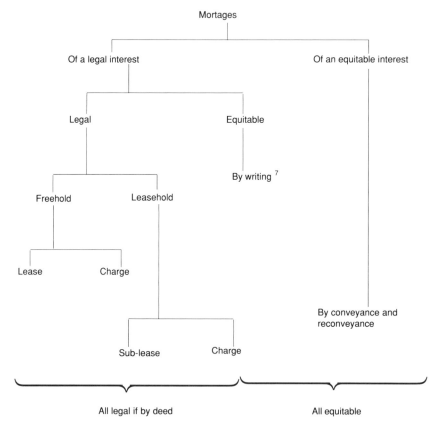

Fig 5.2 Types of mortgage

---

7 Since s. 2, Law of Property (Miscellaneous Provisions) Act 1989 (see Chapter 2, pp. 47–51), according to the Law Commission (No. 204, para. 2.8 – see below – but also see G. Hill 100 LQR (1990) 396), there can no longer be an equitable mortgage of land simply by deposit of the title deeds. Writing incorporating all the terms and signed by both parties is necessary in every case.

debt'. Typically, a lender attempts to repossess a home, and the wife (or other partner) responds by claiming that the mortgage – usually a second mortgage made directly in the husband's interests – must be set aside because of his undue influence or misrepresentation. Often the claim is that the man managed the finances and the woman did as he told her; sometimes he exerted pressure on her, and sometimes he lied, and sometimes both. The argument is that the bank ought to have taken steps to make sure that there was no wrong-doing before making the loan. Cases cited here concern married people, but the rules apply to all co-owners who have emotional ties to one another.

Barclays Bank plc v *O'Brien and another* [1993] 4 All ER 417 (HL), Lords Templeman, Lowry, Browne-Wilkinson, Slynn and Woolf

Mr O'Brien's business was in serious difficulties and he tried to resolve them by a second mortgage on the family home. Mrs O'Brien, who had an equitable interest in the land,[8] went with him to the bank and signed the charge without any legal advice and without reading the documents. Within six months the bank was seeking to take possession because of the unpaid debts. Mrs O'Brien alleged that the mortgage should be set aside; her husband-trustee had told her the loan was only £60,000 for merely three weeks but it was in fact for £135,000.

Lord Browne-Wilkinson gave the unanimous opinion, first reviewing the policy considerations:

The large number of cases of this type coming before the courts in recent years reflects the rapid changes in social attitudes and the distribution of wealth which have recently occurred...

In parallel with these financial developments, society's recognition of the equality of the sexes has led to a rejection of the concept that the wife is subservient to the husband in the management of the family's finances ... Yet ... although the concept of the ignorant wife leaving all financial decisions to the husband is outmoded, the practice does not yet coincide with the ideal. In a substantial proportion of marriages it is still the husband who has the business experience and the wife is willing to follow his advice without bringing a truly independent mind and will to bear on financial decisions. The number of recent cases in this field shows that in practice many wives are still subjected to, and yield to, undue influence by their husbands. Such wives can reasonably look to the law for some protection when their husbands have abused the trust and confidence reposed in them.

On the other hand, it is important to keep a sense of balance in approaching these cases. It is easy to allow sympathy for the wife who is threatened with the loss of her home at the suit of a rich bank to obscure an important public interest, *viz* the need to ensure that the wealth currently tied up in the matrimonial home does not become economically sterile. If the rights secured to wives by the law renders vulnerable loans granted on the security of matrimonial homes, institutions will be unwilling to accept such security, thereby reducing the flow of loan capital to

---

8 See Chapter 9 at p. 258.

business enterprises. It is therefore essential that a law designed to protect the vulnerable does not render the matrimonial home unacceptable as security to financial institutions.

As far as the law is concerned, he held:

A wife who has been induced to stand as a surety for her husband's debts by his undue influence, misrepresentation or some other legal wrong has an equity as against him to set aside that transaction. Under the ordinary principles of equity, her right to set aside that transaction will be enforceable against third parties (e.g. against a creditor) if either the husband was acting as the third party's agent or the third party had actual or constructive notice of the facts giving rise to her equity. Although there may be cases where, without artificiality, it can properly be held that the husband was acting as the agent of the creditor in procuring the wife to stand as surety, such cases will be of very rare occurrence. The key to the problem is to identify the circumstances in which the creditor will be taken to have had notice of the wife's equity to set aside the transaction.

The doctrine of notice lies at the heart of equity. Given that there are two innocent parties, each enjoying rights, the earlier right prevails against the later right if the acquirer of the later right knows of the earlier right (actual notice) or would have discovered it had he taken proper steps (constructive notice). In particular, if the party asserting that he takes free of the earlier rights of another knows of certain facts which put him on inquiry as to the possible existence of the rights of that other and he fails to make such an inquiry or take such other steps as are reasonable to verify whether such earlier right does or does not exist, he will have constructive notice of the earlier right and take subject to it. Therefore where a wife has agreed to stand surety for her husband's debts as a result of undue influence or misrepresentation, the creditor will take subject to the wife's equity to set aside the transaction if the circumstances are such as to put the creditor on inquiry as to the circumstances in which she agreed to stand surety...

Therefore, in my judgment a creditor is put on inquiry when a wife offers to stand surety for her husband's debts by the combination of two factors:
(a) the transaction is on its face not to the financial advantage of the wife; and
(b) there is a substantial risk in transactions of that kind that, in procuring the wife to act as surety, the husband has committed a legal or equitable wrong that entitles the wife to set aside the transaction.

It follows that, unless the creditor who is put on inquiry takes reasonable steps to satisfy himself that the wife's agreement to stand surety has been properly obtained, the creditor will have constructive notice of the wife's rights...

Normally in such circumstances, the bank should see the wife separately from her husband, the transaction should be explained to her and she should be advised to take separate legal advice. Here the bank had failed to take these reasonable steps to discover her equity and, therefore, had constructive notice of her right against her husband to have the mortgage set aside, and was bound by it. However, this was probably merely a temporary setback to the bank; under s. 30 Law of Property Act, [9] the house would probably be sold to pay the husband's debts.

---

9 See Chapter 9, at p. 237.

CIBC Mortgages plc v *Pitt* [1993] 4 All ER 433 (HL), Lords Templeman, Lowry, Browne-Wilkinson, Slynn and Woolf[10]

Mr Pitt arranged a mortgage of £150,000, ostensibly to buy a second home. Mrs Pitt was joint legal owner and therefore signed all the papers with him but did not read any of them and did not know the amount of the loan. In fact, the money was for share speculation, and the trial judge found that Mr Pitt had exerted undue influence on her. Eighteen months later, after the 1987 stock market crash, the repayments were in arrears and the lender sought possession.

The question for the House of Lords was whether the lender should be fixed with constructive notice.

Lord Browne-Wilkinson:

So far as the plaintiff [lender] was aware, the transaction consisted of a joint loan to the husband and wife to finance the discharge of an existing mortgage on 26 Alexander Avenue and, as to the balance, to be applied in buying a holiday home. The loan was advanced to both husband and wife jointly. There was nothing to indicate to the plaintiff that this was anything other than a normal advance to a husband and wife for their joint needs...

If third parties were to be fixed with constructive notice of undue influence in relation to every transaction between husband and wife, such transactions would become almost impossible ... [and] would not benefit the average married couple and would discourage financial institutions from making the advance.

What distinguishes the case of the joint advance from the surety case [for example, that of Mrs O'Brien] is that, in the latter, there is not only the possibility of undue influence having been exercised but also the increased risk of it having in fact been exercised because, at least on its face, the guarantee by a wife of her husband's debts is not for her financial benefit. It is the combination of these two factors that puts the creditor on inquiry.

It may seem that a difficult problem which has challenged the courts for many years has now been resolved, but doubts remain about the extent of the lender's duty to counsel the wife. In addition, the justice of the present rule seems open to question: the House of Lords' easy distinction between the loan 'on the face of it' to the financial benefit of only one or to both parties is patently unrealistic, for, clearly, a dependent wife gains at least as much 'financial benefit' from the continuation of her husband's business as she does from a holiday home.

THE RIGHTS OF THE BORROWER

The equity of redemption

The court of equity's intereference in mortgage transactions gave the borrower the equity of redemption. More recently, Parliament has also intervened to protect the

---

10 See M.P. Thompson [1994] Conv 140.

borrower in the form of the Consumer Credit Act 1974.

The rights of borrowers can be listed:

1. Rights concerning free redemption:
    (a) legal right to redeem on the date agreed;
    (b) equitable right to redeem after the legal date has passed – this right is only ended by the remedy of 'foreclosure' or by sale;
    (c) equitable right to have set aside any term which hinders the equitable right to redeem;
    (d) equitable right to have unfair terms ('collateral advantages') set aside;
    (e) statutory rights to have grossly unconscionable interest rates varied (Consumer Credit Act 1974).
2. Right to be given time to pay arrears (in a mortgage of a dwelling house) under the Administration of Justice Acts.
3. The general rights of a fee simple owner – to grant and accept surrenders of leases for example (s. 99, Law of Property Act 1925).

As will be seen in the following cases, equity's interference in mortgage contracts overlaps with other areas where the courts' policy has been to intervene in contracts, including the laws of usury (against moneylenders) and against monopolies.

The extracts indicate the general development of the law in this century, from a rather rigid approach in the early years to a more flexible 'case by case' approach more recently.

Terms delaying redemption

James Fairclough v *Swan Brewery Co Ltd* [1912] AC 565 (PC)
Lord Macnaghten, Lord Atkinson, Lord Shaw of Dunfermline,
Lord Mersey

A lessee of an Australian hotel granted a mortgage to the brewery company which contained a term that the borrower could not redeem the mortgage virtually until the remaining period of the lease expired (just over 17 years). At first instance, the term was held to be a clog on the equity of redemption and therefore void, but the Supreme Court of Western Australia allowed the appeal. In the Privy Council:

Lord Macnaghten:
The arguments of counsel ranged over a very wide field. But the real point is a narrow one. It depends upon a doctrine of equity which is not open to question.

'There is', as Kindersley VC said in *Gossip* v *Wright* [(1863) 32 LJ (Ch) 648, 653], 'no doubt that the broad rule is this: that the Court will not allow the right of redemption in any way to be hampered or crippled in that which the parties intended to be a security either by any contemporaneous instrument with the deed in question, or by anything which this Court would regard as a simultaneous arrangement or part of the same transaction.' The rule in comparatively recent times was unsettled by certain decisions in the Court of Chancery in England which seem to have misled the learned judges in the Full Court. But it is now firmly established by the House of Lords that the old rule still prevails and that equity will not permit any device or contrivance being part of the mortgage transaction or contemporaneous with it to prevent or impede redemption ... Here the provision for redemption is nugatory. The incumbrance on the lease the subject of the mortgage according to the letter of the bargain falls to be discharged before the lease terminates, but at a time when it is on the very point of expiring, when redemption can be of no advantage to the mortgagor even if he should be so fortunate as to get his deeds back before the actual termination of the lease. For all practical purposes this mortgage is irredeemable. It was made irredeemable in and by the mortgage itself.

Thus, the term was void and Fairclough was able to redeem his mortgage when he chose to do so.

Knightsbridge Estates Trust Ltd v *Byrne and others* [1939] 1 Ch 441 (CA) Sir Wilfred Green MR, Scott and Farwell LJJ

In 1931 the trust granted a mortgage of 'high-class' freehold land in Knightsbridge to Byrne and others (trustees of a friendly society). The sum advanced was £310,000. It was repayable by half-yearly instalments over 40 years. Six years later, in 1937, they wished to redeem the mortgage and claimed that the term preventing redemption before 1971 was 'illegal and void as a clog on their right to redeem'. At first instance, they won. In the Court of Appeal:

Sir Wilfred Green MR:

The first argument was that the postponement of the contractual right to redeem for forty years was void in itself, in other words, that the making of such an agreement between mortgagor and mortgagee was prohibited by a rule of equity. It was not contended that a provision in a mortgage deed making the mortgage irredeemable for a period of years is necessarily void. The argument was that such a period must be a 'reasonable' one, and it was said that the period in the present case was an unreasonable one by reason merely of its length...

The resulting agreement was a commercial one between two important corporations experienced in such, and has none of the features of an oppressive bargain where the borrower is at the mercy of an unscrupulous lender. In transactions of this kind it is notorious that there is competition among the large insurance companies and other bodies having large funds to invest, and we are not prepared to view the agreement made as anything but a proper business transaction...

But it is said not only that the period of postponement must be a reasonable one, but that in judging the 'reasonableness' of the period the considerations which we have mentioned cannot be regarded; that the Court is bound to judge 'reasonableness' by a consideration of the terms of the mortgage deed itself and without regard to extraneous matters. In the absence of clear authority we emphatically decline to consider a question of 'reasonableness' from a standpoint so unreal. To hold that the law is to tell business men what is reasonable in such circumstances and to refuse to take into account the business considerations involved, would bring the law into disrepute. Fortunately, we do not find ourselves forced to come to any such conclusion...

[E]quity does not reform mortgage transactions because they are unreasonable. It is concerned to see two things – one that the essential requirements of a mortgage transaction are observed, and the other that oppressive or unconscionable terms are not enforced. Subject to this, it does not, in our opinion, interfere. The question therefore arises whether, in a case where the right of redemption is real and not illusory and there is nothing oppressive or unconscionable in the transaction, there is something in a postponement of the contractual right to redeem, such as we have in the present case, that is inconsistent with the essential requirements of a mortgage transaction? Apart from authority the answer to this question would, in our opinion, be clearly in the negative. Any other answer would place an unfortunate restriction on the liberty of the contract of competent parties who are at arms' length – in the present case it would have operated to prevent the respondents obtaining financial terms which for obvious reasons they themselves considered to be most desirable. It would, moreover, lead to highly inequitable results.

Thus, this borrower was not able to redeem the mortgage until 1971.

Collateral advantages

Noakes & Co Ltd v *Rice* [1902] AC 24 (HL) Earl of Halsbury LC, Lord Macnaghten, Lord Shand, Lord Davey, Lord Brampton, Lord Robertston, Lord Lindley

The borrower, a pub landlord, borrowed money on the security of his lease from the brewery company and promised that he would only buy beer from the company for the rest of his lease, even after he redeemed the mortgage. He then wished to redeem the mortgage and sought a declaration that this promise would not bind him after redemption. At first instance, and on appeal, the brewery company lost and the term was struck out. The House of Lords dismissed the appeal unanimously.

Earl of Halsbury;

Under these circumstances, my Lords, it is and must be in each case a question of the particular thing which is advanced as a clog or a fetter, and in some cases it may seem to come very near the line. Whatever rule is laid down one can reduce it to something like an absurdity by taking an extreme case. But, my Lords, taking this case, it appears to me that undoubtedly this was a mortgage, and that the equity of redemption is clogged and fettered here by the continuance of an obligation which would render this house less available in the hands of its owner during the whole period and beyond the whole period of the term, apart from the realisation of the security. Under those circumstances, as a matter of the merest and simplest reasoning, I am wholly unable to come to any other conclusion than that there is a clog and fetter here which the law will not permit.

Lord Davey:

My Lords, there are three doctrines of the Courts of Equity in this country which have been referred to in the course of the argument in this case. The first doctrine to which I refer is expressed in the maxim, 'Once a mortgage always a mortgage.' The second is that the mortgagee shall not reserve to himself any collateral advantage outside the mortgage contract; and the third is that a provision or stipulation which will have the effect of clogging or fettering the equity of redemption is void.

My Lords, the first maxim presents no difficulty: it is only another way of saying that a mortgage cannot be made irredeemable, and that a provision to that effect is void. My Lords, the second doctrine to which I refer, namely that the mortgagee shall not reserve to himself any collateral advantage outside the mortgage contract, was established long ago when the usury laws were in force ... I think it will be found that every case under this head of equity was decided either on this gound, or on the ground that the bargain was oppressive and unconscionable. The abolition of the usury laws has made an alteration in the view the Court should take on this subject and I agree that a collateral advantage may now be stipulated for by a mortgagee, provided that no unfair advantage be taken by the mortgagee which would render it void or voidable, according to the general principles of equity, and provided that it does not offend against the third doctrine...

The third doctrine to which I have referred is really a corollary from the first, and might be expressed in this form: Once a mortgage always a mortgage and nothing but a mortgage. The meaning of that is that the mortgagee shall not make any stipulation which will prevent a mortgagor, who has paid principal, interest, and costs, from getting back his mortgaged property in the condition in which he parted with it.

Kreglinger v *New Patagonia Meat and Cold Storage Co Ltd* [1914] AC 25 (HL) Viscount Haldane LC, Earl of Halsbury, Lord Atkinson, Lord Mersey, Lord Parker of Waddington

There was a mortgage by a company floating charge.[11] The borrower agreed to sell its sheepskins (by-products of the meat business) to the lender for five years, provided they paid the best price. This term was to take effect even if the mortgage were redeemed before the five years passed. Kreglinger paid off the mortgage after less than three years and claimed that the sheepskin term was void. At first instance and in the Court of Appeal the term was held to be void as a clog on the right to redeem, but the House of Lords disagreed.

Viscount Haldane LC:

My Lords, the respondents have now, as they were entitled to do under the

---

11 Effectively, a mortgage on company property, and subject to the same principles as land mortgages.

agreement, paid off the loan. They claim that such payment has put an end to the option of the appellants to buy the respondents' sheepskins. Under the terms of the agreement this option, as I have already stated, will, if it is valid, continue operative until August 24, 1915 ... The Legislature during a long period placed restrictions on the rate of interest which could legally be exacted. But equity went beyond the limits of the statutes which limited the interest, and was ready to interfere with any usurious stipulation in a mortgage. In so doing it was influenced by the public policy of the time. The policy has now changed, and the Acts which limited the rate of interest have been repealed. The result is that a collateral advantage may now be stipulated for by the mortgagee provided that he has not acted unfairly or oppressively, and provided that the bargain does not conflict with the third form of the principle. This is that a mortgage (subject to the apparent exception in the case of family arrangements to which I have already alluded) cannot be made irredeemable, and that any stipulation which restricts or clogs the equity of redemption is void...

My Lords, the rules ... have now been applied by Courts of Equity for nearly three centuries, and the books are full of illustrations of their application. But ... it is inconsistent with the objects for which they were established that these rules should crystallise into technical language so rigid that the letter can defeat the underlying spirit and purpose. Their application must correspond with the practical necessities of the time. The rule as to collateral advantages, for example, has been much modified by the repeal of the usury laws and by the recognition of modern varieties of commercial bargaining.

The question is one not of form but of substance and it can be answered in each case only by looking at all the circumstances, and not by mere reliance on some abstract principle, or upon the *dicta* which have fallen *obiter* from judges in other and different cases.

My Lords, after the most careful consideration of the authorities, I think it is open to this House to hold and I invite your Lordships to hold, that there is now no rule in equity which precludes a mortgagee, whether the mortgage be made upon the occasion of a loan or otherwise, from stipulating for any collateral advantage, provided such collateral advantage is not either (1) unfair and unconscionable, or (2) in the nature of a penalty clogging the equity of redemption, or (3) inconsistent with or repugnant to the contractual and equitable right to redeem.

Interest rates

Rates of interest were once controlled by the usury laws.[12] Equity also intervened between moneylenders and their 'victims' but today the courts' view of money-lenders has changed.

Multiservice Bookbinding Ltd v *Marden* [1979] 1 Ch 95

Marden lent the company £36,000 on a mortgage. He was a private individual looking to invest money to provide security for his retirement and the company

---

12 Note, building societies are allowed to change their interest rates unilaterally.

was a small business looking to expand. The mortgage contained the unusual term that the rate of interest should be linked to the value of the Swiss franc.

Browne-Wilkinson J:

Since 1966, the pound sterling has greatly depreciated as against the Swiss franc. The September 1966 rate of exchange stated in the mortgage was just over 12 Swiss francs to the pound. The rate at the beginning of October 1976, when a redemption statement was prepared, was just over 4 Swiss francs to the pound. Although by October 15, 1976, some £24,355.57 had been repaid on capital account, these repayments had operated to reduce the nominal amount of the debt by only £15,000. This left £21,000 nominal to be discharged, which, after adding the Swiss franc uplift, would require a further actual payment of £63,202.65.

Accordingly, if redemption had occurred on October 15, 1976, the defendant who had advanced £36,000 in 1966 would have received £87,588.22 in repayment of capital.

In these circumstances it is not surprising that the plaintiffs sought to redeem as soon as they were able. By letter dated Feburary 24, 1976, they duly gave notice to redeem on September 7, 1976. At the date of the notice it was impossible to calculate the sum required for redemption, since the rate of exchange on September 6, 1976 was, of course, unknown. In fact between the date on which notice was given and October 15, 1976, the date down to which a redemption statement was eventually made up, the amount required to pay off the outstanding capital, £21,000 nominal, increased by some £14,500, due to a further sharp depreciation of the pound against the Swiss franc.

However, there is another side to the coin. Although the evidence is that in 1966 the plaintiff company was prosperous, its growth in the last 10 years has been considerable. Comparing the years 1965–66 and 1975–76, turnover has risen from £39,323 to £184,879: profits, after charging directors' emoluments and interest on the land, from £674 to £14,759; directors' remuneration from £5,000 to £21,898. It would be wrong to attribute these increases entirely to the new premises acquired in 1966; much must be due to the skill and hard work of Mr and Mrs Mara and the extra working capital introduced by them. But at least part of the increase must have been due to the availability of the larger premises, purchased with the loan made by the defendant. Perhaps most relevantly the property itself now stands in the books of the plaintiff company at a value of £93,075, after deducting moneys expended since 1966 ... it has doubled in value and in my judgment there is not likely to be much difference between the capital growth, in terms of sterling, of the loan, from £36,000 to £87,588 and the capital growth of the property purchased by means of that loan.

Secondly, considering the morgage bargain as a whole, in my judgment there was not great inequality of bargaining power as between the plaintiffs and the defendant ... Therefore the background does not give rise to any pre-supposition that the defendant took an unfair advantage of the plaintiffs.

The defendant made a hard bargain. But the test is not reasonableness. The parties made a bargain which the plaintiffs, who are businessmen, went into with their eyes open, with the benefit of independent advice, without any compelling necessity to accept a loan on these terms and without any sharp practice by the defendant. I cannot see that there was anything unfair or oppressive or morally reprehensible in such a bargain entered into in such circumstances.

Cityland & Property (Holdings) Ltd v *Dabrah* [1968] 1 Ch 166

Dabrah had a lease of a house from the company, and when it expired they sold him the freehold for £2,900, lending him £2,300 of the price on a mortgage. He could not repay it and they sought possession against him. The interest rate was fixed at an annual rate of 19 per cent; at this time the standard rate was 5.7 per cent.

Goff J:

The defendant ... presented a much more formidable argument that the large premium which brought the loan of £2,300 up to no less than £4,553 was in itself harsh and unconscionable, and such a collateral advantage as a court of equity would not allow.

Unlike the facts in *Kreglinger* v *New Patagonia Meat and Cold Storage Co Ltd*, this was not a bargain between two large trading concerns. It was the case of a man who was buying his house and a man who was obviously of limited means because he was unable to find more than £600 towards the purchase, whereas in evidence filed for another purpose, the plaintiffs have stated that all the other persons who had purchased property from them had been able themselves to finance or to arrange finance for the purchases. The premium which was added to the loan was, as I understand, no less than 57 per cent of the amount of the loan. I do not think it is really open to the plaintiffs to justify this premium as being in lieu of interest because they claim interest on the aggregate of the loan and the premium; but even if it should be, then, taking the mortgage as a six-year mortgage – and of course, they bound themselves not to call it in within that time if the instalments were duly paid – it would still represent interest at 19 per cent, which is out of all proportion to any investment rates prevailing at the time. Moreover, it was expressly provided by the charge that, on default, the whole should immediately become due.

I have further to bear in mind that this was not an unsecured loan: a security was being offered with a reasonable margin, not, it is true, a one-third/two-thirds margin as one usually expects in trustee investments, but still the defendant provided £600 and there was that margin in the property to secure the plaintiffs. I think they would have been entitled to charge a higher rate of interest than the normal market rate, or a reasonable premium comparable therewith, but nothing like the extent of 19 per cent, looked at as an interest rate, or 57 per cent, looked at as a capital sum; and it must be borne in mind that this premium was so large that it forthwith destroyed the whole equity and made it a completely deficient security. If default were made, and all that had been secured was the principal and interest, it was unlikely that on any exercise of the plaintiffs' powers as mortgagees, there would be a surplus for the mortgagor, but this premium destroyed any possibility of that, and it also made the security which was offered deficient.

For these reasons, in my judgment this was not reasonable.

Goff J imposed an interest rate of 7 per cent, with the proviso that each case should be decided on its own merits.

Consumer credit protection

The Consumer Credit Act 1974 is a complicated piece of legislation, which covers borrowing agreements between credit companies (not building societies) and private individuals.[13] The sections which replace the Moneylenders Acts are of the most importance in relation to mortgages.

Consumer Credit Act 1974

Extortionate credit bargains

137 (1) If the court finds a credit bargain extortionate it may reopen the credit agreement so as to do justice between the parties.

(2) In this section and sections 138 to 140 –
(a) 'credit agreement' means any agreement between an individual (the 'debtor') and any other person (the 'creditor') by which the creditor provides the debtor with credit of any amount, and
(b) 'credit bargain' – (i) where no transaction other than the credit agreement is to be taken into account in computing the total charge for credit, means the credit agreement; or; (ii) where one or more other transactions are to be so taken into account, means the credit agreement and those other transactions, taken together.

When bargains are extortionate

138 (1) A credit bargain is extortionate if it
(a) requires the debtor or a relative of his to make payments (whether unconditionally, or on certain contingencies) which are grossly exorbitant[14] or;
(b) otherwise grossly contravenes ordinary principles of fair dealing.

(2) In determining whether a credit bargain is extortionate, regard shall be had to such evidence as is adduced concerning –
(a) interest rates prevailing at the time it was made,
(b) the factors mentioned in subsections (3) to (5), and
(c) any other relevant considerations.

(3) Factors applicable under subsection (2) in relation to the debtor include –
(a) his age, experience, business capacity and state of health; and
(b) the degree to which, at the time of making the credit bargain, he was under financial pressure, and the nature of that pressure.

(4) Factors applicable under subsection (2) in relation to the creditor include –
(a) the degree of risk accepted by him, having regard to the value of any security provided; and

---

13 See also R, Lowe and G.F. Woodroffe *Consumer Law and Practice* (Sweet & Maxwell: 1991), pp. 361–3.
14 Defined in *Davies* below.

(b) his relationship to the debtor; and
(c) whether or not a colourable cash price was quoted for any goods or services included in the credit bargain.

(5) Factors applicable under subsection (2) in relation to a linked transaction include the question how far the transaction was reasonably required for the protection of debtor or creditor, or was in the interest of the debtor.

Cases on these sections have shown how hard it is to prove an 'extortionate' bargain. The borrowers are usually under such financial pressure that they represent poor risks to the lenders, and so harsh terms are deemed reasonable by the courts. In 1909 Darling J said: 'If you had to lend a mutton chop to a ravenous dog, on what terms would you lend it?' (*Jackson* v *Price* (1909) 25 TLR 106 at p. 108). This describes pretty well the modern approach too.

Davies and another v *Directloans Ltd.* [1986] 2 All ER 783

Davies agreed a mortgage with the loan company for £17,450, at an annual interest rate of 21.6% (the building society rate at the time varied from 11 to 15%). He was unable to repay the instalments, so he sold the house to redeem the mortgage and claimed that the interest rate was 'extortionate' under the Act.

Edward Nugee QC:

On these facts the question posed by s. 138 of the 1974 Act is whether the defendant has proved that the legal charge required the plaintiffs to make payments which were not grossly exorbitant. These words are not defined by the Act and must be given their ordinary meaning. 'Exorbitant' is defined by the *Shorter Oxford England Dictionary* as 'Exceeding ordinary or proper bounds; excessive, outrageously large'; 'grossly' is defined as 'excessively; flagrantly'. I am more than satisfied that the payments which the defendant required the plaintiffs to make in the present case fall far short of rendering the credit bargain constituted by the legal charge extortionate within the meaning of s. 138 of the 1974 Act. I take into account that the rate of interest was fixed throughout the term of the mortgage although the plaintiffs could of course redeem at any time if they could obtain finance more cheaply elsewhere or they wished to sell. But this is an inevitable feature of an agreement under which a loan is repayable by equal fixed instalments over a period of years and one that may operate in favour of either party...
  Sir John Donaldson MR said in *Wills* v *Wood* [1984] I CCLR 7 at 15:

'It is of course clear that the Consumer Credit Act 1974 gives and is intended to give the court the widest possible control over credit bargains which, for a variety of reasons might be considered 'extortionate'. But the word is 'extortionate', not 'unwise'. The jurisdiction seems to me to contemplate at least a substantial imbalance in bargaining powers of which one party has taken advantage.'

If the plaintiffs appear in retrospect to have been unwise, their lack of wisdom lay in contracting to buy the house at a time when their finances were not established on a sufficiently firm foundation. Given that initial decision, which was taken with the full benefit of advice from their own solicitor, I do not consider that it was unwise of them to have entered into the legal charge so as to enable them to complete the contract and I am wholly satisfied that the defendant did not, either then or at the earlier contract stage, take advantage of such imbalance in bargaining power as existed, and that there was nothing extortionate about the terms of the legal charge. Accordingly the plaintiffs' claim fails and I dismiss this action.

THE RIGHTS OF THE LENDER

The lender's rights in general

The lender has the right to:

1. hold the Charge Certificate (or title deeds, in unregistered land) as evidence of the mortgage;
2. take possession of the land, because he is either a lessee or has the rights of a lessee. Normally, the lender will only take possession if he is going to sell the land. If he is in possession, he also has the right to grant leases and accept their surrenders (s. 99, LPA 1925) but obviously this is rare;
3. insure, and reclaim the cost from the borrower;
4. if a mortgagee has lent money on more than one mortgage on a piece of land, the mortgagee may reserve the right to refuse to allow the borrower to redeem one mortgage without redeeming the other ('consolidation');
5. if the borrower defaults on the agreement by breaching one of the mortgage terms the lender may:
   (a) foreclose (a court order declaring the equity of redemption is at an end) – extremely rare;
   (b) appoint a receiver (more likely in a commercial mortgage);
   (c) sell the land.

The lender's power of sale

Law of Property Act 1925

Powers incident to estate or interest of mortgagee

101 (1) A mortgagee, where the mortgage is made by deed, shall, by virtue of this Act, have the following powers, to the like extent as if they had been in terms conferred by the mortgage deed, but not further (namely):
   (i) A power, when the mortgage money has become due, to sell, or to

concur with any other person in selling, the mortgaged property, or any part thereof, either subject to prior charges or not, and either together in lots, by public auction or by private contract, subject to such conditions respecting title, or evidence of title, or other matter, as the mortgagee thinks fit, with power to vary any contract for sale, and to buy in at an auction, or to rescind any contract for sale, and to re-sell, without being answerable for any loss occasioned thereby; and

(ii) A power, at any time after the date of the mortgage deed, to insure and keep insured against loss or damage by fire any building, or any effects of property of an insurable nature, whether affixed to the freehold or not, being or forming part of the property which or an estate or interest wherein is mortgaged, and the premiums paid for any such insurance shall be a charge on the mortgaged property or estate or interest, in addition to the mortgage money, and with the same priority, and with interest at the same rate, as the mortgage money; and

(iii) A power, when the mortgage money has become due, to appoint a receiver of the income of the mortgaged property, or any part thereof; or, if the mortgaged property consists of an interest in income, or of a rentcharge or an annual or other periodical sum, a receiver of that property of any part thereof; and

(iv) A power, while the mortgagee is in possession, to cut and sell timber and other trees ripe for cutting, and not planted or left standing for shelter or ornament, or to contract for any such cutting and sale, to be completed within any time not exceeding twelve months from the making of the contract.

Regulation of exercise of power of sale

103 A mortgagee shall not exercise the power of sale conferred by this Act unless and until –

(i) Notice requiring payment of the mortgage money has been served on the mortgagor or one of two or more mortgagors, and default has been made in payment of the mortgage money, or of part thereof for three months after such service; or

(ii) Some interest under the mortgage is in arrears and unpaid for two months after becoming due; or

(iii) There has been a breach of some provision contained in the mortgage deed or in this Act, or in an enactment replaced by this Act, and on the part of the mortgagor, or of some person concurring in making a mortgage, to be observed or performed, other than and besides a covenant for payment of the mortgage money or interest thereon.

Conveyance on sale

104 (1) A mortgagee exercising the power of sale conferred by this Act shall have power, by deed, to convey the property sold, for such estate and interest therein as he is by this Act authorised to sell or convey or may be the subject of the mortgage, freed from all estates, interests and rights to which the mortgage has priority, but subject to all estates, interests and rights which have priority to the mortgage.

(2) Where a conveyance is made in exercise of the power of sale conferred by this Act, or any enactment replaced by this Act, the title of the purchaser shall not be impeachable on the ground –

(a) that no case had arisen to authorise the sale; or

(b) that due notice was not given; or

(c) where the mortgage is made after the commencement of this Act, that leave of the court, when so required, was not obtained; or

(d) whether the mortgage was made before or after such commencement, that the power was otherwise improperly or irregularly exercised;

and a purchaser is not, either before or on conveyance, concerned to see or inquire whether a case has arisen to authorise the sale, or due notice has been given, or the power is otherwise properly and regularly exercised; but any person damnified[15] by an unauthorised, or improper, or irregular exercise of power shall have his remedy in damages against the person exercising the power.

Application of proceeds of sale

105 The money which is received by the mortgagee, arising from the sale, after discharge of prior incumbrances to which the sale is not made subject, if any, or after payment into court under this Act of a sum to meet any prior incumbrance, shall be held by him in trust to be applied by him, first, in payment of all costs, charges and expenses properly incurred by him as incident to the sale or any attempted sale, or otherwise; and secondly, in discharge of the mortgage money, interest, and costs, and other money, if any, due under the mortgage; and the residue of the money so received shall be paid to the person entitled to the mortgaged property, or authorised to give receipts for the proceeds of the sale thereof.

Social Trends No. 24 (HMSO: 1994)

In 1992 the number of [possession] warrants issued dropped for the first time since 1984 to 124,000, a seven per cent decrease on 1991. Despite this, the number of warrants executed increased to just over 62,000, including some which will have been issued in previous years. Between 1984 and 1992 warrants issued and executed both increased two-and-a-half times. [See Figs. 5.1 and 5.3 on p. 155]

Choosing the time of sale

Where there are mortgage arrears and the lender wishes to take possession and sell the property, there may be conflict over the timing of the sale. A borrower who wishes to delay sale may rely on the provisions of the Administration of Justice

---

15 'Suffering loss'.

Repossession!

Acts 1970 and 1973. The 1970 Act was introduced to give owner–occupiers[16] similar rights of security as tenants and s. 36 gives the court power to delay sale of a dwelling house if it appears that the borrower could repay 'the sums due under the mortgage' within a reasonable time. It soon became clear that the section failed to protect borrowers in the case of mortgages where the *whole* loan became 'due' in the event of instalment arrears. Section 8 of the 1973 Act therefore amended s. 36 so that 'sums due' refers only to outstanding instalments.

The extra time has gradually been extended by the courts in the face of recession. Further, in *Target Home Loans Ltd* v *Clothier* [1994] 1 All ER 439 (CA) the borrower was given three months' delay – not to repay the arrears in the normal way, but to find a purchaser and redeem the mortgage.

Regional Trends No. 27 (HMSO: 1994)

The fall in house prices has resulted in a significant number of owner–occupiers being affected by negative equity, that is where the size of the mortgage [loan] is greater than the value of the property. In the third quarter of 1993, it was estimated that 800 thousand households in England had negative equity, of which 60 per cent were in the South-East and 20 per cent in East Anglia and the South- West.

Where there is a negative equity, whether or not the repayments are in arrears, again the lender and borrower may disagree about sale, but here it is the borrower who may wish to sell in order to reduce their liabilities and the lender who may

---

16 It does not apply to any mortgage in respect of land other than a dwelling, but in any other action the court *may* adjourn possessions for a brief time.

Regional Trends No. 29 (HMSO: 1994)

Table 5.1 Mortgage lenders: number of mortgages, arrears and possessions

United Kingdom		Loans in arrears at end-period		Thousands
	Number of mortgages	By 6-12 months	By over 12 months	Properties taken into possession in period
1971	4,506	17.6		2.8
1976	5,322	16.0		5.0
1981	6,336	21.5		4.9
1986	8,138	52.1	13.0	24.1
1987	8,283	55.5	15.0	26.4
1988	8,564	42.8	10.3	18.5
1989	9,125	66.8	13.8	15.8
1990	9,415	123.1	36.1	43.9
1991	9,815	183.6	91.7	75.5
1992	9,922	205.0	147.0	68.5
1993	9,998	191.6	158.0	31.8

Source: Council of Mortgage Lenders

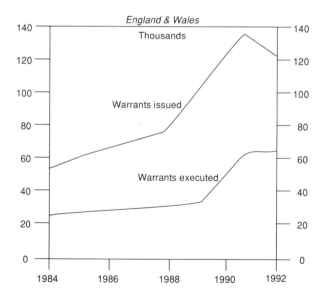

Fig. 5.3 Repossession of properties: warrants issued and executed
Source: Lord Chancellor's Department

wish to prevent sale at a price below the level of debt. Building societies have refused to allow borrowers to sell at a price below the mortgage loan and to carry the deficit on to another property, preferring instead to lease the house to cover interest repayments until the market improves.

Palk v *Mortgage Services Funding plc* [1993] 2 WLR 415 (CA), Sir Ronald Nicholls VC, Butler-Sloss LJ and Sir Michael Kerr

In this case the borrower's position was so dire in comparison with that of the lender that sale was ordered without the lender's consent under s. 91(2), Law of Property Act 1925 for the very first time. The debt stood at £409,000 and was increasing at the rate of about £43,000 a year; the house was worth £280,000 and the maximum yearly rent attainable was only £14,000. The value of the house could never catch up with the runaway interest on the debt.

Sir Donald Nicholls VC:
I have given two examples where the law imposes a duty on a mortgagee when he is exercising his powers: if he lets the property he must obtain a proper market rent, and if he sells he must obtain a proper market price. I confess I have difficulty in seeing why a mortgagee's duties in and about the exercise of his powers of letting and sale should be regarded as narrowly confined to these two duties...

In the present case Mortgage Services is exercising its rights over the house. It has obtained an order for possession, suspended at present. The company has embarked on a course of realisation, initially by letting the property with a sale to follow. This course is likely to be highly prejudicial to Mrs Palk's financial position as a borrower ... Unless good fortune shines on the parties, she is bound to suffer financially by a postponement of the sale. For its part Mortgage Services wishes to preserve the possibility of good fortune. Its commercial judgment is that it is likely to do better by waiting. In other words, it hopes that house prices will not merely rise but that they will do so at a rate which will compensate for the financial disadvantage suffered by postponing receipt of the proceeds of sale. And the company can always fall back on Mrs Palk's personal covenant for whatever it may be worth...

The question on this appeal is how ought the court to exercise its discretion under the statute in the particular circumstances...

He concluded that it was 'just and equitable' to order sale because of four factors:
(1) the gap between the annual interest payments and the maximum rental;
(2) a substantial (and unlikely) rise in house prices was the only possible solution to the problem;
(3) the borrower's loss far exceeded the lender's gain and was therefore oppressive to her;
(4) the mortgagee could still choose to buy the property itself and play its waiting game at its own risk.

Sir Michael Kerr noted that the court's power to order sale would only be exercised against the wishes of the lender 'in exceptional and extreme circumstances'.[17] This case, with Mrs Palk's indefinite 'financial haemorrhage', was a correct exercise of the court's discretion.

The question of family debt and repossession has inevitably been much in the public eye during the 1980s. Recent changes in economic and social life suggest that mortgage borrowers and lenders must come to terms with a new world:

R. Davis and Y. Dhooge *Living with Mortgage Arrears* (HMSO: 1993)

There is no such thing as a typical household in mortgage arrears. The reasons why households get into difficulties with their mortgages, their attitudes towards their debt and the strategies they adopt to deal with their situation vary enormously...

Lenders' policies for granting loans and for dealing with arrears need to be re-examined in the light of the social and economic environment in which they operate. The changing context of the 1990s has implications for the situations borrowers get into, the way they react to debt, and their ability to resolve their own situations. Compared to the 1980s, lenders have changed their approach to some extent, but not yet enough to deal with the growing volume of mortgage debt.

Lenders' approaches to granting mortgages are largely based on the assumption of secure income derived from stable salaried employment. This is becoming increasingly inappropriate to current economic conditions. We have identified changing employment patterns as the major cause of mortgage arrears. Unemployment is only part of the problem. In 1991, more than a million fewer men were employed in full-time jobs than ten years earlier. The number of part-time workers and women workers have both increased. The number of people who are self-employed has also grown. These trends are likely to continue, and will have a growing impact on borrowers' abilities to meet regular mortgage repayments. Once arrears have developed, a sustained period of stable income is required for arrears to be cleared. For those whose arrears have arisen through loss of income, there is often not much prospect of this.

Today's mortgage defaulters are generally in more complex situations than they were five or ten years ago. Firstly, many defaulters have been in debt for some time, and lenders and borrowers alike allow the situation to drag on without resolution. Because of the fall in house prices, selling or trading down is rarely an option for borrowers, and the ultimate solution for lenders of repossession is less attractive because they will in many cases be unable to recover the debt from resale of the property. Secondly, most defaulters have multiple debts, and have extended their mortgages, or taken out additional secured loans on their properties. This is to a large extent a legacy of the financial situation of the financial deregulation of the mid-1980s, and the involvement of brokers and other intermediaries who, in the view of some borrowers, encouraged and assisted them to enter into irresponsible borrowing.

---

17 However, it is unclear at this stage to what extent other borrowers are taking advantage of this precedent: see *Sunday Times*, 14 August 1994.

The attitudes of many borrowers with mortgage arrears are markedly different from those identified in previous research. In particular, they are less likely to blame themselves, and more likely to see themselves as victims of Government policy (in promoting owner–occupation, for example), or of the recession, or of the lending policies of their creditors. Furthermore, people who have multiple or long-term debts get used to living with debts as part of their own lives, and as a feature of society as a whole, and are therefore less likely to feel anxious about their debts.

A more relaxed attitude towards debt among defaulters combined with the perception that mortgage lenders are now more flexible towards arrears, has led to a shift of power away from the lender towards the borrower. Often defaulters feel that lenders' options are severely curtailed because of the extent of the arrears problem and the current state of the housing market. This has immediate implications for mortgage lenders. While there is certainly a need for greater flexibility in dealing with people in arrears, they must also recognise that their flexibility causes some borrowers to take fewer active steps to deal with their mortgage arrears...

This new world might spell the end of the 'real-property-mortgaged-to-a-building-society-owning democracy' as we have come to know it.

Reasonable care in exercising the power of sale

A mortgagee exercising the power of sale is not a trustee, but becomes a trustee of the money received from the sale and must hold the surplus money for the person next entitled, that is the next mortgagee or, if none, the borrower. However, the mortgagee selling repossessed land must exercise reasonable care.[18]

Cuckmere Brick Co v *Mutual Finance Ltd* [1971] 1 Ch 949 (CA)
Salmon, Cross and Cairns LJJ

It was alleged that the mortgagee sold the land for £44,000 at an auction without advertising that the land had planning permission for 100 flats. At first instance, Plowman J agreed that this was unreasonable: the price should have been around £65,000. The mortgagee appealed.

Cairns LJ:

The issues in this appeal are: (1) Does the duty of a mortgagee to a mortgagor on the sale of the mortgaged property include a duty to take reasonable care to obtain a proper price or is it sufficient for the mortgagee to act honestly and without a reckless disregard of the interests of the mortgagor? (2) Was the advertising of the auction without reference to the planning permission for flats (a) right; (b) an error of judgment; (c) negligent; or (d) reckless? (3) A similar question in relation to the

---

18 See also *Tse Kwong Lam* v *Wong Chit Sen* [1983] 1 WLR 1349 (PC) and *Parker-Tweedale* v *Dunbar Bank plc* [1991] AC 12 (CA).

refusal to postpone the auction. (4) If anybody on the defendants' side was at fault, was the fault that of the defendants themselves or of their agents Caering and Colyer, or both? (5) If the fault was that of the agents only, can it be attributed to the defendants? (6) If there was negligence for which the defendants are responsible, did the plaintiffs suffer any damage thereby? (7) If so, what value is to be attributed to the land in assessing the damages?

(1) I find it impossible satisfactorily to reconcile the authorities, but I think the balance of authority is in favour of a duty of care ... and I would hold that the present defendants had a duty to take reasonable care to obtain a proper price for the land in the interest of the mortgagors.

(2) I think there was abundant evidence to support the finding that the land should have been advertised for sale as land which had planning permission for building flats ... [and] if the permission for flats had been advertised a wider range of buyers might have attended the auction and a better price might have been obtained.

(3) When it came to the question of whether the auction should be postponed, everybody was fully alive to the existence of the planning permission for flats. If once it is accepted that a better price might have been obtained for flat-building than for house-building, I think it follows that it would have been wise to postpone the auction. And if it was negligent not to advertise the permission in the first instance then it was negligent not to postpone the auction and re-advertise. Not that there were no good reasons for pressing on with the sale: interest was accruing every day, the future of the market in land was uncertain, and people who had already shown some interest in buying might have lost interest if the sale had been put off. These were considerations of weight but I do not think they are sufficient to outweigh, in the mind of a reasonable man, the chance by postponement and re-advertising of getting a better price. I would therefore accept the judge's conclusion that in this respect too there was negligence on the defendants' side.

There was a breach of the duty to take reasonable care here, but it was held that there should be further enquiry into the real value of the land in order to assess the damages.

REFORM OF THE LAW OF MORTGAGES

The Law Commission (Report No. 204 1991)

2.5 The artificiality and complexity ... are largely attributable to problems in the structure of English mortgage law. In particular there are two broad structural problems to which most of the unnecessary complications in the law can be ascribed. First, English law recognises too many types of consensual mortgage or charge, and too many methods of creating some of the types. Secondly, the methods used to create legal and equitable mortgages in the present law give rise to inappropriate relationships between the parties, which have had to be modified by equity, by piecemeal statutory reform, and by contract...

3.1 It is central to our proposal for the creation of a new kind of mortgage that the attributes of the mortgage should be expressly defined by statute, rather than defined by reference to pre-existing forms of mortgage or by analogy to any other legal relationship...

3.2 The guiding principle we have adopted ... is that the only function of the mortgaged property is to provide security for the performance of the mortgagor's payment obligations. It follows from this that the nature and extent of the mortgagee's interest ought to be dictated by the need to preserve the value of the security and, where necessary, to enforce it...

The Report covers all areas of mortgage law, including the registration implications. Only a few of the summarised recommendations are included here.

10.2 All methods of consensually mortgaging or charging interests in land should be abolished and replaced by new forms of mortgage (the formal land mortgage and the informal land mortgage) the attributes of which would be expressly defined by statute and which would be the only permissible methods of mortgaging any interest in land whether legal or equitable.

The formal land mortgage would be the equivalent of today's legal mortgage and, in registered land, would have to be registered on the Land Register. The informal mortgage would be 'any consensual security over any interest in land that does not amount to a formal land mortgage' (para. 10.7). The mortgagee in the latter would only be able to enforce their security by going to court (para. 10.8).

10.4 The statutory provisions defining the rights, power, duties and obligations of the parties to a land mortgage should be categorised as either 'variable' or 'overriding'. Variable provisions should be variable or excludable, either directly by an express term of the mortgage or indirectly by necessary implication from any express term. Overriding provisions should apply notwithstanding any provision to the contrary contained in the mortgage or in any other instrument. Any provision of a mortgage or any other instrument should be void to the extent that it (i) purports to impose a liability which has the effect of allowing the mortgagee to escape or mitigate the consequences of any overriding provision or to be reimbursed for the consequences of complying with it or (ii) has the effect of preventing or discouraging the mortgagor or any other person from enforcing or taking advantage of an overriding provision.

10.5 The rights, remedies and powers of a mortgagee under a land mortgage should be expressly stated to be exercisable only in good faith and for the purposes of protecting or enforcing the security. This should apply to all the mortgagee's rights, remedies and powers, whether derived from statute, contract or elsewhere.

10.16 There should be a class of protected mortgage consisting of all formal and informal land mortgages of any interest in land which includes a dwelling house except those where either (a) the mortgagee is a body corporate, or (b) enforcement of the mortgage would not affect the occupation of the dwelling-house or (c) the dwelling-house is occupied under a service tenancy.

10.17 The front page of a protected land mortgage should be in a form to be prescribed by regulations. The document should set out all the statutorily implied overriding and variable mortgage provisions (as varied, in the case of variable provisions) and also comply with regulations to be made about form and content of protected mortgages...

10.37 If the mortgage is a protected mortgage, the mortgagee should not be entitled to exercise the power of sale without leave of the court [having served an 'enforcement notice' – para. 10.39].

The Report includes details of the proposed variable and overriding terms. Variable terms include provisions for insurance and repair. Overriding terms include a provision that the mortgagor could grant leases (although these would not bind the mortgagee unless he had consented). It also proposes (para. 10.57) that the jurisdiction in equity and under the Consumer Credit Act to set aside unconscionable terms should be codified.

There is at this point no indication that legislation is forthcoming to implement these recommendations.

6 Easements and profits

INTRODUCTION

It has already been pointed out (see Chapter 2) that land is a particular kind of property: interests in land can be in permanent physical contact unlike, for example, cars or stocks and shares. Because of this, it is inevitable that there are arguments about boundaries, but these are often within the category of tort law, such as trespass to land.

Because of the proximity of one piece of land to its neighbour, and the potential flexibility of land use, it is also natural that rights should emerge to use a neighbour's land for certain purposes – such as to walk over it (an easement), or to fish from it (a profit). Often, of course, these activities are simply a question of good neighbourliness, but because of the value of land they have, for centuries, been capable of formal legal protection. These rights are categorised as easements and profits. They benefit anyone who buys the 'dominant' land or 'tenement' and burden anyone who buys the 'servient' land (subject to the rules about registration and notice). They may be attached to any interest in land, including a leasehold interest. Thus, a tenant may own the dominant land, and enjoy an easement over her landlord's remaining land. There are many examples of this, including *Liverpool City Council* v *Irwin* (1977) (see below at pp.172–3).

Easements and profits usually confer positive rights, which are rights to do something (such as walk along a path or take firewood). There are also 'negative' easements, which require the owner of the servient tenement not to do something, for example not to obstruct the passage of light to a window. There is, in addition, the 'spurious easement of fencing', which is the servient owner's duty to fence his land as in *Crow* v *Wood* [1971] 1 QB 77.

Even when the existence of an easement is not in argument, there may be debate over the extent of it. *London and Suburban Land and Building Co (Holdings) Ltd* v *Carey* (1992) 62 P & CR 480 is an example. The owner of an easement giving the right of access along a road on the servient land claimed she also had the right to load and unload her lorries on the road. Millett J denied this because a right to pass does not necessarily include a right to stop, especially on the facts of this case where there was also a forecourt for unloading.

If an easement or a profit is wrongly interfered with, the owner may sue for an injunction to stop the interference and/or damages, or may put matters right personally. The latter is called 'abatement' and only reasonable force may be used.

It is because property in land is 'exclusive'[1] that it is necessary to recognise legal rights for other people to enter and use the land. This is true even for large estates in private ownership in rural areas. There could, however, be a different approach altogether. In Sweden, for example, there is an ancient presumption of a right to walk on any land:

National Board of Urban Planning *Physical Planning in Sweden* (Boktryckeri: 1972)

A fundamental legal principle in Sweden is the so-called right-of-way prerogative. The right-of-way gives each and every person the right to pass over land without the permission of the owner. The provision is based on ancient custom and is affected by only a very few provisions in modern legislation.

But this right is not unlimited. It is unlawful to exercise this prerogative in such a way that it causes the owner of the land appreciable material damage or disturbs his privacy. It is forbidden to walk through a field of growing crops or through the garden of an occupied dwelling...

As it is forbidden to pass through the garden of [a] house without the permission of the owner, the right-of-way prerogative is null and void in the case of such land as that on which leisure housing is built near lake or sea shores. This means that the access of the general public to the shores of the lakes or beaches can be barred, if leisure housing is built near lake or sea shores. In order to prevent [this] ... it is possible, pursuant to the Nature Conservation Act, to forbid building within 300 metres of a lake shore or sea beach. On the strength of this regulation, a great many of Sweden's shore stretches are safeguarded against building.

THE CHARACTERISTICS OF EASEMENTS AND PROFITS

Easements

S.G. Maurice *Gale on Easements* 15th edn (Sweet & Maxwell: 1988)

An easement was defined by Lord Esher MR in *Metropolitan Railway* v *Fowler* [1893] AC 416 as 'some right which a person has over land which is not his own' but this definition lacks precision, as not every right which one has over another's land is necessarily an easement, and perhaps no precise definition is possible. The question of easement or no easement usually arises where (1) the right has been

---

1 On property in land as an exclusive right, see Chapter 1 at pp. 23–4 and Chapter 3.

granted and (a) the allegedly dominant tenement or the allegedly servient tenement has since changed hands or (b) the grantee of the right seeks to restrain obstruction by a stranger to the allegedly servient tenement; or (2) a 'right' long enjoyed is alleged to have been acquired, by prescription, or lost grant, as an easement. In such cases it is safer to try to discover the essential characteristics of an easement, and see whether the right in question has them, than to rely on some pretended definition which may or may not be wholly accurate.

The four 'essential characteristics' of easements originally set out in *Gale* above were judicially approved in the next case.[2] (Many of the cases in this chapter illustrate the influence of academics in this area of law.)

In Re Ellenborough Park [1956] 1 Ch 131 (CA) Evershed MR, Birkett and Romer LJJ

The owners of nearby houses claimed the right of compensation after the war for loss of their property right – to walk in and enjoy the park. They could only win compensation if the right amounted to an easement, not merely a contractual licence.

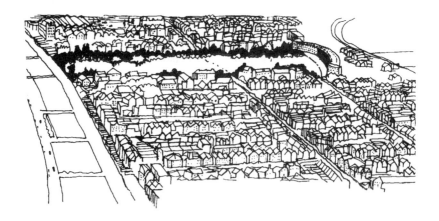

Ellenborough Park, Weston-super-Mare

Lord Evershed MR:

It is clear ... that, if the house owners are now entitled to an enforceable right in respect of the use and enjoyment of Ellenborough Park, that right must have the character and quality of an easement as understood by, and known to, our law. It has, therefore, been necessary for us to consider carefully the qualities and

---

2 See also AWB Simpson (1967) 83 LQR 240 on *Gale* as an authority.

characteristics of easements, and, for such purpose, to look back into the history of that category of incorporeal rights in the development of real property law...[3]

For the purposes of the argument before us Mr Cross and Mr Goff were content to adopt, as correct, the four characteristics formulated in Dr Cheshire's *Modern Real Property*, 7th edn, pp. 456 *et seq*. They are (1) there must be a dominant and a servient tenement; (2) an easement must 'accommodate' the dominant tenement; (3) dominant and servient owners must be different persons; and (4) a right over land cannot amount to an easement, unless it is capable of forming the subject-matter of a grant.

The four characteristics stated by Dr Cheshire correspond with the qualities discussed by Gale in his second chapter ... Two of the four may be disregarded for present purposes, namely, the first and third ... The exact significance of [the] fourth and last condition is, at first sight perhaps, not entirely clear.[4] As between the original parties to the 'grant', it is not in doubt that rights of this kind would be capable of taking effect by way of contract or licence. But ... the cognate questions involved under this condition are: whether the rights purported to be given are expressed in terms of too wide and vague a character; whether, if and so far as effective, such rights would amount to rights of joint occupation or would substantially deprive the park owners of proprietorship or legal possession; whether, if and so far as effective, such rights constitute mere rights of recreation, possessing no quality of utility or benefit; and on such grounds cannot qualify as an easement...

We pass, accordingly, to a consideration of the first of Dr Cheshire's conditions – that of the accommodation of the alleged dominant tenements by the rights as we have interpreted them. For it was one of the main submissions by Mr Cross on behalf of the appellant that the right of full enjoyment of the park, granted to the purchaser by the conveyance of December 23, 1864, was insufficiently connected with the enjoyment of the property conveyed, in that it did not subserve some use which was to be made of that property; and that such a right accordingly could not exist in law as an easement. In this part of his argument Mr Cross was invoking a principle which is, in our judgment, of unchallengeable authority, expounded, in somewhat varying language, in many judicial utterances, of which the judgments in *Ackroyd* v *Smith* [(1850) 10 CB 164] are, perhaps, most commonly cited. We think it unnecessary to review the authorities in which the principle has been applied; for the effect of the decisions is stated with accuracy in Dr Cheshire's *Modern Real Property*, 7th edn, at p. 457. After pointing out that 'one of the fundamental principles concerning easements is that they must be not only appurtenant to a dominant tenement, but also connected with the normal enjoyment of the dominant tenement' and referring to certain citations in support of that proposition the author proceeded: 'We may expand the statement of the principle thus: a right enjoyed by one over the land of another does not possess the status of an easement unless it accommodates and serves the dominant tenement, and is reasonably necessary for the better enjoyment of that tenement, for if it has no necessary connexion therewith, although it confers an advantage upon the owner and renders his

---

3 An 'incorporeal' right (or hereditament) is an intangible right over land.
4 It can only really be grasped by reading the cases, such as those below.

ownership of the land more valuable, it is not an easement at all, but a mere contractual right personal to and only enforceable between the two contracting parties.' ...

It is clear that the right did, in some degree, enhance the value of the property, and this consideration cannot be dismissed as wholly irrelevant. It is, of course, a point to be noted; but we agree with Mr Cross's submission that it is in no way decisive of the problem; it is not sufficient to show that the right increased the value of the property conveyed, unless it is also shown that it was connected with the normal enjoyment of that property. It appears to us that the question whether or not this connexion exists is primarily one of fact, and depends largely on the nature of the alleged dominant tenement and the nature of the right granted...

The park became a communal garden for the benefit and enjoyment of those whose houses adjoined it or were in its close proximity. Its flower beds, lawns and walks were calculated to afford all the amenities which it is the purpose of the garden of a house to provide: and, apart from the fact that these amenities extended to a number of householders instead of being confined to one (which on this aspect of the case is immaterial), we can see no difference in principle between Ellenborough Park and a garden in the ordinary signification of that word. It is the collective garden of the neighbouring houses, to whose use it was dedicated by the owners of the estate and as such amply satisfied, in our judgment, the requirement of connexion with the dominant tenements to which it is appurtenant...

We turn next to Dr Cheshire's fourth condition for an easement – that the right must be capable of forming the subject-matter of a grant. As we have earlier stated, satisfaction of the condition in the present case depends on a consideration of the questions whether the right conferred is too wide and vague, whether it is inconsistent with the proprietorship or possession of the alleged servient owners, and whether it is a mere right of recreation without utility or benefit.

To the first of these questions the interpretation which we have to the ... deed provides, in our judgment, the answer; for we have construed the right conferred as being both well defined and commonly understood. In these essential respects the right may be said to be distinct from the indefinite and unregulated privilege which, we think, would ordinarily be understood by the Latin term '*jus spatiandi*', a privilege of wandering at will over all and every part of another's field or park, and which, though easily intelligible as the subject-matter of a personal licence, is something substantially different from the subject-matter of the grant in question, namely, the provision for a limited number of houses in a uniform crescent of one single large but private garden.

Our interpretation of the deed also provides, we think, the answer to the second question; for the right conferred no more amounts to a joint occupation of the park with its owners, no more excludes the proprietorship or possession of the latter, than a right of way granted through a passage, or than the use by the public of the gardens of Lincoln's Inn Fields (to take one of our former examples) amount to joint occupation of that garden with the London County Council, or involve an inconsistency with the possession or proprietorship of the council as lessees. It is conceded that, in any event, the plaintiff owners of the park are entitled to cut the timber growing on the park and to retain its proceeds. We have said that in our judgment, under the deed, the flowers and shrubs grown in the garden are equally the park owner's property. We see nothing repugnant to a man's proprietorship or possession of a piece of land that he should decide to make it and maintain it as an ornamental garden, and should grant rights to a limited number of other persons to come into it for the enjoyment of its facilities...

As appears from what has been stated earlier, the right to the full enjoyment of Ellenborough Park, which was granted by the 1864 and other relevant conveyances, was, in substance, no more tha[n] a right to use the park as a garden in the way in which gardens are commonly used. In a sense, no doubt, such a right includes something of a *jus spatiandi*, inasmuch as it involves the principle of wandering at will round each part of the garden, except of course, such parts as comprise flower beds, or are laid out for some other purpose, which renders walking impossible or unsuitable. We doubt, nevertheless, whether the right to use and enjoy a garden in this manner can with accuracy be said to constitute a mere *jus spatiandi*...

The Court of Appeal thus 'had little difficulty in applying the terminology of easements to the civilised user by civilised people of a communal garden situated in an excessively bourgeois location ...' Gray *Elements of Land Law* (Butterworths: 1993 2nd edition) at p. 1068.

The easement must be 'appurtenant'

The rule that an easement must be attached to a dominant tenement (cannot 'lie in gross') has recently been affirmed by the Court of Appeal:

London and Blenheim Estates Ltd v *Ladbroke Retail Parks Ltd* [1993] 4 All ER 157 (CA), Ralph Gibson, Beldam and Peter Gibson LJJ

The plaintiffs bought land with an easement to park cars on land retained by the seller.[5] They also had the right to buy other (unspecified) land from the seller and to attach the easement also to this new land providing they gave notice within five years of the purchase. They duly bought another piece of land. By the time they gave notice (within the five years), the defendants had become the owner of the servient land. The defendants denied the easement in relation to the new land because there had been no dominant tenement at the time of the grant. The plaintiffs argued that the right was either an equitable easement or an estate contract (an enforceable right to a legal easement).

Peter Gibson LJ:
It is trite law that there can be no easement in gross...

None of the ... authorities cited to us by Sir William [for the plaintiffs] seems to me to lend support to his submission that the absence of an identified dominant

---

5 On the issue of the right to park as an easement, S. Bridge comments that 'The courts have drawn a single yellow line. Sometimes you can park by right of an easement, and sometimes you can't' (1994) CLJ 229 at 231.

tenement was not fatal to his case on both estate contract and on equitable easement.

If one asks why the law should require that there should be a dominant tenement before there can be a grant, or a contract for the grant, of an easement sufficient to create an interest in land binding successors in title to the servient land, the answer would appear to lie in the policy against encumbering land with burdens of uncertain extent. As was said by Fox LJ in *Ashburn Anstalt* v *Arnold* [1988] 2 All ER 147 at 167: 'In matters relating to the title to land, certainty is of prime importance'.[6] A further related answer lies in the reluctance of the law to recognise new forms of burden on property conferring more than contractual rights ... A right intended as an easement and attached to a servient tenement before the dominant tenement is identified would, in my view, be an incident of a novel kind.

Thus, the easement could only have come into existence had the notice been given before the alleged servient land changed hands.

The rule that easements cannot exist without a dominant tenement has been criticised:

M.F. Sturley 'Easements in Gross' 96 *LQR* (1980) 55

Conclusions

This survey of the rule against easements in gross leads to the conlusion that it exists on the weakest of authority for reasons that are no longer compelling. The judicial statements cited for the proposition are either unreasoned *dicta* or essentially irrelevant. (In the only decision which is directly on point, the Court of King's Bench actually permitted an easement in gross [*Senhouse* v *Christian* (1787) 1 TR 560; 99 Eng Rep 1251 (KB)].)

It was in Gale's treatise on easements that the campaign for the rule effectively began, and ironically enough the current edition of *Gale on Easements* is now the last authority to cast any doubt on the rule's position in English law [14th edn, 1972, pp. 7–8, 42]...

One important policy of the law which has been evident for centuries is the encouragement of maximum utilisation of land. This was evident in the medieval developments to eliminate restrictions on alienability, and evident in the passage of the 1925 legislation (such as the Settled Land Act).[7] In the nineteenth century, when changing industrial and commercial needs required a more refined law of easements than Gale had found in 1839, this policy was a principle force behind the rule against easements in gross. At that time, easements in gross would have been clogs on title doing more to restrict the use of land than to benefit it. Today, though, the nineteenth-century objections are outdated, and the same policy of encouraging maximum utilisation of land should be applied to permit easements in gross. Constant repetition should not be sufficient to support a rule without authority or justification.

---

6 See also p. 290.
7 See Chapter 8.

Clearly, the Court of Appeal is not in a mood currently to accept this argument. In some US jurisdictions, however, it is possible to have easements without a dominant tenement:

Maranatha Settlement Association v *Evans* 385 Pa 208, 122A 2d 679 (1956)

Stern CJ:

The sole question involved in this appeal is whether a bathing right, granted in deeds to purchasers of certain lots, constituted a licence, an easement in gross, or an easement appurtenant. We are of opinion that the court below correctly decided that it was an easement appurtenant.

The [Evans-Yale] corporation, having constructed a swimming pool on the tract, inserted in all its deeds to purchasers of the lots a provision that 'The grantee and his immediate family only, shall enjoy the free use of the swimming pool.' However, plaintiff ... which ... received title to the tract from Evans-Yale ... forbade defendants, the then owners of some of the lots, from enjoying the use of the pool, claiming that the privilege was limited to the immediate grantees from Evans-Yale ... on the ground that it was merely a license or easement in gross and did not pass to the assignees of the original purchasers. Defendants, on the other hand, interpreted the grant of the privilege as extending to them, their heirs and assigns, claiming that it attached to the estates and not merely to the persons of the owners of the lots, in short, that it was an easement appurtenant...

The extent of the grant ... depends entirely on the intent of the parties as determined by a fair interpretation of the language employed and consideration of all the attendant circumstances. So viewing the question it seems utterly impossible to believe that the intention was to give the privilege of bathing in the pool only to the original purchasers of the lots as a mere easement in gross, much less a revocable license. It may well be asked why should the right have been given to the original purchasers as individuals wholly apart from their status as owners of the neighbouring lots in view of the fact that such a purchaser might remain the owner merely for a very short time and then deed the title to an assignee, in which case, if plaintiff's position were correct, he would still have the right to bathe in the pool as possessing an easement in gross, but on the other hand the new owner of the property and all subsequent owners and occupants would have no right to the bathing privilege at all...

Easements must lie in grant

The fourth of Cheshire's required characteristics is that the easement or profit must 'lie in grant', that it must fit into the general category as defined by past cases. This is a question of policy in each case, and the courts' view of policy is reflected in virtually every case in this chapter, and especially in the cases on storage (see pp. 179–82).

There are two famous quotations:

'Incidents of a novel kind cannot be devised and attached to property at the fancy or caprice of any owner.'

(Lord Brougham LC, 1834)

'The category of easements must alter and expand with the changes that take place in the circumstances of mankind.'

(Lord St Leonards LC, 1852)

An illustration of the law accepting the 'changes that take place in the circumstances of mankind' is *Dowty Boulton Paul Ltd* v *Wolverhampton Corporation (No 2)* [1976] 1 Ch 13 (CA), where it was held that there could be an easement of a right to use an airfield: 'I do not see in principle why such a right cannot exist as an easement. A tendency in the past to freeze the categories of easements has been overtaken by the decision in *Re Ellenborough Park*' (Russell LJ, 23).

The following cases demonstrate how the courts may respond to claims to new easements.

Protection from the weather

Phipps v *Pears* [1965] 1 QB 76 (CA) Lord Denning MR, Pearson and Salmon LJJ

(This case is also relevant to s. 62, Law of Property Act 1925 – see p. 177 below).

Lord Denning MR:

So there were the two houses – new No. 16 and old No. 14 – standing side by side. In 1962, the Warwick Corporation made an order for the demolition of old No. 14, Market Street, because it was below the required standard. It was, I suppose, unfit for human habitation.[8] In consequence, the governors of the Lord Leycester Hospital demolished it. And when they did so, there was left exposed the flank wall of new No. 16. This was in a very rough state. It had never been pointed. Indeed, it could not have been because of the way it was built, flat up against the old No. 14. So it was not weatherproof. The result was that the rain got in and during the winter it froze and caused cracks in the wall. The plaintiff seeks to recover for the damage done [an argument for an easement of support having failed]...

The plaintiff said ... that at any rate his house No. 16 was entitled to protection from the weather. So long as No. 14 was there, it afforded excellent protection for No. 16 from rain and frost. By pulling down No. 14, the defendant, he said, had infringed his right of protection from the weather. This right he said was analogous to the right of support...

[A] right to protection from the weather (if it exists) is entirely negative. It is a right to stop your neighbour pulling down his own house. Seeing that it is a negative

---

8 See Chapter 4, pp. 96–103.

easement, it must be looked at with caution. Because the law has been very chary of creating any new negative easements.

Take this simple instance: Suppose you have a fine view from your house. You have enjoyed the view for many years. It adds greatly to the value of your house. But if your neighbour chooses to despoil it, by building up and blocking it, you have no redress. There is no such right known to the law as a right to a prospect or a view, see *Bland* v *Moseley* (1587) cited by Lord Coke in *Aldred's* case [(1610) 9 Co Rep 57b]. The only way in which you can keep the view from your house is to get your neighbour to make a covenant with you that he will not build so as to block your view.[9]

The reason underlying these instances is that if such an easement were to be permitted, it would unduly restrict your neighbour in his enjoyment of his own land. It would hamper legitimate development, see *Dalton* v *Angus* [(1881) 6 App. Ca. 740] per Lord Blackburn. Likewise here, if we were to stop a man pulling down his house, we would put a brake on desirable improvement. Every man is entitled to pull down his house if he likes. If it exposes your house to the weather, that is your misfortune. It is not wrong on his part ... There is no such easement known to the law as an easement to be protected from the weather...

However an aggrieved neighbour in a semi-detached or terraced property may yet find a solution:

Bradburn v *Lindsay* [1983] 2 All ER 408[10]

The plaintiff successfully claimed £2,000 damages for negligence in *tort law*. His neighbour had failed to prevent dry rot coming through the party wall.

Blackett-Ord VC:

The case was put on the footing that she [the owner of No. 53] should have taken steps to prevent the dry rot spreading through to No. 55, and also should have maintained it so as to provide support and protection for No. 55...

I find that the defendant should reasonably have appreciated the danger to No. 55 from the dry rot and from the lack of repair of No. 53, and that there were steps which she could reasonably have taken to prevent the damage occurring. In my judgment she owed a duty to the plaintiffs to take reasonable steps. She failed to do so and, therefore, she is liable for the damage caused...

In 1966 the Law Commission (14th Report, Cmnd. 3100) recommended that there should be an easement to be sheltered by an adjacent building: paras 96, 99.

---

9 See Chapter 7.
10 See also A.J. Waite (1987) 51 Conv 47.

Rights in tower blocks or flats

Liverpool City Council v *Irwin* [1977] AC 239 (HL)
Lords Wilberforce, Cross, Salmon, Edmund-Davies, Fraser

The council tenants complained of their lifts being constantly out of order, lack of lighting on, and dangerous conditions of, the stairs, and frequent blockage of the rubbish chutes. The judge said he was appalled by the condition of the premises. There was no written lease, merely 'Rules for Tenants'. They stopped paying rent, and the council started proceedings for possession.

The tenants won their counterclaim for damages at first instance, but the Court of Appeal allowed the council's appeal. In the House of Lords:

Lord Wilberforce:

My Lords this case is of general importance, since it concerns the obligations of local authority, and indeed other, landlords as regards high rise or multi-storey dwellings towards the tenants of these dwellings. Haigh Heights, Liverpool, is one of several recently erected tower blocks in the district of Everton. It has some 70 dwelling units in it. It was erected 10 years ago following a slum clearance programme at considerable cost and was then, no doubt, thought to mark an advance in housing standards. Unfortunately, it has since turned out that effective slum clearance depends upon more than expenditure upon steel and concrete. There are human factors involved too, and it is these which seem to have failed...

We start with the fact that the demise is useless unless access is obtained by the staircase; we can add that, having regard to the height of the block, and the family nature of the dwellings, the demise would be useless without a lift service; we can continue that, there being rubbish chutes built into the structures and no other means of disposing of light rubbish, there must be a right to use the chutes. The question to be answered – and it is the only question in this case – is what is to be the legal relationship between landlord and tenant as regards these matters.

There can be no doubt that there must be implied (i) an easement for the tenants and their licensees to use the stairs, (ii) a right in the nature of an easement[11] to use the lifts, (iii) an easement to use the rubbish chutes.

But are these easements to be accompanied by any obligation upon the landlord, and what obligation? There seem to be two alternatives. The first, for which the council contends, is for an easement coupled with no legal obligation, except as may arise under the Occupiers' Liability Act 1957 as regards the safety of those using the facilities, and possibly such other liability as might exist under the ordinary law of tort. The alternative is for easements coupled with some obligation on the part of the landlords as regards the maintenance of the subject of them, so that they are available for use.

My Lords, in order to be able to choose between these, it is necessary to define what test is to be applied, and I do not find this difficult. In my opinion such obligation should be read into the contract as the nature of the contract itself implicitly requires, no more, no less: a test, in other words, of necessity...

---

11 Is a 'right in the nature of an easement' an easement?

All these are not just facilities, or conveniences provided at discretion: they are essentials of the tenancy without which life in the dwellings, as a tenant, is not possible. To leave the landlord free of contractual obligation as regards these matters, and subject only to administrative or political pressure, is, in my opinion, inconsistent totally with the nature of this relationship. The subject matter of the lease (high-rise blocks) and the relationship created by the tenancy demand, of their nature, some contractual obligation on the landlord ...

It remains to define the standard. My Lords, if, as I think, the test of the existence of the term is necessity, the standard must surely not exceed what is necessary having regard to the circumstances. To imply an absolute obligation to repair would go beyond what is a necessary legal incident and would indeed be unreasonable. An obligation to take reasonable care to keep in reasonable repair and usability is what fits the requirements of the case...

[In the case of lighting areas with no natural light] the grant should carry with it an obligation to take reasonable care to maintain adequate lighting, comparable to the obligation as regards the lifts...

This decision was distinguished in *Duke of Westminster* v *Guild* [1984] 3 WLR 630.[12] Here, the tenant had to repair a drain at a cost of £17,000, and claimed the landlord should pay because it was essential to the use of the leased property. However, the Court of Appeal held that the case was different from *Irwin*'s since here all the terms of the lease were in writing, and this case did not concern a tower block.

The easement of light

The easement of light is a negative easement of great age (it is often called 'ancient lights'). Today, the law is contained in the Rights of Light Act 1959. It is still hard to decide *how much* light a dominant owner is entitled to.

Colls v Home and Colonial Stores Ltd [1904] AC 179 (HL) Lord Halsbury LC, Lord Shand, Lord Davey, Lord Robertson, Lord Macnaghten and Lord Lindley

Much of the case is concerned with the Prescription Act 1832, by which twenty years' enjoyment of light can give rise to an easement of light (see p. 187). However, the House also had to decide whether a proposed building, by reducing available light, would infringe the claimed easement.

Lord Lindley:

My Lords, Joyce J, who tried this case and was asked to grant an injunction before the defendant's building had been erected, considered that although the buildings would sensibly diminish the plaintiff's light, the diminution would not materially affect his comfort or convenience, and would not be sufficient to entitle the plaintiffs to

---

12 See also P. Jackson (1985) 49 Conv 66.

any relief, and he dismissed their action. The Court of Appeal, however, took a different view, and granted a mandatory injunction ordering the defendant to pull down part of his building which had been completed after the injunction had been refused. Hence the appeal to Your Lordships...

[G]enerally speaking an owner of ancient lights is entitled to sufficient light according to the ordinary notions of mankind for the comfortable use and enjoyment of his house as a dwelling-house, if it is a dwelling-house, or for the beneficial use and occupation of the house if it is a warehouse, a shop, or other place of business ... The expressions 'the ordinary notions of mankind', 'comfortable use and enjoyment', and 'beneficial use and occupation' introduce elements of uncertainty; but similar uncertainty has always existed and exists still in all cases of nuisance, and in this country an obstruction of light has commonly been regarded as a nuisance, although the right to light has been regarded as a peculiar kind of easement.

If a more absolute standard had been adopted in all cases, certainty would, no doubt, have been gained; but the consequences would frequently have been very oppressive on the owner of the servient tenement. The owner of the servient tenement could have done nothing on his own land which, in fact, diminished the light acquired by his neighbour, even if all of it was not wanted for comfortable enjoyment or business purposes. It would follow that the owner of a piece of vacant land opposite to a house in an ordinary street could not build on it at all after twenty years. The adherence to the old but uncertain standard of comfort and convenience avoids the danger of oppression and extortion, and renders it necessary to take a wider view of each case, especially when an injunction is asked for...

The general principle ... appears to be that the right to light is in truth no more than a right to be protected against a particular form of nuisance, and that an action for the obstruction of light which has in fact been used and enjoyed for twenty years without interruption or written consent cannot be sustained unless the obstruction amounts to an actionable nuisance ... There are elements of uncertainty which render it impossible to lay down any definite rule applicable to all cases... But, notwithstanding these elements of uncertainty, the good sense of judges and juries[13] may be relied upon for adequately protecting rights to light on the one hand and freedom from unnecessary burdens on the other...

In this case the Court of Appeal have, in my opinion, gone too far, and the appeal ought to be allowed with costs here and below...

The more modern case below sheds a little more light on the question:

Lyme Valley Squash Club Ltd v *Newcastle-under-Lyme Borough Council & Another* [1985] 2 All ER 405

Blackett-Ord VC:

I hold therefore that the [squash club] company has a right to light to its windows. Then the questions arise which are not the easiest in the case. Has the right been

---

13 Does the modern absence of juries from civil cases make any difference here?

infringed? Or, rather, will the right be infringed by the erection of the proposed building? And if it will be, what effect will that have on the value of the club? And, thirdly, taking those matters into account, to what remedy, if any, is the club entitled?

As far as the question of infringement is concerned, light experts gave evidence on both sides. They disagreed as to the amount of natural light now being received into the bar lounge through the windows at table height, but they were in substantial agreement as to the amount of light that would be left if the new building were to be erected; something like 30% or 35%, a theoretical maximum, as against something like 50%, which, though not by any means a hard and fast rule, has been regarded in some cases by the courts as a minimum.

But, of course, in cases concerning light there are always many factors to take into account. What light does a bar lounge actually need? ... In my judgment the reduction of daylight proposed will not seriously affect the amenities of the club. I think it must follow from that, I think, that it will not very seriously affect its value either. But I should deal with the valuer's evidence...

In my judgment, the defendants are threatening an actionable interference with the plaintiff's rights, but, in all the circumstances, the case is not one for the grant of an injunction. The court has, however, under the successor to Lord Cairn's Act, jurisdiction to grant damages in lieu of an injunction, and I think that the plaintiff club would be properly compensated by an award of damages, which I would assess at £10,000.

New technology may raise the possibility of 'modern' lights.

D.N. Zillman and R. Deeny 'Legal Aspects of Solar Energy Development' 25 *Ariz St L Jo* (1976) 26[14]

The solar homeowner needs the protection of a negative easement. He must be able to prevent the owner of the servient estate from blocking his access to direct sunlight. An express agreement between landowners can solve this problem.

Under any set of circumstances it would seem desirable to secure an express or consensual easement. But the newness of solar technology may work against the landowner. His neighbor, who may be quite willing to grant a portion of his land for a footpath or a driveway, may be unsure of the consequences of relinquishing rights to a portion of the airspace over his land. The servient owner may be giving up the right to construct a second storey to his residence or to plant trees. His offer of a short-term easement may not be encouraging to the solar energy user contemplating a $10,000 investment. The solar energy user must also consider the types of uses to which he may later put the property. If initially he wishes only to provide sufficient panelling for water heating, he may need to renegotiate the easement if he later converts to solar space heating and cooling. The solar energy user must also consider how many separate landowners must join in the easement. The construction of a 14-storey building two lots over may nullify easement agreements with the immediately adjoining neighbor. The easement's virtue, of course, may be its relative permanency...

---

14 On new technology and land law, see also Chapter 2 at p. 51.

Overall, the burdens facing the potential solar energy user seeking an easement may be substantial. But if adjoining property owners are not forbidden by other means (restrictive covenants, zoning) from screening the solar user's property, resorts to easements may be necessary. One possible way to avoid the painstaking individual agreement approach would be to create statutory easements. Such easements have been legalised for power companies and cable television.

Profits

Profits are rights to 'take and carry away' something from another's land, such as the ancient rights of common (to graze animals, or take fuel). Rights of common must now be registered, although the Commons Registration Act 1965 seems to have become largely a mechanism to destroy rather than to preserve common rights.[15] Unlike easements, profits do not have to be attached to dominant land but can exist 'in gross'.

The law of profits is couched in particularly poetic legal language:

Sir Robert Megarry and H.W.R. Wade *The Law of Real Property* (Stevens: 1984)

A profit of pasture is a true profit; the taking and carrying away is effected by means of the mouths and stomachs of the cattle in question.

1. *Forms of profit* A profit of pasture may exist in the following forms.
    (a) *Appendant.*[16] A profit of pasture appendant is limited to horses, oxen, cows and sheep, The numerical test is that of levancy and couchancy.[17]
    (b) *Appurtenant.*[18] A profit of pasture appurtenant is not confined to any particular animals, but depends on the terms of the grant ... Thus it may extend to sheep, when it is known as a 'foldcourse' or 'sheepwalk'. The number of animals may either be limited by levancy or couchancy, or fixed; it cannot be unlimited.
    (c) *Pur cause de vicinage.* Under a common of pasture pur cause de vicinage, the commoners of one common may not put more cattle on it than it will maintain...
    (d) *In gross.* A profit of pasture in gross may exist for a fixed number of animals or sans nombre. The last phrase means literally 'without number' (an alternative form is 'without stint'), but such a right is limited to not more cattle than the servient tenement will maintain in addition to any existing burdens...

Profit of turbary

A profit of turbary is the right to dig and take from the servient tenement peat or turf for use as fuel in a house on the dominant tenement.

---

15 See R. Oswald *Common Land and the Commons Registration Act 1965* (ESC: 1989).
16 'Attached to land'.
17 How many animals the land can maintain.
18 'Attached to land by grant'.

THE CREATION OF EASEMENTS AND PROFITS

Methods of acquisition

Each of the methods of acquisition is dealt with in turn below (See Fig. 6.1).

Theoretically, there are two separate questions in easement and profit cases:
1. does this right amount to an easement (or profit)? and
2. has it been acquired by the plaintiff?

In practice, however, these two questions are inextricably linked together; in addition, many of the cases were decided before the clarification in *Re Ellenborough Park* (see p. 164) and the judges therefore did not have the advantage of the 'four characteristics'.

A *grant* is where the seller retains the servient land; a *reservation* is where she retains the dominant land and 'reserves' to herself an interest in the land she is selling. The courts interpret reservations against the grantor/reserver, and take some persuasion to find an implied reservation.

In the case of express grant or reservation, by s.19, Land Registration Act 1925 the easement or profit must be registered: otherwise, it will be equitable only.[19]

Implied grant: Section 62

Law of Property Act 1925

General words implied in conveyances

62 (1) A conveyance of land shall be deemed to include and shall by virtue of this Act operate to convey, with the land, all buildings, erections, fixtures, commons, hedges, ditches, fences, ways, waters, watercourses, liberties, privileges, easements, rights, and advantages whatsoever, appertaining or reputed to appertain to the land or any part thereof, or, at the time of conveyance, demised, occupied, or enjoyed with, or reputed or known as part or parcel of or appurtenant to the land or any part thereof.

(2) A conveyance of land, having houses or other buildings thereon, shall be deemed to include and shall by virtue of this Act operate to convey, with the land, houses, or other buildings, all outhouses, erections, fixtures, cellars, areas, courts, courtyards, cisterns, sewers, gutters, drains, ways, passages, lights, watercourses, liberties, privileges, easements, rights, and advantages whatsoever, appertaining or reputed to appertain to the land, houses, or other buildings conveyed, or any of them, or any part thereof, or, at the time of

---

19 See Chapter 10 at p. 283.

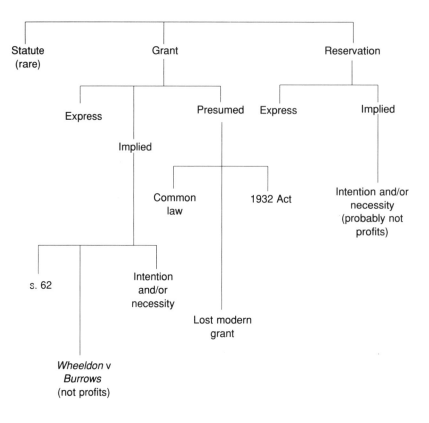

Fig. 6.1 Methods of acquisition of easements and profits

conveyance, demised, occupied, or enjoyed with, or reputed or known as part or parcel of or appurtenant to, the land, houses, or other buildings conveyed, or any of them, or any part thereof...

(4) This section applies only if and as far as a contrary intention is not expressed in the conveyance, and has effect subject to the terms of the conveyance and to the provisions therein contained.[20] Cases on s. 62 include *Phipps* v *Pears* (above p. 170), *Duke of Westminster* v *Guild* (above p. 173) and the *Lyme Valley Squash Club case* (above p. 174).

International Tea Stores Co v *Hobbs* [1903] 2 Ch 165

Farwell J:

I am therefore thrown back on the inquiry whether it is or not the fact that at the date of

---

20 A contrary intention must be very clearly expressed if it is to defeat s. 62.

the conveyance[21] the way in question was a way used and enjoyed with the property conveyed. If it was in fact so used and enjoyed, then it passed to the plaintiffs by the very words of the grant.

Now the facts are these. Mr Hobbs owned the property on both sides of the roadway or yard in question, and in 1888 or 1889 let the plaintiff's premises to Mr Sharp. He allowed Mr Sharp to make a hole in the wall which then bounded the roadway, for the purpose of carrying in some printing presses. That opening in the wall was there at the date of the lease to the plaintiff's predecessor in title...

I think ... that on the true construction of the lease the predecessors in title of the plaintiffs did not get any right of way by demise over this particular roadway. But after they had entered under their lease, their first manager, Mr Gardner, obtained permission from Mr Hobbs to use the roadway which was then constructed into Chapel Street from the door in the wall of the plaintiffs' premises; that permission was asked for and given once for all to Mr Gardner. Two succeeding managers obtained a like permission in the same way.

In 1895 the plaintiff company took an assignment of the lease, and took over and carried on the business of the original lessees, and I find as a fact that their first manager also obtained from the defendant a like permission to go on using this road in the same way in which it had been used before...

I find as a fact that the roadway has been used for all purposes of the company's business whenever they wanted to use it...

Down to this point, therefore, I find that there was a way used in fact, and used for several years, by the plaintiffs before and at the date of the conveyance. But then Lord Coleridge says that such use was wholly permissive ... The use of the road by them was not as of right, because the lease did not give it to them. They must, therefore, have used the road either by licence or without licence...

[T]he fact of licence makes no difference ... The real truth is that you do not consider the question of title to use, but the question of the fact of user; you have to inquire whether the way has in fact been used, not under what title it has been used, although you must of course take into consideration all the circumstances of the case ... whether it has, or has not, been enjoyed within the meaning of the statute...

The road was being used with permission at the time of the conveyance, and therefore the licence became a legal easement by s. 62.

Section 62 thus applies where, for example, a tenant is actually enjoying a use of the landlord's property and this use is capable of being an easement or profit. If the landlord grants a new lease to the tenant, then the use enjoyed (whether or not by permission) is transformed by s. 62 into a true, legal easement or profit.

Wright v *Macadam* [1949] 2 KB 744 (CA) Tucker, Jenkins and Singleton LJJ

Jenkins LJ:

The plaintiffs claimed an injunction to restrain the defendant from trespassing or

---

21 The date when the plaintiff company bought the freehold of their lease.

otherwise interfering with their lawful use of the coal shed, a declaration that their tenancy of the flat included the right to use the coal shed, and damages limited to 10/–. I may mention that, as matters stand at present, the last of those claims appears to be the only relevant one, inasmuch as we were informed in the course of the hearing that the defendant has in fact pulled down the coal shed. The question therefore is simply this: whether the plaintiffs, as tenants of the top floor flat at 13, Mount Ararat Road, were entitled to the use of the coal shed in question. It is argued for the plaintiffs that they were so entitled, by virtue of s. 62 of the Law of Property Act, 1925, which is the section ... providing by statute the general words which it was customary to insert in full in the parcels of conveyances and other dispositions of land.[22] The plaintiffs claim that this section covers the case. The defendant, on the other hand, claims that, although the coal shed was admittedly used, it was used under no sufficiently definite arrangement; that it was used purely as a matter of personal licence and precariously; and that the arrangement under which it was used could not be said to confer a right in any way appurtenant to the flat, but was an arrangement of a kind to which s. 62 of the Act had no application...

The question in the present case, therefore, is whether the right to use the coal shed was at the date of the letting of August 28, 1943, a liberty, privilege, easement, right or advantage appertaining or reputed to appertain, to the land ... it is enough for the plaintiffs' purposes if they can show that the right was at the time of the material letting demised, occupied or enjoyed with the flat or any part thereof...

[T]he right was, as I understand it, a right to use the coal shed in question for the purpose of storing such coal as might be required for the domestic purposes of the flat. In my judgment that is a right or easement which the law will clearly recognise ... Therefore, applying to the facts of the present case the principles which seem deducible from the authorities, the conclusion to which I have come is that the right to use the coal shed was at the date of the letting of August 28, 1943, a right enjoyed with the top floor flat within the meaning of s. 62 of the Law of Property Act, 1925, with the result that (as no contrary intention was expressed in the document) the right in question must be regarded as having passed by virtue of that letting, just as it would have passed if it had been mentioned in express terms...

The Court of Appeal therefore allowed the tenant's appeal and awarded the damages claimed. Tucker LJ added:

The result is that the defendant, through his act of kindness in allowing this lady to use the coal shed is probably now a wiser man, and I may perhaps regret that the decision in this case may tend to discourage landlords from acts of kindness to their tenants; but there it is: that is the law.

Subsequently, doubt was cast on whether a right to store goods could amount to an easement, for it 'is virtually a claim to possession of the servient tenement, if necessary to the exclusion of the owner; or, at any rate, to a joint user, and no

---

22 At that time it was said that solicitors were 'paid by the yard'. For a similar 'word-saving' provision, see s. 78, below p. 200.

authority has been cited to me which would justify the conclusion that a right of this wide and undefined nature can be the proper subject-matter of an easement ...' (Upjohn J in *Copeland* v *Greenhalf* [1952] 1 Ch 488, 498).

However, Brightman J in *Grigsby* v *Melville* [1973] 1 All ER 385, 393 (in which case the claimed easement – a right to store goods in a cellar – failed) commented on the *Wright* and *Copeland* cases:

I am not convinced there is any real inconsistency between the two cases. The point of the decision in *Copeland* v *Greenhalf* was that the right asserted amounted in effect to a claim to the whole beneficial user of the servient tenement and for that reason could not exist as a mere easement. The precise facts in *Wright* v *Macadam* in this respect are not wholly clear from the report and it is a little difficult to know whether the tenant had exclusive use of the coal shed or of any defined portion of it. To some extent a problem of this sort may be one of degree...[23]

Implied grant: the rule in *Wheeldon* v *Burrows*

Wheeldon v *Burrows* (1879) 12 Ch D 31 (CA) Thesiger, James and Baggalay LJJ

The case turned on whether the plaintiff had reserved an easement of light. The famous quote is technically an *obiter dictum*.

Thesiger LJ:

We have had a considerable number of cases cited to us, and out of them I think that two propositions may be stated as what I may call the general rule governing cases of this kind. The first of these rules is, that on the grant by the owner of a tenement of part of that tenement as it is then used and enjoyed, there will pass to the grantee all those continuous and apparent easements (by which, of course, I mean *quasi*-easements), or, in other words, all those easements which are necessary to the reasonable enjoyment of the property granted, and which have been and are at the time of the grant used by the owners of the entirety for the benefit of the part granted. The second proposition is that, if the grantor intends to reserve any right over the tenement granted, it is his duty to reserve it expressly in the grant. Those are the general rules governing cases of this kind, but the second of those rules is subject to certain exceptions [including a right of way by necessity]...

Both of the general rules which I have mentioned are founded upon a maxim which is as well established by authority as it is consonant to reason and common sense, viz ... that a grantor shall not derogate from his grant...

These cases ... support the propositions that in the case of a grant you may imply a grant of such continuous and apparent easements or such easements as

---

23 Similar questions arise in relation to the right to park cars – consider, for example, the recent case of *London and Suburban Building* v *Carey* (above p. 167).

are necessary to the reasonable enjoyment of the property conveyed, and have in fact been enjoyed during the unity of ownership...

Thus the rule applies where a person sells a part of his or her land, and has been enjoying a use in the nature of an easement, for the benefit of the part sold, over the part that is retained. The buyer will then gain the right to that use of the retained land as a legal easement.

The relationship between s. 62 and *Wheeldon* v *Burrows*

Wheeldon v *Burrows*	Section 62
Applies in wills, deeds or contracts but only to easements.	Applies in deeds only, but to easements and profits.
Both tenements in the same ownership or occupation.	Tenements in separate owner-ship or occupation.
Easement used by the grantor for the benefit of the part granted, continuously and apparently and/ or this right is reasonably necessary.	Easement 'appertained' etc. to the dominant tenement.

Differences between these two methods of obtaining an easement by implied grant are shown in:

Sovmots Investments Ltd v *Secretary of State for the Environment* [1979] AC 144 (HL) Lords Wilberforce, Edmund-Davies, Fraser, Russell, Keith

The question was whether the London Borough of Camden had properly carried out a compulsory purchase of maisonettes in Centre Point, a tower office block in central London. This depended on whether they had gained, with the land, easements of access by either s. 62 or the rule in *Wheeldon* v *Burrows*.

Lord Wilberforce:

The rule [in *Wheeldon* v *Burrows*] is a rule of intention, based on the proposition that a man may not derogate from his grant. He cannot grant or agree to grant land and at the same time deny to his grantee what is at the time of the grant obviously necessary for its reasonable enjoyment. To apply this to a case where a public

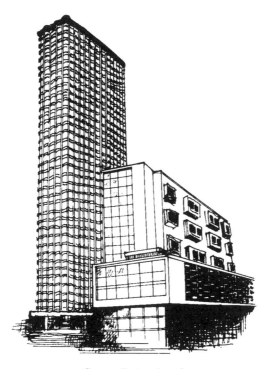

Centre Point, London

authority is taking from an owner his land without his will is to stand the rule on its head: it means substituting for the intention of a reasonable voluntary grantor the unilateral, opposed, intention of the acquirer.

Moreover ... the words ... show that for the rule to apply there must be actual, and apparent, use and enjoyment at the time of the grant. But no such use or enjoyment had, at Centre Point, taken place at all.

Equally, section 62 does not fit this case. The reason is that when land is under one ownership one cannot speak in any intelligible sense of rights, or privileges, or easements being exercised over one part for the benefit of another. Whatever the owner does, he does as owner and, until a separation occurs, of ownership or at least of occupation, the condition for the existence of rights, etc., does not exist: see *Bolton* v *Bolton* (1879) 11 Ch D 968, 970 per Fry J and *Long* v *Gowlett* [1923] 2 Ch 177, 189, 198, in my opinion a correct decision.

A separation of ownership, in a case like the present, will arise on conveyance of one of the parts (e.g. the maisonettes), but this separation cannot be projected back to the stage of the compulsory purchase order so as, by anticipation, to bring into existence rights not existing in fact...[24]

---

24 See also C. Harpum (1977) 41 Conv 415.

Implied grant or reservation: intention and/or necessity

An easement will be implied into a deed where it is clear to the court that the parties must have intended it, as in *Liverpool City Council* v *Irwin* (see above, p. 172). An easement will also be implied where it is *essential* to any enjoyment of the land conveyed.

P. Jackson, 'Easements of Necessity' *Current L Problems* (1981) 133

The origin of the law relating to easements of necessity is to be found in decisions and dicta relating to access to agricultural property. A way of necessity is a way without which land is inaccessible and unusable. From the earliest times it has been recognised that it is to the 'prejudice del weal publick que terre gisser fresh & unoccupied' [*Packer* v *Welstead* (1658) 2 Sid 111, 112 per Glyn CJ]; and that it 'est pro bono publico que le terre ne serra unoccupy' [*Dutton* v *Taylor* (1701) 2 Lut. 1457]. Since such a state of affairs is contrary to the public good the law is prepared to imply a right of way where a vendor sells part of his land whether the implication is one of grant or reservation ... The attitude of the English courts is clearly expressed in the words of Lord President (Inglis): 'No one can possess a piece of land without having a right of ish and entry'...

The test of necessity is a strict one. Thus a way is not one of necessity if there is another means of access to the property, however inconvenient...

Attempts to show necessity have often proved very difficult. For example, in *Manjang* v *Drammeh* (1991) 61 P & CR 194, the Privy Council decided that the availability of access to land by water was sufficient to negative an easement of necessity on dry land in all the circumstances of the case.

The two grounds of intention and necessity are often similar in practice, and are difficult to disentangle.

Wong v *Beaumont Property Trust* [1965] 1 QB 173 (CA) Lord Denning MR, Pearson and Salmon LJJ

Salmon LJ:

Whether or not an easement of necessity is here to be implied seems to me to depend solely on this question: in 1957, at the date when the lease was granted, could the business of a popular restaurant have been lawfully carried on on these premises without some system of ducting whereby smell and odours were taken from the restaurant up the back of the building to the roof of the premises ... The judge has come to the conclusion (and in my view there is evidence to support this finding) that even in 1957 the existing flue was insufficient and some form of ducting from the restaurant to the roof was necessary. This is not a very surprising conclusion when one considers that this restaurant was in a cellar with no windows at all ... Therefore, it seems to me that unless a duct from the cellar to the roof were installed in 1957, it would have been impossible lawfully to carry on the business of a popular restaurant on these premises.

It seems to me to be plain on the authorities, as my Lord has said, that if a lease is granted which imposes a particular use on the tenant and it is impossible for the tenant to use the premises legally unless an easement is granted, the law does imply such an easement as of necessity...

MRA Engineering Ltd v *Trimster Co Ltd* (1988) 58 P & CR 1 (CA)
Dillon, Nourse and Bingham LJJ

The question here concerned the valuation of land: if there were an easement to drive a car over neighbouring land, the plot in question would be worth much more.

Dillon LJ:

The law as to ways of necessity is in some respects archaic, and it may be that it is time it was given closer consideration as against modern circumstances...

As I have said, at the back of the red land and down one side of it there are public footpaths. It appears therefore that it is possible to obtain access to the red land and the house on it by foot along the public footpaths. Mr Shaw certainly took a car in, although he garaged it on the green land, and a car could not go along the public footpath. As the judge said:

'... nowadays one seems to think and it is very natural so to think, that everybody must have a car and the house must be approached by a car. It is certainly very inconvenient and could be inconvenient to a very large extent.'

This court could not differ from his conclusion of fact in view of the public footpaths that the property is usable in the ordinary sense of the word. It is not absolutely inaccessible or useless without the right of way claimed; merely difficult and inconvenient.

Here the claims based both on necessity and on s. 62 failed: the section did not operate because the servient land had previously been sold by the seller of the dominant tenement, and he could not give a right over land he did not own at the time of the conveyance.[25]

Stafford v *Lee* (1993) 65 P & CR 172 (CA), Nourse and Russell LJJ

The plaintiff bought a wood in 1955 with an easement of way. Thirty-five years later, it was claimed that, either by necessity or by common intention, the easement included the right of access for cars to a house. There was no doubt that the plaintiff had a right of access, but the defendant argued that the easement was only for the enjoyment of the wood, not for building and enjoying a house. The claim based on necessity failed because there was an easement of access, but the claim on common intention succeeded.

---

25 See also JEM 53 Conv (1989) 355.

Nourse LJ:

If the grantee can establish the requisite intention, the law will then imply the grant of such easements as may be necessary to give effect to it.

There are therefore two hurdles which the grantee must surmount. He must establish a common intention as to some definite and particular user. Then he must show that the easements he claims are necessary to give effect to it...

The requirement that the parties should have intended a definite and particular use for the land does not require that the intention be proved as a certainty. As always, it is enough that it is proved on the balance of the probabilites. What help do we get from the 1955 deed in this regard?

The deed showed that the original buyer of the woodland lived a hundred miles away; further, the plan attached to the deed indicated a house on the land. The court, therefore, held that there was sufficient evidence of common intention.

Presumed grant: prescription

Here, the courts presume that there once was a deed granting the easement or profit, although they know that this is probably a fairy story.[26]

There are three routes to this presumption:

1. common law;
2. lost modern grant;
3. Prescription Act 1832.

(Prescription is quite different from adverse possession. Here, a legal easement or profit is created by long use; in adverse possession, the paper owner is prevented from enforcing his or her claims in court.)

Three rules must be fulfilled for any claim of prescription to succeed. The use of the other person's land must be:

1. as of right, without any force, secrecy or permission (*'nec vi, nec clam, nec precario'*); and
2. by a fee simple owner against a fee simple owner; and
3. continuous.

Common law prescription

Twenty years' use gives rise to a presumption that the right was granted before 1189 (the official start of legal memory). The presumption can be rebutted by proof that this would have been impossible (for example, because solar panels had not been invented then).

---

26 See also A.W.B. Simpson *A History of the Land Law* (Clarendon: 1986).

Lost modern grant

Twenty years' use gives rise to a presumption that there was a modern deed, but it has been lost.

Prescription Act

'The Act is a classic example of an incompetent attempt to reform, the law.'
(A.W.B. Simpson, *A History of the Land Law* (Clarendon: 1986), p. 269)

Prescription Act 1832

Claims to right of common and other *profits à prendre*, not to be defeated after thirty years' enjoyment by merely showing the commencement; after sixty years' enjoyment the right to be absolute, unless had by consent or agreement.

1 No claim which may be lawfully made at the common law, by custom, prescription, or grant, to any right of common or other profit or benefit to be taken and enjoyed from or upon any land of our sovereign Lord the King or any land being parcel of the Duchy of Lancaster or of the Duchy of Cornwall, or of any ecclesiastical or lay person, or body corporate, except such matters and things as are herein specially provided for, and except tithes, rent, and services, shall, where such right, profit, or benefit shall have been actually taken and enjoyed by any person claiming right thereto without interruption for the full period of thirty years, be defeated or destroyed by showing only that such right, profit, or benefit was first taken or enjoyed at any time prior to such period of thirty years, but nevertheless such claim may be defeated in any other way by which the same is now liable to be defeated; and when such right, profit, or benefit shall have been so taken and enjoyed as aforesaid for the full period of sixty years, the right thereto shall be deemed absolute and indefeasible, unless it shall appear that the same was taken and enjoyed by some consent or agreement expressly made or given for the purpose by deed or writing.

Section 2 provides similarly for easements, that is for 'any way or other easement, or to any watercourse, or the use of any water...'

Claim to use of light enjoyed for twenty years

3 When the access and use of light to and for any dwelling house, workshop, or other building shall have been actually enjoyed therewith for the full period of twenty years without interruption, the right thereto shall be deemed absolute and indefeasible, any local usage or custom to the contrary notwithstanding, unless it shall appear that the same was enjoyed by some consent or agreement expressly made or given for that purpose by deed or writing.

Before-mentioned periods to be deemed those next before suits

4 Each of the respective periods of years hereinbefore mentioned shall be

deemed to be taken to be the period next before some suit or action wherein the claim or matter to which such period may relate shall have been or shall be brought into question, and no act or other matter shall be deemed to be an interruption, within the meaning of this statute, unless the same shall have been or shall be submitted to or acquiesced in for one year after the part interrupted shall have had or shall have notice thereof, and of the person making or authorising the same to be made.

Section 7 provides that periods of infancy or mental disability are to be excluded in the counting of time for these sections.

Mills v *Silver* [1991] 2 WLR 324 (CA) Dillon, Parker, and Stocker LJJ

Mills sued Silver for trespass. Silver claimed a right of way by prescription, and also that he had the right to pave the roadway. The trial judge decided against Silver. The main dispute concerned 'tolerance', whether Mills' predecessor in title had given permission for the track to be used by Silver's predecessor.

Dillon LJ:

The first and second defendants' case has to be founded on use of the disputed track with vehicles for access to and egress from Coed Major during the lifetime of Joe Phillips, who occupied Coed Major from 1922 until a few days before his death in 1981...

I turn now to the judge's point of tolerance. The question is whether the judge has correctly directed himself in law. To put it another way, did the tolerance of the successive servient owners ... of such vehicular use of the disputed track as there was in Joe Phillips' time preclude a prescriptive right being acquired, even though no express permission was ever granted to Joe Phillips and no reservations as to his use of the disputed track with vehicles were ever communicated to him by anyone.

The topic of tolerance has bulked fairly large in recent decisions of this court dealing with claims to prescriptive rights, since the decision in *Alfred F Beckett Ltd* v *Lyons* [1967] Ch 449. If passages in successive judgments are taken on their own out of context and added together, it would be easy to say, as with all respect, it seems to me that the judge did in the present case, that there is an established principle of law that no prescriptive right can be acquired if the user by the dominant owner of the servient tenement in the particular manner for the appropriate number of years has been tolerated without objection by the servient owner. But there cannot be any such principle of law because it is, with rights of way, fundamentally inconsistent with the whole notion of acquisition of rights by prescription.[27] It is difficult to see how, if there is such a principle, there could ever be a prescriptive right of way...

On the facts of the present case as set out in the judgment of Judge Micklem it is, in my judgment, plain that James Price acquiesced in all use of the disputed

---

27 Compare the 'implied licence' in adverse possession – see Chapter 3 at p. 68.

track with vehicles. He knew of it, had power to prevent it, and did not intervene ... In my judgment, the user with vehicles for the purposes of Coed Major in Joe Phillips' time was user as of right, and the plaintiffs have no defence in law on the ground of tolerance to the defendants' claim to a prescriptive easement by the presumption of a lost grant...

Accordingly, in my judgment the defendants succeed to the extent that there is to be presumed a lost grant before the death of Joe Phillips of a right, appurtenant to Coed Major, and which thus endures to the benefit of the first and second defendants, to pass and repass with or without vehicles, but for domestic or agricultural purposes only, over the disputed track, in so far as its condition permitted passage, between Coed Major and the Hay Road...

The making of the stone road [by the defendants] involved the putting down of between 600 and 700 tons of stone along the disputed track. That is an improvement of the track which in my judgment went far beyond mere repair. The prescriptive right to which the defendants were entitled did not authorise them to do that to the plaintiff's detriment. Accordingly, the laying of the stone road was a trespass to the plaintiff's land...

Therefore, the defendant had gained an easement by prescription, but the plaintiff was entitled to damages for the trespass by wrongful improvement.

In 1966 the Law Reform Committee (Cmnd. 3100, para. 3.2) recommended the abolition of prescription. It would be replaced by 12 years' enjoyment (for either easements or profits), the same period as for adverse possession.

ENDING EASEMENTS AND PROFITS

An easement or profit, unless attached to a lease, will last for ever. It can be ended by statute or by agreement ('release'), or if dominant and servient land are owned by the same person. There is also abandonment (implied release), but the courts are reluctant to hold that a person has given away a valuable legal right merely on the grounds that she has not used it lately:

Benn v *Hardinge* (1992) 66 P & CR 257 (CA), Dillon, Kennedy and Hirst LJJ

The easement of way arose from an enclosure grant made in 1818:

Dillon LJ:

I take the law to have been laid down in clear terms by the judgment of the court in *Gotobed* v *Pridmore* (1971) EG 759. In view of that and the many expressions of high authority in the cases to which I have referred, to the effect that there must be an intention to abandon, I do not feel that it is open to us in this court to say that the way must be presumed to have been abandoned merely because no one had occasion to use it, even for so long as 175 years. It is important in this context that the photographs show such a rural and unchanged situation on the servient owner's side of the boundary line...

In all these circumstances, and with considerable regret on my part, I would hold that there has been no abandonment of this right of way...

Hirst LJ:

This right of way was always a piece of property of latent value, though not actually exploited because of the alternative means of egress ... The abandonment of such a valuable latent piece of property should not be lightly inferred since it might be of significant importance in the future...

Huckvale v *Aegean Hotels Ltd* (1989) 58 P & CR 163 (CA) Slade, Nourse and Butler-Sloss LJJ

Here a new argument about the ending of easements was raised. Huckvale had reserved a right of way across the red land and then across the hotel's land, to the road. The easement over the red land was equitable only and was lost through non-registration (the land was unregistered: see Appendix 1). The hotel argued therefore that the right of way over the hotel's land no longer accommodated the dominant tenement since there was now no complete route to the road.

Nourse LJ:

In this court, Mr Patten has submitted that ... the plaintiffs' rights of way over the red land ceased to accommodate the plaintiffs' property and were thereupon extinguished...

As I have said, Mr Patten submits, correctly, that it is one of the essential characteristics of an easement that it should confer a real and practical benefit on it and be reasonably necessary for its better enjoyment. In support of that submission, he has referred us to the decision of this court in *Re Ellenborough Park*, but neither that case nor any other which has been cited is authority for the proposition that, in the case of any easement founded in grant, the question of accommodation is to be determined at any date other than that of the grant. Mr Patten accepts that the rights of way over the red land did accommodate the plaintiffs' property at the date of the reservation on June 18, 1982, because at that time those rights, together with the complementary rights over the remainder of the hotel property, conferred on the plaintiffs' property a real and practical benefit in fact and were reasonably necessary for its better enjoyment...

For the purposes of this appeal it is unnecessary to decide whether an easement which accommodated the dominant tenement at the date of the grant, but which thereafter ceases to accommodate it, is extinguished by operation of law, notwithstanding the continued existence of the dominant tenement. Although the proposition is novel and unsupported by any authority which has been cited to us, it could not be said that there might not be a case whose facts would attract its operation.

In the present case it is clear, on the evidence as it stands, that it cannot be said that the rights of way over the red land have ceased to accommodate the plaintiffs' property. It is certainly not possible to say either that they have ceased to confer a real and practical benefit on it or that they might not be reasonably necessary for its better enjoyment in the future ... I do not think that it would be possible for us to be certain that at some time in the future, in altered circumstances, the plaintiffs or their successors in title might not be able to obtain a regrant of the complementary rights of way over the remainder of the hotel property, so that the rights over the red land could thereupon be enjoyed to the fullest extent once more...

Thus the hotel failed: the easement subsisted.

The 1966 Report (Cmnd. 3100) of the Law Commission recommended that the Lands Tribunal should have power to discharge easements and profits (see also Chapter 7, p. 218).

In 1985, in Report No. 151 (*Rights of Access to Neighbouring Land*, Cmnd 9692, para. 3.42), the Law Commission recommended that there should be a right of access to neighbouring property to carry out repair work, under an order available at the discretion of the county court.

This has now become law in the Access to Neighbouring Land Act 1992 (see also 142 NLJ (1992) 858).

Access to Neighbouring Land Act 1992

Access Orders[28]

1 (1) A person –

(a) who for the purpose of carrying out works to any land (the 'dominant land'), desires to enter upon any adjoining or adjacent land (the 'servient land'), and
(b) who needs, but does not have, the consent of some other person to that entry,

may make an application to the court for an order under this section (an 'access order') against that other person.

(2) On an application under this section, the court shall make an access order if, and only if, it is satisfied –

(a) that the works are reasonably necessary for the preservation of the whole or any part of the dominant land; and
(b) that they cannot be carried out, or would be substantially more difficult to carry out, without entry on the servient land;

but this subsection is subject to subsection (3) below.

Subsection (3) provides that an order will not be made if the respondent would 'suffer interference with, or disturbance of, his use of the servient land' or would 'suffer hardship' to such a degree that it 'would be unreasonable to make the order'. Such an order is registrable under the Land Charges Act or the Land Registration Act (s. 5).

---

28 This section came into effect from 31 January 1993.

7 Covenants in freehold land

INTRODUCTION

The idea that a promise can be attached to land so that rights and responsibilities ('benefits and burdens') pass on any transfer of the land to the new owner is a familiar one in the law of leases. Benefits and burdens can also be transferred without a leasehold relationship through the concept of 'restrictive' covenants.

For historical reasons,[1] a right to enforce a restrictive covenant is equitable interest only: in registered land it can only ever be a minor interest. The normal remedy for breach of a restrictive covenant is an injunction, but damages may be awarded as well as, or instead of, an injunction.[2]

The justification for the limited role of restrictive covenants is that:

H.W.R. Wade 'Licences and Third Parties' 68 *LQR* (1952) 337

If there were no frontier, there would be no limit to the new incidents of property which could be invented. But rights which can bind third parties ought to be of a limited and familiar kind; for otherwise purchasers might have to investigate an infinite variety of incumbrances, and would often have no means of knowing the real effect of some fancy or imaginative transaction to which they were strangers. Therefore the law has striven to draw lines of demarcation round the special interests which, exceptionally, may be created by contract or covenant.

The major function of the rules about restrictive covenants, is the control of land use. When the rules were initially developed in the nineteenth century, there was no public planning law so landowners were much more free to do what they liked on their land, whatever their neighbours thought about it. A person selling land for building might extract a promise that only homes would be built (no shops or factories), and initially this was only enforceable in contract law, that is only against the person who made the promise (the covenantor) and not against his

---

1 See *Tulk* v *Moxhay* below.
2 For discussion of remedies, see for example the *Federated Homes case* (below p. 201) and *Chatsworth Estates* v *Fewell* (below p. 210).

successors on the land. The first famous case in which a promise made by a predecessor in title was enforced against a later owner is a good example of the planning function of these covenants:

Tulk v *Moxhay* (1848) 41 ER 1143, Lord Cottenham[3]

In 1808 the plaintiff, then owner of Leicester Square and of several of the houses around it, sold the freehold central area to Elms. The conveyance contained an express covenant by Elms, for himself, his heirs and assigns that he would 'keep and maintain' the square garden 'as a pleasure ground, uncovered with any buildings'. By a series of conveyances, the land came into the hands of the defendant, whose purchase deed contained no similar covenant with his vendor although he had known about the 1808 covenant.

The defendant wanted to build on the garden. The plaintiff sued for an injunction to prevent this. An injunction was granted by the Master of the Rolls and the defendant sought its discharge.

Lord Cottenham LC:

[T]he owner of certain houses in the square sells the land adjoining, with a covenant from the purchaser not to use it for any other purposes than as a square garden. And it is now contended, not that the vendee could violate that contract, but that he might sell the piece of land, and that the purchaser from him may

---

3 See also C.D. Bell 45 Conv (1981) 55: S. Gardner 46 Conv (1982) 279.

violate it without this Court having any power to interfere. If that were so, it would be impossible for an owner of land to sell part of it without incurring the risk of rendering what he retains worthless. It is said that, the covenant being one which does not run with the land, this Court cannot enforce it; but the question is, not whether the covenant runs with the land, but whether a party shall be permitted to use the land in a manner inconsistent with the contract entered into by his vendor, and with notice of which he purchased. Of course, the price would be affected by the covenant, and nothing could be more inequitable than that the original purchaser should be able to sell the property the next day for a greater price, in consideration of the assignee being allowed to escape from the liability which he had himself undertaken...

[I]f an equity is attached to the property by the owner, no one purchasing with notice of that equity can stand in a different situation from the party from whom he purchased.

The injunction was therefore not discharged.

It was clear by the mid-nineteenth century that a healthy city needed 'lungs' in order to breathe, and Leicester Square was seen as one of these breathing spaces in the crowded city. It remains 'uncovered with buildings' to this day (although a lot goes on underneath the surface of the land – see for example *R* v *Westminster County Council ex p Leicester Square Coventry Street Association* [1989] 87 LGR 675).[4]

Although the covenant in *Tulk* v *Moxhay* was expressed in a positive fashion – 'keep the land uncovered with buildings' – it was in substance restrictive – not to build. By the end of the nineteenth century the rule that only negative promises were enforceable had become clear. It has recently been restated:

Rhone v *Stephens* [1994] 2 All ER 65 (HL), Lords Templeman, Oliver, Woolf, Lloyd, Nolan

A single leaky roof covered both a house and a cottage which were in separate ownership. The roof belonged to the house, and, when the cottage was first sold, the owners of the house promised that they would maintain the roof. The current owner of the cottage was trying to get the current owner of the house to carry out the positive obligation to repair the roof.[5]

Lord Templeman:
At common law a person cannot be made liable upon a contract unless he was a party to it ... The rigours of the common law which do not allow covenants to be enforced by and against successors in title were relaxed first by the doctrines ...

---

4 The modern possibility of using restrictive covenants as a mechanism of conservation of the countryside is canvassed in R. Castle and I. Hodge 'Covenants for the Countryside' (1994) Conv 122.

5 What do you think they should have done? See also N.P. Gravells (1994) 110 LQR 346.

now in ss. 141 and 142 of the Law of Property Act 1925.[6] In the result, as between landlord and tenant both the burden and the benefit of a covenant which touches or concerns the land demised and is not merely collateral run with the reversion and the term at law whether the covenant be positive or restrictive. As between persons interested in land other than as landlord and tenant, the benefit of a covenant may run with the land at law but not the burden...

My lords, equity supplements but does not contradict the common law. When freehold land is conveyed without restriction, the conveyance confers on the purchaser the right to do with the land as he pleases provided that he does not interfere with the rights of others or infringe statutory restrictions. The conveyance may however impose restrictions which, in favour of the covenantee, deprive the purchaser of some of the rights inherent in the ownership of unrestricted land...

Equity does not contradict the common law by enforcing a restrictive covenant against a successor in title of the covenantor but prevents the successor from exercising a right which he never acquired. Equity did not allow the owner of Leicester Square to build because the owner never acquired the right to build without the consent of the persons (if any) from time to time entitled to the benefit of the covenant against building...

Equity can thus prevent or punish the breach of a negative covenant which restricts the user of land or the exercise of other rights in connection with land. Restrictive covenants deprive an owner of a right which he could otherwise exercise. Equity cannot compel an owner to comply with a positive covenant entered into by his predecessors in title without flatly contradicting the common law rule that a person cannot be made liable upon a contract unless he was a party to it. Enforcement of a positive covenant lies in contract: a positive covenant compels an owner to exercise his rights. Enforcement of a negative covenant lies in property: a negative covenant deprives the owner of a right over property...

For over 100 years it has been clear and accepted law that equity will enforce negative covenants against freehold land but has no power to enforce positive covenants against successors in title of the land. To enforce a positive covenant would be to enforce a personal obligation against a person who has not covenanted. To enforce negative covenants is only to treat the land as subject to restriction...

Lord Templeman referred to counsel's attempt at persuading the House of Lords to overrule this old rule in light of 30 years of recommendations for its reform of the old rule. However:

To do so would destroy the distinction between law and equity and to convert the rule of equity into a rule of notice. It is plain from the articles, reports and papers to which we were referred that judicial legislation to overrule the *Austerberry* case [(1885) Ch D 750] would create a number of difficulties, anomalies and uncertainties and affect the rights and liabilities of people who have for over 100 years bought and sold land in the knowledge, imparted at an elementary stage to every student of the law of real property, that positive covenants affecting freehold land are not directly enforceable except against the original covenantor.

---

6 See Chapter 4 at 107–12.

Parliamentary legislation to deal with the decision in the *Austerberry* case would require careful consideration of the consequences...

The argument that the rule had been reversed 'remarkably but unremarked' 60 years earlier by s. 79, Law of Property Act 1925[7] was rejected. So was the proposition that there was a mutual benefit and burden here: that the house owner could not take the benefit of the cottage's support of the house without suffering the burden of repairing the roof. This was because these two rights were not 'reciprocal'.

'Mutual covenants', such as the mutual rights of support in this case, are one way of ensuring that a positive promise will remain enforceable. Other common ways of getting around the restrictive rule are to use a lease.[8]

Private and public planning

The case of *Tulk* v *Moxhay* shows the potential of covenants: a landowner can sell part of his/her land and make sure that it retains a particular character. Normally, of course, this means that the retained land will keep its value because buyers will pay more for the right to prevent a neighbour being able to hold pop festivals.

Restrictive covenants are still created today (see, for example, s. 40, Land Registration Act 1925), although their importance is diminished by the development of public planning law.[9] Under the Town and Country Planning Act 1971 (replacing the Act of 1947), a complicated system of public planning is carried out by local government, under the ultimate control of central government.

M. Grant *Urban Planning Law* (Sweet & Maxwell: 1982)

The roots of modern planning law

Modern land use planning is entirely the product of statutory legislation. The common law regulated private rights, but recognised no supervening public or governmental interest in the private use of land.[10] Land use regulation was instead a product primarily of tenure, and restrictions on use and new building were imposed as conditions upon which the land was held from the superior landlord. A limited extension of that doctrine emerged in the mid-nineteenth century as the break-up of the large estates and the spread of freehold ownership loosed the traditional controls, and made it necessary to allow the enforcement of similar restrictive conditions between the freehold owners of adjacent land...

The other relevant limb of the common law was that of nuisance. The courts came to insist that the full right of enjoyment and exploitation of land which the

---

7 See below p. 205, and compare the Court of Appeal's use of s. 78 in the *Federated Homes* case, below p. 201.

8 See J. Snape (1994) L S Gaz 22–3.

9 See also J.D.C. Harte *Landscape, Land Use and the Law* (Spon: 1985); P. Macauslan *The Ideologies of Planning Law* (Pergamon: 1980).

10 Compare the Swedish law on easements – see Chapter 6, pp. 163.

common law recognised as a benefit of ownership, was nonetheless subject to some limitation in order to preserve the enjoyment and exploitation rights of adjoining occupiers...

Whatever the scope of the debate today, it was clear to the social reformers of the nineteenth century that the *laissez-faire* ideology of the common law was unlikely to offer any relief to the overcrowding, congestion and disease of the Victorian cities, and certainly not at the suit of those who lacked resources and property rights. The law of nuisance, moreover, offered no means of overcoming established nuisances in order to improve badly polluted and unhealthy urban areas. It was primarily a means of preserving the status quo, and 'what would be a nuisance in Belgrave Square would not necessarily be so in Bermondsey' [*Sturges v Bridgman* (1879) 11 Ch D 852 at 865] was the philosophy by which the judges were guided. New laws were necessary, but Parliamentary legislation offered the only realistic possibility for reform...

But much of the content of the Town and Country Planning Act 1947 [now 1971] was more a consolidation and refinement of earlier measures than a revolutionary departure from them, and despite reforms in procedure and methodology, and the ever-shifting balance between private property and state power, there is a continuity of purpose and ideology which links directly the nineteenth century measures with contemporary planning.

It is normally necessary to ask permission of the local authority before changing the use of land. A home owner who wants to build an extension, or a shopkeeper who wants to sell fruit rather than clothes, must not only check against leasehold and restrictive covenants but also against public planning law.

The interpretation of covenants

Academics mostly study cases concerning the benefits and burdens of covenants passing automatically with land. In practice, another important question is, 'What does the covenant *mean*?' It is possible to ask the court's advice as to whether a covenant binds a piece of land, and as to whether a particular activity would be a breach of it:

Law of Property Act 1925 (as amended by the Law of Property Act 1969)[11]

84 (2) The court shall have power on the application of any person interested –
   (a) to declare whether or not in any particular case any freehold land is or would in any given event be affected by a restriction imposed by any instrument; or
   (b) to declare what, upon the true construction of any instrument purporting to impose a restriction, is the nature and extent of the restriction thereby

---

11 For further examples of this sub-section in use, see *In Re Ecclesiastical Commissioners Conveyance* and *In Re Dolphin's Conveyance*, below.

imposed and whether the same is or would in any given event be enforceable and if so by whom.

Typical restrictive covenants had to be interpreted in:

C & G Homes Ltd v Secretary of State for Health [1991] 2 WLR 715 (CA) Lord Donaldson MR, Nourse and Russell LJJ[12]

A health authority bought two houses on a new estate in Bath for former inpatients at a mental hospital, as part of the policy of enabling them to live, with the necessary support, in the community. The houses were subject to a number of covenants, including (clause 20) not to allow any 'nuisance ... or detriment' to owners on other parts of the estate, and (clause 24) not to carry on any trade or business from the property for the next ten years, or to use the house for any purpose except a 'private dwelling house'. In relation to the 'no business' covenant:

Nourse LJ:

[The] authorities show that the question of fact and degree which has to be answered in each case will involve a consideration of all or some of the following matters: the number of occupants; the degree of permanence of their occupancy; the relationship between them; whether payment is made or not and, if so, whether it is only a contribution to expenses or something more; whether the owner or lessee resides there himself and, if not, whether he has people there to supervise and support those who do...

Although I do not find it necessary to express a concluded view on the first limb of the covenant, I doubt whether the Secretary of State is carrying on a business on or from either of these houses. The small number of residents, the permanence of their residence, the relationship between them and the absence of any payment for their board and lodging together suggest to my mind that it is not the business of a lodging-house. And, while I accept that 'business' is a word of wide application, my impression – and when you have assembled all the features of a case it is really no more than a matter of impression – is that it is not a business of any other kind.

Is then the Secretary of State using these houses for any purpose or purposes other than those of a private dwelling house? I think that he is. The basic proposition ... was that because each house is the private dwelling house of those who reside there, therefore it is being used by the Secretary of State as a private dwelling house. I think that it might well be possible to say that he is using them as dwelling houses. But I cannot agree that he is using them as 'private' dwelling houses...

The Court of Appeal held that there was here a breach of clause 24, but no breach of clause 20.

---

12 See also P. Devonshire 55 Conv (1991) 388.

However, the final result had little to do with the legal arguments. The local people supported the Secretary of State, and there was a public campaign against C & G Homes and the linked Cheltenham and Gloucester Building Society. In the spring of 1991, C & G Homes agreed that the patients could stay if they became tenants of the Secretary of State – see *New Statesman and Society*, 1 March 1991.[13]

THE RULES CONCERNING BENEFITS AND BURDENS

Express transfer of the benefit

The simplest way to transfer the benefit of a promise is to do so expressly in a deed, under:

Law of Property Act 1925

Legal assignments of things in action

136   (1) Any absolute assignment by writing under the hand of the assignor (not purporting to be by way of charge only) of any debt or other legal thing in action, of which express notice in writing has been given to the debtor, trustee or other person from whom the assignor would have been entitled to claim such debt or thing in action, is effectual in law (subject to equities having priority over the right of the assignee) to pass and transfer from the date of such notice –
(a) the legal right to such debt or thing in action;
(b) all legal and other remedies for the same; and
(c) the power to give a good discharge for the same without the concurrence of the assignor...

Benefits of promises can also be transferred automatically when the benefiting land is transferred. This implied transfer is possible both at law and in equity.

Implied transfer of the benefit of a covenant at law

The benefit of a covenant will automatically be transferred with the legal ownership of land if:

1.   the covenant 'touches and concerns' the land: and

---

13 In *National Schizophrenia Fellowship* v *Ribble Estates SA* (1993) 25 HLR 476 (Ch), it was held that housing 12 rehabilitated schizophrenics would not breach a covenant against 'nuisance'. A further development in the effects of the 'community care' policy on land law is in the discharge of covenants (below p. 216).

2. the covenantor and covenantee had legal estates, and the person seeking to enforce the covenant has a legal estate in the land.

If the covenant was made before 1926, it must also be proved that the covenant was intended to run with the land. This could be done by using a well-tried formula, such as: 'The covenant is taken for the benefit of land owned by the covenantee adjacent to Leicester Square'. Since 1925, this is implied into all covenants:

Law of Property Act 1925

Benefits of covenants relating to land[14]

78 (1) A covenant relating to any land of the covenantee shall be deemed to be made with the covenantee and his successors in title and the persons deriving title under him or them, and shall have effect as if such successors and other persons were expressed.

For the purposes of this subsection in connection with covenants restrictive of the user of land 'successors in title' shall be deemed to include the owners and occupiers for the time being of the land of the covenantee intended to be benefited.

This section was interpreted in:

Smith & Snipes Hall Farm Ltd v *River Douglas Catchment Board* [1949] 2 KB 500 (CA) Tucker, Summervell and Denning LJJ

In 1938 the Board promised the owners of land it would maintain the river banks, and the owners paid a contribution to the cost. However, the Board failed to carry out the work properly, and the land was seriously flooded in 1944. The landowner and his tenant both sued the Board for damages.[15]

The freeholder could sue the Board, but could the tenant farmer who was in possession of the benefiting land? Under s. 78, he could:

Denning LJ:

It was always held ... at common law that, in order that a successor in title should be entitled to sue, he must be of the same estate as the original owner. That alone was a sufficient interest to entitle him to enforce the contract. The covenant was supposed to be made for the benefit of the owner and his successors in title, and not for the benefit of anyone else. This limitation ... has been removed by s. 78...

The covenant of the catchment board in this case clearly relates to the land of the covenantees. It was a covenant to work on the land for the benefit of the land. By the statute, therefore, it is to be deemed to be made, not only with the original

---

14 This section applies also to leases.
15 At this time, food production for the war effort was a very high priority.

owner, but also with the purchasers of the land and their tenants as if they were expressed.

Thus, the *benefit* of any promise may automatically pass with the land.

No implied transfer of the burden of a covenant at law

Only equity enforces a burden on a new owner of land (see *Rhone* v *Stephens* p. 194, above). There is no enforcement of burdens at law.

Implied transfer of the benefit of a covenant in equity

The courts of equity developed their own rules about the transfer of both burdens and benefits. The *benefit* of a covenant would pass in equity if:

1. it touched and concerned the land; and
2. it was intended to run, as indicated by either annexation, or assignment.

For *annexation*, it is necessary to prove that the benefit was 'glued' to the covenantee's land by the use of the appropriate words. For *assignment*, it is necessary to prove that there is an unbroken chain of express assignments (according to s. 136, Law of Property Act 1925 above) of the benefit of the covenant. (The difference between the legal and the equitable rules on the benefit of a covenant is that equity does not require *legal* ownership of land in order for the promise to be enforced.)

There are a number of complicated cases about annexation and assignment, but they have all gathered dust since a Court of Appeal decision in 1980:

Federated Homes Ltd v *Mill Lodge Properties Ltd* [1980] 1 All ER 371 (CA) Megaw, Browne and Brightman LJJ[16]

A builder owned three neighbouring areas of land, described as the blue, the red and the green. He sold the blue to Mill Lodge who promised to build not more than 300 houses. He then sold his remaining land. Later, Federated Homes eventually became the owners of both the red and green areas, but via different intermediate owners.

Mill Lodge decided to build more than the 300 houses and Federated Homes took them to court to prevent this, seeking enforcement of the promise.

As far as the green land was concerned, Federated Homes was able to prove that there was an unbroken chain of assignments to them from the original covenantee. Therefore, under the rules of assignment they could enforce the covenant, since it clearly 'touched and concerned' the land.

---

16 See also 46 Conv (1982) 313: Newsom 98 LQR (1982) 202. Compare the interpretation of s. 79 in *Rhone* v *Stephens*, above p. 194.

However, to make doubly sure (and also, no doubt, to increase the value of the red land), they also wished to enforce the covenant as owners of the red land. There was no chain of assignments here or annexation, but they argued that either s. 62 or s. 78 allowed them to enforce the covenant. Much of the case was concerned with planning permission issues, but the Court of Appeal made a revolutionary decision on s. 78:

Brightman LJ:

Although the section [78] does not seem to have been extensively used in the course of argument in this type of case, the construction of s. 78 which appeals to me appears to be consistent with at least two cases decided in this court ...[17]

In my judgment the benefit of this covenant was annexed to the retained land, and I think that this is a consequence of s. 78...

Counsel for the defendants submitted that there were three possible views about s. 78. One view, which he described as the orthodox view hitherto held, is that it is merely a statutory shorthand for reducing the length of legal documents. A second view, which was the one that counsel for the defendants was inclined to place in the forefront of his argument, is that the section only applies, or at any rate only achieves annexation, when the land intended to be benefited is signified in the document by express words or necessary implication as the intended beneficiary of the covenant. A third view is that the section applies if the covenant in fact touches and concerns the land of the covenantee, whether that be gleaned from the document itself or from evidence outside the document.

For myself, I reject the narrowest interpretation of s. 78, the supposed orthodox view, which seems to me to fly in the face of the working of the section. Before I express my reasons I will say that I do not find it necessary to choose between the second and third views because, in my opinion, this covenant relates to land of the covenantee on either interpretation of s. 78...

If, as the language of s. 78 implies, a covenant relating to land which is restrictive of the user thereof is enforceable at the suit of (1) a successor in title of the covenantee, (2) a person deriving title under the covenantee or under his successors in title, and (3) the owner or occupier of the land intended to be benefited by the covenant, it must, in my view, follow that the covenant runs with the land, because *ex hypothesi* every successor in title to the land, every derivative proprietor of the land and every other owner and occupier has a right by statute to the covenant. In other words, if the condition precedent of s. 78 is satisfied, that is to say, there exists a covenant which touches and concerns the land of the covenantee, that covenant runs with the land for the benefit of his successors in title, persons deriving title under him or them and other owners and occupiers. This approach to s. 78 has been advocated by distinguished textbook writers...

In the end I come to the conclusion that s. 78 of the Law of Property Act 1925 caused the benefit of the restrictive covenant in question to run with the red land and therefore to be annexed to it, with the result that the plaintiff company is able to enforce the covenant against Mill Lodge, not only in its capacity as owner of the green land, but also in its capacity as owner of the red land.

For these reasons I think that the judge reached the correct view on the right of

---

17 The first was *Smith* v *River Douglas Catchment Board*, above, and the second *Williams* v *Unit Construction Co Ltd* (1951) 19 Conv NS 262.

the plaintiff company to enforce the covenant, although in part he arrived there by a different route [s. 62].

There remains only the question whether we ought to interfere with the remedy granted by the judge of an injunction against the building of the 32 extra dwellings. *Shelfer* v *City of London Electric Lighting Co* [[1895] 1 Ch 287] is authority for the proposition that a person who has the benefit of a restrictive covenant is, as a general rule, entitled to an injunction on the trial of the action as distinct from an award of damages unless (1) the injury to the plaintiff's legal rights is small, (2) it is capable of being estimated in terms of money, (3) it can adequately be compensated for by a small payment, and (4) it would be oppressive to the defendant to grant an injunction. In my view, the first, third and fourth of these conditions have not been shown to be satisfied. I would, therefore, uphold the injunctions and I would dismiss the appeal.

Therefore, by s. 78, any promise which touches and concerns the land will automatically pass when the land is transferred; this is a 'statutory annexation' of the benefit and means that the old rules about annexation and assignment are unnecessary. It was interpreted again in the next case.

Roake v *Chadha* [1984] 1 WLR 40[18]

A suburban semi-detached house was first sold in 1934 subject to a covenant that not more than one house would be built on the plot. The burdened and the benefiting lands came into the hands of Chadha and Roake respectively. Chadha proposed to build another house in the garden (and obtained planning permission to do so) and Roake went to court to stop him.

The original deed stated that the covenant would not pass unless 'the benefit ... be expressly assigned'. The judge had not only to determine exactly what the Court of Appeal had decided in *Federated Homes*, but also what to do on the facts of this case, because s. 78 does not allow for a 'contrary intention'.

Judge Paul Baker QC:

Mr Henty [for the defendant] made a frontal attack on this use of section 78, which he reinforced by reference to an article by Mr G.H. Newsom QC in (1981) 97 *LQR* 32 [see below] which is critical of the decision...

Now, all this is very interesting ... All the same, despite Mr Henty's blandishments, I am not going to succumb to the temptation of joining in any such discussion. Sitting here as a judge of the Chancery division, I do not consider it to be my place either to criticise or to defend the decisions of the Court of Appeal. I conceive it my clear duty to accept the decision of the Court of Appeal as binding on me and apply it as best I can to the facts I find here.

The true position as I see it is that even where a covenant is deemed to be made with successors in title as section 78 requires, one still has to construe the covenant as a whole to see whether the benefit of the covenant is annexed. Where

---

18 See also P.N. Todd 48 Conv (1984) 68.

one finds, as in the *Federated Homes* case, the covenant is not qualified in any way, annexation may be readily inferred; but where, as in the present case, it is expressly provided, 'this covenant shall not enure'... one cannot just ignore these words. One may not be able to exclude the operation of the section in widening the range of the covenantees, but one has to consider the covenant as a whole to determine its true effect. When one does that, then it seems to me that the answer is plain and in my judgment the benefit was not annexed. That is giving full weight to both the statute in force and also what is already there in the covenant...

Therefore, Chadha was not bound: Roake failed because the benefit had not been transferred to him with his land.

Another case after *Federated Homes* had to consider a covenant not to use the land except for private houses, but this covenant had been made before s. 78 came into effect. In *Sainsbury PLC* v *Enfield LBC* [1989] 1 WLR 590, Moritt J held that the predecessor of s. 78 (s. 58, Law of Property and Conveyancing Act 1881) was 'in radically different terms' from the modern section, and did not automatically annex the benefit to the land.

Some experts did not easily accept the revolutionaries in the Court of Appeal in *Federated Homes*. Newsom had concluded in the article referred to in the case above:

The purpose of this article is to show of the decision in the *Federated Homes* case, so far as it concerns section 78, that:

1. It was perhaps *obiter*, for the green land alone, where there was an express assignment, justified the whole of the relief claimed and granted.
2. It may well be overruled in the House of Lords, as not giving adequate weight to the parliamentary history of section 78 or indeed to the older cases or to the proposition that annexation is a matter of intention.

Perhaps the most remarkable thing about the grounds on which the *Federated Homes* case was decided is that they apply to every restrictive covenant created since 1925, but that it had never occurred to any counsel to argue, or Judge to decide, in that sense before... If the *Federated Homes* case is eventually upheld in the House of Lords, the sitting owners and the insurance companies will become vulnerable in respect of these very numerous cases. It is therefore imperative that the matter should be litigated further as soon as possible and that a decision of the House of Lords shall be obtained which is directly upon the point raised by the observations of Brightman LJ which are criticised in this article.[19]

Implied transfer of the burden of a covenant in equity

The burden of a covenant will pass in equity if:

---

19 See also P.N. Todd 49 Conv (1985) 177.

1. it is negative (that is, it can be complied with without spending money), and
2. it touched and concerned land owned by the covenantee and now owned by the plaintiff. (Note also the registration requirements, see Chapter 10, p. 309, and Appendix 1.)

The first of these rules was affirmed in *Rhone* v *Stephens* (above p. 194). Regarding the second rule, for covenants made before 1926, it must also be proved that the burden of the covenant was intended to run with the land. For covenants made after 1925, this is implied by:

Law of Property Act 1925

Burden of covenants relating to land

79 (1) A covenant relating to any land of a covenantor or capable of being bound by him, shall, unless a contrary intention is expressed, be deemed to be made by the covenantor on behalf of himself his successors in title and the persons deriving title under him or them, and, subject as aforesaid, shall have effect as if such successors and other persons were expressed...

(2) For the purpose of this section in connection with covenants restrictive of the user of land 'successors in title' shall be deemed to include the owners and occupiers for the time being of such land...

Two cases illustrate the rules:

London County Council v *Allen* [1914] 3 KB 642 (CA) Buckley and Kennedy LJJ and Scrutton J

The Council obtained a promise not to build on the site of a proposed road from Allen's predecessor. However, Allen argued, successfully, that she was not bound by it because the Council did not own any benefiting land.

Buckley LJ:

The reason given [for the doctrine in *Tulk* v *Moxhay*] is that, if [it] were not so, it would be impossible for an owner of land to sell part of it without incurring the risk of rendering what he retains worthless. If the vendor has retained no land which can be protected by the restrictive covenant, the basis of the reasoning is swept away...

In the present case we are asked to extend the doctrine of *Tulk* v *Moxhay* so as to affirm that a restrictive covenant can be enforced against a derivative owner taking with notice by a person who never has had or who does not retain any land to be protected by the restrictive covenant in question. In my judgment the doctrine does not extend to that case ... The doctrine ceases to be applicable when the person seeking to enforce the covenant against the derivative owner has no land to be protected by the negative covenant. The fact of notice is in that case irrelevant.

This has now been reversed in limited circumstances by statutes giving powers to local authorities, and some other bodies such as the National Trust, to enforce promises without owning benefiting land. An example is s. 609 Housing Act 1985.

A head lessor has sufficient interest in land to enforce a restrictive covenant against a sub-tenant:

Hall v Ewin (1887) XXXVII Ch D 74 (CA) Cotton, Lopes and Lindley LJJ

Figure 7.1 represents the position of the parties. The covenant in question, 'not to exercise any noisome or offensive trade or business', was contained in the head lease. However, the sub-sub-tenant, McNeff, was keeping lions for public exhibition in the garden.

Cotton LJ:

[T]herefore Ewin was merely an underlessee and was not bound at law by the covenants in the original lease... If the Plaintiff is entitled to relief in this case it must be not on the ground of breach of covenant, but on the ground that he is equitably bound, on the principle laid down in *Tulk* v *Moxhay*...

It was held that, if it were Ewin who was keeping the wild beasts, or if he had given McNeff permission to do so, an injunction would be awarded to Hall against him (Ewin). However, on the particular facts of this case, the plaintiff did not win his injunction.

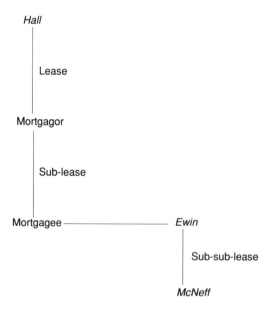

Fig. 7.1

Schemes of development

The third set of equitable rules about restrictive covenants shows even more clearly the 'planning' function of this doctrine. If a scheme of development (or building scheme) is proved, it is as if a local by-law existed. Everyone owning land within the area can enforce, and is bound by, the covenants. Even with modern public planning laws, schemes of development can be very attractive to buyers (and, therefore, to developers) both because they can have many more and more detailed rules, and also because the local people enforce the covenants and maintain the character of the estate themselves.

The case of *Elliston* v *Reacher* [1908] Ch 654 laid down four requirements of a building scheme, and this was sometimes treated almost as if it were a statute. However, it was refined in the next case.

In Re Dolphin's Conveyance [1970] 1 Ch 654 Stamp J

Dolphin was a solicitor and landowner in Birmingham in the mid-nineteenth century. The plaintiff seeking to avoid the covenant was the local authority, but it failed because the court held there was a scheme of development here.

Stamp J:

This originating summons is concerned with some land forming part of an estate known, or formerly known, as the Selly Hill Estate. The estate is now within the area of the city of Birmingham.

The plaintiff's predecessor in title, one Coleman, bought the land nearly a hundred years ago, subject to certain restrictions which Coleman covenanted to observe. That the plaintiffs bought their land with notice of these covenants is not in question. There are numerous persons who, being owners of other parts of the Selly Hill Estate, claim to be entitled to enforce the covenants against the plaintiffs. The plaintiffs ... wish, as part of their housing programme, to redevelop their land in a way inconsistent with the restrictions which, on one view, are designed to secure the preservation of the Selly Hill Estate as an exclusively residential estate, to use modern parlance, of low density, and to that end provide that no building other than a detached dwelling-house shall be built on the estate, such detached dwelling-house having not less than one-quarter acre of land including the site of the dwelling-house...

I find that all the conveyances of the several portions of the Selly Hill Estate by the Dolphin family, except the last, were, so far as material, in identical form...

That it was the intention of the two Miss Dolphins, on the sale of the parcel comprised in Coleman's conveyance, that there should be imposed upon each and every part of the Selly Hill estate the restrictions set out in the conveyance ... cannot be doubted. And each conveyance evidenced the same intention. Nor can it be doubted that each purchaser, when he executed his conveyance, was aware of that intention. The covenant by the vendor in each conveyance, to the effect that the same restrictions would be placed on all future purchasers and lessees, makes this clear. Furthermore, I would, unless constrained by authority to the contrary, conclude as a matter of construction of Coleman's conveyance, and of all the others, that the vendor was dealing with the Selly Hill estate on the footing of imposing obligations for the common benefit, as well of himself, as of the several purchasers of that estate. It is trite law that if you find conveyances of these several parts of an estate all containing the same or similar restrictive covenants with the vendor that is not enough to impute an intention on the part of that vendor that the restrictions should be for the common benefit of the vendor and of the several purchasers *inter se*; for it is at least as likely that he imposed them for the benefit of himself and of the unsold part of the estate alone. That is not this case. Here there is the covenant by the vendors that on a sale or lease of any other part of Selly Hill Estate:

> 'it shall be sold or leased subject to the [seven] stipulations above ... and that the vendors their heirs or assigns will procure a covenant from each purchaser or lessee upon Selly Hill estate to the effect of those seven stipulations.'

What was the point of it? For what possible reason does a vendor of part of an estate who has extracted restrictive covenants from a purchaser, covenant with that purchaser that the other parts of the estate, when sold, shall contain the same restrictions, unless it be with the intention that the purchaser with whom he covenants, as well as he himself, shall have the benefits of the restrictions when imposed? In view of these covenants by the vendor in the several conveyances, I cannot do otherwise than find that the covenants were imposed, not only for the benefit of the vendors or of the unsold part of their estate, but as well for the benefit of the several purchasers. As a matter of construction of the conveyances, I find that what was intended, as well by the vendors as the several purchasers, was to lay down what has been referred to as a local law for the estate for the common benefit of all the several purchasers of it. The purpose of the covenant by the vendors was to enable each purchaser to have, as against the other purchasers, in one way or another, the benefit of the restrictions to which he had made himself subject...

Re Dolphin's Conveyance must be compared with a more recent decision with a quite different result: the court at first instance and on appeal in Trinidad and in the Privy Council were unanimous that there was no building scheme established here.

Emile Elias and Co Ltd v *Pine Grove Ltd* [1993] 1 WLR 305 (PC)

Lord Browne-Wilkinson:
In this case the plaintiff seeks to enforce against the defendant restrictive covenants affecting a parcel of land which formerly formed part of the St Andrews Gold Club in Trinidad. Both the plaintiff's and the defendant's land were part of a small development which took place in 1938 when the then common owner ... sold five parcels of land to four different purchasers, each of the purchasers entering into restrictive covenants affecting the land bought by them. The plaintiff alleges that those covenants are now mutually enforceable between the owners of the lots by reason of a building scheme...

Having reviewed the history of the land and the authorities, he continued:

In this case there was one plan, which was attached to all four 1938 conveyances, but this plan did not show lot 5. If, therefore, lot 5 falls to be treated as part of the designated scheme area, it has not been proved that in 1938 the purchasers of lots 1, 2 and 3 were aware of that fact ... Accordingly lot 5 being part of any scheme that could be established and it not having been shown that the purchasers of lots 1–3 were aware of that fact, the requirements of a defined scheme area known to the original purchasers cannot be satisfied...

It is one of the badges of an enforceable building scheme ... that they accept a common code of covenants. It is most improbable that a purchaser will have any intention to accept the burden of covenants affecting the land which he acquires being enforceable by other owners of the land in the scheme area unless he himself is to enjoy reciprocal rights over the land of such other owners ... That does not mean that all lots within the scheme must be subject to identical covenants ... But if, as in the present case, the lots are all of a similar nature and all intended for high-class development consisting of one dwelling on a substantial plot, a disparity in the covenants imposed is a powerful indication that there was no intention to create reciprocally enforceable rights.

If one steps back and looks at the matter generally, there is no convincing proof that the parties' intention was to produce mutually enforceable covenants.

Extending the class of people who may benefit from a covenant: s. 56

Law of Property Act 1925

Persons taking who are not parties and as to indentures

56 (1) A person may take an immediate or other interest in land or other property, or the benefit of any condition, right of entry, covenant or agreement over or respecting land or other property, although he may not be named as a party to the conveyance or other instrument.

In *In Re Ecclesiastical Commissioners for England's Conveyance* [1935] 1 Ch 430 Luxmoore J held that the section only operates where the people who may enforce the covenant are identifiable at the date of the conveyance.

ENDING RESTRICTIVE COVENANTS

Introduction

Covenants can be ended by mutual agreement, and it is important to bear in mind, when advising people who are bound by a covenant, that they might be able to 'buy it' off the land. Local authorities also have special powers to get rid of covenants (see s. 610, Housing Act 1985).

Other ways in which covenants end are:

1. abandonment (compare the ending of easements, see Chapter 6, p. 189);
2. merger;
3. an application under s. 84, Law of Property Act.

Abandonment

If it is proved that a covenant has been abandoned, equity will not grant a remedy to enforce it. This was argued in:

Chatsworth Estates v Fewell [1931] 1 Ch 224

The covenant here had been made in 1897 and stated that the land was to be used 'as a private dwelling-house only' but Fewell was using it as a boarding-house. Chatsworth owned the benefiting land and wished to prevent this.

Farwell J:

The result of the evidence is that in my view the area in question still remains a residential area. In considering whether an area is residential or not there is a clear distinction between residential flats and boarding houses. The defendant contended that for this purpose there was no distinction and that a really well conducted paying guest house was just as residential as a block of flats. I cannot accept that view. A residential area means an area in which persons reside more or less permanently.[20] A hotel or boarding-house is quite different. This area remains mainly residential, although there are many flats, some few boarding-houses, some schools and so on. Although the area is no longer confined to single dwelling-houses, and the covenants have been somewhat relaxed in the sense that some boarding-houses or guest houses have been permitted, and some other houses have been put to uses not strictly within the covenants, still, on the whole, and taking it broadly, the area still retains its character of being a residential area.

That does not, however, determine the question before me, because although a block of flats does not necessarily render the area non-residential, its erection, or the conversion of a house into a block of flats, is undoubtedly a technical breach of the covenants. In those circumstances I have to consider whether it would be equitable for me to give the plaintiffs any relief by injunction or damages, or whether I must refuse all relief.

Nothing can be said against the defendant's conduct of his establishment except that it is a breach of covenants. That being so, ought I to refuse the plaintiffs relief?

The defendant's first ground of defence is that there has been such a complete change in the character of the neighbourhood, apart from the plaintiffs' acts or omissions, that the covenants are now unenforceable. But to succeed on that ground the defendant must show that there has been so complete a change in the character of the neighbourhood that there is no longer any value left in the covenants at all ... It is quite impossible here to say that there has been so complete a change in the character of this neighbourhood as to render the covenants valueless to the plaintiffs...

---

20 Compare the interpretation of 'private dwelling house' in *C & G Homes* (above p. 198).

The defendant really relied on the acts and omissions of the plaintiffs and their predecessors as a bar to equitable relief.

Now the plaintiffs are not unduly insistent on the observance of these covenants in this sense, that they do not conduct inquisitorial examinations into their neighbours' lives, and do not make it their business to find out very carefully exactly what is being done, unless the matter is brought to their notice, either by complaints of other inhabitants, or by seeing some board or advertisement. I cannot think that plaintiffs lose their rights merely because they treat their neighbours with consideration.[21] They are doing what they think sufficient to preserve the character of the neighbourhood...

But whether they are entitled to relief depends on the exact effect of their past acts and omissions.

Now, as stated in my authorities, the principle upon which this equitable doctrine rests is that the plaintiffs are not entitled to relief if it would be inequitable to the defendant to grant it. In some of the cases it is said that the plaintiffs by their acts and omissions have impliedly waived performance of the covenants. In other cases it is said that the plaintiffs, having acquiesced in past breaches, cannot now enforce the covenants. It is in all cases a question of degree. It is in many ways analogous to the doctrine of estoppel[22] and I think it is a fair test to treat it in that way and ask, 'Have the plaintiffs by their acts and omissions represented to the defendant that the covenants are no longer enforceable and that he is therefore entitled to use his house as a guest house?'...

The answer in my judgment is in the negative...

As to the form of relief I must grant an injunction ... Damages are no remedy, because the object of the covenant is not to make persons pay for committing breaches but to prevent those breaches...

Therefore, Chatsworth won his case.

This case is often compared with:

Shaw v *Applegate* [1977] 1 WLR 970 (CA) Buckley, Goff and Shaw LJJ

Applegate had promised in 1967, when he bought his land, that he would not run an amusement arcade on it. By 1971 he was in breach of the covenant, and two years later the owner of the benefit, Shaw, sued for an injunction. Applegate argued that Shaw had delayed too long to gain his equitable remedy.

Buckley LJ:

The parties seem to have been really confused in their own minds as to whether what was being done was in law a breach of the covenant. They knew all the relevant facts, and had they been as well advised as they will be after we have delivered judgment today, they would have known that there was a breach of the covenant. But it is clear that the parties were not clear in their own minds whether

---

21 How do you think what goes on behind the front door might be discovered?
22 See Chapter 2, pp. 54.

there had been a breach of the covenant; and, moreover, in the earlier years it is probably true to say that the plaintiffs were not particularly upset by what the defendant was doing because his activities probably did not compete very strongly with their own activities...

The real test, I think, must be whether upon the facts of the particular case the situation has become such that it would be dishonest or unconscionable for the plaintiff or the person having the right sought to be enforced to continue to seek to enforce it.

In the present case, having regard to the doubtful state of mind of the parties during the period from the spring of 1971 to August 1973, I do not think that one could reach the conclusion that in this case the plaintiffs would be acting dishonestly or unconscionably in seeking to enforce the rights under the contract because of their failure to sue at an earlier date. After all, it should not I think, be the policy of the courts to push people into litigation until they are really sure that they have got a genuine complaint and have got a case in which they are likely to be able to succeed, and acquiescence at a time when the parties are in doubt as to what their true rights are could, it seems to me, seldom satisfy the tests I have been discussing. Accordingly, in my judgment, there is not here sufficient acquiescence to bar the plaintiffs from all remedy in respect of this covenant, or to deprive them of any continuing cause of action.

But that is not the end of the matter for we then have to proceed to consider whether, in the circumstances of the case, it is a proper case for an injunction or whether we ought not, under the Chancery Amendment Act 1858 (Lord Cairns' Act) to award damages in lieu of an injunction... It is now 1977, almost six years since he [the defendant] first began to operate this property as an amusement arcade and I think that it would be extremely hard after that length of time to restrain him by injunction from continuing to carry on this business...

In these circumstances, I think that the appropriate remedy in this case is not an injunction but damages...

Merger

If the burdened and the benefiting lands come into the hands of a single owner, the covenant ends just as an easement would end: it is not possible to have rights against oneself. However, in the case of a building scheme, the covenant is only temporarily ineffective and it comes back to life if the land returns to separate ownership.

Section 84 and the Lands Tribunal

P. Polden 'Private Estate Planning and the Public Interest' 49 *MLR* (1986) 195

The popularity of such [restrictive] covenants, which were ... enforceable as equitable interests in land soon led to a particular difficulty, for they enclosed individual properties and often whole streets and neighbourhoods in a legal straightjacket which inhibited a flexible response to changes in social habits (such as reduction in the size of households) or in the social status or economic function of a locality. In London this result had become apparent before the Great War, for a long-term centrifugal trend was accelerated by the coming of the motor bus and the electric train, and high quality housing estates were left marooned in areas deserted by the only class who could use them in accordance with the covenants. In the political climate of post-war reconstruction, when the land law was being remodelled around the cult of a fee simple owner who was to be as little hampered in his dealings as possible, it is not surprising that proposals to reduce this inconvenience were put forward...

These proposals resulted in a section virtually unnoticed in 1925 in the flood of legislation:

Law of Property Act 1925 (as amended by the Law of Property Act 1969)

Power to discharge or modify restrictive covenants affecting land

84 (1)[23] The Lands Tribunal shall (without prejudice to any concurrent jurisdiction of the court) have power from time to time, on the application of any person interested in any freehold land affected by any restriction arising under covenant or otherwise as to the user thereof or the building thereon, by order wholly or partially to discharge or modify any such restriction on being satisfied –

(a) that by reason of changes in the character of the property of the neighbourhood or other circumstances of the case which the Lands Tribunal may deem material, the restriction ought to be deemed obsolete[24] or

(aa) that in a case falling within subsection (1A) below the continued existence thereof would impede some reasonable user of the land for public or private purposes or, as the case may be, would unless modified so impede such user; or

(b) that the persons of full age and capacity for the time being or from time to time entitled to the benefit of the restriction, whether in respect of estates in fee simple or any lesser estates or interests in the property to which the benefit of the restriction is annexed, have agreed, either expressly or by implication, by their acts or omissions, to the same being discharged or modified; or

(c) that the proposed discharge or modification will not injure the persons entitled to the benefit of the restriction:

and an order discharging or modifying a restriction under this subsection may direct the applicant to pay to any person entitled to the benefit of the restriction such sum by way of consideration as the Tribunal may think it just to award under one, but not both, of the following heads, that is to say, either –

(i) a sum to make up for any loss or disadvantage suffered by that person in consequence of the discharge or modification; or

---

23 In what ways is this section wider than the equitable discretion regarding remedies?
24 Defined in the *Truman* case, below.

(ii) a sum to make up for any effect which the restriction had, at the time when it was imposed, in reducing the consideration then received for the land affected by it.

(1A) Subsection (1)(aa) above authorises the discharge or modification of a restriction by reference to its impeding some reasonable user of land in any case in which the Lands Tribunal is satisfied that the restriction, in impeding that user, either –
(a) does not secure to persons entitled to the benefit of it any practical benefits of substantial value or advantage to them; or
(b) is contrary to the public interest;
and that money will be an adequate compensation for loss or disadvantage (if any) which any such person will suffer from the discharge or modification.

(1B) In determining whether a case is one falling within subsection (A) above, and in determining whether (in any such case or otherwise) a restriction ought to be discharged or modified, the Lands Tribunal shall take into account the development plan and any declared or ascertainable pattern for the grant or refusal of planning permission in the relevant areas, as well as the period at which and context in which the restriction was created or imposed and any other material circumstances.

(1C) It is hereby declared that the power conferred by this section to modify a restriction includes power to add such further provisions restricting the user of or the building on the land affected as appear to the Lands Tribunal to be reasonable in view of the relaxation of the existing provisions, and as may be accepted by the applicant; and the Lands Tribunal may accordingly refuse to modify a restriction without some such addition.

(8) This section applies whether the land affected by the restrictions is registered or not, but, in the case of registered land, the Land Registrar shall give effect on the register to any order under this section in accordance with the Land Registration Act 1925.

(9) Where any proceedings by action or otherwise are taken to enforce a restrictive covenant, any person against whom the proceedings are taken may in such proceedings apply to the court for an order giving leave to apply to the Lands Tribunal under this section, and staying the proceedings in the meantime.

A covenant may be upheld by the Lands Tribunal even though planning permission has been granted. This is so even if it is the same local authority which (through different departments) has both granted the permission and seeks to prevent the development (see *In Re Hopcrafts Application* (1993) 66 P & CR 475).

There are many cases on s. 84, and each turns on its own particular facts. Two illustrations are provided here.

In Re Truman Hanbury Buxton & Co Ltd's Application [1956] 1 QB 201 (CA) Evershed MR, Romer and Birkett LJJ

The brewery company wished to open a pub on the main road from London to Southend, but the land was subject, as was most of the land in the locality, to a covenant forbidding the 'trade of a hotel keeper, innkeeper, victualler of wines, spirits or beer'. The land was useless to the company unless the covenant could be discharged.

Romer LJ:

The particular ground upon which the application was made, and upon which it is now still sought to support it, is that the covenant in question ought to be deemed obsolete within the meaning of subsection (1)(a) of section 84, having regard to the changes which have taken place in the character of the property or the neighbourhood since 1908.

It seems to me that if, as sometimes happens, the character of an estate as a whole or of a particular part of it gradually changes, a time may come when the purpose to which I have referred can no longer be achieved, for what was intended at first to be a residential area has become, either through express or tacit waiver of the covenants, substantially a commercial area. When that time does come, it may be said that the covenants have become obsolete, because their original purpose can no longer be served and, in my opinion, it is in that sense that the word 'obsolete' is used in section 84(1)(a)...

If serious injury would result to the opponents and others if the covenant was discharged (and having regard to the proposed user for the benefit of motor-coach travellers between Southend and London, it is very easy to imagine the kind of result that would happen) I cannot see how, on any view, the covenant can be described as obsolete, because the object of the covenant is still capable of fulfilment, and the covenant still affords a real protection to those who are entitled to enforce it.

In Re Bass Ltd's Application (1973) 26 P & CR 156

The covenants (to use the land only for private houses) had been made in 1903 and 1911. Bass Ltd wanted to use the land as a lorry park beside their existing brewery but local people (entitled to the benefit) objected because of the increased noise and pollution this would cause. This case was decided after the 1969 amendments and still provides a model of how to go about judging such cases.

J.S. Daniel QC:

I am by no means satisfied that to stop this proposal would be contrary to public interest. There is a private interest, of course, and to serve the private interest of so large a concern as Bass Limited which performs so useful and agreeable a function does to some extent serve the public interest, but that is really as far as it goes, and I do not think it goes far enough...

The proposition that this operation is in the public interest[25] is strange indeed

---

25 On public and private interest, see Kennedy (1982) U Pa L Rev 1332.

unless the public interest is to be equated to the economic benefits to this particular part of the beer trade. Of course such benefits are not to be ignored; they are part of the situation as a whole, but they cannot possibly be allowed to override everything else. It is difficult to isolate this issue...

He found that it had not been shown that the public interest required the covenant to be discharged. He continued:

The residents of City Road are already subjected to noise which is not only undesirable but is beyond the limit of what is acceptable. And this application proposes to increase it.

In that situation I feel quite unable to be satisfied that impeding this proposal does not secure to the objectors benefits of substantial value or advantage. The objectors' evidence made it very clear how they feared and disliked this proposal. It does not seem to me that any authority is needed for the proposition that prevention of such a proposal and therefore the assuaging of the fear and dislike it engenders is indeed a benefit of substantial advantage.

It is not only the noise. That perhaps is the factor most amenable to measurement, difficult though that is. Fumes, vibration, dirt, the appearance of things and the risk of accidents, all add to the aggregation of debits, and cumulatively strengthen my opinion that in impeding this proposal the objectors do secure practical benefits of substantial value and advantage...[26]

It follows that the application must be refused.

The power to declare a covenant contrary to the public interest has been exercised only three times.

In Re Lloyd and Lloyd's Application (1993) 66 P & CR 112 (Lands Tribunal), Judge Marder QC[27]

The Lloyds wished to use their house in a select residential area of Worthing as a community care home for mental patients ready to re-enter the community. Neighbours wished to prevent this, and relied on a covenant prohibiting business use. The Lloyds, therefore, applied to have the covenants declared obsolete under s. 84(1)(a), or modified as contrary to public policy under s. 84(1)(aa). After inspecting the land, Marder QC held that the covenant was not obsolete:

Marder QC:
As to ground (aa) it is not disputed that the applicants' proposal would represent a

---

26 The tribunal judge usually visits the site of the case.

27 See also *In Re Barclays Bank plc's Application* (1990) 60 P & CR, the mortgagee bank won its action to have a 'farm workers only' covenant discharged as obsolete because the overall farm development scheme was unworkable. In *Re Fisher and Ginson Ltd's Application* (1992) 65 P & CR 312, public interest required a covenant preventing building to be discharged as the alternative would mean the new building would have to be demolished; here the objectors received £6,000 in compensation.

reasonable use of the property which is impeded by the restriction. In my judgment the restriction in impeding that user is contrary to the public interest.

I am conscious that the Lands Tribunal in considering the public interest point on many occasions has never before modified or discharged a covenant on this ground in similar cases...

However, in the light of government policy, local need, the adequacy of the Lloyds' house and their suitability to run the proposed home, he concluded:

In the light of these findings, I am satisfied that the restrictive covenant in preventing that use is contrary to the public interest, and I would be prepared to grant the proposed modification on this ground.

Furthermore, in relation to the other limb of ground (aa), I do not consider that in impeding the user of the subject property as a residential care home, the restriction confers any substantial benefit or advantage on the beneficiaries...

There is no evidence to suggest that the conduct of the proposed occupiers, being people with problems of mental illness in course of rehabilitation, would be more or less objectionable or anti-social than if the property were occupied, for example, as a boarding house [permitted under the restrictive covenant] for 10 residents chosen at random from the community at large.

As to ground (c), for reasons already stated, I do not consider the modification sought will injure those entitled to benefit...

It can be argued that the s. 84 jurisdiction amounts to a taking of property (the covenant) without the owner's consent, and thus contrary to human rights. This was proposed by a plaintiff from Northern Ireland to the European Court of Human Rights:

N. Dawson 'Restrictive Covenants and Human Rights' 50 *Conv* (1986) 124

In relation to the benefit of the covenants, the Commission found that the Lands Tribunal decision to extinguish the covenants *interfered with* Mrs Scott's right to peaceful enjoyment of her interest in the land, but *did not deprive her of* her possessions. She could still collect the fee farm rent and enforce the other covenants of the fee farm grant. It therefore appears that the Commission took the view that the benefit of a covenant is not a possession in itself...

It might have been more logical for the Commission to accept that to an extent the applicant had been deprived of her possessions, after all, the benefit of a covenant is a chose in action, and therefore 'property' in our law, but that the deprivation was justified in the public interest...

The Commission agreed with the Tribunal that the facts of the case justified the discharge of the covenants as obsolete, and found that extinction of the 'covenants upon payment of compensation was disproportionate to the legitimate aim of ensuring the most efficient use of the land for the benefit of the community.' Thus, it would now seem that appeal lies, on the facts, from a decision of the Land Tribunal (in favour of the servient owner) to the European Convention of Human Rights.

REFORM

There have been several examinations of the rules relating to covenants, all of which have included proposals for reform.

Law Commission Report No. 127 *Transfer of Land: The Law of Positive and Restrictive Covenants* (1984)[28]

(a) Positive covenants

4.3 The main defect in the present law about positive covenants is of course both simple and devastating; they do not run in any circumstances with the burdened land. None of the devices sometimes used to mitigate the consequences of this rule is apt to do so satisfactorily, but all of them result in conveyancing and other complexities for which there should be no need. It must also be remembered that there are, as it were, two sides to this rule. Not only do later owners not take the burden: the original owner does not lose it. The outcome, therefore, may well be not merely that the covenant cannot be enforced against someone who should be liable, but that it can be enforced against someone who should not.

The Commission condemned the equitable rules relating to the running of the burden of restrictive covenants on the grounds of complexity and uncertainty (para. 4.8). Because of *Federated Homes*:

[A] traveller in this area of the law, old though it is, walks on ground which is still shifting... If a landowner sought legal advice periodically about the enforceability of a particular covenant, he would have to be told different things at different times; and his lot would not be a happy one if he had acted in good faith on advice given one year only to find it invalidated the next. [Paras 4.10–11]

The Commission therefore recommended 'comprehensive reform': the creation of a new interest in land, the 'land obligation':

4.22 ... [T]he new interest will, like an easement, normally subsist as a legal interest in land, and be enforceable by legal remedies, including an action for common law damages. The highly technical rules determining whether the benefit and the burden of restrictive covenants may pass to new owners of the land affected will also disappear; and any doubt which might otherwise arise as to whether an obligation was intended to run with the land or operate only between the parties will be removed by requiring parties who intend to create an obligation

---

28 See also H.W. Wilkinson (1984) NLJ 459, 481; S.R. Edell (1984) J Pl L 222, 317, 401, 485; H.W.R. Wade (1972) 31 Cam L Jo 157; Lord Templeman in *Rhone* v *Stephens* (above p. 195). Castle and Hodge (above note 4) have suggested that positive covenants to preserve the countryside would be of particular value.

running with the land to label it by express words as a 'land obligation'... It will not be enforceable between the original parties after they have parted with the land.

Following this, in 1991 the Law Commission recommended provisions for converting established restrictive covenants into land obligations, and, at the same time, a simpler method of disposing of old covenants.

Law Commission No. 201 *Transfer of Land: Obsolete Restrictive Covenants* (HC No. 546, 1991)[29]

2.13 ... The scheme consists of two main recommendations: first, all restrictive covenants should cease to have effect eighty years after their creation, with transitional provisions for covenants which are older when the new legislation comes into force; secondly, any covenant which is shown not to be obsolete should be replaced with an equivalent land obligation.

2.14 Experience has shown that even though restrictive covenants are patently obsolete, many are allowed to remain on titles to land. This may result from ignorance either of the existence of the restrictions or of what can be done about them, lack of economic incentive or just apathy. Whatever the cause, the inconvenience of their continuing to be recorded has become clear.[30] It seems doubtful whether any change or simplification in the removal procedure would significantly increase the number of owners of burdened land applying to discharge obsolete covenants.

2.15 We therefore consider that, in effect, the burden of proof should be reversed. Once a restriction has been in existence for a substantial period, it should be for the person claiming its benefit to show that there is good reason for it to continue in force, albeit by replacement by a land obligation.

---

29 Editorial comment 56 Conv (1992) 2.

30 Because 'they hamper conveyancing without offering compensating benefit'. Compare the law on the ending of easements (above p. 189).

8 Strict settlements

INTRODUCTION

The orthodox view of the strict settlement is that it was a concept which, along with statutory devices like the Enclosure Acts (see Chapter 1, p. 11), stabilised the power, wealth and social position of the older aristocratic families and eighteenth-century Whigs. In turn, this inhibited the social pretensions of smaller land owners and the nouveau riche. Certainly, the concept of the strict settlement allowed – and was itself largely the creation of – individual families who drew their own complex, particular regimes of inheritance and land ownership.

Keeping it in the family

A.W.B Simpson *A History of the English Land Law* (Clarendon: 1986)

The sixteenth century saw the rise of a new aristocracy and a new landed gentry, which seems to have been obsessed with a desire to entrench its position in society. The landowners, many of whom were lawyers themselves, aided by their conveyancers, attempted expedient after expedient to give permanence to their families; the confused state of the land law and the passion for litigation gave rise to case after case in which this or that form of settlement came under review, to be upheld or struck down for reasons which appeared incomprehensible at times to lawyers, let alone to clients. Towards the end of the seventeenth century, however, the activities of a number of eminent conveyancers – notable amongst them Sir Orlando Bridgman, who, it is said, 'betook himself to conveyancing in the time of the Civil Wars' – produced some order by designing model conveyances which satisfied the desires of the landowners and kept within reasonably well settled doctrines of the law ... The most notable achievement of the conveyancers was the classical strict settlement...

The strict settlement, by perpetuating and consolidating the wealth and power of the wealthy families, and by preserving their estates intact through the years, had an immense effect upon the social and political life of the country until very recent times... The settlement was the legal regime of the landed interest, powerful in both national and local political life; there is inevitably a problem in saying whether the legal institution was cause or effect of the political and social phenomenon. Death duties have in this century brought about the destruction of the social structure which the strict settlement enshrined, though the institution still lingers on.

THE CONCEPTUAL FEATURES AND AIMS OF THE STRICT SETTLEMENT

The foundations of the strict settlement

The strict settlement appeared, as indicated above, in many varied forms. However, its basic nature and purpose is effectively explained in the following extract.

K. Gray and P. Symes *Real Property and Real People* (Butterworths: 1981)

The strict settlement reflected the living arrangements ordained by a patriarchal family figure; it provided a medium for the conferment of family largesse. The settlement could be made to mirror a number of important and complex social evaluations within the family context, through the dispensing of differing grades of interest to differing kinds of family member ... Imagine the position of a wealthy but moribund member of the landed aristocracy of a previous social era. This paterfamilias owned the ancestral home and estate in fee simple, but wished to provide for the members of his family upon his imminent decease. What living arrangements could he fashion which might appropriately govern the land in his absence? How could he provide for his widow and for his eldest son (the new representative of the proud family line)? The difficulty inherent in providing simultaneously for both was accentuated by the extremely important social fact that, if there were two persons whom a moribund testator did well not to trust, those persons were precisely his own widow and his prodigal son. The widow could not be entrusted with the fee simple absolute in the ancestral home – for several reasons. First, she might remarry with the consequence that the ancestral homestead might pass into the hands of another family. Second, there was a common assumption that a widow, being a female, could be guaranteed to be quite incompetent in business matters, and would doubtless be prone to administer and dispose of the family estate in an irresponsible manner. Nor was the eldest son necessarily worthy of any greater confidence. It might also be *de rigeur* for that son to waste his substance in riotous living at such institutions as the University of Cambridge!

The resolution of the dilemma disclosed in this slightly hyperbolic account of times past was achieved in the institution of the strict settlement ... The testator could draw upon a strict settlement to take effect on his death, under which his widow would receive a life interest in the ancestral home and estate. His eldest son would receive an entailed interest in remainder – an interest which would of course fall into possession on the widow's death but which would never enable him to lay his hands on the capital investment represented by the land ... Thus, by making arrangements which conferred merely limited beneficial interests upon the widow and son, the testator could effectively ward off the possibility of depredation against the family inheritance committed either through negligence or through overweening self-interest...

In the event that the family line should terminate at some future date, the ultimate remainder in fee simple[1] could be conferred upon, say, some charity. In this way, if and when all possible temporal benefit had been extracted from the land in favour of one's family, one could finally buy a little spiritual credit by leaving the property for the purposes of some charitable object.

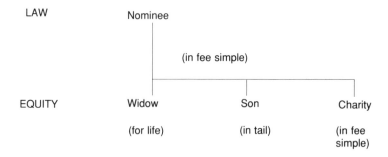

Fig. 8.1

These manifold motivations could be conveniently reconciled within the framework of a strict settlement which vested the bare legal title to the land in a nominee while ensuring that the intrinsic benefit to be derived from the land was

1 See Chapter 2, p. 42.

diverted to the beneficiaries at the appropriate time and in the appropriate proportions:

The essence of this arrangement was that the paper title to the land (i.e., the legal estate) was vested in a nominee who was entrusted with purely administrative functions (powers of management and disposition) and who was bound by fiduciary duties in relation to those functions. However, the valuable as distinct from nominal ownership of the land vested in the beneficiaries behind the trust arrangement thus devised. The enjoyment function therefore devolved upon the beneficiaries in turn, and it became possible in this way to reconcile the conflicting objectives of commerciability and endowment.[2]

Of course, the evolution of the strict settlement in its final form occurred over a long period of time, and the device of landholding described above contains some fairly sophisticated developments which were not perfected until the enactment of the Settled Land Act 1925.[3]

A flavour of the strict settlement, together with an indication of the kind of family conflict which settlements could engender, is provided by Jane Austen. In this extract Mrs Bennet, mother of several daughters, decries the favoured method for maintaining wealth within families, particularly when entailed[4] through the male line:

J. Austen *Pride and Prejudice* (Everyman: 1968)

'I hope, my dear,' said Mr Bennet to his wife, as they were at breakfast the next morning, 'that you have ordered a good dinner today, because I have reason to expect an addition to our family party.'

'Who do you mean, my dear? I know of nobody that is coming I am sure unless Charlotte Lucas should happen to call...'

'The person of whom I speak is a gentleman and a stranger.'

Mrs Bennet's eyes sparkled. 'A gentleman and a stranger! It is Mr Bingley, I am sure. Why Jane – you never dropt a word of this – you sly thing! Well, I am sure I shall be extremely glad to see Mr Bingley...'

'It is *not* Mr Bingley,' said her husband; 'it is a person whom I never saw in the whole course of my life.'

This roused a general astonishment; and he had the pleasure of being eagerly questioned by his wife and five daughters at once.

After amusing himself some time with their curiosity, he thus explained. 'About a month ago I received this letter, and about a fortnight ago I answered it, for I thought it a case of some delicacy, and requiring early attention. It is from my cousin, Mr Collins who, when I am dead, may turn you all out of this house as soon as he pleases.'

'Oh! my dear,' cried his wife, 'I cannot bear to hear that mentioned. Pray do not talk of that odious man. I do think it is the hardest thing in the world, that your estate should be entailed away from your own children; and I am sure if I had been you, I should have tried long ago to do something or other about it.'

---

2 See Chapter 9, p. 234.
3 See Chapter 2, p. 41.
4 An interest which can only be inherited by the children of the grantee.

Jane and Elizabeth attempted to explain to her the nature of an entail. They had often attempted it before, but it was a subject on which Mrs Bennet was beyond the reach of reason; and she continued to rail bitterly against the cruelty of settling an estate away from a family of five daughters, in favour of a man whom nobody cared anything about.

'It certainly is a most iniquitous affair', said Mr Bennet, 'and nothing can clear Mr Collins from the guilt of inheriting Longbourn. But if you will listen to his letter, you may perhaps be a little softened by his manner of expressing himself.'

'No, that I am sure I shall not; and I think it was very impertinent of him to write to you at all, and very hypocritical. I hate such false friends. Why could not he keep on quarrelling with you, as his father did before him?'

If Mrs Bennet wanted a foretaste of her own fate as a widow, or that of many other women in her class, she need look no further than another of Miss Austen's books. The widow with a life interest determinable upon marriage might perceive herself as sorely treated. However, the greatest pity should be reserved for those whose livelihood was a matter of moral, rather than fiduciary, obligation. The position of women whose 'interests' in the family wealth were not enforceable in equity are amply demonstrated in the next extract.

Sense and Sensibility is the story of the Dashwoods. It opens with a description of how the 'Norland estate' is settled solely in the male line. Mr Henry Dashwood, on his deathbed, calls his son, John, and begs him 'to promise to do everything in his power to make ... comfortable' John's stepmother and stepsisters, given that all the wealth is settled upon John. The young man agrees.

J. Austen *Sense and Sensibility* (Penguin: 1986)

When he gave his promise to his father, he meditated within himself to increase the fortunes of his sisters by the present of a thousand pounds a-piece. He then really thought himself equal to it. The prospect of four thousand a year, in addition to his present income ... warmed his heart and made him feel capable of generosity. – Yes, he would give them three thousand pounds: it would be liberal and handsome! It would be enough to make them completely easy ... No sooner was his father's funeral over, than Mrs John Dashwood, without sending any notice of her intention to her mother-in-law, arrived with her children and their attendants ... Mrs John Dashwood did not at all approve of what her husband intended to do for his sisters. To take three thousand pounds from the fortune of their dear little boy, would be impoverishing him to the most dreadful degree. She begged him to think again on the subject. How could he answer it to himself to rob his child, and his only child too, of so large a sum? And what possible claim could the Miss Dashwoods, who were related to him only by half blood, which she considered as no relationship at all, have on his generosity to so large an amount. It was very well known that no affection was ever supposed to exist between the children of any man by different marriages; and why was he to ruin himself, and their poor little Harry, by giving away all his money to his half sisters?

'It was my father's last request to me...'

'He did not know what he was talking of, I dare say; ten to one but he was

A common intention?[5]

light-headed at the time. Had he been in his right senses, he could not have thought of such a thing as begging you to give away half your fortune from your own child.'

'He did not stipulate for any particular sum, my dear Fanny; he only requested me, in general terms, to assist them ... Something must be done for them whenever they leave Norland and settle in a new home.'

'Well, then *let* something be done for them; but that something need not be three thousand pounds. Consider,' she added, 'that when the money is parted with, it can never return...'

'Perhaps, then, it would be better ... if the sum were diminished one half ... I think I may afford to give them five hundred pounds a-piece ... As it is ... they will each have three thousand pounds on their mother's death − and a very comfortable fortune for any young woman.'

'To be sure it is; and indeed, it strikes me that they can want no addition at all ...'

'That is very true ... I do not know whether, upon the whole, it would not be more advisable to do something for their mother while she lives rather than for them − something of the annuity kind I mean...'

'... An annuity[6] is a very serious business; it comes over and over every year and there is no getting rid of it. You are not aware of what you are doing. I have known a great deal of trouble with annuities...'

'... I believe you are right, my love; it will be better that there should be no annuity in the case; whatever I give them occasionally will be of far greater assistance than a yearly allowance, because they would only enlarge their style of living if they felt sure of a larger income, and would not be sixpence the richer for it at the end of the year ... A present of fifty pounds, now and then, will prevent their

---

5 For a very rich reading of this famous painting by Gainsborough, see G. Rose 'Feminism and Geography: The limits of Geographical knowledge' (Polity, 1993) at p. 91.

6 'A yearly sum payable out of the income of land; a rentcharge.'

ever being distressed for money, and will, I think, be amply discharging my promise to my father.'

'To be sure it will. Indeed, to say the truth, I am convinced within myself that your father had no idea of your giving them any money at all. The assistance he thought of, I dare say, was only such as might be reasonably expected of you; for instance, such as looking out for a comfortable small house for them, helping them to move their things, and sending them presents of fish and game, and so forth, whenever they are in season. I'll lay my life he meant nothing farther; and indeed it would be very strange and unreasonable if he did.'

Did the strict settlement effectively preserve aristocratic property?

The extracts in the previous section suggest some support for Simpson's view that the strict settlement effectively 'fenced in' family wealth. Jane Austen supports the notion that the settlement succeeded in keeping landed property intact, 'safely' under the control of the male family members. However, another story of the importance of strict settlements has been put forward.

M.R. Chesterman 'Family Settlements on Trust: Landowners and the Rising Bourgeoisie' in G. Rubin and D. Sugarman *Law, Economy and Society* (Professional Books: 1984)

It has ... been argued, chiefly by Sir John Habbakuk, that between the Civil War and the mid-eighteenth century there was a great deal of land acquisition by the larger landowners (many of whom had moved into this class in Tudor or Jacobean times by means of newly-acquired mercantile wealth, and who mortgaged existing holdings to facilitate new acquisitions), but that thereafter land acquisition slowed down as, with the aid of the strict settlement, the great landed families sat firm on their estates...

This account of the impact of the strict settlement was accepted as orthodox for some time after it was put forward (about 1950) and was supported to some extent by empirical study ... More recent writers ... have however challenged it on a number of points. [They] ... argue first that a general pattern of increase in the size of large landed estates between the Civil War and the mid-eighteenth century is not discernible; indeed, in at least one ... county chosen for empirical study, Cumbria, it did not occur. Secondly, they assert, with empirical evidence from Lincolnshire and Cumbria particularly, that throughout the period under discussion merchants and industrialists could buy land if they wished; there was no 'squeeze' after the mid-eighteenth century due to strict settlements. It is thus misleading to talk in terms of a single-minded desire to tie up heavily mortgaged estates for the foreseeable future. Thirdly, they argue that the strict settlement did not really work along the lines claimed by Habbakuk. Not only was it fragile in the senses conceded by him ... in particular, that it could be scattered to the four winds by a decision of father and heir not to resettle, or by a private Act – but it also could fail to keep the family estates in bondage if successions were not in the direct line or if the father died before the majority or marriage of the heir. As to the last of these contingencies ... at least until the latter half of the eighteenth century it was more likely than not that an aristocratic father would die before the marriage of his heir ... Fourthly, there is clear evidence that in many cases some of an aristocratic family's land was left out of settlement, though it is of course impossible to estimate any overall proportion. Finally, Habbakuk's critics point to evidence that between the Civil War and the mid-eighteenth century – when, according to Habbakuk, large landowners were mortgaging existing holdings in order to acquire new land – mortgage interest rates were significantly higher than the rates of return to be had from leasing agricultural land. It would thus have been economic suicide to indulge extensively in [such] a practice...

As a result of these attacks ... one can no longer safely regard the strict settlement as a major compelling force within a uniform process of aggregation and consolidation of large landed estates. It does not follow that it played no significant role ... even if there is inadequate evidence to support Habbakuk's assertion that the larger landed estates grew at the expense of the smaller ones ... it is still arguable that strict settlements assisted significantly in averting the counter-tendency, *viz.*, the break-up of large estates through division on inheritance, sales by life tenants under financial pressure and so on. The concurrent existence of similar attempts to tie up land – sometimes called 'vinculism' – amongst aristocratic families on the Continent as well as England confirms that the settlement had at least this defensive role, given that in several of those countries (notably France), the partition of smaller holdings went to considerable lengths...

Accordingly, while one has to agree with the opponents of Habbakuk's thesis that as a generalised account of aspects of the land market after the Civil War it must be deemed unproven, it is possible at the same time to assert that a significant pressure towards consolidation of landed estates – or, at the very least, against short-sighted dissipation by individual family members – was exerted by the widespread use of strict settlements amongst landowners from the Civil War to the late nineteenth century.

THE ROLE OF THE STRICT SETTLEMENT IN THE LATE TWENTIETH CENTURY

The strict settlement has suffered a decline in the twentieth century.[7] Successive government legislation, particularly with respect to taxation, has made the strict settlement less and less attractive to the wealthy landowner.[8] As Gray and Symes point out in *Real Property and Real People* (Butterworths: 1981), 'it is ironical that just as the strict settlement reached its zenith of refinement as a legal institution', [in the Settled Land Act 1925] 'other factors began to operate in such

---

7 A.R. Mellows *The Law of Succession* (1983), p. 304.

8 The wide powers given to the tenant for life may also be unattractive when the next incumbent is considered to be irresponsible and unbusiness-like. See *Hambro and Others* v *Duke of Marlborough and Others* [1994] 3 All ER 332.

a way as to render the strict settlement an unsuitable (if not fiscally disastrous) form of land-holding' (pp. 156–7). Occasionally strict settlements may be created by accident as a result of poor drafting[9] or indeed as a result of judicial intervention. A recent example of the latter follows. (But compare also *Binions* v *Evans* (1974) Ch 359 and *Greasley* v *Cooke* (1980) 1 WLR 1306, and cases in Chapter 9.)

Ungurian v *Lesnoff* [1989] 3 WLR 840

The defendant – Mrs Lesnoff – who was Polish, gave up secure accommodation in her home country, together with a promising academic career, in order to live with the plaintiff – Mr Ungurian. She met him, a successful international businessman, through a marriage bureau and in 1970 he bought a London house in his sole name. The defendant and her two sons by a previous marriage lived with him in the house during a relationship which spanned four years. During this period she made considerable improvements to the property including the installation of central heating, rewiring, replumbing and decoration. (Compare *Thomas* v *Fuller-Brown*, Chapter 9, p. 264.) Part of the work was carried out by the defendant herself and the remainder by skilled craftsmen. When the parties separated she remained in the house and claimed either all of or a share in the equitable estate. The plaintiff sought to recover possession.

Vinelott J:

In my judgment, the inference to be drawn from the circumstances in which the property was purchased and the subsequent conduct of the parties – the intention to be attributed to them – is that Mrs Lesnoff was to have the right to reside in the house during her life. It would be to that extent her house ... I do not think that full effect would be given to this common intention by inferring no more than an irrevocable licence to occupy the house.[10] I think the legal consequences which flow from the intention to be imputed to the parties was that Mr Ungurian held the house on trust to permit Mrs Lesnoff to reside in it during her life unless and until Mr Ungurian, with her consent, sold the property and bought another residence for her in substitution for it.

If that is the right conclusion, then the house became settled land within the Settled Land Act 1925 and Mrs Lesnoff is tenant for life and entitled to call for the execution of a vesting deed and for the appointment of trustees...[11]

---

9 For a recent example of poor drafting – in the form of a home-made will – giving rise to a strict settlement, see *Muir* v *Lloyds Bank plc* (1992), 89 Law Soc Gazette 34. See also *Costello* v *Costello* (CA) (1994: Lexis).

10 See Chapter 11, p. 325 *et seq.*

11 What if Mr Ungurian had sold the house? The answer lies in Chapter 10.

9 Trusts for sale

INTRODUCTION

Co-ownership and the trust for sale

Chapter 8 described the essential components of the strict settlement, which developed in order to satisfy the needs of the land-holding classes. However, in the modern period family settlements, with their system of successive owners, have been largely replaced by forms of concurrent ownership. This simultaneous entitlement of two or more persons to possession of an interest in land is usually termed co-ownership.

Co-ownership finds its legal expression in the trust for sale. Indeed one of the major aims of the 1925 legislation is that whenever co-ownership arises it will be subject to a trust for sale, so that the shared beneficial ownership is curtained off from buyers. Trusts for sale can be created expressly, in which case they may give effect to either concurrent or successive beneficial interests. An express trust for sale of land, to be enforceable, must be created in writing:

Law of Property Act 1925

Instruments required to be in writing

53 (1) Subject to the provisions hereinafter contained with respect to the creation of interests in land by parol –

(b) ... a declaration of trust respecting any land or any interest therein must be manifested and proved by some writing and signed by some person who is able to declare such trust or by his will; ...

(2) This section does not affect the creation or operation of resulting, implied or constructive trusts.

Strict settlements are now rarely a consequence of deliberate formal action but the result of a mistake or poor drafting[1] on the part of the settlor's legal adviser, or they arise because the settlor/testator has no legal adviser (see, for example, *Muir*

---

1 For an interesting discussion of the effects of inadequate drafting see *Costello* v *Costello* (CA) (1994: Lexis).

v *Lloyds Bank plc* (1992), 89 Law Soc Gazette 34). Express trusts for sale of successive interests are more common. In the absence of an express trust for sale, implied trusts for sale arise in situations where land is conveyed into the names of two or more persons:

Law of Property Act 1925

Effect of future dispositions to tenants in common

34 (1) An undivided share in land shall not be capable of being created except as provided by the Settled Land Act 1925 or as hereinafter mentioned.

(2) Where, after the commencement of this Act, land is expressed to be conveyed to any persons in undivided shares and those persons are of full age, the conveyance shall (notwithstanding anything to the contrary in this Act) operate as if the land had been expressed to be conveyed to the grantees, or, if there are more than four grantees, to those four first named in the conveyance, as joint tenants upon the statutory trusts hereinafter mentioned and so as to give effect to the rights of the persons who would have been entitled to the shares had the conveyance operated to create those shares:

Provided that, where the conveyance is made by way of mortgage the land shall vest in the grantees or such four of them as aforesaid for a term of years absolute (as provided by this Act) as joint tenants subject to cesser on redemption in like manner as if the mortgage money had belonged to them on a joint account, but without prejudice to the beneficial interests in the mortgage money and interest.

Meaning of the statutory trusts

35 For the purposes of this Act land held upon the 'statutory trusts' shall be held upon the trusts and subject to the provisions following, namely, upon trust to sell the same and to stand possessed of the net proceeds of sale, after payment of costs, and of the net rents and profits until sale after payment of rates, taxes, costs of insurance, repairs, and other outgoings, upon such trusts, and subject to such powers and provisions, as may be requisite for giving effect to the rights of the persons (including an incumbrancer of a former undivided share or whose incumbrance is not secured by a legal mortgage) interested in the land and the right of a person who, if the land had not been made subject to a trust for sale by virtue of this Act, would have been entitled to an entailed interest in an undivided share in the land, shall be deemed to be a right to a corresponding entailed interest in the net proceeds of sale attributable to that share.

Where –
(a) an undivided share was subject to a settlement, and
(b) the settlement remains subsisting in respect of other property, and
(c) the trustees thereof are not the same persons as the trustees of sale,
then the statutory trusts include a trust for the trustees for sale to pay the proper proportion of the net proceeds of sale or other capital money attributable to the

share to the trustees of the settlement to be held by them as capital money arising under the Settled Land Act 1925.

Joint tenancies

36 (1) Where a legal estate (not being settled land) is beneficially limited to or held in trust for any persons as joint tenants, the same shall be held on trust for sale, in like manner as if the persons beneficially entitled were tenants in common, but not so as to sever their joint tenancy in equity.

(2) No severance of a joint tenancy of a legal estate, so as to create a tenancy in common in land, shall be permissible, whether by operation of law or otherwise, but this subsection does not affect the right of a joint tenant to release his interest to the other joint tenants, or the right to sever a joint tenancy in an equitable interest whether or not the legal estate is vested in the joint tenants:

Provided that, where a legal estate (not being settled land) is vested in joint tenants beneficially, and any tenant desires to sever the joint tenancy in equity, he shall give to the other joint tenants a notice in writing of such desire or do such other acts or things as would, in the case of personal estate, have been effectual to sever the tenancy in equity, and thereupon under the trust for sale affecting the land the net proceeds of sale, and the net rents and profits until sale, shall be held upon the trusts which would have been requisite for giving effect to the beneficial interests if there had been an actual severance.

Nothing in this Act affects the right of a survivor of joint tenants, who is solely and beneficially interested, to deal with his legal estate as if it were not held on trust for sale.

(3) Without prejudice to the right of a joint tenant to release his interest to the other joint tenants no severance of a mortgage term or trust estate, so as to create a tenancy in common, shall be permissible.

A statutory trust for sale will also arise where the owner of property, whether real or personal, dies without leaving a valid will:

Administration of Estates Act 1925

Trust for Sale

33 (1) On the death of a person intestate as to any real or personal estate, such estate shall be held by his personal representatives –
(a) as to the real estate upon trust to sell the same; and
(b) as to the personal estate upon trust to call in sell and convert into money such part thereof as may not consist of money, with power to postpone such sale and conversion for such a period as the personal representative, without being liable to account, may think proper, and so that any reversionary

interest be not sold until it falls into possession, unless the personal representatives see special reason for sale, and so also that, unless required for purposes of administration owing to want of other assets, personal chattels be not sold except for special reason.

The nature of the trust for sale

The following extract describes, in general terms, the trust concept.

R. Cotterrell 'Power, Property and the Law of Trusts: A Partial Agenda for Critical Legal Scholarship' 14 *Journal of Law and Society* (1987) 77

As Maitland suggested long ago, it was, above all, the device of the trust which made it possible for English law to recognise many forms of property ownership by collectivities without attracting some of the technical difficulties and ideological conflicts centred on aspects of the doctrinal problem of corporate personality in continental civil law systems ... the trust makes possible the creation of enduring objects of property ('things', clusters of value) in the form of funds which can be invested in various ways to preserve and enhance their value. In this way the trust greatly facilitates the concentration and preservation of capital – and thereby helps guarantee the power and security which the property-form embodies. The recognition of the trust fund, in many trusts, as the embodiment of abstract value, a 'cluster of value', rather than tangible assets (for example, land) is a sophisticated recognition in legal doctrine of the ideological nature of property as an embodiment of power. Ultimately what is important is not the particular assets which are owned at any given time but the abstract value of what is owned which determines the degree of power of the property-holder ... The major ideological significance of this structure is the far greater flexibility in manipulation of property-power which is made possible by it, and a further 'disguising' in ideological forms of the nature of that power.[2] ... The trust form tends to disguise the actual nature of the power relationship between trustees and beneficiaries. The ideology of the trust is such that the legal owner (trustee) is the person who 'looks most like' an owner since she or he is the one who (usually) can carry out most of the ordinary legal transactions possible to an owner – sale, mortgage, lease, exchange, etc. The beneficiary under a trust is seen as passive. Typically the beneficiary cannot interfere in management of the trust property except by procuring the intervention of the courts (for example, in claiming breach of duty by the trustee). During the existence of the trust, control of capital typically rests with trustees.

The trust for sale manifests all the classic features of the trust concept: administration of the trust property is separated from enjoyment, the former being in the hands of active trustees, the latter in the hands of largely passive beneficiaries. However, perhaps more clearly than any other species of trust, the trust for sale translates tangible assets into 'abstract value'. For the trust for sale has some quite unique characteristics.

---

2 See also Chapter 1, p. 16–19.

Sir Robert Megarry and H.W.R. Wade *The Law of Real Property* (Stevens, 1984)

1. *Objects of trusts for sale.* A trust for sale is a trust which directs the trustees to sell the trust property, invest the proceeds, and hold the resulting fund upon the trusts declared by the settlor ... Dividing it among the family was therefore easy, and there was the convenience that a mixed fund of land and personalty could be disposed of under the same set of trusts. This form of settlement was ideal for settling fortunes made in commerce, and for this reason trusts for sale were sometimes called 'traders' settlements'...

3. *Position pending sale.* In a trust for sale the legal estate was vested in the trustees upon trust to sell the land and hold the income until sale and the proceeds thereafter upon specified trusts for the beneficiaries. The trustees were usually given power to postpone the sale in their discretion, and to manage the land until sale. Thus the trustees did not have to sell until market conditions were suitable. Often the consent of the beneficiaries entitled in possession was made requisite to a sale, and in the meantime they could usually have the benefit of the property itself if they wished, as by living in a house, or enjoying the rents if the land was let...

4. *The doctrine of conversion.* The effect of creating a trust for sale is that even before sale the rights of the beneficiaries are for certain purposes deemed to be rights in personalty. This is a case of equity treating that as done which ought to be done. As soon as there is a binding obligation to sell ... the interests of the beneficiaries are notionally converted into the money into which the land is destined to be converted. Even if there is a power to invest the proceeds of sale in the purchase of other land, that land will, unless there is some provision to the contrary, be held on trust for sale and so be treated as money.

There is considerable dispute as to whether the equitable interests of beneficiaries under a trust for sale comprise rights in personalty rather than rights in land. This is not merely a theoretical debate because whether a person has an interest in land or merely in money may determine their rights. (See Chapter 10, pp. 290–303.) An alternative view to that above is offered in the next extract.

S. Anderson 'The Proper, Narrow Scope of Equitable Conversion in Land Law' 100 *LQR* (1984) 86

It has become a trite assertion that interests under trusts for sale of land are to be treated as interests in personalty or the notional proceeds of sale even before the land is sold. This, the principle of equitable conversion, entails in its most absolute form that such interests will fall outside rules concerning interests in land. Such conversion-absolutism, as I shall call this view, presents itself as both logical and timeless, being logically deduced from the (albeit near magical) principle that 'equity regards as done that which ought to be done'. It plays an important part in the academic explanation of the 1925 Property Acts but also, being timeless, can be used to argue that parts of them, Law of Property Act 1925 section 2(1)(ii) in particular, are misconceived. It is also, of course, a standard for evaluating judicial decisions. Yet ... judicial decisions themselves have until recently given little support for the theory of conversion-absolutism. It is true that support from academic writers during this century can be found easily, though much less so for earlier; but if 1925 is taken as a convenient bench-mark, the cases and lines of cases until then seem to divide equally between those seeking a conceptual answer to the question 'does this interest under a trust for sale count as an interest in land?' and those seeking an answer in the policy of the particular rule in question. Moreover, the cases which do fall into the first category again divide about equally between those finding their conceptual answer in conversion-logic and those asserting that 'really' these interests are interests in land.

Perhaps if the responsible maxim had remained as 'equity looks to the substance rather than the form' conversion-absolutism would not have arisen. 'Substance' and 'form' when applied to something as insubstantial as an interest can only be metaphors for relative degrees of proximity between beneficiary and res, and as such very likely to be sensitive to the various contexts in which the question could arise.[3]

TRUSTS FOR SALE UNDER THE LAW OF PROPERTY ACT 1925

The trust for sale as a conveyancing device

The trust for sale, under the 1925 legislative scheme, has the necessary characteristics to make it, in principle, an ideal method for conveying land. For it offers the possibility of reconciling two fundamentally opposing objectives which face any system of land law operating in a modern capitalist world: (1) that land must be freely and easily alienable; and (2) that ownership of land should be both capable of fragmentation and provide a degree of security for those co-owners. One of the ways in which the 1925 legislation sought to meet its two objectives was through the imposition of the doctrine of overreaching. This ensures that when land, held upon a trust for sale, is sold the equitable interests automatically attach to the proceeds of that sale. It is then the duty of the trustees to distribute the money amongst the beneficiaries. The third-party purchaser, in theory, acquires good title to the land free from the beneficiaries' interests.

Law of Property Act 1925

Conveyances overreaching certain equitable interests and powers

2 (1) A conveyance to a purchaser of a legal estate in land shall overreach any equitable interest or power affecting that estate, whether or not he has notice thereof, if −

---

3 See also J. Warburton 50 Conv (1986) 415.

(i) the conveyance is made under the powers conferred by the Settled Land Act 1925, or any additional powers conferred by a settlement, and the equitable interest or power is capable of being overreached thereby, and the statutory requirements respecting the payment of capital money arising under the settlement are complied with;

(ii) the conveyance is made by trustees for sale and the equitable interest or power is at the date of the conveyance capable of being overreached by such trustees under the provisions of subsection (2) of this section or independently of that sub-section, and the statutory requirements respecting the payment of capital money arising under a disposition upon trust for sale are complied with;

(iii) the conveyance is made by a mortgagee or personal representative in the exercise of his paramount powers, and the equitable interest or power is capable of being overreached by such conveyance, and any capital money arising from the transaction is paid to the mortgagee or personal representative;

(iv) the conveyance is made under an order of the court and the equitable interest or power is bound by such order, and any capital money arising from the transaction is paid into, or in accordance with the order of, the court.

(2) Where the legal estate affected is subject to a trust for sale, then if at the date of a conveyance made after the commencement of this Act under the trust for sale or the powers conferred on the trustees for sale, the trustees (whether original or substituted) are either –

(a) two or more individuals approved or appointed by the court or the successors in office of the individuals so approved or appointed; or

(b) a trust corporation,[4]

any equitable interest or power having priority to the trust for sale shall, notwithstanding any stipulation to the contrary, be overreached by the conveyance, and shall, according to its priority, take effect as if created or arising by means of a primary trust affecting the proceeds of sale and the income of the land until sale.

Purchaser is not to be concerned with the trusts of the proceeds of sale which are to be paid to two or more trustees or to a trust corporation

27 (1) A purchaser of a legal estate from trustees for sale shall not be concerned with the trusts affecting the proceeds of sale of land subject to a trust for sale (whether made to attach to such proceeds by virtue of this Act or otherwise), or affecting the rents and profits of the land until sale, whether or not those trusts are declared by the same instrument by which the trust for sale is created.

---

4 Note three vital conditions – conveyance by trustees for sale; overreachable; payment to at least two trustees.

Definition of the trust for sale

Law of Property Act 1925

General definitions

205 (1)... (xxix) 'Trust for sale', in relation to land, means an immediate binding trust for sale, whether or not exercisable at the request or with the consent of any person, and with or without a power at discretion to postpone the sale; 'trustees for sale' mean the persons (including a personal representative) holding land on trust for sale; and 'power to postpone the sale' means power to postpone in the exercise of a discretion;

As a definition this lacks a certain clarity, perhaps because it includes as part of that definition the concept which it seeks to define. Two of the terms – 'immediate' and 'binding' – have excited a degree of judicial and academic debate. The use of the word 'immediate' does not mean that the land must be sold at once, because, as indicated in the definition, the trustees may have a discretion to postpone the sale. Rather the word 'immediate' refers not to the sale but to the trust. No trust for sale arises unless and until the land is impressed with a duty of sale in the trustees. According to the statutory definition any attempt to create a trust to sell at some time in the future will not be a trust for sale under the Law of Property Act.

There has been judicial conflict as to whether the word 'binding' in the statutory definition has any specific meaning at all. In *In Re Leigh's Settled Estates* [1926] 1 Ch 852 Tomlin J (857) stated: 'There must be, it seems to me, some significance in the word "binding" here. It is incredible that the word should have no meaning.' By contrast Romer J (257) in *In Re Parker's Settled Estates* [1928] 1 Ch 247 concluded that 'the word may quite conceivably have been inserted to meet a case of a revocable trust for sale ... and even if this be not so I should prefer to treat the word as mere surplusage ... rather than give to it a meaning that would exclude from being trusts for sale innumerable trusts which are indubitably trusts for sale hitherto ...' Such attempts at ascribing meaning to the word 'binding' have arisen in cases where the court has had to ascertain the moment at which a strict settlement of land gave way to a trust for sale and are, therefore, of declining importance.

Powers and duties of the trustees for sale

Section 205(1)(xxix) makes clear that a 'trust for sale' imposes a paramount duty upon the trustees to sell the land. However, in practice this sale is frequently delayed by the trustees unanimously exercising a power to postpone the sale.

Law of Property Act 1925

Power to postpone sale

25 (1) A power to postpone sale shall, in the case of every trust for sale of land, be implied unless a contrary intention appears.

(2) Where there is a power to postpone the sale, then (subject to any express direction to the contrary in the instrument, if any, creating the trust for sale) the trustees for sale shall not be liable in any way for postponing the sale, in the exercise of their discretion, for any indefinite period; nor shall a purchaser of a legal estate be concerned in any case with any directions respecting the postponement of a sale.

The power to postpone the sale is a discretion and must be exercised unanimously. The duty to sell is an obligation. If one trustee wishes to sell the land it should be sold. In the real world a trustee may disregard this duty and refuse to sell, thereby presenting a difficulty for other trustee/s. It is for instance necessary that all trustees sign the documents to make a legal conveyance. Third-party purchasers (especially mortgagees – see Chapter 10, pp. 290–303) are also unlikely to buy from only one trustee. In a dispute situation over sale the trustee/s who wish to fulfil their duty to sell, one of the beneficiaries, or 'any person interested' such as a mortgagee, may apply to the court for an order.

Law of Property Act 1925

Powers of court where trustees for sale refuse to exercise powers

30 If the trustees for sale refuse to sell or to exercise any of the powers conferred by either of the last two sections, or any requisite consent cannot be obtained, any person interested may apply to the court for a vesting or other order for giving effect to the proposed transaction or for an order directing the trustees for sale to give effect thereto, and the court may make such order as it thinks fit.

The above section is geared towards circumstances where one party to a trust for sale wishes to ensure that the sale takes place. However, the court has a discretion under s. 30 to make whatever order 'it thinks fit'. In exercising their discretion the courts have developed a test of 'underlying purposes' to the trust for sale. These 'underlying purposes', if still in existence at the time of the application for a s. 30 order, may displace the primacy of the duty to sell. The test may not be sufficient to resolve a dispute and the court may also ask the question: Whose voice ought to prevail in equity? This is illustrated in the following case:

Abbey National plc v *Moss and Others* [1994] 1 FLR 307 (CA), Ralph Gibson, Hirst and Peter Gibson LJJ

Mrs Moss was persuaded to transfer her house to herself and her daughter, Mrs Leto, who then obtained a mortgage loan of £30,000. Both Mrs Leto and Mrs Moss appeared on the mortgage deed as mortgagors. It was held, however, that

Mrs Moss's signature was forged and that she had been unaware of the mortgage at the time of its creation. The mother and daughter fell out and the daughter stopped paying the mortgage instalments. The mother appealed against the trial judge's order of sale:

Peter Gibson LJ:

... I start with the position in law created by the transfer of the property into the joint names of Mrs Moss and Mrs Leto subject to the agreement that the property was not to be sold in Mrs Moss's lifetime. The effect was that the trust for sale thereby brought into being could not be implemented without Mrs Moss's consent in her lifetime. It was not in dispute that a restriction in the form of a requirement of the consent of a designated person is not inconsistent with a valid trust for sale ... Moreover, the clear purpose of the agreement was that Mrs Moss could live in the house for the rest of her life if she wanted to do so. There was no agreement that Mrs Leto was to live there with Mrs Moss during their joint lives or at all. On the contrary, as the findings of fact by the judge make clear, Mrs Leto persuaded her mother to create a joint tenancy because on her mother's death survivorship would make the transfer of the property to her so much simpler. In other words, it was for the purpose of convenience only at the point of Mrs Moss's death that the joint tenancy was created by way of gift and that was done only subject to the stipulation made by Mrs Moss.

In circumstances such as these, in proceedings apart from s. 30, the court will not allow the trustees for sale to ignore the requirement of consent ... I would add that in my opinion if the court considers the wider merits apart from the bare requirement of consent, it is hard to conceive of a stronger case for that requirement not to be overridden than one where the owner of the property is induced to create a joint tenancy by way of gift for the purpose of simplifying the passing of the property on her death and does so on the express condition accepted by the donee that the property is not to be sold in the donor's lifetime without her consent. It could not have been within either party's contemplation that the assignment, whether voluntary or involuntary, of Mrs Leto's interest could lead to the sale of the property against the wishes of Mrs Moss. Again apart from s. 30, I apprehend that an assignee of the donee would be held not to be in any better position than the donee to ignore the requirement of Mrs Moss's consent to a sale. It is elementary law and, I would say, only equitable that the assignee cannot acquire a better right than the assignor had, but takes his interest subject to all the equities affecting that interest in the hands of the assignor...

What then is the position in proceedings under s. 30 when consent is refused? It is common ground between Mr Reid and Miss Jackson that s. 30 confers a wide discretion on the court which empowers it to dispense with a consent which is refused. An illustration of circumstances where the court will override a consent requirement is provided by *Re Beale's Settlement Trusts* [1932] 2 Ch 15. There the person whose consent was required but who by reason of his bankruptcy has ceased to have a beneficial interest unreasonably refused his consent.

The approach of the court to the exercise of its discretion can be seen from the cases recently reviewed and analysed by Nourse LJ in *Re Citro* [1991] Ch 142. I shall refer to them only so far as necessary for the purpose of explaining my reasoning in this judgment.

I start with *Re Buchanan-Wollaston's Conveyance* [1939] Ch 738. There land had been conveyed to four persons as joint tenants who shortly afterwards entered into a deed of covenant by which they mutually agreed that any transaction in connection with one part of the land needed the unanimous agreement of all the parties and that any question arising with reference to the remainder of the land was to be determined by a majority vote. On the application of one party for an order under s. 30 this court held that it would not aid that party to break his contractual obligations and so refused to order sale. Sir Wilfred Greene MR (with whom Clauson and du Parcq LJJ agreed) said (at p. 747):

'... it seems to me that the court of equity, when asked to enforce the trust for sale, whether one created by a settlement or a will or one created by the statute, must look into all the circumstances of the case and consider whether or not, at the particular moment and in the particular circumstances when the application is made to it, it is right and proper that such an order shall be made. In considering a question of that kind, in circumstances such as these, the court is bound to look at the contract into which the parties have entered and to ask itself the question whether or not the person applying for execution of the trust for sale is a person whose voice should be allowed to prevail.'

He supported the view of Farwell J that it was not right for the court to act on the invitation of the contract-breaker in the face of opposition by other persons interested, but pointed out that the court might in other circumstances at some future time lend its aid, and cited as an example of changed circumstances the death of all the parties and the sale of their houses for the benefit of which the deed of covenant had been made. That example was one where the collateral purpose had ceased to exist.

The test posed in that case by the Master of the Rolls, *viz* whose voice should be allowed to prevail has been applied in all the subsequent cases. In *Jones* v *Challenger* [1961] 1 QB 176, further light was thrown by this court on what should be the correct approach on an application under s. 30. That was a case where a matrimonial home was purchased in the joint names of the husband and wife. The husband then divorced the wife who left the house. The husband continued to live in the house and refused the wife's request for a sale. Devlin LJ at pp. 180–181 referred to *Re Mayo* [1943] Ch 302 in which Simonds J had said that the trust for sale will prevail in the absence of agreement by all the trustees to postpone sale. Devlin LJ pointed out that in that case there was no suggestion that any beneficiary was intended to occupy the property and referred to the simple principle that in a trust for sale there is a duty to sell and a power to postpone sale. 'But', he continued (at p. 181) 'this simple principle cannot prevail where the trust itself or the circumstances in which it was made show that there was a secondary or collateral object besides that of sale.' He then referred to the facts of *Re Buchanan-Wollaston's Conveyance* and said:

'It is plain from the judgment that in such circumstances the court has a complete discretion to do what is right and proper, and will not allow the voice of the man who is in breach of his obligation to prevail.'

At p. 182 he referred with approval to the decision of Upjohn J in *Stevens* v *Hutchinson* [1953] Ch 299 as showing that where property is acquired by husband

and wife for the purpose of providing a matrimonial home, neither party has a right to demand sale while that purpose still exists, as that might defeat the object behind the trust and the court must do what is right and proper in all the circumstances. At p. 183 Devlin LJ referred to *Re Buchanan-Wollaston's Conveyance* and three other cases, saying that in each one of them:

'...there was a trust for sale because there was a joint tenancy, and the joint tenancy had been created for a particular purpose ... In the case we have to consider, the house was acquired as the matrimonial home. That was the purpose of the joint tenancy and, for so long as that purpose was still alive, I think that the right test to be applied would be that in *Re Buchanan-Wollaston's Conveyance*. But with the end of that marriage that purpose was dissolved and the primary duty, to sell, was restored.'

That first sentence in the last passage cited prompts this comment: it is not surprising that the courts will allow the collateral purpose, while it subsists, to prevail over the trust for sale, given the use of the trust for sale by the 1925 property legislation as the conveyancing device by which beneficial interests are kept off the title to the land. To ordinary people to whom land is conveyed as joint tenants it is artificial to regard the primary purpose of the conveyance as being to sell that which they have just acquired. However, as Devlin LJ pointed out at p. 184, once the collateral purpose goes, then effect must be given to the trust for sale if there is no inequity in selling the property. The true question, he said, was whether it was inequitable for the wife, once the collateral purpose of the provision of a matrimonial home had gone, to want to realise her investment:

'The conversion of the property into a form in which both parties can enjoy their rights equally is the prime object of the trust, the preservation of the house as a home for one of them is simply not an object at all.'

Accordingly, in the circumstances of the case this court ordered the sale of the property.

Jones v *Challenger*, in my judgment, therefore, is clear authority for the principle that so long as there is a collateral purpose still subsisting requiring that retention of the property the trust for sale will not be enforced, but that once the collateral purpose has come to an end, one beneficial owner cannot insist on the retention of the property against the wishes of another beneficial owner who wants the property sold.

There then followed a series of cases in which the effect of the bankruptcy of one of the parties to a marriage and of the consequent vesting in the trustee in bankruptcy of the bankrupt's interest in the jointly owned matrimonial home was considered. In all the cases bar one it was held that the voice of the trustee ought to prevail. The exception was in *Re Holliday* [1981] Ch 405 in which the court allowed the voice of the wife to prevail to the extent that the house was not to be sold until the youngest of the children of the marriage attained 17. The circumstances of that case were somewhat unusual and included the fact that it was highly unlikely that postponement of payment of the debts would cause any great hardship to the creditors (see *Re Citro* (above) at pp. 157 and 161). Nourse LJ in the *Citro* case at p. 157 summarised the broad effect of these authorities as follows:

'Where a spouse who has a beneficial interest in the matrimonial home has become a bankrupt under debts which cannot be paid without the realisation of that interest, the voice of the creditors will usually prevail over the voice of that other spouse and the sale of the property ordered within a short period. The voice of the other spouse will only prevail in exceptional circumstances. No distinction is to be made between a case where the property is still being enjoyed as the matrimonial home and one where it is not.

At p. 158 Nourse LJ turned to consider whether the bankruptcy cases were consistent with the principles in *Jones* v *Challenger*. He pointed out that there was no problem where the property was no longer being enjoyed as the matrimonial home, the collateral purpose having ended. But he continued:

'The more interesting question is whether there is an inconsistency in the case where the property is still being enjoyed as the matrimonial home ... It would have been open to the wife ... to argue that the secondary purpose was still existing, that the husband's beneficial interest to which the trustee had succeeded was, in the words of Buckley LJ in *Re Holliday* ... at p. 424c, "an asset in the bankruptcy which is liable to be affected by the interest of any other party interested in that land" and that the trustee had no greater right to demand a sale than the husband himself ... Perhaps it was unfortunate there that the husband and wife represented themselves, because after that the point appears to have got lost. In none of the decisions is there to be found any overt consideration of the argument or any reasoned explanation of its rejection. They simply assume that there is no distinction between the two cases.'

He then sought to reconcile those ... decisions with *Jones* v *Challenger* by a unifying principle. It is important to observe that this formed part of the *ratio* of his decision. In the *Citro* case two brothers, Domenico and Carmine Citro, had become bankrupt, the only substantial asset of each being his share in the matrimonial home. But whereas Domenico Citro's marriage had come to an end (so that the secondary purpose behind his and his wife's joint acquisition of their matrimonial home had ended with his judicial separation from his wife), the secondary purpose behind the joint acquisition by Carmine Citro and his wife of their matrimonial home had not. Nourse LJ said (at pp. 158–159):

'Here I should state that Mr Cameron, who appears for the bankrupt's wives, has not argued for any distinction between these two cases, notwithstanding that the secondary purpose behind the joint acquisition of Carmine and Josephine Citro's home still exists. Having been puzzled by the point myself and having thought it right to consider it, I have come to the clear conclusion that the assumption made in the earlier decisions is correct. Shortly stated, my reasoning is this. In the husband and wife cases exemplified by *Jones* v *Challenger* ... it is held that neither spouse has a right to demand a sale of the property while the purpose of its enjoyment as a matrimonial home still exists. In order to be so enjoyed it must be occupied by the spouses jointly. As a matter of property law, the basis of their joint occupation is their joint ownership of the beneficial interest in the home. Although the vesting of one of their interests in a trustee for creditors does not in itself destroy the secondary purpose of the trust, the basis for their joint occupation has gone. It must, I think, be implicit in the principle of

Jones v *Challenger*, that the secondary purpose can only exist while the spouses are not only joint occupiers of the home but joint owners of it as well.'

It is to be observed that the reasoning of Nourse LJ expressly includes the proposition that the secondary purpose, *viz* that the property can be occupied as the matrimonial home, can only exist while the spouses are both joint occupiers and also joint owners of the home, and this he founds on the fact that as a matter of property law, the basis of the husband's and wife's joint occupation is their joint ownership of the beneficial interest in the home. It follows that Nourse LJ treats a case where the husband and wife are still living together in the matrimonial home, but one of them become bankrupt, as a case where the collateral purpose has come to an end. This reconciliation of the bankruptcy authorities with the principles of *Jones* v *Challenger* may or may not stand further scrutiny in the House of Lords, but, as part of the *ratio* of Nourse LJ, with whom Bingham LJ agreed, it is plainly binding on this court. It is entirely consistent with what seems to me to be the manifestly correct and principled proposition that where the collateral purpose has not come to an end the court will ordinarily not allow the trust for sale to defeat that purpose, even where there has been an assignment to another by an original party to that purpose. The assignee cannot normally be in a better position than the assignor. In the present case it is impossible to say that the collateral purpose, *viz* that Mrs Moss should continue to live in the property during her life, has come to an end by reason of Mrs Leto losing her beneficial interest through the mortgage, because the collateral purpose is wholly unaffected by that event. It would, of course, have been otherwise if the collateral purpose had been that she and Mrs Moss would live together in the property.

I should mention two other cases to which we were referred. In *Lloyds Bank plc* v *Byrne and Byrne* [1993] 1 FLR 369, another matrimonial home case, this court held that a bank which obtained a charging order on the husband's interest in the property was in the same position as a trustee in bankruptcy when seeking an order for sale. There are aspects of what was said in Parker LJ's judgment which, I have to say, I find difficult, but I, of course, accept that the decision is binding on this court and clearly supports the judge's view, to which he came without the benefit of the *Byrne* case, that the position of a chargee and that of a trustee in bankruptcy can be equated. But that case is of the same type as that of Carmine Citro, and the decision in *Re Citro* was expressly followed by this court. Accordingly, it is distinguishable in the same way as *Re Citro*. The second case was the earlier decision of this court in *Stott* v *Ratcliffe* reported briefly in (1982) 126 Sol Jo 310 ... In that case a married man, Mr Stott, formed an association with the defendant, Mrs Ratcliffe. Both contributed to the purchase of a house in Mr Stott's sole name. Later they put the property into their joint names on a beneficial joint tenancy in common in equal shares. They lived together for 20 years, Mr Stott told Mrs Ratcliffe that he intended to leave his share to her in his will but never got round to it. On his death his half-share became vested in his wife, the plaintiff. She sought an order for sale under s. 30. Mrs Ratcliffe gave evidence that there was an understanding between Mr Stott and herself that the two of them and the survivor should live in the house. The court below found that the intentions of the parties was not fulfilled or terminated on the death of either of them: the house had been bought as their home and was meant to remain a home for the survivor. The court refused to order a sale, both Lord Denning MR and Eveleigh LJ saying that the purpose of the trust was not completely fulfilled on the death of Mr Stott. In my judgment that decision too is entirely in line with the principles of *Jones* v *Challenger* in recognising that a subsisting collateral purpose will not be overridden by the trust for sale notwithstanding that the beneficial interest of one of the original parties to that purpose has passed to another who is being kept out of the enjoyment both of the property and of the proceeds of sale.

I come back to the decision of the judge. In my judgment he plainly erred in treating *Re Citro* as establishing that the court would not normally take a subsisting collateral purpose into account when one of the original parties to that purpose has parted with his share. On the contrary, *Re Citro* only establishes that the collateral purpose will not be treated as subsisting when that purpose is to provide a matrimonial home and one of the parties ceases through bankruptcy or the like to own his share. It does not purport to apply where a different collateral purpose continues to subsist and where such purpose is not affected by the alienation by a party to that purpose of his share. The judge also erred in holding that the collateral purpose established by the agreement of Mrs Moss and Mrs Leto was not a factor to inhibit him from ordering a sale and that by reason of *Re Citro* it was for Mrs Moss to show that there were no exceptional circumstances present. Again I fear he has not appreciated the distinction between *Re Citro* and the present case, nor taken any account of the fact that in every reported case where a collateral purpose has been held to continue (and I therefore exclude cases like that of Carmine Citro) the court has not allowed the trust for sale to prevail.

The consequence of that error is that the court must exercise the discretion under s. 30 afresh. The judge expressed the view that the failure by Mrs Moss to speak out when she discovered that there was a mortgage on the property would have weighed heavily against her and would disentitle her to any substantial postponement of sale. But that *obiter* opinion appears to have been dependent on a point on which no evidence was led or given and which appears only to have occurred to the judge in writing his reserved judgment. The point was that the plaintiff's chances of effectively chasing Mr and Mrs Leto and possibly obtaining a *Mareva* injunction against them must be much reduced by that silence. There is no evidence that the plaintiff suffered any prejudice as a result of Mrs Moss's silence. I am therefore unable to give this factor the weight that the judge would have given to it.

Looking at all the circumstances, it seems to me plain that the most important consideration is the continuing collateral purpose, particularly when viewed against the background of how it came about that Mrs Leto acquired any interest at all. Further, in the judge's own words:

'Mrs Moss has, in effect, been defrauded, and she stands to lose the home to which she is deeply attached and which she shows every intention of not leaving except under compulsion. The original debacle is not remotely her fault.'

On the other side of the scales can be put the fact that the plaintiff did not know of the collateral purpose and the condition subject to which Mrs Leto acquired her interest. It is owed a substantial sum of money and it may well be that Mrs Leto's interest in the circumstances is not readily saleable and that without an order for sale of the property it will be kept out of the monies due from Mr and Mrs Leto for even longer, with interest mounting all the while. But I feel bound to observe that I do not agree with the judge's comment that there was no fault on the part of the plaintiff. The detriment it is suffering comes from its failure to obtain Mrs Moss's signature to the mortgage deed. It should have ensured, through its solicitor, that all the intended parties to the mortgage did in fact execute the mortgage deed. I must also observe that the way that deed was completed should have caused the plaintiff, again through its solicitor, to check whether each party did in fact duly execute the deed. I say that because the places in the deed opposite the parties' signatures, which were intended for the signature of the witness to each party's signature and for details about the witness, were incorrectly filled in with details about the parties themselves and only at the bottom of the deed under what appear to be the three signatures of the three parties does one find the manuscript words 'Witnessed by' and then the signature of Mr Russell. The plaintiff, through its solicitor, should, in my view, have been alerted by that oddity to inquire whether Mr Russell did, in fact, witness the three signatures. In fact he witnessed none of the signatures on the deed. A final point against the plaintiff is that it takes its interest as assignee of Mrs Leto, who could not herself have obtained an order for sale.

I am left in no doubt that the court's discretion should be exercised against ordering a sale. To order a sale seems to me not to be right and proper but to be grossly inequitable. For my part I would allow this appeal and dismiss the plaintiff's proceedings against Mrs Moss.

As indicated in *Abbey National* v *Moss* there are particular problems with respect to petitions made under s. 30, Law of Property Act 1925, where land is held jointly and one party becomes insolvent. When someone is declared bankrupt, in general, their property automatically vests in the trustee in bankruptcy. Where land is held jointly, by the bankrupt and another, the legal title cannot vest in the trustee. However, the beneficial interest of the bankrupt can vest in the trustee, who to fulfil his duty on behalf of the bankrupt's creditors will apply to the court for an order of sale. Such a petition may, and frequently will, be challenged by the co-owner of the property.

The Insolvency Act 1986, s. 336(3), requires all applications by the trustee in bankruptcy for sale of the property under s. 30 to be made to the court with jurisdiction in the bankruptcy. The 1986 Act provides criteria for guidance to the court in exercising its discretion.

Insolvency Act 1986

Rights of occupation etc. of bankrupt's spouse

336 (4) On such an application as is mentioned in subsection ... (3) the court shall make such an order under ... section 30 of the Act of 1925 as it thinks just and reasonable having regard to –
    (a) the interests of the bankrupt's creditors,
    (b) the conduct of the spouse or former spouse, so far as contributing to the bankruptcy,
    (c) the needs and financial resources of the spouse or former spouse,
    (d) the needs of any children, and

(e) all the circumstances of the case other than the needs of the bankrupt.

(5) Where such an application is made after the end of the period of one year beginning with the first vesting ... of the bankrupt's estate in a trustee, the court shall assume, unless the circumstances of the case are exceptional, that the interests of the bankrupt's creditors outweigh all other considerations.

There has been no decision directly on these provisions of the Insolvency Act but the next extract provides some useful ideas regarding their likely interpretation:

G. Howell *Family Breakdown and Insolvency* (Butterworths:1993)

As far as is known there are no decided cases as to what constitutes 'exceptional circumstances' under s. 336(5), although the point is anticipated in *Re Citro* [1990] 3 All ER 952 ... That the homelessness of the spouse and the children alone will not be sufficient is spelt out in *Re Citro*...

In that case, however, Nourse LJ states (at p. 962e): 'I do not say that in other cases there might not be other exceptional circumstances. They must be identified if and when they arise'. Nourse LJ goes on to specifically mention that if it was highly unlikely that the postponement or payment of the creditor's debts would cause any great hardship to any of them this could amount to an exceptional circumstance.

To speculate otherwise, as that is all that can be done in the absence of case law ... the following could perhaps be suggested as being 'exceptional circumstances' for the purpose of s. 336(5):

- where the house has been specifically adapted for a handicapped spouse or child;
- where the spouse is terminally ill;
- where the spouse plans to emigrate on a specified date in the relatively near future;
- where the creditors are not prejudiced by a postponement of the realising of the bankrupt's interest due to a secured commercial rate of interest;
- where the remaining amount to be realised to satisfy the creditors in full from the sale of the home is purely nominal in view either of the extent of the rest of the bankrupt's estate or the level of his or her debts or both;
- where the spouse satisfies the court that although unable to buy out the trustee in bankruptcy's interest in the home immediately, there is no doubt that this will be done at a specified date in the relatively near future;
- where the spouse is involved in proceedings against a third party, the result of which may mean that the spouse can afford to buy out the trustee in bankruptcy (see *Re Gorman* [1990] 1 All ER 717...).

In both law and practice, therefore, as long as the home is not owned and occupied solely by the bankrupt ... there will be a breathing space of 12 months for the bankrupt, the spouse and their family to have an opportunity to sell the home voluntarily or, if possible, to enter into arrangements to buy out the trustee in bankruptcy's interest in the home to avoid a forced sale. However ... if such arrangements cannot be reached with the trustee in bankruptcy and the trustee in bankruptcy chooses to issue an application then the court will order a sale of the property. In practice, much will depend upon the trustee in bankruptcy's willingness to force the matter through the courts.[5]

The trustee's duty to sell may be subject to the consent of any person, or persons, whether or not they have an interest under the trust. There is statutory limitation upon the number of consents trustees for sale are required to obtain and provision is further made for judicial intervention in circumstances where consent is either unobtainable or is refused. In addition there is a duty placed upon trustees holding upon statutory trusts to consult the beneficiaries prior to any sale.

Law of Property Act 1925

Consents to the execution of a trust for sale

26 (1) If the consent of more than two persons is by the disposition made requisite to the execution of a trust for sale of land, then in favour of a purchaser, the consent of any two of such persons to the execution of the trust or to the exercise of any statutory or other powers vested in the trustees for sale shall be deemed sufficient.

(2) Where the person whose consent to the execution of any such trust or power is expressed to be required in a disposition is not *sui juris* or becomes subject to disability, his consent shall not, in favour of a purchaser, be deemed to be requisite to the execution of the trust or the exercise of the power; but the trustees shall, in any such case, obtain the separate consent of the parent or testamentary or other guardian of an infant or of the receiver (if any) of a person suffering from mental disorder.

(3) Trustees for sale shall so far as practicable consult the persons of full age for the time being beneficially interested in possession in the rents and profits of the land until sale, and shall, so far as consistent with the general interest of the trust, give effect to the wishes of such persons, or, in the case of dispute, of the majority (according to the value of their combined interests) of such persons, but a purchaser shall not be concerned to see that the provisions of the subsection have been complied with. In the case of a trust for sale, not being a trust for sale created by or in pursuance of the powers conferred by this or any other Act, this subsection shall not apply unless the contrary intention appears in the disposition creating the trust.[6]

---

5 The provisions of the Insolvency Act do not apply to cohabitees (see M.P. Thompson *Coownership* (Sweet and Maxwell: 1988), pp. 108–12).
6 See also, *In Re Beale's Settlement Trusts* [1932] 2 Ch 15.

The above provision is supplemented by the jurisdiction awarded to the Court under s. 30 of the same Act[7] and by Trustee Act 1925, s. 57.

Trustee Act 1925

Power of court to authorise dealings with trust property

57 (1) Where in the management or administration of any property vested in trustees, any sale, lease, mortgage, surrender, release, or other disposition, or any purchase, investment, acquisition, expenditure, or other transaction, is in the opinion of the court expedient, but the same cannot be effected by reason of the absence of any power for that purpose vested in the trustees by the trust instrument, if any, or by law, the court may by order confer upon the trustees, either generally or in any particular instance, the necessary power for the purpose, on such terms, and subject to such provisions and conditions, if any, as the court may think fit and may direct in what manner any money authorised to be expended, and the costs of any transaction, are to be paid or borne as between capital and income.

The duty under s. 26(3), Law of Property Act 1925, is to consult but not necessarily to fulfil the wishes of the beneficiaries. However, in certain circumstances this provision may be an important weapon in the hands of a beneficiary who wishes to halt or delay the sale of land. A useful illustration is offered by the next case.

Waller v *Waller* [1967] 1 WLR 451

A house had been purchased using the resources of both husband and wife, but in the name of the husband alone. Without consulting his wife, the other beneficiary, as to her wishes regarding the house, the husband entered into an agreement with a Mr Jeffs to sell the house. The wife sought an interlocutory injunction to restrain her husband from continuing without her consent.

Stamp J:

I have no doubt that the husband ought to be restrained. The wife is entitled to be protected from what may be an improvident sale by the appointment of an additional trustee, and to have her wishes considered. What is submitted on behalf of the husband is that whatever might be the position at law and in equity as between two strangers, it is different as between husband and wife, and that where a property has been purchased by husband and wife as a matrimonial home, and the wife is no longer in possession – as, so it is submitted, is the case here – she cannot prevent her husband from selling the property.

The purpose for which the property was purchased, so the argument runs, having come to an end, it is open to the husband to sell the property without regard

---

7 See *Abbey National Building Society* v *Moss* (above).

to his wife's wishes ... Neither the authorities nor the submissions satisfy me, however, that a tenant in common in equity who is the wife of the other tenant in common in equity is in any worse a position to prevent the sale of the property by the husband, who is the sole trustee, than would be the position if the parties were complete strangers to each other ... The fact that at the time this motion opened before me Jeffs was not a party to the proceedings has occasioned me more anxiety, but the general principle is that where the equities are equal, *qui prior est tempore potior est jure.*[8]

Notwithstanding the fact that Jeffs has an equitable interest in the property because the husband as legal owner has entered into a contract with him to sell it, I think that the wife has made a prima facie case for restraining the husband...

Trustees for sale have a variety of statutory powers which enable them to administer and manage the trust property. These discretions derive from s. 28(1), Law of Property Act 1925, which gives trustees for sale 'all the powers of a tenant for life and the trustees of a settlement under the Settled Land Act 1925'. The trustees may, for example, grant leases, raise money on a mortgage for improvements to the land, or invest the proceeds from selling a part of the land held upon trust in the purchase of new land. In addition s. 29(1), Law of Property Act 1925, gives trustees for sale the right to delegate their powers of management 'by writing, signed by them, to any person of full age ... for the time being beneficially entitled in possession' until sale. Under s. 29(3), Law of Property Act 1925, the trustees for sale are not 'liable for the acts or defaults of the person to whom the power is delegated'.

REFORM

Law Commission Report No.181 (1989) *Transfer of Land: Trusts of Land*

3.5 Our proposals in relation to concurrent interests are focused upon two features of the trust for sale. Our principal recommendations are, firstly, that all land which previously would have been held under an implied trust for sale (including cases of equitable co-ownership behind a sole legal title ... achieved in the draft Bill by the comprehensive definition of 'trust of land' in clause 1) should now be held under the new system by trustees with a power to retain and a power to sell, (this will be one consequence of giving trustees of land the powers of an absolute owner) and, secondly, that the doctrine of conversion should cease to apply. Thus, the main purpose of the trust will no longer be the realisation of the capital value of the land ...

3.6 ... This scheme will ... put the exercise of judicial discretion under s.30 on a rather better footing than at present. Although the courts have exercised this discretion rather broadly, the starting point has always been that there is a duty to

---

8 'Who is first in time, is first in right.' (The first person has the best right.)

sell ... If the trustees have ... a power either to sell or to retain rather than a power merely to postpone the sale, the terms of the discretionary jurisdiction will be more in accord with the circumstances which they are required to accommodate...

12.6 As regards the circumstances in which applications to the court should be allowed, our general view is that the courts should be able to intervene in any dispute relating to a trust of land ... We recommend that any interested person should be able to apply to the court either to force or prevent a sale, or to force or prevent the exercise of the trustee's powers...

12.9 ... it is our view that the court's discretion should be developed along the same lines as the current 'primary purpose' doctrine. This approach was moulded to practical requirements (even though it may have developed 'in spite of' the statutory formulation of the trust for sale) and we consider that it more or less gets the balance right. The criteria which the courts have evolved for settling disputes over trusts for sale are ones which will continue to have validity in the context of the new system ... the guidelines will ... put these criteria on a statutory footing. For example, although it seems clear that the courts will not be slow to protect the interests of children ... Our recommendation here is that the welfare of children should be expressly defined as an independent consideration. The aim is to ensure that the interests of children are not linked to the interests of particular beneficial owners.[9]

12.10 Aside from the welfare of children, the court is directed to have regard to five other factors: the intentions of the settlor; the purpose for which the land was acquired; the wishes of any adults entitled to interests in possession; the interests of any creditor who has obtained a charging order ... against any person for whose benefit the land is held; and any other matter which appears to the court to be relevant.

CO-OWNERSHIP

Types of co-ownership

The common law provided four possible kinds of co-ownership: (a) tenancy by entireties; (b) coparcenary; (c) joint tenancy; (d) tenancy in common. In practice only the joint tenancy and the tenancy in common are found.

The former is characterised by the 'four unities' and the 'right of survivorship'. The 'four unities', easily remembered by the acronym 'PITT', are unity of possession, interest, time and title. A joint tenant, it may be said, owns everything and nothing. The joint tenant, along with the other co-owners, is entitled to enjoy possession and enjoyment of all the property. Alone, the joint tenant owns no specific or individual part of the property. This last point is reinforced by the

---

9 How does this fit with Insolvency Act provisions? See p. 244–46.

'right of survivorship' or *jus accrescendi*. When one joint tenant dies without severing the share *inter vivos*, the interest simply accrues to the surviving joint tenants. A problem may arise where two or more joint tenants die in circumstances where it is difficult to ascertain who survived whom, as in road, rail or air accidents. Legislation makes provision for such situations:

Law of Property Act 1925

Presumption of survivorship in regard to claims to property

184 In all cases where, after the commencement of this Act, two or more persons have died in circumstances rendering it uncertain which of them survived the other or others, such deaths shall (subject to an order of the court), for all purposes affecting the title to property be presumed to have occurred in order of seniority, and accordingly the younger shall be deemed to have survived the elder.

In contrast only one of the four unities applies to tenancies in common – unity of possession. Thus each tenant in common has an equal right to occupy the co-owned land. One co-owner cannot, in general, maintain an action for trespass against another, nor is one co-owner in sole occupation of the property usually obliged to pay rent to the others.[10]

Each tenant in common, therefore, can hold a different share in the property. For example, one may be entitled to a third share, another to a quarter share and so on. The land itself is not marked in any way with boundaries between each individual share, but that does not detract from a tenant in common's entitlement to a specific share. Consequently, the right of survivorship plays no part in the tenancy in common. Each tenant in common can deal with his/her own share in whichever way he/she prefers and may nominate, in a will, his/her successor to the property. There is no automatic accrual to the surviving co-owners.

Co-ownership after 1925

One of the avowed purposes of the 1925 legislation was to simplify conveyancing. In this regard the joint tenancy is more convenient than the tenancy in common because, due to the unity of title, any purchaser of land from joint tenants will need to investigate only one title prior to conveyance. Moreover, the right of survivorship doctrine means that there is a gradual, but inevitable, progression from joint tenancy to sole ownership, which in its turn makes conveyancing simpler. By contrast, the tenancy in common fragments title making it unattractive from a conveyancer's point of view. Legal tenancies in common were, therefore, abolished by Parliament in s. 1(6), Law of Property Act 1925.

In addition, a legal joint tenancy may *never* be severed:

---

10 See *In Re Pavlou (A Bankrupt)* [1993] 2 FLR 751.

Law of Property Act 1925

Joint tenancies

36 (2) No severance of a joint tenancy of a legal estate, so as to create a tenancy in common in land, shall be permissible, whether by operation of law or otherwise, but this subsection does not affect the right of a joint tenant to release his interest to the other joint tenants, or the right to sever a joint tenancy in an equitable interest whether or not the legal estate is vested in the joint tenants:

Provided that, where a legal estate (not being settled land) is vested in joint tenants beneficially, and any tenant desires to sever the joint tenancy in equity he shall give to the other joint tenants a notice in writing of such desire or do such other acts or things as would, in the case of personal estate, have been effectual to sever the tenancy in equity and thereupon under the trust for sale affecting the land the net proceeds of sale, and the net rents and profits until sale, shall be held upon the trusts which would have been requisite for giving effect to the beneficial interests if there had been an actual severance.

Whilst stating that no tenancy in common can be created at law s. 36(2), therefore, expressly preserves their existence in equity. Indeed, equity may prefer tenancies in common since equity aims for equality, a feature singularly lacking under the *jus accrescendi* doctrine. It is possible, therefore, for land to be held by joint tenants at law upon trust for sale on behalf of either joint tenants or tenants in common in equity.

It is of course crucial in co-ownership to know whether a person is an equitable joint tenant or tenant in common. 'Equity follows the law' and so in the absence of other evidence a beneficial joint tenancy will be created. On the other hand evidence of a tenancy in common may be derived from the destruction of the four unities, for instance where the co-owners obtained their interests under different titles and at different times. If the co-ownership was created in one document it is essential to look for so-called 'words of severance'. Where land is conveyed 'to A and B in fee simple', without any further words explaining the co-owners' individual shares, the law will give effect to an equitable joint tenancy. However, where land is conveyed to 'A and B in equal shares', or 'to share and share alike', 'equally', or any other words or phrases which indicate a distinct share for each party then the law will give effect to an equitable tenancy in common. Equity may also presume a tenancy in common where the parties made unequal contributions to the purchase price or where the co-owners are partners or run separate businesses.[11]

This last point was reinforced in the following extract from a Privy Council decision emphasising a continuing preference for equitable tenancies in common.

---

11 See *Barton* v *Morris* [1985] 2 All ER 1032.

Malayan Credit Ltd v *Jack Chia-MPH Ltd* [1986] 1 All ER 711 (PC)
Lord Keith of Kinkel, Lord Brandon of Oakbrook, Lord Brightman, Lord
Mackay of Clashfern, Sir Denys Buckley

The appellant and respondent were joint tenants in law of leasehold business
premises in Singapore. They shared the premises but ran separate businesses and
paid rent and service charges in agreed unequal proportions.

Lord Brightman:

Their Lordships will deal first with the general principles involved in the case. As
the lease itself contains no words of severance, it necessarily takes effect as a
grant to the lessees as joint tenants at law. As regards the beneficial interest in the
lease in equity, there are three possible situations. Situation A: the lessees at the
inception of the lease hold the beneficial interest therein as joint tenants in equity.
This will be the case if there are no circumstances which dictate to the contrary. On
subsequent severance, the lessees would hold the beneficial interest in equal
shares. Situation B: the lessees at the inception of the lease hold the beneficial
interest as tenants in common in equity in equal shares. Situation C: the lessees at
the inception of the lease hold the beneficial interest as tenants in common in
equity in unequal shares.

Situation A is that which is advocated by the Chia company. The argument is
that, in the absence of an express agreement, persons who take as joint tenants at
law hold as tenants in common in equity only in three classes of case: first, where
they have provided the purchase money in unequal shares ...; second, where the
grant consists of a security for a loan and the grantees were equal or unequal
contributors to the loan ...; and, third, where they are partners and the subject
matter of the grant is partnership property...

It seems to their Lordships that, where premises are held by two persons as joint
tenants at law for their several business purposes, it is improbable that they would
intend to hold as joint tenants in equity. Suppose that an accountant and an
architect take a lease of premises containing four rooms, that the accountant uses
two rooms, and that the architect uses two rooms. It is scarcely to be supposed
that they intend that if, for example, the accountant dies first without having gone
through the formalities of a severance the beneficial interest in the entire premises
is to survive to the architect. Their Lordships do not accept that the cases in which
joint tenants at law will be presumed to hold as joint tenants in common in equity
are as rigidly circumscribed as the Chia company asserts. Such cases are not
necessarily limited to purchasers who contribute unequally, to co-mortgagees and
to partners. There are other circumstances in which equity may infer that the
beneficial interest is intended to be held by the grantees as tenants in common. In
the opinion of their Lordships, one such case is where the grantees hold the
premises for their several individual purposes ...

However, an equitable joint tenancy can, over the period of the existence of
co-ownership and a trust for sale in land, be changed into a tenancy in common.
This process is known as severance.

Determination of an equitable joint tenancy

Section 36(2) Law of Property Act 1925 provides a statutory means of severance, by written notice given to the other joint tenants. Further guidance as to the service of such notices is provided by the same statute.

Law of Property Act 1925

Regulations respecting notices

196 (3) Any notice required or authorised by this Act to be served shall be sufficiently served if it is left at the last known place of abode or business in the United Kingdom of the lessee, lessor, mortgagee, mortgagor...

(4) Any notice required or authorised by this Act to be served shall also be sufficiently served, if it is sent by post in a registered letter addressed to the lessee, lessor, mortgagee, mortgagor, or other person to be served, by name, at the aforesaid place of abode or business, office, or counting house, and if that letter is not returned through the post-office undelivered; and that service shall be deemed to be made at the time at which the registered letter would in the ordinary course be delivered.[12]

Gray, in *Elements of Land Law* (Butterworths: 2nd edition 1993) at p. 488, argues that, under a strict analysis of s. 36(2), 'it ... may well be inapplicable to cases in which the names on the legal title are not identical to the beneficiaries behind the trust.'[13]

Severance has long been accepted within the common law and the classic statement was issued by Sir William Page-Wood VC, in *Williams* v *Hensman* (1861) 1 John & Hem. 546, 557, who categorised three basic types:

1. *An act of a joint tenant 'operating upon his own share'*. Although an individual joint tenant owns no particular beneficial share in the land held upon trust for sale, it has long been the general rule that such a tenant may, *inter vivos*, alienate his or her share to a stranger. This alienation may arise through a sale, a specifically enforceable contract to sell or where a joint tenant mortgages his or her interest under the trust. Further, the effect of a bankruptcy by one joint tenant is to 'operate upon his own share', sever the joint tenancy and to pass that beneficial share immediately to the trustee in bankruptcy.

   There is considerable academic and judicial dispute as to whether an oral statement by one joint tenant to another, or others, of a wish to sever will have the desired effect. Certainly Plowman J in *In Re Draper's Conveyance* [1967] 1 Ch 490 accepted that severance could occur in such circumstances. An alternative position was adopted by Walton J in *Nielsen Jones* v *Fedden* [1975] Ch 222.

2. *By mutual agreement.*

---

12 See also *Re 88 Berkeley Road NW9* [1971] Ch 648.
13 See also D.J. Hayton, (1976) CLJ 20 at 24.

3. *By course of conduct.*

Sir William Page-Wood VC made a clear distinction between these two latter means of severance. However, their precise meaning is unclear. The following extract, which explores many of the most important judicial decisions surrounding severance, indicates that the case law cannot be divided into a neat typology:

McDowell v Hirschfield Lipson & Rumney and Smith [1992] 2 FLR 126

Judge Eric Stockdale:

The plaintiff is the executrix and sole beneficiary under the will of the late Ivan Clavell Smith (hereinafter called the husband). She was never married to him, but had two children by him. The first defendants are a firm of solicitors who acted for the husband from the beginning of 1987 until his death on 30 April 1988 at the age of 54. The deceased's wife was a few years older than him, and is the second defendant.

The husband and wife were married in March 1961 and had their only joint child, a daughter, in the following January. By a conveyance dated 17 July 1981 they jointly purchased a semi-detached bungalow ... but they lived together for less than a year: the husband left the matrimonial home and his wife in about May 1982. Thereafter, the wife took no steps to obtain a divorce at any time ... However, the husband did take some steps towards a divorce on two separate occasions: in January 1985 instructing ... [a firm of] solicitors, and in January 1987 instructing the first defendants. Both solicitors discussed with the wife and her solicitors the possibility of using the two years' separation for a petition, and both suggested that a sale of the former matrimonial home and a division of the net proceeds of sale would make sense. The first solicitors suggested that the wife should accept a little over half of the proceeds. The wife went to the same solicitors on both occasions, and they stated that their client was not prepared to agree to a sale, but was prepared to buy out the husband for £10,000 ... Eventually, the offer was raised to £18,000, but this was never accepted by the husband before his death, which occurred a mere two months after his petition for divorce. That petition was dated 29 February 1988 and filed in the Bow County Court. It was based on five years' separation...

It is to be noted that at no time during the negotiations, some of which were expressed to be without prejudice, did the wife or her solicitors express the least interest in severing that which is agreed to have been the beneficial joint tenancy of the parties. There were, of course, equal advantages and disadvantages for both parties if the joint tenancy were to continue. Each one has an even chance of surviving the joint tenant and of becoming the sole owner of the bungalow ... Each one similarly ran the risk of dying first ... The gamble for each was not unlike that enjoyed by the many people who like the risks involved in the well-known gamble of double or quits. That may partly account for equity's dislike of the joint tenancy and its marked preference for the tenancy in common. It is not suggested by anyone that the negotiations between the husband's first solicitors and the wife's solicitors, which lasted throughout 1985, resulted in a severance of the joint tenancy. However, it is now argued on behalf of the defendant solicitors that they did effect such a severance by virtue of their correspondence with the wife's solicitors during 1987 and 1988 ... What is said for the defendant solicitors is that [the correspondence was] ... sufficient to effect a severance, despite the fact that neither solicitor and neither lay client ever referred to the need or desire for such a step, and despite the fact that both lay clients had been happy to continue as joint tenants for six years after their separation. On the face of it, this would seem to be a startling proposition: nobody suggested or referred to severance, yet they managed to achieve it, it is submitted. The argument was based on the third manner of effecting a severance referred to in ... *Williams* v *Hensman*...

It should be noted that apart from the survivorship point – which cuts both ways – there was no advantage to be gained by either spouse from a severance. If they agreed on a price for the wife to buy the husband out, or agreed to a sale with a division of the net proceeds on a given basis, there was no conveyancing problem. If they could not agree, and the divorce had proceeded to a hearing of their property dispute, the registrar would have made his decision on the basis of the statutory provisions continued in Part II of the Matrimonial Causes Act 1973. It would not have mattered to him whether the parties were joint tenants or tenants in common, nor whether the bungalow was in the sole name of one or other spouse. His powers would have been adequate to deal with a division of the matrimonial assets, no matter how complicated the situation had become. Lord Denning MR pointed out in *Burgess* v *Rawnsley* [1975] Ch 429...:

'The thing to remember today is that equity leans against joint tenants and favours tenancies in common.'

That leaning would appear, on the facts of this case, to be the only support available for the submission put forward on behalf of the defendant solicitors – who accept that the burden of proof on the issue of severance is on them.

In *Burgess* v *Rawnsley*, the court was concerned with a couple who had never married or lived together, and who had agreed to a sale price for the interest of one party before the death. Lord Dennin MR ... concluded...:

'That agreement was not in writing and it was not specifically enforceable. Yet it was sufficient to effect a severance. Even if there was not any firm agreement but only a course of dealing, it clearly evinced an intention by both parties that the property should henceforth be held in common and not jointly.'

It is pertinent to ask of the husband and wife in the present case: when and how did both parties firmly evince such an intention – or even one of them? I find it impossible to say that either evinced such an intention at any time.

The facts in *Burgess* v *Rawnsley* were significantly different from those of the present case, and ... each one of the cases considered by the court of Appeal had turned on its own facts. In the earlier case of *Re Draper's Conveyance; Nihan* v *Porter* [1969] 1 Ch 486, which was relied upon by the defendant solicitors, Plowman J had been concerned with proceedings under s. 17 of the Married Women's Property Act 1882. He said...:

'...I take the view that in this case the summons issued by the wife in the Divorce Division coupled with the affidavit which she swore in support of that summons did operate to sever her beneficial joint tenancy.'

Under s. 17, the court had only limited powers, but the court would have had very wide powers in the matrimonial dispute between husband and wife. The registrar would not have been limited in the way that a judge hearing a s. 17 application was: this is why s. 17 is now almost a dead letter and why applications under it are rarely heard.

In *Harris* v *Goddard* [1984] FLR 209 ... the wife had petitioned for divorce and had included in her petition a prayer for a property adjustment order. The Court of Appeal agreed with the trial judge that this conduct did not constitute a severance. The court distinguished *Re Draper's Conveyance* ... Dillon LJ saying:

'In *Re Draper's Conveyance* the relief claimed by the originating summons which had been issued and by the affidavit in support included, as Lawton LJ has pointed out, a claim that the property might be sold and that the proceeds be distributed equally in accordance with the rights of the parties. This plainly involved severance of the beneficial joint tenancy as I understand the term "severance".

In the present case, however ... the prayer of the petition merely seeks relief in the most general and unparticularised terms under s. 24 of the Matrimonial Causes Act 1973. Apart from the fact that any relief for Mrs Harris under s. 24 lay in the future and was contingent on the court's exercising its discretion under the section in her favour, she had not yet specified what she desired by the time Mr Harris died and the general prayer could have been satisfied by relief which did not involve severance, e.g. an order extinguishing Mr Harris's interest in the property and directing that the property be vested in Mrs Harris as sole absolute beneficial owner, or an order directing a resettlement of the property on Mr and Mrs Harris successively and not as concurrent owners. Therefore the petition in this case cannot be notice of a desire to sever the joint tenancy.'

Many of these observations apply to the present case: Mr Smith has also asked for a property adjustment order in the prayer of his petition, but who can say what the outcome would have been? Severance was not an inevitable step for either spouse.

In all the circumstances, I cannot find that the defendant solicitors have discharged the burden of proving that a severance took place. There was no course of dealing on the part of the parties or of the husband to justify such a finding, and it is conceded that no other means of effecting a severance falls to be considered...

There is a further method of severance, not mentioned in *Williams* v *Hensman*, that comes into play when one joint tenant kills another.

M.P. Thompson 'Beneficial Joint Tenancies: A Case for Abolition' 51 *Conv* (1987) 29

A long-established principle of equity has been that a criminal shall not profit from his own crime. To this end, a constructive trust is imposed upon a killer who inherits under his victim's will. In the context of joint tenancies, it has not been clear how this principle operates if one joint tenant kills the other in circumstances when equity would deprive him of the benefit of the right of survivorship. As will be seen, owing to the provisions of the Forfeiture Act 1982, this issue has assumed rather greater importance than in the past.

Traditionally, the English approach to this matter is to take the view that the homicide causes severance of the equitable joint tenancy. The result of this is that if A and B are joint tenants and A kills B, A becomes the sole owner at law but holds on trust for himself and B's estate in equal shares. Until recently, no English authority existed on the point but elsewhere in the Commonwealth a different view is taken. In *Schobelt* v *Barker* (1967) [60 DLR (2nd) 519] it was held ... to the contrary, that in these circumstances survivorship operated normally, both at law and equity, but that a constructive trust is imposed upon A as to one-half of the property. In England, however, an essential part of the reasoning in *Re K (dec'd)* [1985] Ch 85 was that the homicide itself caused severance of the joint tenancy rather than a later constructive trust being imposed to prevent the offender benefiting from his crime.

Which of these views is correct is by no means academic. Under section 2(1) of the Forfeiture Act 1982, a court, except if the killing amounts to murder, has power to relieve an offender against the rule of equity which prevents an offender acquiring property as a result of an unlawful killing, where it considers that course to be appropriate. The difficulty is that if the homicide causes severance to take place, it may not be the forfeiture rule that has this effect. Suppose A and B are beneficial joint tenants and A is guilty of the manslaughter of B, in circumstances where a court would be prepared to relieve A from the forfeiture rule. B has died intestate and C is entitled to his property upon intestacy. If the homicide causes severance to occur, then C is entitled to B's share not by dint of the forfeiture rule but under the rules of intestate succession. Accordingly the court would appear to lack jurisdiction under the Act to modify this result. If the Commonwealth view was adopted, or A had been entitled under B's will or intestacy, then the court would under the Act be able to let him retain the property beneficially.

Similar problems could arise if there were more than two joint tenants. If E, F and G were joint tenants and E killed F, this according to *Re K (dec'd)* would cause F's interest to be severed in equity. The result would be that E and G would hold as joint tenants at law upon trust for themselves as to two-thirds and for F's estate as to one-third. G, upon severance, would then have a one-third share in the property. If, however, the Commonwealth view was adopted, E and G would take by survivorship and subject to the court's discretion, E would hold his share on constructive trust leaving G with a half share in the property. It is not obvious why G should be prejudicially affected by E's crime. While it is submitted that the better view is to be found in the recent Commonwealth decisions as opposed to *Re K (dec'd)*, it is nevertheless evident that beneficial joint tenancies can create problems in this admittedly slightly arcane area.

One important question regarding severance remains: what share does each new tenant in common acquire upon severance of a joint tenancy? The Court of Appeal in *Goodman v Gallant* [1986] 1 All ER 311 made clear that, in the absence of any express statement to the contrary, severance of a joint tenancy will give rise to a tenancy in common of equal shares.

COHABITATION AND IMPUTED TRUSTS

The importance of land law principles in *de facto* family disputes

Trusts for sale can be created expressly and whenever land is conveyed at law into the names of two or more people a trust for sale will be implied by statute. However, in certain circumstances, even where land is conveyed into the name of one person alone the courts may still imply equitable co-ownership in the property. In general, the mechanism the courts adopt is an elaboration of what they call either a resulting or constructive trust.

Much of the case law has arisen in the context of the matrimonial home or, more importantly, in the context of various forms of cohabitation. The most obvious example of the latter is that of an unmarried heterosexual couple who live in a property owned at law by the man alone. When the relationship comes to an end the woman, who may by this time have children to support, makes an equitable claim upon the house. It has been estimated[14] that in the period 1990–92 7–8% of people aged 16–39 were cohabiting. The possible forms of cohabitation are multifarious and include gay couples, extended families and 'communes'.

There is no principle in English law, despite the efforts of Lord Denning in the 1960s and 1970s, of 'community of property' or 'family assets'. In 1882 Parliament, through the Married Women's Property Act, provided for strict legal equality between husbands and wives with respect to property (see Chapter 1, p. 16). Section 17 gave the courts power to hear and resolve disputes concerning possession and ownership of matrimonial property and make such order as they 'thought fit'. From 1970 such disputes came to be resolved under the divorce legislation, which gives the court considerable powers regarding the distribution of property held by parties to a marriage.

However, for unmarried couples, and married couples who cannot or will not bring their problems under the aegis of the Matrimonial Causes Acts, disputes concerning their homes have to be decided upon general land law principles, specifically those relating to trusts. The context of those land law rules was the principle of separate property, evinced so clearly in the Married Women's Property Act 1882, i.e. ownership lies with the provider of the purchase money.

The remedial constructive trust?

A.J. Oakley *Constructive Trusts* (Sweet & Maxwell: 1987)

In the years immediately before and after 1970, a number of decisions emanating from the Court of Appeal imposed constructive trusts as a result of conduct which the individual judges were prepared to classify merely as inequitable. The

---

14 *Regional Trends No. 29* (Central Statistical Office: 1994) at 3.17.

underlying and indeed often expressed objective of the judges in question was to prevent results which would, otherwise, have been inequitable. If application of the basic principles of property law led to a result which, in the view of the court in question, was contrary to good conscience, that court acted upon the conscience of the party who would otherwise have obtained this unjust benefit and imposed a constructive trust upon him to bring the result into line with the requirements of justice. ... However, the approach manifested in this series of cases has not been followed up in the more recent decisions of the Court of Appeal in which there has been a return to the more traditional approach.

The modern approach

In a recent decision the House of Lords had the opportunity to review the existing authorities and set out the modern framework for the courts in making decisions regarding the imposition of trusts upon 'family' homes.

Lloyds Bank v *Rossett* (1990) 1 AER 1111 (HL)
Lord Bridge of Harwich, Lord Griffiths, Lord Ackner, Lord Oliver of Aylmerton and Lord Jauncey of Tullichettle[15]

Lord Bridge:

The first and fundamental question which must always be resolved is whether, independently of any inference to be drawn from the conduct of the parties in the course of sharing the house as their home and managing their joint affairs, there has at any time prior to acquisition, or exceptionally at some later date, been any agreement, arrangement or understanding reached between them that the property is to be shared beneficially. The finding of an agreement or arrangement to share in this sense can only, I think, be based on evidence of express discussions between the partners, however imperfectly remembered and however imprecise their terms may have been. Once a finding to this effect is made it will only be necessary for the partner asserting a claim to a beneficial interest against the partner entitled to the legal estate to show that he or she acted to his or her detriment or significantly altered his or her position in reliance on the agreement in order to give rise to a constructive trust or proprietary estoppel.[16]

In sharp contrast with this situation is the very different one where there is no evidence to support a finding of an agreement or arrangement to share, however reasonable it might have been for the parties to reach such an arrangement if they had applied their minds to the question, and where the court must rely entirely on the conduct of the parties both as the basis from which to infer a common intention to share the property beneficially and as the conduct relied on to give rise to a constructive trust. In this situation direct contributions to the purchase price by the partner who is not the legal owner, whether initially or by payment of mortgage

---

15 See also P.J. Clarke, (1992) Fam Law 72.
16 The overlap between proprietary estoppel and the constructive trust has become such that in *Burrows & Burrows* v *Sharp* (1991) 23 HLR 82 the Court of Appeal deemed it unnecessary to consider any distinction between the concepts.

instalments, will readily justify the inference necessary to the creation of a constructive trust. But, as I read the authorities, it is at least extremely doubtful whether anything less will do...[17]

Lord Bridge's first category

Eves v Eves [1975] 1 WLR 1338 (CA) Lord Denning MR, Browne LJ and Brightman J

Lord Denning:

The problem in this case is a familiar one. If often happens that a man and a woman set up house together and have children. They cannot marry because one or other or both are already married. But they intend to marry as soon as they are free to do so. She takes his name. They live as husband and wife. They get a house; but it is put in his name alone. Then, before they get married, the relationship breaks down. In strict law she has no claim on him whatever. She is not his wife. He is not bound to provide a roof over her head. He can turn her into the street. She is not entitled to maintenance from him for herself. All she can do is to go to the magistrates and ask for an affiliation order against him on the footing that she is a 'single woman': and get an order for him to pay maintenance for the children. If he does not pay, she may have great difficulty in getting any money out of him, even for the children. Such is the strict law. And a few years ago even equity would not have helped her. But things have altered now...

Although Janet did not make any financial contributions, it seems to me that this property was acquired and maintained by both of their joint efforts with the intention that it should be used for their joint benefit until they were married and thereafter as long as the marriage continued. At any rate Stuart Eves cannot be heard to say to the contrary. He told her that it was to be their home for them and their children. He gained her confidence by telling her that he intended to put it in their joint names (just as married couples often do) but that it was not possible until she was 21. The judge described this as a 'trick', and said that it 'did not do him much credit as a man of honour.' The man never intended to put it in joint names but always determined to have it in his own name. It seems to me that he should be judged by what he told her – by what he led her to believe – and not by his own intent which he kept to himself.[18]

Another 'trick' was played in the following case.

Grant v Edwards [1986] 2 All ER 426 (CA) Sir Nicolas Browne-Wilkinson VC, Nourse and Mustill LJJ

A house was purchased in the names of a man – Mr Edwards – and his brother. Mr Edwards had informed his cohabitee – Mrs Grant – that if her name appeared

---

17 See also S. Gardiner (1991) 54 MLR 126.
18 For an interesting analysis of this case see A. Bottomley (1993) 20 *Jo of Law & Soc* 57.

on the legal title it might prejudice the property settlement arising out of her divorce from Mr Grant. Mrs Grant made some financial contributions towards one of the mortgages raised on the property.

Sir Nicolas Browne-Wilkinson VC:

There is little guidance in the authorities on constructive trusts as to what is necessary to prove that the claimant ... acted to her detriment ... In my judgment where the claimant has made payments which, whether directly or indirectly, have been used to discharge the mortgage instalments, this is a sufficient link between the detriment suffered by the claimant and the common intention. The court can infer that she would not have made such payments were it not for her belief that she had an interest in the house. On this ground therefore I find that the plaintiff had acted to her detriment in reliance on the common intention that she had a beneficial interest in the house and accordingly that she had established such beneficial interest.

I suggest that, in other cases of this kind, useful guidance may in the future be obtained from the principles underlying proprietary estoppel[19] ... In both, the claimant must to the knowledge of the legal owner have acted in the belief that the claimant has or will obtain an interest in the property. In both, the claimant must have acted to his or her detriment in reliance on such belief. In both, equity acts on the conscience of the legal owner to prevent him from acting in an unconscionable manner by defeating the common intention. The two principles have been developed separately without cross-fertilisation between them; but they rest on the same foundation and have on all other matters reached the same conclusions.

Reviewing the authorities in her chosen area of 'detrimental reliance' the author of the following extract isolated and critically analysed an apparently simple test adopted by the judges:

A. Lawson *Acquiring a Beneficial Interest in the Family Home: The Detrimental Reliance Test* (WG Hart Legal Workshop: 1993)

The test is, that for conduct to amount to detrimental reliance:

'...it must be conduct on which the [claimant] could not reasonably have been expected to embark, unless she was to have an interest in the house.' (Nourse LJ in *Grant* v *Edwards*)

In order to decide whether or not conduct amounts to detrimental reliance, the judge must decide whether it is conduct that the claimant could reasonably have been expected to perform had she not owned an interest in land. In the type of case with which this paper is primarily concerned – that of a once cohabiting

---

19 A dialogue concerning the possible overlap between proprietary estoppel and the common intention constructive trust can be found in P. Ferguson (1993) 109 LQR 114 and D Hayton (1993) 109 LQR 485.

heterosexual couple who have parted – the judge must decide whether it is reasonable to expect a party to such a relationship to have performed the allegedly detrimental conduct out of any other motive, such as love or affection for the other party, or a desire to live in a comfortable well-appointed home. Only when the conduct is not of such a type will it amount to detrimental reliance. Thus the property rights of the couple who once cohabited, are determined by the judge's conceptions of how it is reasonable to expect men and women to behave in the context of such a relationship. From the cases it is possible to glean some idea of what some of these conceptions are...

[They] reflect traditional stereotypes of women and women's work. This is perhaps not surprising, since they are expressions of how judges expect women to behave in relationships with men. In order to succeed, female claimants must show that they 'did much more than most women would do' (*Cooke* v *Head* [1972] 1 WLR 518 at 519), or rather that they did more than judges would expect most women to do. The use of the stereotype as a norm, from which deviation has to be established, is an almost inevitable consequence of the adoption of Nourse LJ's test...

...a word should be said about the evidential problems it may create for claimants. Financial contributions are not likely to be difficult to prove ... However, female claimants, relying on their physical labour to establish detrimental reliance, and whose work was not witnessed by anybody but their estranged lovers, may well encounter great difficulty in convincing judges that they did actually perform types of conduct which do not fall within the ambit of what is traditionally thought of as women's work. For instance, in *Ungurian* v *Lesnoff* [1990] Ch 206 (see Ch. 8, p. 228 above) Mrs Lesnoff ... alleged ... work [which] included using a pickaxe to remove door-frames from brickwork. Vinelott J's ... attitude ... can be seen from the following passage:

'Mrs Lesnoff gave a graphic account of wielding a pickaxe. No doubt her solicitors had retailed to her the facts in *Eves* v *Eves* ... I doubt whether Mrs Lesnoff used a tool as clumsy as a pickaxe at all, unless possibly she picked one up that had been left lying around by workmen and put it to some temporary, and possibly inappropriate, use.'

This does not bode well for women who seek to rely on their heavy physical labour to establish detrimental reliance.

Lord Bridge's second category

What amounts to a direct contribution towards the purchase price, capable of demonstrating, or referring to, a common intention that the party not named on the legal title is to enjoy a beneficial share, as indicated in Lord Bridge's own description of the second category, appears from the cases to be subject to strict limitations. The best explanation of the judicial policy in this area can be found in a 1984 Court of Appeal decision:

Burns v *Burns* (1984) FLR 215 (CA) Waller, Fox, May LJJ

A man and woman cohabited for 19 years, but did not marry. They had two children and two years after they began living together moved into a house purchased in the man's sole name. The property was bought using his savings and a mortgage for which he assumed responsibility. The woman looked after the house and the children. In the last decade of the relationship she obtained a part-time job and then started a small business. From this income she bought a variety of gifts for the children, her partner and for the home. There was no suggestion that she and her partner were pooling their resources. When the relationship broke down she claimed an interest in the house. The High Court dismissed her application and she appealed:

May LJ:

I think that the approach which the courts should follow, be the couples married or unmarried, is now clear. What is difficult, however, is to apply it to the facts and circumstances of any given case. Where the family home is taken in the joint name, then, unless the facts are very unusual, I think that both the man and the woman are entitled to a share in the beneficial interest. Where the house is bought outright and not on a mortgage, then the extent of their respective shares will depend upon a more-or-less precise arithmetical calculation of the extent of their contributions to the purchase price. Where, on the other hand and as is more usual nowadays, the house is bought with the aid of a mortgage, then the court has to assess each of the parties' respective contributions in a broad sense...

The inquiry becomes even more difficult when the home is taken in only one of the two names. For present purposes I will assume that it is the man ... Where a matrimonial or family home is bought in the man's name alone on mortgage by the mechanism of deposit and instalments, then if the woman pays or contributes to the initial deposit this points to a common intention that she should have some beneficial interest in the house. If thereafter she makes direct contributions to the instalments, then the case is a fortiori and her rightful share is likely to be greater. If the woman, having contributed to the deposit but although not making direct contributions to the instalments, nevertheless uses her own money for other joint household expenses so as to enable the man the more easily to pay the mortgage instalments out of his money, then her position is the same.[20] Where a woman has made no contribution to the initial deposit, but makes regular and substantial contributions to the mortgage instalments, it may still be reasonable to infer a common intention that she should share the beneficial interest from the outset or a fresh agreement after the original conveyance that she should acquire such a share ... Finally, when the house is taken in the man's name alone, if the woman makes no 'real' or 'substantial' financial contributions towards either the purchase price, deposit or mortgage instalments by the means of which the family home was acquired, then she is not entitled to any share in the beneficial interest in that home even though over a very substantial number of years she may have worked just as hard as the man in maintaining the family in the sense of keeping the house, giving birth to and looking after and helping to bring up the children of the union.

---

20 See *Pietrantoniou* v *Fazzari* (Lexis: 1993) below p. 270.

As the above extracts indicate, the courts recognise that most houses are bought with the help of a mortgage obtained from a bank or building society and that payment of mortgage instalments may be clear evidence of 'common intention'. However, this evidence can be rebutted on the grounds that the payments were made for some other reason agreed between the parties. There has been some dispute as to whether a small number of mortgage payments will suffice to give a share in equity, especially when the dispute arises soon after the mortgage has been created: see the Court of Appeal in *Young* v *Young* [1984] FLR 375 and *Marsh* v *Von Sternberg* [1986] 1 FLR 526. However, if the land is conveyed to joint tenants, an equal division will probably be inferred: *In Re Gorman (A bankrupt) ex parte the Trustee of the Bankrupt* v *the Bankrupt and Another* [1990] 2 FLR 284.

Substantial physical improvements to a property, by the partner without legal title, such as the building of additional rooms, may provide evidence from which the court can infer a common intention to give that partner a beneficial interest. However, the claimant may find that such actions are not interpreted as indicators of a common intention.

Thomas v *Fuller-Brown* [1988] 1 FLR 237 (CA) Slade LJ and Sir Denys Buckley

The plaintiff and defendant lived together in a house purchased in the plaintiff's sole name. The defendant was unemployed and kept by the plaintiff. She obtained a grant for improvements to her house and made an agreement with the defendant that he would carry out the work in return for his board and pocket money. He carried out substantial improvements but then the relationship broke down and the plaintiff left the house. She sought to remove him from the property and he counterclaimed that he was entitled to a two-thirds share in it. His counterclaim was dismissed by the judge and he appealed.

Slade LJ:

Can ... an inference of any common intention properly be made in the present case? I emphasize the word 'common' in that phrase ... The judge thought not but the defendant has submitted to us that she was quite wrong ... I think his strongest point was this. He submitted that it was not realistic to suppose that he would have designed and constructed what he described in his notice of appeal as a valuable two-storey extension, made major alterations and other improvements in return for meals, lodgings on site, pocket money and cohabitation ... Translated into legal terms, his submission is that the only reasonable inference from the parties' conduct is that they both intended that, in exchange for what he was doing for the plaintiff and for the house, he should have a beneficial interest in it.

I see the force of that submission but for my part I am not able to accept it ... in my judgment the conduct of both parties was still perfectly capable of being rationally explained in the manner in which the judge thought it was to be explained. And this was the explanation which she preferred after seeing both parties and hearing all the evidence. She was sure that the defendant went to

Bosham with the plaintiff on the same terms as those on which he had been living with her at Selsey, namely, as a licensee doing the odd job here and there and being, as she put it, a kept man provided by the plaintiff with board and lodging ... The judge was sure that after the arrangement had been made that he would do the work covered by the council grant, the arrangement between them continued on exactly the same basis as before, save that he was to receive some additional money by way of what he called weekly pocket-money ... I have no doubt that the defendant for his part hoped, and may well have expected, that the plaintiff would in due course marry him and that he would receive a beneficial interest in the house. But as I have already emphasized, it is the common intention of the parties that is relevant. It takes two parties to make an agreement or form a common intention, not merely one. On the basis of the judge's findings of primary fact ... the plaintiff never did agree to marry him and never did lead him to suppose that by doing these improvements he would ever acquire an interest in the house...

In the case of matrimonial property statute confers a beneficial interest on the husband or wife who makes a substantial improvement to the house:

Matrimonial Proceedings and Property Act 1970

Contributions by spouse in money or money's worth to the improvement of property

37 It is hereby declared that where a husband or wife contributes in money or money's worth to the improvement of real or personal property in which or in the proceeds of sale of which either or both of them has or have a beneficial interest, the husband or wife so contributing shall, if the contribution is of a substantial nature and subject to any agreement between them to the contrary express or implied, be treated as having then acquired by virtue of his or her contribution a share or an enlarged share, as the case may be, in that beneficial interest of such an extent as may have been then agreed or, in default of such agreement, as may seem in all the circumstances just to any court before which the question of the existence or extent of the beneficial interest of the husband or wife arises (whether in proceedings between them or in any other proceedings).

Problems and possible solutions

A judge in the Family Division outlined the challenge he faced in applying the existing property law to former cohabitation relationships.

Hammond v Mitchell [1991] 1 WLR 1127

Waite J:

[T]he law these days when dealing with the financial consequences of divorce adopts a forward-looking perspective in which questions of ownership yield to the higher demands of relating the means of both to the needs of each, the first consideration given to the welfare of children. Since this couple did not marry, none of that flexibility is available to them ... In general, their financial rights have to be worked out according to the strict entitlements in equity, a process which is anything but forward-looking and involves, on the contrary, a painfully detailed retrospect ... The court first has to ask itself whether there have at any time prior to acquisition of the disputed property ... been discussions between the parties leading to any agreement, arrangement or understanding reached between them that the property is to be shared beneficially ... If there have been no such discussions ... the investigation of subsequent events has to take the form of an inferential analysis involving a scrutiny of all events potentially capable of throwing evidential light on the question whether ... a presumed intention can be spelt out of the parties' course of dealing. This operation was vividly described by Dixon J in Canada as, 'The judicial quest for the fugitive or phantom common intention' (*Pettkus* v *Becker* (1980) 117 DLR (3d) 257) ... The difficulties of applying that formula can be alarming, as this present case has well illustrated. The hearing has occupied no less than 19 days of High Court time and has cost the parties, one of whom is legally aided, more than £125,000 between them in legal fees. Given the mounting pressure on the courts as cases of this kind increase with the growing numbers of the population who choose to live together outside marriage, procedures will clearly have to be worked out to keep such hearings within sensible bounds in the future ... The primary emphasis accorded by the law in cases of this kind to express discussions between the parties ... means that the tenderest exchanges of a common law courtship may assume an unforeseen significance many years later when they are brought under equity's microscope and subjected to an analysis under which many thousands of pounds of value may be liable to turn on fine questions as to whether the relevant words were spoken in earnest or in dalliance and with or without representational intent. This requires that the express discussions to which the court's initial inquiries will be addressed should be pleaded in the greatest detail, both as to language and to circumstance.[21]

The 'difficulties' raised by cohabitation have also concentrated the minds of legal commentators:

S. Gardner 'Rethinking Family Property' (1993) 109 LQR 263:

We have seen, then, that the present treatment of family property cases at common law is unsatisfactory. In broad terms, there seems a measure of agreement as to the desirability of providing relief. However, the doctrines articulated to date are all individualistic, requiring certain thinking on the part of the parties as a precondition for such relief. In reality, the relief is only able to be given by fabricating this thinking, because it is typically absent from the situations with which we are concerned. Its place is taken, as the parties' means of organising their relationship, by trust and collaboration. It has thus been argued that it would

---

21 For a fascinating reading of this decision see A. Bottomley (1994) III *Feminist Legal Studies* 83. See also P.J. Clarke [1992] Fam Law 72.

be more appropriate to devise a jurisprudence which would provide the desired relief on the foundation of these values instead. Two suggestions have been made.

The first implants trust and collaboration into the familiar framework of unjust enrichment, in place of individualistic substratum from which there would otherwise arise problems as to voluntariness and subjective devaluation. This approach would provide resititutionary relief. It would be appropriate in cases where the parties trust and collaborate with one another, but on an ad hoc basis. That is, they maintain essentially separate responsibility for their own well-being, but pool efforts and resources on particular matters, which might include the securing of a home. This is in contrast to situations where the parties organise their whole lives collaboratively, so that the well-being of each is made dependent on the co-operation of the other. These situations – or communality – are the target of the second suggestion. This recognises a relationship of this kind as in effect a mutually fiduciary relationship, and so gains access to the law's existing learning about fiduciaries. It is thus able to give the parties relief by way of either a half-share in, or adequate support from, each other's assets.

Finally, attending to the values inherent in the parties' relationship requires us to observe their thinking where it does exist. It follows that it is open to parties to agree to exclude these obligations. But such agreements would be vitiated if they were procured by oppression, and then the standard relief would arise again.

So how much of a stretch would it be for the law to follow this analysis? At one level, hardly a stretch at all. The guiding principle throughout this article has been to put sustainable doctrinal clothing on the practical *status quo*. The thesis has been that the relief currently being granted or at any rate hankered for is based on certain intuitions about policy, and that these intuitions provide at least a rough working model of the results the law ought to be producing. So the suggestions here would involve comparatively little change as to the practical outcome of cases. The most notable difference would be to remove English law's 'referability' filter, which discriminates against non-financial contributions: all forms of contribution would count equally well under the modified unjust enrichment analysis, and communality operates independently of contributions. But of course there is already a swell of opinion that this change would be to the good. Beyond that, the change would largely take the form of a more structured pattern of relief. Both restitutionary remedies and ones based on communality are to be found in the existing materials, but the analysis suggested here would provide clarity as to which should lie when.

Doctrinally, of course, the stretch is greater. But the novelty should not be overestimated. The two suggested analyses adopt the existing superstructures of unjust enrichment and fiduciary obligations. The extent of their claim is to be able to base these superstructures on what appear to be new foundations – the values of trust and collaboration – as a substitute for the individualism of the current law of restitution and for the commercial quality of the relationships which are usually characterised as fiduciary.

As Gardiner indicates, everything he advocates 'is already standard – though unexplicated – in existing statutory treatments' (p. 299) most notably in the De Facto Relationship Act 1984 (NSW). Legislation designed specifically to deal with property disputes between cohabitees must be under review by the Law Commission as it investigates the law on unmarried couple's property rights. A spirited argument in favour of such legislation is made in the following extract taken from an article on the position of cohabitees in Sweden who, in 1987, were granted limited property rights by statute:

M. Fawcett 'Taking the Middle Path: Recent Swedish Legislation Grants Minimal Property Rights to Unmarried Cohabitants' (1990) XXIV *Family Law Quarterly* 179:

Legal theorists often argue that non-marital cohabitation should not be regulated, as people choose this form of living in order to stand outside the law. Statistics simply do not support this notion. People choose to live together without marrying for a multitude of personal reasons. Thus, it is a fallacy to presume that these people choose to live outside the protections of the law and only give remedies to people who can satisfy significant evidentiary burdens. It is in society's best interest to presume that these people's intent was to deal fairly with each other, and then let parties do their best to disprove that presumption...

This author has personally concluded that neither the arguments for nor the arguments against such regulation can be made to form a clear pattern that leads to one logical conclusion. The place that non-marital cohabitation occupies in society is not sufficiently certain to allow for a conclusion that will satisfy all people...

Despite this lack, the guiding policy concerning cohabitation should be that society regards it as important as that in marriage-like cohabitation ... What appears to be a breakdown of traditional values may also be part of a reorganisation of family concepts and structures. Not keeping this process within some social and legal constraints is even less desirable than leaving parties to fend for themselves.

Anders Angell characterises the Swedish legislation as a journey without destination. Although his judgement of the legislation is disputable, his characterization is apt. Society's destination is not known. Given that the destination is not known, it is a more responsible approach to make sure that the road to wherever we are going is sound and can bear the largest number of people possible.

Classification and quantification

The following extract is primarily concerned with a discussion of the means by which courts, having made a decision that a cohabitee without any legal title is entitled to an interest in equity, quantify the precise share. The debate inevitably also raises the practical importance attached to distinguishing between a constructive and a resulting trust.

P. Sparkes 'The Quantification of Beneficial Interests: Problems Arising from Contributions to Deposit, Mortgage Advances and Mortgage Instalments' 11 *Oxford Jo. Legal Studies* (1991) 39

Quantification is only useful as an exercise if the courts exercise their equitable jurisdiction in such a way as to reflect the contributions of the parties. In order to assess whether this is so, it is necessary to review the basis on which resulting and constructive trusts are imposed...

There are two clear cases of true resulting trusts. One is where a property is purchased outright without a mortgage ... In the second, analogous, case a mortgage is assessed as a cash contribution on acquisition...

Apart from these two cases, current usage is unclear about exactly where resulting trusts end and constructive trusts begin ... Identification of that special feature which creates a constructive trust is important for our purposes, because it is important to know whether the beneficial interests are to be related in size to the amount of the resources introduced ... Browne-Wilkinson VC identified in *Grant* v *Edwards* [see above] one essential unifying concept behind the constructive trust jurisdiction; that when a property is purchased there is an intention common to both partners to the relationship that the claimant should be entitled to a defined beneficial interest; and the claimant has acted to his or her detriment in reliance upon that common intention...

Superficially therefore there is a very limited scope for quantification of beneficial interests arising under constructive trusts. There are clear examples of constructive trusts where the beneficial interests arising are unrelated to the contribution of the parties. The parties may arrange, for example, before acquisition to share equally in a property irrespective of the contributions. When the beneficial interests are derived from an express agreement, there is no necessary link between the contributions and the quantum of beneficial interest derived from them. Such cases can only be described as constructive trusts. However, the more recent pronouncements of the House of Lords do suggest that constructive trusts in which the beneficial interests are totally unrelated to the financial contributions are quite restricted. Lord Bridge has said in *Lloyds Bank* v *Rosset* [see above] that there must be evidence of explicit discussion between the parties of their arrangement usually prior to the purchase, though in exceptional cases a later arrangement may be sufficient. This class of constructive trust is thus based on an express oral agreement which is enforceable because of detrimental reliance upon it ... In no sense could the shares of the claimants in these cases have been regarded as proportionate to what the judge in *Lloyds Bank* v *Rosset* described as a 'qualifying contribution' in terms of the indirect contributions to the acquisition enhancements of the values of the houses made by the female partners ... For purposes of quantification it is akin to an express trust, in that size of beneficial interests may be unrelated to the contributions.

Recent judicial statements support the above view that once a claimant has 'got a foot in the door', by establishing a right to a beneficial share, 'all payments made and acts done by the claimant are to be treated as illuminating the common intention as to the extent of the beneficial interest' (per Nourse LJ, *Stokes* v *Anderson* [1991] 1 FLR 391 at 400). The practical difficulties which the courts experience in assessing beneficial interests are expressed in the following case:

Pietrantoniou v *Fazzari* (1993) (Unreported: Lexis) (CA), Dillon, Butler-Sloss, Hoffmann LJJ

The trial judge had been asked to determine whether the applicant (referred to in the case as 'the wife', although she was not in fact married to the defendant), had a beneficial interest in a house where she had lived for 20 years with the defendant. The court inferred a 'common intention' that she had a one-third beneficial share since she had made indirect financial contributions to its purchase. Her 'husband' appealed.

Hoffmann LJ:

On the judge's findings of fact, therefore, the inference of a beneficial interest of some kind is in my view well justified. The difficulty is in ascertaining precisely how the judge came to fix that interest at one-third. The degree to which the husband was able to save to a greater extent in the period before the house was purchased by reason of the wife's income being used for the household is by no means easy to establish, and the judge did not try to do so.

Mr Iwi (counsel for the husband) submitted to us that for that reason it should be ignored altogether. I do not agree. Provided that the judge considers that the indirect contribution was a substantial one, that is to say not something which can be ignored as insignificant, he must in my view simply do the best he can to ascertain what, in terms of quantum, it represents.

A greater difficulty is to ascertain what importance he attached to the £1,000 and £900 which were paid after the purchase. It would in my view be wrong to treat those contributions as being on the same footing for the purposes of calculating the beneficial interest as sums paid directly or indirectly to the purchase price. As the judge rightly says in his judgment, the beneficial interest has to be taken as crystallising at the time of acquisition. Unless later payments give rise to a new proprietary estoppel, it seems to me that they can be looked at only for the purposes of allowing one to infer, or to confirm, other evidence of, a previous understanding as to what the quantum should be of the original beneficial interest. Thus if the judge had reasoned that £1,900 should simply be added to the wife's indirect contribution, whatever it was, and treated as a proportion of the value of the house, that would be wrong.

On the other hand, I think it would be legitimate for him, in doing his best to arrive at what the common intention was likely to have been, to take into account that the wife would not ordinarily have been expected to pay substantial sums for improvements in the way of central heating, and even for carpeting in a house in which she had only a minimal beneficial interest.

There is, however, nothing in the judgment to show that the judge misdirected himself in this matter. It has frequently been said that calculations of this kind are not susceptible of nice mathematical precision.

For my part I would regard his conclusion that the wife should have a one-third beneficial interest as generous to the wife. I rather doubt whether on the same evidence I would have arrived at the same figure. On the other hand, there does seem to me to have been evidence upon which the judge was entitled to take the view that one-third was the right figure, even though it may have been at the upper end of the scale.

I do not think, therefore, that we ought to modify the figure. For those reasons I would dismiss the appeal.

10 Registering title to land

INTRODUCTION

HM Land Registry *Explanatory Leaflet No. 15* (1990)[1]

The object of registering title to land is to create and maintain a register of land owners whose title is guaranteed by the State and thus simplify the sale (transfer) and mortgage of such land...

HM Land Registry *Completing the Land Register in England and Wales* (1992)

The land register is a valuable and authoritative record of unique and important information about ownership and interests in property. It is central to the effective operation of conveyancing and the credit markets. Over 15 million applications and enquiries are handled each year. Its rapid computerisation enhances its potential as the comprehensive and multi-purpose land information data-base for England and Wales.

With nearly 14 million titles the register includes the great majority of active and marketable residential and commercial properties...

In the early years of this century, Lloyd George's radical Liberal government aimed at a 'new Domesday', a public register of land titles which could be the basis of taxing land ownership. This was merely the most recent attempt: both Henry VIII and Cromwell, for example, had tried to register the ownership of land. The present system, established by a Conservative government in 1922–5, was introduced merely 'to improve conveyancing'.

---

1 The Registry publishes information to explain its services, as well as its own discussion papers concerning reform. See also R.J. Smith 39 CLP (1986) 111.

T.B.F. Ruoff *An Englishman Looks at the Torrens System (Being some provocative Essays on the operation of the System after one hundred years* (Law Book Co: 1957)

Cynics may ask what all this fuss is about. It is all too easy to regard the transfer of title to land merely as a dry-as-dust subject for lawyers. Yet, as a little reflection will show, land is our sole source of life...

[In mid-nineteenth century Australia Sir Robert Torrens] ... was placed in charge of the South Australian deeds registers, which, of course, were kept on the conventional British lines. He instantly perceived the complications and the chaos that pervaded conveyancing affairs and noted a marked contrast with the orderly and efficient ease with which sales and mortgages of shares in merchant ships were transacted. In the teeth of derisive and bitter opposition from the legal profession – opposition for which their successors today, as they have told me, have nothing but regret – this tenacious layman carried through the South Australian Parliament legislation which fundamentally reorganised the system of land transfer...[2]

The essential features of every system of registered title are that the State authoritatively establishes title by declaring, under a guarantee of indemnity, that it is vested in a named person or persons, subject to specified incumbrances and qualifications. Anterior defects of title are cured, and thenceforth all investigations of the history of how the named owner came to be entitled is ruled out for ever and all future transactions are carried out by simple forms and simple machinery. No transaction is effective until it has been entered on the official record kept by the State, but once this has happened it cannot (apart from fraud) be upset – that is the broad theory.

It remains for me to indicate what I believe to be the merits or faults of this system. I suggest that in each particular country or state, it succeeds or fails according to the degree with which the local law and the local administration accord, or do not accord, with certain fundamental principles. I will call these:

(1) The mirror principle.
(2) The curtain principle.
(3) The insurance principle.

The mirror principle involves the proposition that the register of title is a mirror which reflects accurately and completely and beyond all argument the current facts that are material to a man's title...

The curtain principle is one which provides that the register is the sole source of information for proposing purchasers, who need not and, indeed, must not concern themselves with trusts and equities which lie behind the curtain.[3] ... The aims of the mirror principle and the curtain principle are to make land transfer simple, and simplicity has an intrinsic value...

In conclusion, I think we lawyers should occasionally remind ourselves that although the adoption of improved methods in any work that we undertake benefits us, the person who really counts all the time is the client. An American writer once said that 'the Torrens law is essentially the creation of a business man for business

2 Other countries organised this much earlier, for example Denmark – see p. 285.
3 See conversion, Chapter 9, p. 233.

purposes. If it has failed to make the progress that it should have made, this is due to the fact that it has fallen into the hands of lawyers and has become a matter of legal contest and of judicial construction; that is, a vehicle of interpretation rather than of action.'

I find it impossible to doubt that the most efficient system of land tenure and transfer in the world today is the system of registered titles.[4] ... When established on a sufficient scale and boldly administered it has proved more reliable, simple, cheap and speedy than any other system ... Like anything that is man-made it is unlikely to be perfect, but it will stand or fall according to the way in which it is used and managed both by practising lawyers and by the officials who are entrusted with the keeping of the register.[5]

Given the bureaucratic complexity of registering titles and interests in land, it is perhaps inevitable that the administrators become the main experts on the system. It may be that registered land should be treated as a part of administrative law, not land law at all.

Pottage argues that the development of registration has depended on two related movements: the increasing reliance of conveyancers on documentary evidence (and see now the Law of Property (Miscellaneous Provisions) Act 1989, Chapter 2), and the process of reducing the landscape onto paper in the form of maps. He describes the move from feudal conveyancing to the Land Register as 'local recollection' being replaced by 'institutional memory', a move from contractual to bureaucratic relations:

A. Pottage *The Measure of Land* (1994) 57 MLR 361

In the era which preceded registration of titles, property was essentially contractual. The validity of a title was determined according to the terms of the 'special' contract. This practice of contract formation was a play on the 'property code' of the conveyancing treatise. Given that the formal ideal of a good root of title was often unattainable, contract formation became a practical art, which referred only obliquely to the theory of conveyancing. In practice, conveyancing was an exercise in evaluating the plausibility of a paper title against practical senses of property which had arisen from land use, and which lay in local memory or in the memory of an estate inventory. The most distinctive feature of registration was that it reduced questions of devolution and identity to paper. In so doing, it codified not only the practice of conveyancing, but also the practical senses of property which conveyancing practice itself relied upon when it wove book law and living law into a plausible narrative of title. Given this double codification, documents of title could indeed be treated simply as commentaries upon preceding documents. Registration extricated land from the network of relations and understandings which formed the 'local knowledge' of different communities, relocated it on an abstract geometric

---

4 Compare Shick and Plotkin at p. 285 below, and reform proposals at pp. 305, 308 and 320 below.
5 See also S.R. Simpson *Land Law and Registration* (Cambridge University Press: 1976), Book 1, Chapter 5.

map and deciphered it according to a highly conventionalised topographic code. This process marked a transformation of the idea of land in law: property ceased to be a contractual construct and became a bureaucratic artifact.[6]

THE LAND REGISTER

The Land Register was established, and is regulated by, the Land Registration Acts 1925–88, and the Land Registration Rules made thereunder. (In this chapter, the Act referred to is the 1925 one, unless otherwise specified.) The Register is held in 15 District Land Registries, all of which are to be computerised by 1998.[7] The Registry enjoys a 'vast surplus income' from fees Gray *Elements of Land Law* (Butterworths: 1993 at p. 239).

In 1925, it was planned that the Register would be secret, not open to the public. However, since 3 December 1990, titles held on it can be inspected by anyone on payment of a fee (s. 1, Land Registration Act 1988).

The Register is divided into three sections:

1. Property;
2. Proprietorship;
3. Charges.

A specimen is given in Fig. 10.1.

COMPULSORY REGISTRATION

From 1 December 1990, by s. 2(1), Land Registration Act 1986, all land in England and Wales must be registered when it is sold. In this context 'land' means the legal freehold, and legal leases for more than 21 years. Section 123 of the 1925 Act provides the sanction if the land is not registered:

Land Registration Act 1925

Effect of Act in areas where registration is compulsory

123 (1) ... every conveyance on sale of freehold land and every grant of a term of years absolute of more than twenty-one years from the date of delivery of the grant, and every assignment on sale of leasehold land held for a term of years absolute having more than twenty-one years to run from the date of delivery of the assignment, shall (save as hereinafter provided), on the expiration of two months from the date thereof or of any authorised extension

---

6 See also G. Dworkin (1961) 24 MLR 136 on the Land Registry and administrative law.
7 See also E.J. Pryer 41 (1990) Law Soc Gaz 19.

HM Land Registry

TITLE NUMBER : CS72510

Edition date : 31 August 1990

Entry No.	A. PROPERTY REGISTER containing the description of the registered land and the estate comprised in the Title
	COUNTY DISTRICT CORNSHIRE MARADON
1.	(19 December 1989) The Freehold land shown edged with red on the plan of the above Title filed at the Registry and being 13 Augustine Way, Kerwick.
2.	(19 December 1989) The land has the benefit of a right of way on foot only over the passageway at the rear leading into Monks Mead.

Entry No.	B. PROPRIETORSHIP REGISTER stating nature of the Title, name, address and description of the proprietor of the land and any entries affecting the right of disposing thereof TITLE ABSOLUTE
1.	(31 August 1990) Proprietor's PAUL JOHN DAWKINS and ANGELA MARY DAWKINS both of 13 Augustine Way, Kerwick, Maradon, Cornshire.
2.	(31 August 1990) RESTRICTION : Except under an order of the registrar no disposition by the proprietor(s) of the land is to be registered without the consent of the proprietor(s) of the Charge dated 29 July 1990 in favour of Weyford Building Society referred to in the Charges Register.

Entry No.	C. CHARGES REGISTER containing charges, incumbrances etc. adversely affecting the land and registered dealings therewith
1.	(19 December 1989) A Conveyance of the land in this title and other land dated 19 May 1924 made between (1) Allen Ansell (Vendor) and (2) Frances Amelia Moss (Purchaser) contains the following covenants:- "And the purchaser for herself her heirs executors administrators and assigns hereby covenants with the Vendor his heirs and assigns that she will perform and observe the stipulations set out in the First Schedule hereto so far as they relate to the hereditaments hereby assured THE FIRST SCHEDULE above referred to (a) No caravan shall be allowed upon the premises and the Vendor or owner or owners of adjoining premises may remove and dispose of any such caravan and for that purpose may forcibly enter upon

Continued on the next page

Fig. 10.1 Land Registry entry
(Reproduced with the permission of the Controller of Her Majesty's Stationery Office)

HM Land Registry

Entry No.	C. CHARGES REGISTER (continued)
	any land upon which a breach of this stipulation shall occur and shall not be responsible for the safe keeping of any such caravan or for the loss thereof or any damage thereto or to any fence or wall
	(b) No earth gravel or sand shall at any time be excavated or dug out of the land except for the purpose of excavations in connection with the buildings errected on the land and no bricks or tiles shall at any time be burnt or made nor any clay or lime be burnt on the land."
2.	(19 December 1989) The passageway at the side included in the title is subject to rights of way on foot only.
3.	(31 August 1990) A Transfer of the land in this title dated 29 July 1990 made between (1) JOHN EDWARD CHARLES BROWN and (2) PAUL JOHN DAWKINS and ANGELA MARY DAWKINS contains restrictive covenants. *NOTE:-Copy in Certificate.*
4.	(31 August 1990) REGISTERED CHARGE dated 29 July 1990 to secure the moneys including the further advances therein mentioned.
5.	(31 August 1990) Proprietor(s) : WEYFORD BUILDING SOCIETY of Society House, The Avenue, Weymouth, Cornshire.

***** END OF REGISTER *****

NOTE A :	A date at the beginning of an entry is the date on which the entry was made in the Register.
NOTE B :	This certificate was officially examined with the register on **31 August 1990.** This date should be stated on any application for an official search based on this certificate.

Fig. 10.1 (cont.)

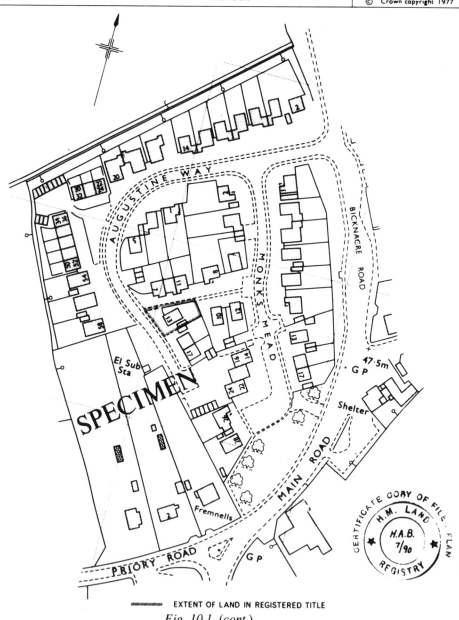

H.M. LAND REGISTRY	TITLE NUMBER
	CS72510

ORDNANCE SURVEY PLAN REFERENCE	TL 7802	SECTION U	Scale 1/1250 Enlarged from 1/2500

| COUNTY CORNSHIRE | DISTRICT MARADON | © Crown copyright 1977 |

EXTENT OF LAND IN REGISTERED TITLE

Fig. 10.1 (cont.)

of that period, become void so far as regards the grant or conveyance of the legal estate in the freehold or leasehold land comprised in the conveyance, grant, or assignment ... unless the grantee (that is to say, the person who is entitled to be registered as proprietor of the freehold or leasehold land) or his successor in title has in the meantime applied to be registered as proprietor of such land...

Thus, in registered land, a buyer must register title or she will not retain legal ownership.

Land not yet registered[8]

A buyer of land not yet registered will need to check the title deeds, the land itself, and the Land Charges Register in order to be sure of a good title. The rule is that:

If a burden on the land is discovered in the Land Charges Register, the answer to the question 'Does this bind the buyer?' will be found in the Land Charges Act 1972.

If a burden which is not registrable in that Register is discovered, a conflict will be resolved according to the rules of registered land.

The unregistered system of land law will eventually wither away as all the land is registered, but an understanding of the Land Charges Act 1972, which is relevant at first registration of title, is nonetheless necessary. In addition, the unregistered conveyancing system will still be relevant for transactions such as mortgages of unregistered land.

Registered land certificates

The land registry issues various documents as evidence of the state of the register:

Land Registration Act 1925

Issue of land and charge certificates

63 (1) On the first registration of a freehold or leasehold interest in land, and on the registration of a charge, a land certificate, or charge certificate, as the case may be, shall be prepared in the prescribed form: it shall state whether the title is absolute, good leasehold, qualified or possessory, and it shall be either delivered to the proprietor or deposited in the registry as the proprietor may prefer.

(2) If so deposited in the registry it shall be officially endorsed from time to time, as in this Act provided, with notes of all subsequent entries in the register affecting the registered land or charge to which it relates.

---

8 See Appendix I for more detail.

(3) The proprietor may at any time apply for the delivery of the certificate to himself or to such person as he may direct, and may at any time again deposit it in the land registry.

(4) The preparation, issue, endorsement, and deposit in the registry of the certificate shall be effected without cost to the proprietor.

Certificates to be produced and noted on dealings

64 (1) So long as a land certificate or charge certificate is outstanding, it shall be produced to the registrar –
    (a) on every entry in the register of a disposition by the proprietor of the registered land or charge to which it relates; and
    (b) on every registered transmission; and
    (c) in every case (except as hereinafter mentioned) where under this Act or otherwise notice of any estate right or claim or a restriction is entered or placed on the register, adversely affecting the title of the proprietor of the registered land or charge, but not in the case of the lodgment of a caution or of an inhibition or of a creditor's notice, or of the entry of a notice of a lease at a rent without taking a fine or a notice of a charge for inheritance tax.

(2) A note of every such entry or transmission shall be officially entered on the certificate and the registrar shall have the same powers of compelling the production of certificates as are conferred on him by this Act as to the production of maps, surveys, books and other documents.

(3) On the completion of the registration of a transferee or grantee of any registered land or charge, the registrar shall deliver to him a land certificate or charge certificate, and where part only of the land is dealt with shall also deliver to the transferor or grantor a land certificate containing a description of the land retained by him.

OWNERSHIP OF REGISTERED LAND

Categorisation of interests

There are three main categories of interest in registered land:

1. Title (ownership) interests, which can be substantively registered and receive their own title number and Land Certificate. These are, normally, the legal fee simple absolute in possession and legal leases of more than 21 years.
2. Overriding interests, which bind everyone.
3. Minor interests, which include everything else.

The registered proprietor

Land Registration Act 1925

Effect of first registration with absolute title

5 Where the registered land is a freehold estate, the registration of any person as first proprietor thereof with an absolute title shall vest in the person so registered an estate in fee simple in possession in the land, together with all rights, privileges and appurtenances belonging or appurtenant thereto, subject to the following rights and interests, that is to say –

(a) Subject to the incumbrances, and other entries, if any, appearing on the register; and

(b) Unless the contrary is expressed on the register, subject to such overriding interests, if any, as affect the registered land; and

(c) Where the first proprietor is not entitled for his own benefit to the registered land subject, as between himself and the persons entitled to minor interests, to any minor interests of such persons of which he has notice.

Therefore, the registered proprietor is normally bound only by:

1. any interest on the register; and
2. any interest defined as overriding (s. 70).

Interests which appear on the register are either:

1. registrable ('title') interests (see above);
2. minor interests – interests which are not registrable as titles.

Land Registration Act 1925

Effect of registration on the legal estate

69 (1) The proprietor of land ... shall be deemed to have vested in him without any conveyance, where the registered land is freehold, the legal estate in fee simple in possession, and where the registered land is leasehold the legal term created by the registered lease, but subject to the overriding interests, if any, including any mortgage term or charge by way of legal mortgage created by or under the Law of Property Act 1925, or this Act or otherwise which has priority to the legal estate.

There is provision for freehold titles which are not quite as good as 'absolute' – ss. 6–7. Sections 8–12 provide similarly for leasehold estates.

Table 10.1 summarises the titles in registered land.

Once the land is registered, the registered proprietor must carry out all dealings through the register. However, provided the registered proprietor acts as prescribed, she can carry out all the transactions that would be possible if the land had not been registered, as shown in the following group of sections:

Table 10.1 Titles in registered land

Freehold	Leasehold	Comment
Absolute	Absolute	The best – the registered proprietor has unconditional statutory ownership.
Possessory	Possessory	Where the paper title is inadequate ... adverse possession.
Qualified	Qualified	Where there is a fundamental problem with the title.
—	Good leasehold	Title is guaranteed subject only to the lessor's right to grant the lease.

Land Registration Act 1925

Powers of disposition of registered freeholds

18 (1) Where the registered land is a freehold estate the proprietor may, in the prescribed manner, transfer the registered estate in the land or any part thereof, and, subject to any entry in the register to the contrary, may in the prescribed manner –

(a) transfer the fee simple in possession of all or any mines or minerals apart from the surface; or of the surface without all or any of the mines and minerals;

(b) grant an annuity or rentcharge in possession (either perpetual or for a term of years absolute) in any form which sufficiently refers in the prescribed manner to the registered land charged;

(c) grant in fee simple in possession any easement, right, or privilege in, over, or derived from the registered land or any part thereof, in any form which sufficiently refers, in the prescribed manner, to the registered servient tenement and to the dominant tenement, whether being registered land or not;

(d) transfer the fee simple in possession of the registered land or any part thereof, subject to the creation thereout, by way of reservation, in favour of any person of an annuity or a rentcharge in possession (either perpetual or for a term of years absolute), or of any easement, right, or privilege in possession (either in fee simple or for a term of years absolute);

(e) grant (subject or not to the reservation of any easement, right or privilege) a lease of the registered land or any part thereof, or of all or any mines and minerals apart from the surface, or of the surface without all or any of the mines and minerals, or of an easement, right or privilege in or over the land, or any part thereof, for any term of years absolute for any purpose ... and in any form which sufficiently refers, in the prescribed manner, to the registered land.

Registration of disposition of freeholds

19 (1) The transfer of the registered estate in the land or part thereof shall be completed by the registrar entering on the register the transferee as the proprietor of the estate transferred, but until such entry is made the transferor shall be deemed to remain proprietor of the registered estate; and, where part only of the land is transferred, notice thereof shall also be noted on the register.

(2) All interests transferred or created by dispositions by the proprietor, other than a transfer of the registered estate in the land, or part thereof, shall, subject to the provisions relating to mortgages, be completed by registration in the same manner and with the same effect as provided by this Act with respect to transfers of registered estates and notice thereof shall also be noted on the register:

Provided that nothing in this section –
(a) shall authorise the registration of a lease granted for a term not exceeding twenty-one years, or require the entry of notice for such a lease; or
(b) shall authorise the registration of a mortgage term where there is a subsisting right of redemption; or
(c) shall render necessary the registration of any easement, right of privilege except as appurtenant to registered land, or the entry of notice thereof except as against the registered title of the servient land.
Every such disposition shall, when registered, take effect as a registered disposition, and a lease made by the registered proprietor under the last foregoing section which is not required to be registered or noted on the register shall nevertheless take effect as if it were a registered disposition immediately on being granted.

(3) The general words implied in conveyances under the Law of Property Act 1925 shall apply, so far as applicable thereto, to dispositions of a registered estate.[9]

Effect of registration of dispositions of freeholds

20 (1) In the case of a freehold estate registered with an absolute title, a disposition of the registered land or of a legal estate therein, including a lease thereof, for valuable consideration shall, when registered, confer on the transferee or grantee an estate in fee simple or the term of years absolute or other legal estate expressed to be created in the land dealt with, together with all rights, privileges, and appurtenances belonging or appurtenant thereto, including (subject to any entry to the contrary in the register) the appropriate rights and interests which would, under the Law of Property Act 1925, have been transferred if the land had not been registered, subject –
(a) to the incumbrances and other entries, if any, appearing on the register

---

9 See, for example. ss. 62, 77–9, at pp. 177, 115, 200, 205.

and any charge for inheritance tax subject to which the disposition takes effect under section 73 of this Act; and

(b) unless the contrary is expressed on the register, to the overriding interests, if any, affecting the estate transferred or created,

but free from all other estates and interests whatsoever, including estates and interests of His Majesty, and the disposition shall operate in like manner as if the registered transferor or grantor were (subject to any entry to the contrary in the register) entitled to the registered land in fee simple in possession for his own benefit...

(4) Where any such disposition is made without valuable consideration, it shall, so far as the transferee or grantee is concerned, be subject to any minor interests subject to which the transferor or grantor held the same, but, save as aforesaid, shall, when registered, in all respects, and in particular as respects any registered dealings on the part of the transferee or grantee, have the same effect as if the disposition had been made for valuable consideration.[10]

Power for proprietors to bind successors and to enforce contracts

107 (1) Subject to any entry to the contrary on the register, the proprietor of any registered land or charge may enter into any contract in reference thereto in like manner as if the land or charge had not been registered, and, subject to any disposition for valuable consideration which may be registered or protected on the register before the contract is completed or protected on the register, the contract may be enforced as a minor interest against any succeeding proprietor in like manner and to the same extent as if the land or charge had not been registered.

(2) A contract entered into for the benefit of any registered land or charge may (if the same would have been enforceable by the owner for the time being of the land or charge, if not registered, or by a person deriving title under the party contracting for the benefit) be enforced by the proprietor for the time being of the land or charge.

ALTERNATIVE VIEWS OF REGISTRATION

Having seen the basic concept of land registration, it is interesting briefly to view it in a wider context. There are many other models of land registration, and, while it may be true that almost any system of registration is better than none (and that a land *title* registration system is certainly better than land *charge* registration (see Appendix 1), the system adopted in this country may not be the best. For example, research in the United States of America (where there is little title registration) suggests some fundamental limitations:

---

10 Sections 21–4 Land Registration Act 1925 provide similarly for leasehold estates.

B.C. Shick and I.H. Plotkin *Torrens in the United States* (Heath: 1979)

The total experience of American jurisdictions with the Torrens approach to establishing and transferring land ownership is essentially negative. The overall picture is one of failure to attract the interest of landowners, failure to recognise and carry out the administrative and financial obligations inherent in operating a complex system affecting important legal interests, and failure to fulfill original expectations ... The broader role of Torrens that was envisioned by its late-nineteenth century proponents has been filled by other title-assurance mechanisms in combination with conventional recording systems. Torrens has been unable to compete with this approach because, for most purposes, it offers fewer benefits at equal or greater cost...

Torrens' lack of success in the United States is best explained by its failure to eliminate the need for search and abstracting of title history, for professional examination of the title and related circumstances that may affect it, and, where required, for the risk-coverage features of title insurance. Nor does the Torrens approach prevent title defects from arising between transfers of ownership or eliminate the need for clearance measures to correct such defects once they occur. These limitations are inherent in the Torrens approach and are not the result of compromise or of inadequacies in legislative language...

An alternative is the *cadastre* system, common in mainland Europe, which not only provides title information but is intimately connected also with mapping, planning law and taxation. The example here is from Denmark.

E. Stubjkaer (ed.) *Land Use, Control and Property Registration in the Nordic Countries* (Institute of Development and Planning, AUC: 1981)

After the introduction of absolute monarchy in Denmark in 1660 it was during the following generation several times attempted to establish a nationwide, systematic index of fixed property (cadastre) to form the basis of [tax] assessment. The effort succeeded in 1688...

At the middle of the 16th century a land reform project was started, aiming at a dissolution of the open field system and giving the farmers the right to dispose of the land they tilled. This consolidation project gained speed from 1769 and onwards. Under the supervision of chartered surveyors the land of the villages was charted on the scale of 1 : 4000 and a computation of the quality of the soil of each parcel was made...

The improvements of the technical basis (maps and methods) were employed in the establishment of a new taxation cadastre which took effect as of 1844. Here we find a clear and uniform identification (title numbers) of the estates and properties as well as a more detailed soil quality assessment...

After the introduction of parliamentary democracy a tax reform was carried into effect in 1903 according to which property taxes were levied after market value. Assessment of property is made by laymen in accordance with instructions from the Ministry, and updating of area data etc. in the assessment register is dealt with by office personnel on the basis of information from the Land Registry Department...

In 1977 this information system was developed to include data concerning buildings and housing and a uniform address code, so that it will interlace with the central population register. In this way the national census can be dealt with automatically in future.

The constant political interest in control and regulation of the size of agricultural holdings has – with the assistance of the chartered surveyors – helped to ensure the updating of the cadastra since 1944. Since the beginning of the twentieth century urbanisation has given rise to improvements in the mapping system of the Land Registry Department...

OVERRIDING INTERESTS

Introduction

Land Registration Act 1925

Liability of registered land to overriding interests

70 (1) All registered land shall, unless under the provisions of this Act the contrary is expressed on the register, be deemed to be subject to such of the following overriding interests as may be for the time being subsisting in reference thereto, and such interests shall not be treated as incumbrances within the meaning of this Act, (that is to say) –

(a) Rights of common, drainage rights, customary rights (until extinguished), public rights, profits à prendre, rights of sheepwalk, rights of way, watercourses, rights of water, and other easements not being equitable easements required to be protected by notice on the register;

(b) Liability to repair highways by reason of tenure, quit-rents, crown rents, heriots, and other rents and charges (until extinguished) having their origin in tenure;

(c) Liability to repair the chancel of any church;

(d) Liability in respect of embankments, and sea and river walls;

(e) [...] payments in lieu of tithe, and charges or annuities payable for the redemption of tithe rentcharges;

(f) Subject to the provisions of this Act, rights acquired or in course of being acquired under the Limitation Acts;

(g) The rights of every person in actual occupation of the land or in receipt of the rents and profits thereof, save where enquiry is made of such person and such rights are not disclosed;

(h) In the case of a possessory, qualified, or good leasehold title, all estates, rights, interests, and powers excepted from the effect of registration;

(i) Rights under local land charges unless and until registered or protected on the register in the prescribed manner;

(j) Rights of fishing and sporting, seignorial and manorial rights of all descriptions (until extinguished), and franchises;

(k) Leases granted for a term not exceeding twenty-one years;[11]

(l) In respect of land registered before the commencement of this Act, rights to mines and minerals, and rights of entry, and user, and other rights and reservations incidental to or required for the purpose of giving full effect to the enjoyment of rights to mines and minerals or of property in mines or minerals, being rights which, where the title was first registered before the first day of January, eighteen hundred and ninety-eight, were created before that date, and where the title was first registered after the thirty-first day of December, eighteen hundred and ninety-seven, were created before the date of first registration:

Provided that, where it is proved to the satisfaction of the registrar that any land registered or about to be registered is exempt from land tax, or tithe rentcharge or payments in lieu of tithe, or from charges or annuities payable for the redemption of tithe rentcharge, the registrar may notify the fact on the register in the prescribed manner.

(2) Where at the time of first registration any easement, right, privilege, or benefit created by an instrument and appearing on the title adversely affects the land, the registrar shall enter a note thereof on the register.

(3) Where the existence of any overriding interest mentioned in this section is proved to the satisfaction of the registrar, or admitted, he may (subject to any prescribed exceptions) enter notice of the same or of a claim thereto on the register, but no claim to an easement, right or privilege created by an instrument shall be noted against the title to the servient land if the proprietor of such land (after the prescribed notice is given to him) shows sufficient cause to the contrary.

Interpretation

3 (xvi) 'Overriding interests' mean all the incumbrances, interests, rights and powers not entered on the register but subject to which registered dispositions are by this Act to take effect...

Some overriding interests are more important than others. Section 70(1)(a), (f), (g) and (i) are examined here.

Section 70(1)(a)

Although at first reading, s. 70(1)(a) seems limited to *legal* easements, the next case held that some *equitable* easements are also protected:

Celsteel Ltd v *Alton House Holdings Ltd & Another No. 1* [1985] 2 All ER 562

A lessee of a flat ('the third plaintiff') had an equitable lease of a basement

---

11 As amended by s. 4, Land Registration Act 1986.

garage, and this lease included an (equitable) easement of access. The lessor leased another part of the basement to Mobil Oil, whose plans to build a car wash would interfere with the equitable easement. Scott J held in favour of the lessee and, although there was a successful appeal on another point ([1987] 1 WLR 291), this judgment was not disturbed. (The case is also discussed in Chapter 4, p. 114.)

Scott J:

It is rightly accepted by counsel for the plaintiffs that, unless the third plaintiff's rights as lessee of garage 52 to easements over the part of the rear driveway comprised in Mobil's lease represented an overriding interest for the purposes of s. 70(1) of the Land Registration Act 1925, Mobil holds its premises free of that right. It is plain, also, that the third plaintiff, although in actual occupation of garage 52 was not in occupation of any part of the rear driveway. He cannot therefore protect his easement over the rear driveway[12] under para. (g) of s. 70(1) and the only paragraph of s. 70(1) under which, he might protect that easement as an overriding interest is para. (a)...

The rights over the rear driveway which the third plaintiff acquired by virtue of the facts pleaded in the ... statement of claim which I have mentioned were certainly rights of way. If they were legal rights of way then Mobil is bound by them. If they were only equitable rights of way then I must decide whether or not they are excepted from para. (a) by the phrase 'not being equitable easements required to be protected on the register'.

The matter stands in my opinion thus. At the time when Mobil acquired its registered leasehold title the third plaintiff's right to an easement of way for the benefit of garage 52 over a part of the property enjoyed under that leasehold title was an equitable and not a legal right... It was not protected by any entry on the register. On the other hand, it was at the relevant time openly exercised and enjoyed by the third plaintiff as appurtenant to garage 52. Section 144 of the Land Registration Act 1925 contains power for rules to be made for a number of specified purposes. The Land Registration Rules 1925 ... were accordingly made and r. 258 provides as follows:

> 'Rights, privileges, and appurtenances appertaining or reputed to appertain to land or demised, occupied, or enjoyed therewith or reputed or known as part or parcel of or appurtenant thereto, which adversely affect registered land, are overriding interests within Section 70 of the Act...'

The third plaintiff's equitable right of way over the rear driveway was, in my view, at the time when Mobil acquired its registered leasehold title, a right enjoyed with land for the purposes of this rule. It was plainly a right which adversely affected registered land, including the part of the rear driveway comprised in Mobil's lease. Rule 258 of the 1925 rules categorises such a right as an overriding interest.[13] Section 144(2) of the 1925 Act provides: 'Any rules made in pursuance of this section shall be of the same force as if enacted in this Act.' Accordingly, in my

---

12 Is it possible to 'occupy' a driveway? Compare *Epps* v *Esso Petroleum Ltd* [1973] 1 WLR 1071.

13 Does this pose a problem for the buyers of registered land? Would this easement have bound Mobil had the company bought unregistered land? (See Appendix 1.)

judgment, the third plaintiff's right ranks as an overriding interest, does not need to be protected by entry of notice on the register and is binding on Mobil...

The Law Commission (Report No. 158, *Third Report on Land Registration*, 1987) has recommended that this decision should be reversed. However:

A.M. Prichard 'Easements and Profits as Overriding Interests' 51 *Conv* (1987) 328:

Where easements are concerned, is it more socially and economically acceptable that the right should be destroyed in favour of a purchaser, knowing or unknowing, or that it should survive, but with the purchaser at least being indemnified properly?

That in turn raises the issue, again unexamined in the [third] report, whether more harm is done by crippling the dominant tenement or by burdening the servient. It is, of course, easy to envisage cases where loss of an easement could render virtually useless the dominant tenement or ones where the existence of an easement could have the same effect on a servient tenement.[14] However, this writer suspects that the latter is likely to be the less dangerous risk, not only rarer but probably occurring only where a small piece of land is encumbered and compensation would be an adequate redress. Moreover, destruction of an easement intentionally created between land-owners may perhaps be regarded as more drastic and less acceptable than a failure to destroy such a one.

Section 70(1)(f)

This para. protects those who have adversely possessed registered land, or part of registered land (see s. 75, Land Registration Act 1925, in Chapter 3, p. 67). An early example is:

Chowood Ltd v *Lyall* [1930] 2 Ch 156 (CA) Lord Hanworth MR, Lawrence and Romer LJJ

Mrs Lyall was sued for trespass by the company, the first registered proprietor of the land; she claimed that she had an overriding interest which defeated the registered proprietor (the company) by reason of adverse possession.

Lord Hanworth MR:

The plaintiffs start their action by saying that they are registered as the proprietors with an absolute title of the land in question at the Land Registry and that this gives them the right to prevent the defendant from interfering with what is their property as shown upon the map which is attached to the land certificate. Luxmoore J has held that the defendant is entitled to succeed, that the disputed strip of land is her property, that the acts which she committed were exercised by her as acts of

---

14 Would it be accepted as an easement if it burdened the servient tenement to this extent? See Chapter 6, pp. 180–1.

ownership upon her own land, and that the plaintiff's certificate and the map attached to it must be rectified[15] by indicating upon it the true limits of the plaintiff's land...

The plaintiffs claim to succeed upon, what I may call, their statutory title. A plaintiff ... must succeed by the strength of his own title. The defendant is entitled to plead that he is in possession and leave the plaintiff by proof of the strength of his title to oust him. All that the plaintiffs have proved prima facie here is that they have good statutory title – that they registered as the first proprietors with an absolute title and therefore have vested in them an estate in fee simple in possession to the land.

The defendant, on the other hand, has proved to the satisfaction of Luxmoore J and to the satisfaction of this court that she is in possession and that she has been in possession, and that for more than twelve years, that there was an actual delimitation of the land in 1911, and that from and after that time there has been no modification of the claim made at that time and acquiesced in by [the former paper owner]. It appears to us therefore that the defendant has proved that she was in possession as owner of this strip.

The plaintiff company therefore lost. 'Statutory title' is subject to adverse possession, whatever the state of the Register.

Section 70(1)(g)

This overriding interest was intended to have the same function as the doctrine of constructive notice in unregistered land. This doctrine provides that a legal purchaser is deemed to have notice of, and to be bound by, any equitable interest in the land which the purchaser would have discovered by a reasonable inspection of the land itself (*Hunt* v *Luck* [1901] 1 Ch 45).

In these cases it is always a question of which one of the two innocent parties should lose, the buyer or the equitable occupier (who is equally a victim of the seller). Constructive notice and s. 70(1)(g) both recognise that the existing occupier of land has a special interest as against all non-occupiers – although such a person may not always win. (For the meaning of actual occupation, see also the unregistered land case of *Kingsnorth Trust Ltd* v *Tizard* [1986] 2 All ER 54, in Appendix 1, p. 345.) It has been held that an interest behind a bare trust [*Hodgson* v *Marks* [1971] 1 Ch 892] and an equitable lease (or estate contract) [*Webb* v *Pollmount* [1966] Ch 584] are both sufficient 'interest in land' for s. 70(1)(g). However, a licence is not enough: see *Ashburn Anstalt Ltd* v *WJ Arnold* [1988] 2 WLR 706 and *Skipton Building Society* v *Clayton* (1993) 66 P & CR 223 (Chapter 4, p. 84.)

Only three of the many decided cases are extracted here, *Boland*, *Flegg* and *Cann*, all from the House of Lords. The claimants in these cases each argued that they were 'in actual occupation' of land which was the subject of a mortgage by

---

15 For indemnity in this case, see p. 318 below.

the registered proprietor(s), and each of the claimants' 'interest in land' comprised a beneficial interest behind a trust for sale. None of the mortgagees had seriously investigated who occupied the land.

Robot Finance

Williams & Glyn's Bank Ltd v Boland [1981] AC 487 (HL)
Lord Wilberforce, Viscount Dilhorne, Lord Salmon, Lord Scarman, Lord Roskill

Mrs Boland had an equitable interest (under a trust for sale) in the family home. Her husband was the registered proprietor and he mortgaged the house to the bank to save his ailing business, but failed to repay the loan. Mrs Boland lost her claim to have an overriding interest at first instance (Templeman J), but won in the Court of Appeal and in the House of Lords. (In fact, there were two separate cases, with two wives in similar portions, heard simultaneously on appeal.)

There were two important issues. The first related to the meaning of 'actual occupation', and whether a wife could occupy 'her husband's' house. The second concerned the question whether an interest behind a trust for sale, which by the doctrine of conversion is theoretically an interest in money and not in land, could be sufficient interest for para. (g).

Lord Wilberforce:

The first question is whether the wife is a 'person in actual occupation' and if so, whether her right as a tenant in common[16] in equity is a right protected by this provision...

Were the wives here in 'actual occupation'? These words are ordinary words of plain English, and should, in my opinion, be interpreted as such...

Then, were the wives in actual occupation? I ask: why not? There was physical presence, with all the rights that occupiers have, including the right to exclude all others except those having similar rights. The house was a matrimonial home, intended to be occupied, and in fact occupied by both spouses, both of whom have an interest in it: it would require some special doctrine of law to avoid the result that each is in occupation...

The only solution which is consistent with the Act (s. 70(1)(g)) and with common sense is to read the paragraph for what it says. Occupation, existing as a fact, may protect rights if the person in occupation has rights. On this part of the case I have no difficulty in concluding that a spouse, living in a house, has an actual occupation capable of conferring protection, as an overriding interest, upon rights of that spouse.

This brings me to the second question, which is whether such rights as a spouse has under a trust for sale are capable of recognition as overriding interests...

I can see no reason why, if these interests, or that of any one of them, is or are protected by 'actual occupation' they should remain merely as 'minor interests'. On the contrary, I see every reason why, in that event, they should acquire the status of overriding interests...

In my opinion, the wives' equitable interests, subsisting in reference to the land, were by the fact of occupation, made into overriding interests, and so protected by section 70(1)(g). I should add that it makes no difference to this that these same interests might also have been capable of protection by the registration of a caution: see *Bridges* v *Mees* [1957] Ch 475, 487 and Land Registration Act, s. 59(6)...

I would only add, in conclusion, on the appeal as it concerns the wives a brief observation on the conveyancing consequences of dismissing the appeal. These were alarming to Templeman J,[17] and I can agree with him to the extent that whereas the object of a land registration system is to reduce the risks to purchasers from anything not on the register, to extend (if it be an extension) the area of risk so as to include possible interests of spouses, and indeed, in theory, of other members of the family or even outside it, may add to the burdens of purchasers, and involve them in enquiries which in some cases may be troublesome.

But conceded, as it must be, that the Act, following established practice, gives protection to occupation, the extension of the risk area follows necessarily from the extension, beyond the paterfamilias, of rights of ownership, itself following from the diffusion of property and earning capacity. What is involved is a departure from an easy-going practice of dispensing with enquiries beyond that of the vendor and

---

16 See Chapter 9, p. 250.
17 For Templeman J's revenge, see the next case.

accepting the risks of doing so. To substitute for this a practice of more careful enquiry as to the fact of occupation, and if necessary, as to the rights of occupiers cannot, in my view of the matter, be considered as unacceptable except at the price of overlooking the widespread development of shared interests of ownership. In the light of section 70 of the Act, I cannot believe that Parliament intended this, though it may be true that in 1925 it did not foresee the full extent of this development.

Lord Scarman:

My Lords, the result of the appeals in the two wives' cases will depend upon the construction to be put upon section 70(1)(g) of the Land Registration Act 1925. But the importance of the House's decision is not to be judged solely by its impact on conveyancing, or banking, practice. The Court of Appeal recognised the relevance, and stressed the importance, of the social implications of the case. While the technical task faced by the courts, and now facing the House, is the construction to be put upon a sub-clause in a subsection of a conveyancing statute, it is our duty, when tackling it, to give the provision, if we properly can, a meaning which will work for, rather than against, rights conferred by Parliament, or recognised by judicial decision, as being necessary for the achievement of social justice. The courts may not, therefore, put aside, as irrelevant, the undoubted fact that, if the two wives succeed, the protection of the beneficial interest which English law now recognises that a married woman has in the matrimonial home will be strengthened whereas, if they lose, this interest can be weakened, and even destroyed, by an unscrupulous husband. Nor must the courts flinch when assailed by arguments to the effect that the protection of her interest will create difficulties in banking or conveyancing practice. The difficulties are, I believe, exaggerated: but bankers, and solicitors, exist to provide the service which the public needs. They can – as they have successfully done in the past – adjust their practice, if it be socially required. Nevertheless, the judicial responsibility remains – to interpret the statute truly according to its tenor...

Fortunately, these appeals call for no judicial ingenuity – let alone distortion. The ordinary meaning of the words used by Parliament meets the needs of social justice.

As a result of this case, spouses and partners are now required to sign their consent to any mortgage of the family home: for a case on forgery of the required consent, see *Abbey National plc* v *Moss* (1994), above, p. 237. This procedure itself has given rise to a new cause of action against a mortgagee: claims of voidability due to duress – see, for example, *Barclays Bank plc* v *O'Brien* [1993] 4 All ER 417 (HL), Chapter 5 at p. 139.

The next two cases together illustrate the current emphasis that the House of Lords places upon 'conveyancing good sense' rather than the 'achievement of social justice'.

City of London Building Society v *Flegg* [1988] AC 54 (HL)
Lord Bridge, Lord Templeman, Lord Mackay, Lord Oliver, Lord Goff

This involved, not a wife in a matrimonial home, but Mr and Mrs Flegg, the parents of one of the two registered proprietors, Mr and Mrs Maxwell-Brown. They all lived together in 'Bleak House'. Unknown to the Fleggs, the Maxwell-Browns granted a mortgage to the society. When they were unable to repay the debt, the building society and the Fleggs fought over the house.

At first instance, the building society won, but this was reversed in the Court of Appeal. Despite the assurance and apparent technical ease of this decision, it was greeted with horror by conveyancers: 'Few decisions on the law of property have excited so much controversy in recent years ...' (S. Bridge, NLJ (1987) 470).[18] The decision of the House of Lords reinstating the building society's success was, however, to be 'welcomed by conveyancers, mortgagees and (not least) law students' (Bridge, above, p. 470). Lord Templeman quoted ss. 27–28, Law of Property Act 1925, and continued:

Lord Templeman:

Section 17 of the Trustee Act 1925 provides:

'No purchaser or mortgagee, paying or advancing money on a sale or mortgage purporting to be made under any trust or power vested in trustees, shall be concerned to see that such money is wanted, or that no more than is wanted is raised, or otherwise as to the application thereof.'

Thus the appellants advancing money in good faith to two trustees for sale on the security of a charge by way of legal mortgage of Bleak House were not concerned with the trusts affecting the proceeds of sale of Bleak House or with the propriety of the trustees entering into the legal charge. As a result of the legal charge the interests of the beneficiaries in Bleak House pending sale were transferred to the equity of redemption vested in the Maxwell-Browns and to the sum of £37,500 received by the Maxwell-Browns from the appellants in consideration for the grant of the legal charge...

The respondents resist the claim of the appellants to possession of Bleak House and rely on section 14 of the Law of Property Act 1925. Sections 27 and 28 of that Act which overreach the interests of the respondents under the trust for sale of Bleak House are to be found in Part I of the Act. Section 14 provides:

'This Part of this Act shall not prejudicially affect the interest of any person in possession or in actual occupation of land to which he may be entitled in right of such occupation or possession.'

The respondents were in actual occupation of Bleak House at the date of the legal charge. It is argued that their beneficial interests under the trust for sale were not overreached by the legal charge or that the respondents were entitled to remain in occupation after the legal charge and against the appellants despite the overreaching of their interests.

My Lords, the respondents were entitled to occupy Bleak House by virtue of their

---

18 See also S. Gardner 51 (1988) MLR 365; R.J. Smith (1987) 103 LQR 520; Swadling 52 Conv (1988) 451.

beneficial interests in Bleak House and its rents and profits pending the execution of the trust for sale. Their beneficial interests were overreached by the legal charge and were transferred to the equity of redemption[19] held by the Maxwell-Browns and to the sum advanced by the appellants in consideration of the grant of the legal charge and received by the Maxwell-Browns. After the legal charge the respondents were only entitled to continue in occupation of Bleak House by virtue of their beneficial interests in the equity of redemption of Bleak House and that equity of redemption is subject to the right of the appellants as mortgagee to take possession. Sections 27 and 28 did not 'prejudicially' affect the interests of the respondents who were indeed prejudiced but by the subsequent failure of the trustees for sale to account to their beneficiaries for capital money received by the trustees. A beneficiary who is entitled to share in the proceeds of sale of land held on trust for sale relies on the trustees. Section 26(3) of the Act (as amended) requires trustees for sale to consult their beneficiaries and to give effect to the wishes of the majority of the beneficiaries 'but a purchaser shall not be concerned to see that the provisions of this subsection have been complied with'. If the argument of the respondents is correct, a purchaser from trustees for sale must ensure that a beneficiary in actual occupation is not only consulted but consents to the sale. Section 14 of the Law of Property Act 1925 is not apt to confer on a tenant in common of land held on trust for sale, who happens to be in occupation, rights which are different from and superior to the rights of tenants in common, who are not in occupation on the date when the interests of all tenants in common are overreached by a sale or mortgage by trustees for sale...

In my view the object of section 70 was to reproduce for registered land the same limitations as section 14 of the Law of Property Act 1925 produced for land whether registered or unregistered. The respondents claim to be entitled to overriding interests because they were in actual occupation of Bleak House on the date of the legal charge. But the interests of the respondents cannot at one and the same time be overreached and overridden and at the same time be overriding interests. The appellants cannot at one and the same time take free from all the interests of the respondents yet at the same time be subject to some of those interests. The right of the respondents to be and remain in actual occupation of Bleak House ceased when the respondents' interests were overreached by the legal charge save in so far as their rights were transferred to the equity of redemption. As persons interested under the trust for sale the respondents had no right to possession as against the appellants and the fact that the respondents were in actual occupation at the date of the legal charge did not create a new right or transfer an old right so as to make the right enforceable against the appellants.

One of the main objects of the legislation of 1925 was to effect a compromise between on the one hand the interests of the public in securing that land held in trust is freely marketable and, on the other hand, the interests of the beneficiaries in preserving their rights under the trusts. By the Settled Land Act 1925 a tenant for life may convey the settled land discharged from all the trusts powers and provisions of the settlement. By the Law of Property Act 1925 trustees for sale may convey land held on trust for sale discharged from the trusts affecting the proceeds of sale and rents and profits until sale. Under both forms of trust the protection and

---

19 Defined in Chapter 5, p. 141.

the only protection of the beneficiaries is that capital money must be paid to at least two trustees or a trust corporation. Section 14 of the Law of Property Act 1925 and section 70 of the Land Registration Act cannot have been intended to frustrate this compromise and to subject the purchaser to some beneficial interests but not others depending on the waywardness of actual occupation.[20] The Court of Appeal took a different view, largely in reliance on the decision of this House in *Williams & Glyn's Bank Ltd* v *Boland*... But in that case the interest of the wife was not overreached or overridden because the mortgagee advanced capital moneys to a sole trustee. If the wife's interest had been overreached by the mortgagee advancing capital moneys to the two trustees there would have been nothing to justify the wife in remaining in occupation as against the mortgagee. There must be a combination of an interest which justifies continuing occupation plus actual occupation to constitute an overriding interest. Actual occupation is not an interest in itself.

Lord Oliver of Aylmerton:

This appeal is of very considerable significance not only to conveyancers but to anyone proposing to lend upon the security of property in respect of which there is a possibility of the existence of beneficial interests which have not been disclosed by the apparent absolute owner. If it be the case, as the Court of Appeal held, that the payment by the appellants in the instant case to two properly constituted trustees for sale, holding upon the statutory trusts, provides no sensible distinction from the *ratio* of the decision of this House in *Boland's* case, the legislative policy of the 1925 legislation of keeping the interests of beneficiaries behind the curtain and confining the investigation of title to the devolution of the legal estate will have been substantially reversed by judicial decision and financial institutions advancing money on the security of land will face hitherto unsuspected hazards, whether they are dealing with registered or unregistered land...

[I]t is tolerably clear that the scheme of the [1925] Act is to enable a purchaser or mortgagee, so long as he pays the proceeds of sale or other capital moneys to not less than two trustees or to a trust corporation, to accept a conveyance or mortgage without reference at all to the beneficial interests of co-owners interested only in the proceeds of sale and rents and profits until sale, which are kept behind the curtain and do not require to be investigated.[21] There are, however, a number of cases in which the question has arisen between beneficiary and trustee as to the rights of the beneficiary in occupation, either alone or in common with his or her co-beneficiary, of the trust property pending sale, particularly where the property has been purchased with a view to its being occupied, for instance, as the matrimonial home of the parties...

My Lords, the ambit of section 14 is a matter which has puzzled conveyancers ever since the Law of Property Act was enacted... What section 14 does not do, on any analysis, is to enlarge or add to whatever interest it is that the occupant has 'in right of his occupation' and in my judgment the argument that places reliance upon it in the instant case founds itself upon an assumption about the nature of the occupying co-owners' interest that cannot in fact be substantiated. The section

---

20 As to occupation being 'wayward', compare, for example, Wade in Appendix 1, p. 343.
21 Compare the views on conversion, Chapter 9, p. 233.

cannot of itself create an interest which survives the execution of the trust under which it arises or answer the logically anterior question of what, if any, interest in the land is conferred by the possession or occupation ... the section cannot, in my judgment, have the effect of preserving, as equitable interests in the land, interests which are overreached by the exercise of the trustees' powers or of bringing onto the title which the purchaser from trustees for sale is required to investigate the equitable interest of every beneficiary who happens to be in occupation of the land. That would be to defeat the manifest purpose of the legislature in enacting the sections to which reference has already been made. Looking at the interest of the tenant in common in actual occupation and considering for the moment only the position in relation to unregistered land, one has, as it seems to me, to bear in mind always the distinction between his rights as against his co-beneficiaries or against the trustee or trustees in whom the legal estate is vested and his rights against a purchaser of the legal estate from the trustees for sale. His interest is overreached and the purchaser is absolved from inquiry only if the statutory requirements respecting the payment of capital money arising under a disposition upon trust for sale are complied with: sections 2(1)(ii) and 27. Until that occurs, he remains entitled to assert against the trustees and, indeed, against any purchaser from the trustees who has not complied with the statutory requirement all the incidents of his beneficial interest in the proceeds of sale of the property and in the net rents and profits until the sale. One of the incidents of that beneficial interest is, or may be according to the agreement between the beneficiaries or to the purpose for which the trust was originally created, the enjoyment of the property *in specie*[22] either alone or concurrently with other beneficiaries. But the enjoyment *in specie*, whilst it may serve to give notice to third parties of the occupier's interest under the trust, is not a separate and severable right which can be regarded as, as it were, free standing. It is and has to be referable to the trust from which, and from which alone, it arises... [T]he framers of that legislation [of 1925] would, I think, have been shocked and surprised to hear it asserted that a purchaser in proper form from the trustees of the statutory trusts was required to investigate the purposes for which the trust property had been acquired by the trustees on the terms of some private and unwritten agreement or understanding between the beneficiaries *inter se* or between one or more of the beneficiaries and the trustees...

[T]he reason why a purchaser of the legal estate (whether by way of outright sale or by way or [sic] mortgage) from a single proprietor takes subject to the rights of the occupying beneficiary is not because section 14 of the Act confers upon the latter some interest in land which is incapable of being overreached but because, having constructive notice of the trust as a result of the beneficiary's occupation, he steps into the shoes of the vendor or mortgagor and takes the estate subject to the same equities as those to which it was subject in the latter's hands, those equities and their accompanying incidents not having been overreached by the sale under the provisions of section 2(1) and section 27 of the Act. Where the purchase has taken effect in accordance with those provisions, it is quite clear from the terms of the statute both that the purchaser, even with express notice, is not concerned with the beneficiary's interest in the proceeds of sale or the net rents and profits until sale and that that interest is overreached. The beneficiary's possession or

---

22 'In its present form'.

occupation is no more than a method of enjoying *in specie* the rents and profits pending sale in which he is entitled to share. It derives from and is ... fathered by the interests under the trust for sale. Once that goes, as it does on the execution of the trust for sale, then the foundation of the occupation goes and the beneficiary has no longer an 'interest ... to which he may be entitled in right of such occupation' ... If I may say so respectfully, the reasoning of the Court of Appeal starts at the wrong end by assuming that there is an interest conferred by occupation which, were it not for section 14, would be in some way prejudiced by the provisions of Part I of the Act, whereas in fact the occupier's interest in this instance is one which stems from, depends on and is co-terminous with the interest in the rents and profits arising under those very provisions and which is displaced by the execution of the trust or the exercise of the trustees' powers to the same extent as that interest.

Lord Oliver, having decided that s. 14 could have no effect on the beneficiaries' rights, went on to consider whether they had an overriding interest:

Considered in the context of a transaction complying with the statutory requirements of the Law of Property Act 1925 the question of the effect of section 70(1)(g) of the Land Registration Act 1925 must, in my judgment, be approached by asking first what are the 'rights' of the person in occupation and whether they are, at the material time, subsisting in reference to the land. In the instant case the exercise by the registered proprietors of the powers conferred on trustees for sale by section 28(1) of the Law of Property Act 1925 had the effect of overreaching the interests of the respondents under the statutory trusts upon which defended their right to continue in occupation of the land. The appellants took free from those trusts (section 27) and were not, in any event, concerned to see that the respondents' consent to the transaction was obtained (section 26). If then, one asks what were the subsisting rights of the respondents referable to their occupation, the answer must, in my judgment, be that they were rights which, *vis-à-vis* the appellants, were, *eo instante*[23] with the creation of the charge, overreached and therefore subsisted only in relation to the equity of redemption. I do not, for my part, find in *Boland's* case anything which compels a contrary conclusion... I cannot for my part accept that, once what I may call the parent interest, by which alone the occupation can be justified, has been overreached and thus subordinated to a legal estate properly created by the trustees under their statutory powers, it can, in relation to the proprietor of the legal estate so created, be any longer said to be a right 'for the time being subsisting'. Section 70(1)(g) protects only the rights in reference to the land of the occupier whatever they are at the material time... Once the beneficiary's rights have been shifted from the land to the capital moneys in the hands of the trustees, there is no longer an interest in the land to which the occupation can be referred or which it can protect. If the trustees sell in accordance with the statutory provisions and so overreach the beneficial interests in reference to the land, nothing remains to which a right of occupation can attach and the same result must, in my judgment, follow *vis-à-vis* a chargee by way of legal mortgage so long as the transaction is carried out in the manner

---

23 'Simultaneously'.

prescribed by the Law of Property Act 1925, overreaching the beneficial interests by subordinating them to the estate of the chargee which is no longer 'affected' by them so as to become subject to them on registration pursuant to section 20(1) of the Land Registration Act 1925. In the instant case, therefore, I would, for my part, hold that the charge created in favour of the appellants overreached the beneficial interests of the respondents and that there is nothing in section 70(1)(g) of the Land Registration Act 1925 or in *Boland's* case which has the effect of preserving against the appellants any rights of the respondents to occupy the land by virtue of their beneficial interests in the equity of redemption which remains vested in the trustees.[24]

Abbey National Building Society v *Cann & Another* [1990] 1 All ER 1085 (HL) Lord Bridge of Harwich, Lord Griffiths, Lord Ackner, Lord Oliver of Aylmerton, Lord Jauncey of Tullichettle

A son, George, bought a new house for his mother; she contributed to the price and therefore had an equitable interest. She believed that he was raising a small amount of money on a mortgage, and (following *Paddington Building Society* v *Mendelsohn* (1985) 50 P & CR 244) she could not claim priority over the building society if he had simply done that. However, he borrowed much more and could not repay it. Her belongings were moved into the house 25 minutes before the purchase was completed and the mortgage deed executed. Thus, she claimed that she had an overriding interest under s. 70(1)(g).

The trial judge, the Court of Appeal and the House of Lords all decided in favour of the building society. The House of Lords held that she could not claim priority over the building society, even though she had not authorised the size of the mortgage: as she had authorised a loan, she was liable, however big the loan actually made. However, the House went further and answered other questions raised by the case. These were: (1) At what moment should 'actual occupation' and 'interest in land' be tested – the moment of execution or of registration of the mortgage deed? (2) Was she in 'actual occupation' at the moment of execution on the facts of this case? (3) Did she have an interest in land at the moment of completion, or did the mortgage take effect first so that all she had was an interest in the equity of redemption?

Lord Oliver of Aylmerton:

First in logical order is the question of the appropriate date for ascertaining the existence of overriding interests under the Land Registration Acts... The question arose directly in *Rosset's* case[25] in which the Court of Appeal decided unanimously that the relevant date was the date of completion of the purchase and not that of registration. Your Lordships are now invited to overrule that decision.

My Lords, the conclusion at which the Court of Appeal arrived makes good conveyancing sense, and, speaking for myself, I should be extremely reluctant to

---

24 See also P. Sparkes 52 Conv (1988) 141.
25 Chapter 9, p. 259.

overrule it unless compulsively driven to do so, the more so because it produces a result which is just, convenient and certain, as opposed to one which is capable of leading to manifest injustice and uncertainty. It has, I think, to be acknowledged, that the interrelation between the provisions of ss. 3(xvi), 20 and 23, 37, 69 and 70(1) is not altogether easy to understand, particularly in relation to the position of a chargee whose charge is created by a purchaser of land who is not yet himself the registered proprietor...

[T]he key to the problem lies in the words of s. 70(1) rather than in the reference to the interests affecting the estate transferred or created in ss. 20(1) and 23(1). The 1925 Act displays a degree of circularity in its general definition of what an overriding interest is...

When regard is had to the list of overriding interests in s. 70(1) it is apparent that all of them are interests which can come into being at any time, and some of them may arise without any volition on the part of the registered proprietor or anyone else seised of an estate in the land. A right of way or a profit à prendre may be acquired by a neighbouring landowner by prescription. A third party may acquire title to the land by adverse possession...

I concluded therefore, like Nicholls LJ, that the relevant date for determining the existence of overriding interests which will 'affect the estate transferred or created' is the date of registration...

The question remains, however, whether the date of registration is also the relevant date for determining whether a claimant to a right is in actual occupation. It is to be noted that it is not the actual occupation which gives rise to the right or determines its existence. Actual occupation merely operates as the trigger, as it were, for the treatment of the right, whatever it may be, as an overriding interest. Nor does the additional quality of the right as an overriding interest alter the nature or quality of the right itself. If it is an equitable right it remains an equitable right...

The case which does give rise to difficulty if the date of registration is the relevant date for determining whether there is a claimant in actual occupation is one in which the sequence of events is that the right, unaccompanied by occupation, is created before completion and before the chargee has advanced his money and then subsequently the claimant enters into actual occupation after completion and remains in occupation up to the date when the registration of the charge is effected. The chargee in that event would have no possibility of discovering the existence of the claimant's interest before advancing his money and taking his charge, but would nevertheless be subject, on registration, to the claimant's prior equitable interest which, *ex hypothesi*, would not have been subject to the charge at its creation.

This does indeed produce a conveyancing absurdity and there is, as Nicholls LJ observed, an internal context for supposing that the legislature, in enacting para. (g), must have been contemplating an occupation which preceded and existed at completion of a transfer or disposition. Not only was the paragraph clearly intended to reflect the rule discussed in *Hunt* v *Luck* with regard to unregistered conveyancing, but the reference to inquiry and failure to disclose cannot make any sense unless it is related to a period in which such inquiry could be other than otiose. That absurdity can, I think, be avoided only by the route which the Court of Appeal adopted and by referring the 'actual occupation' in para. (g) to the date of completion of the transaction by transfer and payment of the purchase money.

Section 70(1) refers to such interests 'as may be for the time being subsisting' and in order to affect 'the estate transferred or created' on registration such interests would no doubt require to be subsisting on that date. But I see no insuperable difficulty in holding that the actual occupation required to support such an interest as a subsisting interest must exist at the date of completion of the transaction giving rise to the right to be registered, for that is the only date at which the inquiry referred to in para. (g) could, in practice, be made and be relevant...

Thus, the answer to the first question is that the date for testing occupation and the existence of the underlying interest is the moment of completion of the transaction. As to whether Mrs Cann had an interest in the land at that moment:

[I]t is difficult to see how she could, at that stage [before completion], have acquired any interest in 7 Hillview. She was not a party to the contract for the purchase of that property which was entered into by George alone. She assumed and, indeed, may have been led to believe that she would have an interest in and the right to occupy that property when George acquired it, but at the stage prior to its acquisition she had no more than a personal right against him. As against this, the society, which had no notice, either actual or constructive, of any rights which Mrs Cann might be minded to claim, had entered into an agreement to advance £25,000 on the security of the first legal charge on the property and that agreement had become binding and specifically enforceable against George on 6 August when the money was advanced at the request of his solicitors. In so far, therefore, as it is relevant to consider the priority of equities, the society, as an equitable chargee for money actually advanced, had an interest ranking in priority to what, at that stage, was merely Mrs Cann's expectation of an interest under a trust for sale to be created if and when the new property was acquired. One can, perhaps, test it in this way. If, prior to the acquisition of 7 Hillview, George Cann had been able to complete the sale of 30 Island Road and had absconded with the proceeds, financing the purchase of 7 Hillview entirely by means of a mortgage advance, could his mother have claimed any interest in the property? I should have thought clearly not, save in so far as she might be entitled to a right of occupation by estoppel based on his promise to accommodate her and her having, in reliance on that promise, vacated 30 Island Road to enable that sale to be completed.

The third question concerned priority between equitable claimant and mortgagee:

It is argued that, however, because the creation of a charge on property in favour of the society necessarily posits that the chargor has acquired an interest out of which the charge can be created, there must notionally be a point of time at which the estate vested in him free from the charge and in which the estoppel affecting him could be 'fed' by the acquisition of the legal estate so as to become binding on and take priority over the interest of the chargee. This is a puzzling problem on which it is not easy to reconcile the authorities...

The reality is that, in the vast majority of cases, the acquisition of the legal estate and the charge are not only precisely simultaneous but indissolubly bound together.

The acquisition of the legal estate is entirely dependent on the provision of funds which will have been provided before the conveyance can take effect and which are provided only against an agreement that the estate will be charged to secure them. Indeed, in many, if not most, cases of building society mortgages there will have been, as there was in this case, a formal offer of acceptance of an advance which will ripen into a specifically enforceable agreement immediately the funds are advanced, which will normally be a day or more before completion. In many, if not most, cases the charge itself will have been executed before the execution, let alone the exchange, or the conveyance or transfer of the property. This is given particular point in the case of registered land where the vesting of the estate is made to depend on registration, for it may well be that the transfer and the charge will be lodged for registration on different days so that the charge, when registered, may actually take effect from a date prior in time to the date from which the registration of the transfer takes effect... The reality is that the purchaser of land who relies on a building society or bank loan for the completion of his purchase never in fact acquires anything but an equity of redemption, for the land is, from the very inception, charged with the amount of the loan without which it could never have been transferred at all and it was never intended that it should be transferred...[26] It follows, in my judgment, that Mrs Cann can derive no assistance from this line of argument.

The answer to the third question is: a building society or bank mortgage takes effect before a beneficial interest vests in the land. As to whether Mrs Cann was in occupation at the time of registration:

It is perhaps dangerous to suggest any test for what is essentially a question of fact, for 'occupation' is a concept which may have different connotations according to the nature and purpose of the property which is claimed to be occupied. It does not necessarily, I think, involve the personal presence of the person claiming to occupy. A caretaker or the representative of a company can occupy, I should have thought, on behalf of his employer. On the other hand, it does, in my judgment, involve some degree of permanence and continuity which would rule out mere fleeting presence. A prospective tenant or purchaser who is allowed, as a matter of indulgence, to go into property in order to plan decorations or measure for furnishing would not, in ordinary parlance, be said to be occupying it, even though he might be there for hours at a time. Of course, in the instant case, there was, no doubt, on the part of the persons involved in moving Mrs Cann's belongings, an intention that they would remain there and would render the premises suitable for her ultimate use as a residential occupier. Like the trial judge, however, I am unable to accept that acts of this preparatory character carried out by courtesy of the vendor prior to completion can constitute 'actual occupation' for the purposes of s. 70(1)(g). Accordingly, all other considerations apart, Mrs Cann fails, in my judgment, to establish the necessary condition for the assertion of an overriding interest.

---

26 Is it not equally true that without Mrs Cann's contribution the land could not have been transferred to George? Why did this not occur to Lord Oliver?

Lord Jauncey:

In my view a purchaser who can only complete the transaction by borrowing money for the security of which he is contractually bound to grant a mortgage to the lender *eo instanti* with the execution of the conveyance in his favour cannot in reality ever be said to have acquired even for a *scintilla temporis*[27] the unencumbered fee simple or leasehold interest in land whereby he could grant interests having priority over the mortgage or the estoppel in favour of prior grantees could be fed with similar results. Since no one can grant what he does not have, it follows that such a purchaser could never grant an interest which was not subject to the limitations on his own interest.[28]

The next case concerns unregistered land, but the principle may apply equally to registered land:

Equity and Law Home Loans Ltd v *Prestidge* [1992] I WLR 137 (CA) Mustill, Butler-Sloss and Mann LJJ[29]

The sole legal owner borrowed £30,000 on mortgage, with the knowledge of Mrs Brown, his equitable co-owner. He then paid off the mortgage by taking out a separate, new mortgage of £42,835 and made off with the proceeds; Mrs Brown had no knowledge of these latest transactions until the new lender sought possession of her home. The question here was whether, and to what extent, she might be bound by the new mortgage.

Mustill LJ:

So it seems to me that one must ask this question: 'What intention must one impute to the parties as regards the position which would exist if the mortgage which had been obtained in order to enable the purchase of the house, and which the parties intended to have priority over the second defendant's [Mrs Brown's] beneficial interest, should be replaced by another mortgage on no less favourable terms?' In my judgement, this question need only to be posed for it to be answered in favour of the plaintiffs [the loan company]. Any other answer would be absurd, for it would mean that if Mr Prestidge had in good faith and without the knowledge of the second defendant transferred the mortgage to another society in order, say, to obtain a more favourable rate of interest, she would suddenly receive a windfall in the shape of the removal of the encumbrance which she had intended should be created in consequence of a transaction which could not do her any harm and of which she was entirely ignorant.

If this answer is correct, it disposes of two objections to the judgement of the recorder, which were canvassed in argument. First, it is said that the second defendant's interest could not be encumbered by a mortgage of which she was

---

27 'For a flash of time'.
28 See also R.J. Smith 106 LQR (1990) 545; P.T. Evans 54 Conv (1990) 155; J. Dewar [1993] Fam Law 231.
29 See also R.J. Smith (1992) 108 LQR 371; J.A. Greed (1992) 142 NLJ 539.

unaware, especially in circumstances where there was ample on the documents to put the plaintiffs on notice of that interest. Well, this would have been right if the mortgage to the plaintiffs had been the first and only transaction. But it was not. The new mortgage was made against the background of a consent by the second defendant to the creation of an encumbrance, so that the transaction could proceed. This imputed consent must, in common sense, apply to the creation of a new encumbrance in replacement of the old, whether the second defendant knew about it or not, provided that it did not change the second defendant's position for the worse.

The second objection receives the same answer. It presupposes that there was a *scintilla temporis* between the discharge of the first mortgage and the attachment of the second when the property was entirely unencumbered and the second defendant's interest therein was also unencumbered. It could be said that this interest could not effectively be re-encumbered by a transaction of which she was unaware. I doubt whether this argument is even technically correct, for it may very well be that if the position in law were closely examined (which very sensibly it was not in the argument before us) it would be found that the transactions were simultaneous. But apart from this, to give effect to such a technicality would go against the grain of the broad equity expounded in *Henning's* case [*Bristol and West Building Society* v *Henning* [1985] 1 WLR 778]. If it was just to enforce the first mortgage it must inevitably be just to enforce the second by virtue of any imputed consent which applied to the creation of both...

The second defendant has been cruelly deceived and has suffered grievous hardship but this is not something to be laid to the account of the plaintiffs.

Mrs Brown was held liable to the new mortgagee for the same sum (£30,000) for which she was liable to the original mortgagee. However, she had priority over the new mortgagee to the extent of the remainder (£12,835).

Even some of those who support the decisions in *Flegg* and *Cann* find this a little hard to take:

M.P. Thompson 'Co-Owners and Mortgagees' (1992) *Conv* 206

[T]his case represents the latest in a line of decisions where the courts have sought to water down the impact of *Williams and Glyns Bank Ltd* v *Boland*. While it is suggested that the results, at least, of the earlier decisions can readily be defended, the decision in *Equity and Law Home Loans Ltd* v *Prestidge* is far more dubious. To a considerable extent, the decision is the result of applying the fiction of imputing to parties intentions that they have never formed but which the courts feel they ought to have formed. Unfortunately, the adoption of this technique leads to the undermining of other accepted principles, in this case subrogation,[30] and also to inconsistencies of approach, in particular to that applied to the question of how a beneficial interest in a house is acquired. It is to be hoped that this dubious line of reasoning is, in the future, quietly abandoned rather than, as here, extended.

---

30 Subrogation is a doctrine which provides that a person (here, the society) who pays a debt for another (the legal owner) stands in the shoes of that other person.

The result of this series of cases on s. 70(1)(g) is that an equitable owner of land may only defeat a mortgage if:

1. the land that had been bought before the mortgage was granted; and
2. such owner was in 'permanent and continuous' occupation before the mortgage was granted; and
3. no inquiry was made of the equitable owner; and
4. there was only one registered proprietor; and
5. the equitable owner had no knowledge of the mortgage and had not consented to any earlier mortgage.

To some authors, the fact that a Mrs Boland might win barely conforms to the registration principle:

R.H. Maudsley 'Bona Fide Purchasers of Registered Land' 36 *MLR* (1973) 25:

Such a decision [as *Hodgson* v *Marks*, on p. 290] raises in their most fundamental form some of the basic questions of a system of registered conveyancing. Even if the register is not to be the one and only arbiter of the binding effect of equitable rights upon a purchaser, the register must count for something. To set up a system of registration and then to decide that a purchaser takes subject to equitable rights created by word of mouth, the existence of which the purchaser may have no possible means of discovering, is to make a caricature of the system.

However, M. Beaumont (junior counsel for Mrs Cann) concluded (in *Law Soc Gaz* (1990) 27, 28) that:

Hard cases make bad law. The *Cann* saga has been no exception. But hard cases make new law and it is to be trusted that the Law Commission will seek to ameliorate the position of the victim of mortgage fraud, whilst, perhaps by way of amendment to s. 70(1)(g) of the 1925 Act, designing the blueprint for balancing what is in essence a conflict between two innocent victims of fraud. Regrettably, it is the failure of the courts to articulate the problem as a contest of innocents, rather than as a contest manifesting clever but imaginary shades of tenuous and tangential blame, which has left legal principle in flux and elderly and confused litigants without a home.[31]

Reform of s. 70(1)(g)

The Law Commission has recommended:[32]

Law Commission Report No. 188 (1989) *Transfer of land: Overreaching – Beneficiaries in Occupation*

3.1 The 1925 legislation compromises between the need to protect beneficiaries

---

31 See also C. Douzinas and R. Warrington 54 MLR (1991) 142.
32 The Report was produced before the decision in *Cann*.

under trusts of land and the demand for certainty and simplicity in conveyancing were satisfactory, and perhaps ideal, in the circumstances in which they were intended to operate. A purchaser from trustees could ignore the beneficial interests so long as he was careful to observe simple precautions in paying the price. This successfully hid the terms of the settlement 'behind the curtain'. Buying from trustees became as simple as buying from a single beneficial legal owner which it certainly had not been previously. At the same time, the financial interest of the beneficiary was safeguarded by transferring his claim to the proceeds of sale. So long as the trustees properly conducted the affairs of the settlement, it was not important to the beneficiary by what assets his interest was secured.

3.2 Doubts about these provisions now arise because, over the years, the patterns of land ownership and the use of settlements have changed...

3.3 For this reason, there is now a very large number of cases in which trust beneficiaries occupy trust property as their own homes... The changes in circumstances have exposed the 1925 rules for the device which they are...

3.5 We remain of the view that reform is required here. There are four main reasons. First, the exclusively financial protection given by the 1925 legislation is no longer appropriate for occupiers of their own homes... Secondly, as the general understanding of many of the beneficiaries with whom we are concerned is that they are joint owners, they should have appropriate ownership rights. There is scant justification for the law giving preference to the wishes of one owner over those of another, simply because the former was constituted trustee of the legal estate. Thirdly, it is unsatisfactory that the consequences which a sale visits upon a beneficiary in occupation are different depending whether the legal estate happens to have been vested in one, or in more than one, person. Fourthly, it is difficult to defend the situation where someone not married to the legal owner in actual occupation of their home, and in which they own a share, has less right to remain there than a husband or wife without any such ownership interest...

4.3 Our principal recommendation, to protect the occupation rights of those with an equitable interest in property, can be succinctly stated:

> A conveyance of a legal estate in property should not have the effect of overreaching the interest of anyone of full age and capacity who is entitled to a beneficial interest in the property and who has a right to occupy it and is in actual occupation of it at the date of the conveyance, unless that person consents...

4.17 It does seem to us necessary to have a procedure by which the court may dispense with the requirement that the occupier give consent.[33] ...

---

33 Compare s. 30., Law of Property Act 1925, Chapter 9, p. 237.

The report concluded with a draft bill to make the necessary amendments to s. 2, Law of Property Act 1925. (For other proposals relating to s. 70, see below.)

Section 70(1)(i)

The owner of any land, whether registered or not yet registered, is bound by any 'local land charges':

Local Land Charges Act 1975

Local land charges

1 (1) A charge or other matter affecting land is a local land charge if it falls within any of the following descriptions and is not one of the matters set out in section 2 below –

(a) any charge acquired either before or after the commencement of this Act by a local authority, water authority or new town development corporation under the Public Health Acts 1936 and 1937, the Public Health Act 1961 or the Highways Act 1980 or any Act repealed by that Act or the Building Act 1984 or any similar charge acquired by a local authority under any other Act, whether passed before or after this Act, being a charge that is binding on successive owners of the land affected;

(b) any prohibition on or restriction on the use of land –

(i) imposed by a local authority on or after 1st January 1926 (including any prohibition or restriction embodied in any condition attached to a consent, approval or licence granted by a local authority on or after that date), or

(ii) enforceable by a local authority under any covenant or agreement made with them on or after that date,

being a prohibition or restriction binding on successive owners of the land affected;

(c) any prohibition of or restriction on the use of land –

(i) imposed by a Minister of the Crown or government department on or after the date of the commencement of this Act (including any prohibition or restriction embodied in any condition attached to a consent, approval or licence granted by such a Minister or department on or after that date), or

(ii) enforceable by such a Minister of the Crown, government department or local authority under any covenant or agreement made with him or them on or after the date of the commencement of this Act and binding on successive owners of the land affected;

(d) any positive obligation affecting land enforceable by a Minister of the Crown, government department or local authority under any covenant or agreement made with him or them on or after the date of the commencement of this Act and binding on successive owners of the land affected;

(e) any charge or other matter which is expressly made a local land charge by a statutory provision not contained in this section.

(2) For the purposes of subsection (1)(a) above, any sum which is recoverable from successive owners or occupiers of the land in respect of which the sum is

recoverable shall be treated as a charge, whether the sum is expressed to be a charge on the land or not.

The registers are kept by local authorities, and they are checked before completion of any transaction. *But*, even charges which have not been registered are binding:

Local Land Charges Act 1975

Compensation for non-registration or defective official search certificate

10 (1) Failure to register a local land charge in the appropriate local land charges register shall not affect the enforceability of the charge but where a person has purchased any land affected by a local land charge, then –

(a) in a case where a material personal search of the appropriate local land charges register was made in respect of the land in question before the relevant time, if at the time of the search the charge was in existence but not registered in that register; or

(aa) in a case where the appropriate local land charges register is kept otherwise than in documentary form and a material personal search of that register was made in respect of the land in question before the relevant time, if the entitlement to search in that register conferred by section 8 above was not satisfied as mentioned in subsection (1A) of that section; or

(b) in a case where a material official search of the appropriate local land charge register was made in respect of the land in question before the relevant time, if the charge was in existence at the time of the search but (whether registered or not) was not shown by the official search certificate as registered in that register,

the purchaser shall (subject to section 11(1) (below)) be entitled to compensation for any loss suffered by him in consequence.

General reform of overriding interests

In addition to the recommended reform of the operation of s. 70(1)(g) (above), the Law Commission No. 158 (1987) proposed reforms to s. 70 as a whole, noting first their earlier report:

Law Commission Working Paper No. 37 (1971) para. 7

From the point of view of purchasers of registered land, it is clearly desirable that as many as possible of the matters which may burden the land should be recorded on the register of the title to the land. We aim at simplifying conveyancing and a reduction of the number of overriding interests would contribute to that end. A balance must, however, be maintained between, on the one hand, the interests of purchasers of land and, on the other, the legitimate interests of those who have rights in the land which might be prejudiced by a requirement that such rights must be recorded on the register to be binding ...

The Commission in 1987 (para 2 : 24) concluded that there should be in future only five categories of overriding interest:
1. legal easements and profits à prendre;
2. rights acquired by adverse possession;
3. legal leases for 21 years or less;
4. rights of persons in actual occupation of land;
5. customary rights.[34]

The relevant date at which to test these should be the date of completion, not the date of registration (compare *Cann*'s case above). There should also be a class of 'general burdens', including local land charges and mineral rights, which would have roughly the same effect as overriding interests.

MINOR INTERESTS[35]

Land Registration Act 1925

Interpretation

3   (xv) 'Minor interests' mean the interests not capable of being disposed of or created by registered disposition and capable of being overridden (whether or not a purchaser has notice thereof) by the proprietors unless protected as provided by this Act, and all rights and interests which are not registered or protected on the register and are not overriding interests, and include –
    (a) in the case of land held on trust for sale, all interests and powers which are under the Law of Property Act 1925 capable of being overridden by the trustees for sale, whether or not such interests or powers are so protected; and
    (b) in the case of settled land, all interests and powers which are under the Settled Land Act 1925 and the Law of Property Act 1925, or either of them, capable of being overridden by the tenant for life or statutory owner, whether or not such interests and powers are so protected as aforesaid.

Dispositions off register creating 'minor interests'

101 (1) Any person, whether being the proprietor or not, having a sufficient interest or power in or over registered land, may dispose of or deal with the same, and create any interests or rights therein which are permissible in like manner and by the like modes of assurance in all respects as if the land were not registered, but subject as provided by this section.

     (2) All interests and rights disposed of or created under subsection 10 of this

---

34 Re-stated Law Commission Report No. 173 (1988) Fourth Report on Land Registration, para. 3.2.
35 See also S. Coveney and A. Pain *Interests in Land, a Practical Guide to Effective Protection at the Land Registry* (Fourmat: 1991).

section (whether by the proprietor or any other person) shall, subject to the provisions of this section, take effect as minor interests, and be capable of being overridden by registered dispositions for valuable consideration.

(3) Minor interests shall, subject to the express exceptions contained in this section, take effect only in equity, but may be protected by entry on the register or such notices, cautions, inhibitions and restrictions as are provided for by this Act or rules.

Since minor interests 'take effect in equity', they take priority according to the date of their creation: 'Where the equities are equal, the first in time prevails'.[36]

Minor interests can be protected on the register as shown in Table 10.2.

An important minor interest in a family home, if the land is registered in the name of a single proprietor, is the 'spouse's right of occupation':

Table 10.2 Protection of minor interests

Type of Interest	Method of Protection	Sections	On the Register	Notes
Equitable easements, charges, restrictive covenants, spouse's rights of occupation	Notice	48–52	Charges Division	Includes any interest burdening the registered title... also here, legal leases over 21 years and legal charges.
Any interest in the land not protected by notice or registration	Caution	53–6	Proprietor-ship	The cautioner has a right to be warned of any dealing. The proprietor is told of the caution.
Any interest which cannot be protected in any other way	Inhibition	57	Proprietor-ship	Prohibits any dealing; used if the proprietor goes bankrupt.
Interests under a settlement or a trust for sale	Restriction	58	Proprietor-ship	Prohibits dealings unless conditions are met.

---

36 This was affirmed in *Mortgage Corporation Ltd* v *Nationwide Credit Corp Ltd* (1992) *The Times*, July 27.

Matrimonial Homes Act 1983

Rights concerning matrimonial home where one spouse has no estate, etc.

1 (1) Where one spouse is entitled to occupy a dwelling house by virtue of a beneficial estate or interest or contract or by virtue of any enactment giving him or her the right to remain in occupation, and the other spouse is not so entitled, then, subject to the provisions of this Act, the spouse not so entitled shall have the following rights (in this Act referred to as 'rights of occupation') –

(a) if in occupation, a right not to be evicted or excluded from the dwelling house or any part thereof by the other spouse except with the leave of the court given by an order under this section;

(b) if not in occupation, a right with the leave of the court so given to enter into and occupy the dwelling house...

(11) It is hereby declared that a spouse who has an equitable interest in a dwelling house or in the proceeds of sale thereof, not being a spouse in whom is vested (whether solely or as a joint tenant) a legal estate in fee simple or a legal term of years absolute in the dwelling house, is to be treated for the purpose only of determining whether he or she has rights of occupation under this section as not being entitled to occupy the dwelling house by virtue of that interest.

Effect of rights of occupation as charge on dwelling house

2 (8) Where the title to the legal estate by virtue of which a spouse is entitled to occupy a dwelling house (including any legal estate held by trustees for that spouse) is registered under the Land Registration Act 1925 or any enactment replaced by that Act –

(a) registration of a land charge affecting the dwelling house by virtue of this Act shall be effected by registering a notice under that Act, and

(b) a spouse's rights of occupation shall not be an overriding interest within the meaning of that Act affecting the dwelling house notwithstanding that the spouse is in actual occupation of the dwelling house.

(9) A spouse's rights of occupation (whether or not constituting a charge) shall not entitle that spouse to lodge a caution under section 54 of the Land Registration Act 1925.

If the minor interest is the 'right of occupation' under the 1983 Act, the court takes all the circumstances of the case into account in deciding whether the spouse or the buyer of the land should win: for an example see *Kashmir Kaur* v *Gill* [1988] 2 All ER 288, where a blind purchaser defeated a wife even though she had registered her right of occupation.

There are two odd cases which suggest that a purchaser with notice might be bound by an *unprotected minor interest*. This is the result of persuasive argument putting together s. 3(xxi), s. 20 (above) and s. 59(6):

Land Registration Act 1925

Interpretation

3 (xxi) 'Purchaser' means a purchaser in good faith or for valuable consideration and includes a lessee, mortgagee, or other person who for valuable consideration acquires an interest in land or in any charge on land; ...

Writs, orders, deeds of arrangement, pending actions, etc.

59 (6) Subject to the provisions of this Act relating to fraud and to the title of a trustee in bankruptcy, a purchaser acquiring title under a registered disposition, shall not be concerned with any pending action, writ, order, deed of arrangement, or other document, matter or claim (not being an overriding interest ... subject to which the disposition takes effect ...) which is not protected by a caution or other entry on the register, whether he has or has not notice thereof, express, implied or constructive.

The first case is *Peffer* v *Rigg*; the second, *Lyus* v *Prowsa*. Both are merely first instance decisions and both are explicable also on other grounds than 'notice'.

Peffer v *Rigg* [1977] 1 WLR 285

Mr Rigg was the sole registered proprietor of a house lived in by his mother-in-law. He shared the beneficial interest with his brother-in-law, Mr Peffer, but the latter's interest was not protected on the register. After the mother-in-law died, Mr Rigg sold the title for £1 to his wife as part of their divorce arrangements. She claimed that, under s. 59(6), she was not affected by the unregistered minor interest, even though she had actual notice of it.

Graham J:

There is a contrast between sections 20 and 59 of the Act. Section 20(1) protects any 'transferee' for valuable consideration. By section 18(5) 'transfer' and 'transferee' in relation to freehold land have very wide meanings but are not specifically defined in section 3. It is to be noted, however, that section 20, though it mentions valuable consideration, does not mention 'good faith' as being necessary on the part of the transferee, nor does it mention notice. It can be argued, therefore, that the section seems to be saying that a transferee whether he has good faith or not, and whether he has notice or not, takes free of all interests (other than overriding interests) provided he has given valuable consideration.

This at first sight seems a remarkable proposition and though undoubtedly the property legislation of 1925 was intended to simplify such matters of title as far as possible, I find it difficult to think that section 20 of this Act can have been intended to be as broad in scope as this... The provisions for rectification in section 82 as against a proprietor in possession who has been a party to a fraud, mistake or an omission in consequence of which rectification of the register is sought also seems to me to show that section 20 must be read with some limitations... Section 59(6) on the other hand speaks of a 'purchaser' not being affected by matters which are not protected by a caution or other entry on the register. By definition, however (see section 3 (xxi)), 'purchaser' means a purchaser in good faith for valuable consideration. It seems clear therefore that as a matter of construction a purchaser who is not in fact one 'in good faith' *will* be concerned with matters not protected by a caution or other entry on the register, at any rate, as I hold, if he has notice thereof. If these sections 20 and 59 are read together in the context of the Act they can be reconciled by holding that if the 'transferee' spoken of in section 20 is in fact a 'purchaser' he will only be protected if he has given valuable consideration and is in good faith. He cannot in my judgment be in good faith if he has in fact notice of something which affects his title as in the present case. Of course if he and, *a fortiori,* if a purchaser from him has given valuable consideration and in fact has not notice he is under no obligation to go behind the register, and will in such a case be fully protected. This view of the matter seems to me to enable the two sections to be construed consistently together without producing the unreasonable result of permitting a transferee purchaser to take advantage of the Act and divest himself of knowledge of defects in his own title, and secure to himself a flawless title which he ought not in justice to be allowed to obtain. This view of the Act produces a result which is also produced by applying the principles applicable in the case of a constructive trust, which I will now consider...

Even if, therefore, I am wrong as to the proper construction of sections 20 and 59, when read together, and even if section 20 strikes off the shackles of the express trust which bound [Mr Rigg], this cannot invalidate the new [constructive] trust imposed on [Mrs Rigg].

Thus, either by the sections of the Land Registration Act, or by means of a constructive trust, the proprietor held the property on trust for herself and Mr Peffer. The court ordered the register to be rectified to take account of this (see p. 314 below).

Lyus v *Prowsa Developments Ltd* [1982] 1 WLR 1044

A development company agreed to sell a house, to be built on registered land, to Mr and Mrs Prowsa. This estate contract was not protected on the register as a minor interest. That company became insolvent and the land came into the hands of the defendant development company 'subject to, but with the benefit of' the estate contract.

Having held that the company should suffer the burden of the estate contract because of the principle of mutuality:

Dillon J:

This does not, however, conclude the matter since I also have to consider the effect of the provisions of the Land Registration Act 1925...

It has been pointed out by Lord Wilberforce in *Midland Bank Trust Co Ltd* v *Green* [1981] AC 513, 531, that it is not fraud to rely on legal rights conferred by Act of Parliament...

It seems to me that the fraud on the part of the defendants in the present case lies not just in relying on the legal rights conferred by an Act of Parliament, but in the first defendant reneging on a positive stipulation in favour of the plaintiffs in the bargain under which the first defendant acquired the land. That makes, as it seems to me, all the difference. It has long since been held, for instance, in *Rochefoucauld v Boustead* [1897] 1 Ch 196, that the provisions of the Statute of Frauds 1677, now incorporated in certain sections of the Law of Property Act 1925, cannot be used as an instrument of fraud, and that it is fraud for a person to whom land is agreed to be conveyed as trustee for another to deny the trust and relying on the terms of the statute to claim the land for himself...

It seems to me that the same considerations are applicable in relation to the Land Registration Act 1925. If, for instance, the agreement of October 18, 1979, between the bank and the first defendant had expressly stated that the first defendant would hold Plot 29 upon trust to give effect for the benefit of the plaintiffs to the plaintiffs' agreement with the vendor company, it would be difficult to say that the express trust was overreached and rendered nugatory by the Land Registration Act 1925...

The plaintiffs are, therefore, entitled to succeed in this action. The appropriate relief in that event is that specific performance should be ordered as against the second defendants of the sale to the plaintiffs of Plot 29, with the completed house thereon, on the terms of the agreement.[37]

The Law Commission's 1987 Report (No. 158 4.14–4.15 – see above p. 308) recommended that only a purchaser *in good faith* for valuable consideration should take free from minor interests which have not been protected on the register.

RECTIFICATION AND INDEMNITY

Rectification

The concept of a list of all land titles necessarily involves the provision of rules for correcting errors on the list ('rectification'), and for compensating anyone who loses out by reason of relying on it ('indemnity').

Land Registration Act 1925

Rectification of the register

82 (1) The register may be rectified pursuant to an order of the court or by the registrar, subject to an appeal to the court, in any of the following cases, but subject to the provisions of this section –

(a) Subject to any express provisions of this Act to the contrary, where a court of competent jurisdiction has decided that any person is entitled to any

---

37 See also P. Bennett 47 MLR (1984) 476.

estate right or interest in or to any registered land or charge, and as a consequence of such decision such court is of opinion that a rectification of the register is required, and makes an order to that effect;

(b) Subject to any express provision of this Act to the contrary, where the court, on the application in the prescribed manner of any person who is aggrieved by any entry made in, or by the omission of any entry from, the register, or by any default being made, or unnecessary delay taking place, in the making of any entry in the register, makes an order for the rectification of the register;

(c) In any case and at any time with the consent of all persons interested;

(d) Where the court or the registrar is satisfied that any entry in the register has been obtained by fraud;

(e) Where two or more persons are, by mistake, registered as proprietors of the same registered estate or of the same charge;

(f) Where a mortgagee has been registered as proprietor of the land instead of as proprietor of a charge and a right of redemption is subsisting;

(g) Where a legal estate has been registered in the name of a person who if the land had not been registered would not have been the estate owner; and

(h) In any other case where, by reason of any error or omission in the register, or by reason of any entry made under a mistake, it may be deemed just to rectify the register.

(2) The register may be rectified under this section, notwithstanding that the rectification may affect any estates, rights, charges, or interests acquired or protected by registration, or by any entry on the register, or otherwise.

(3) The register shall not be rectified, except for the purpose of giving effect to an overriding interest or an order of the court, so as to affect the title of the proprietor who is in possession –

(a) unless the proprietor has caused or substantially contributed to the error or omission by fraud or lack of proper care; or

(c) unless for any other reason, in any particular case, it is considered that it would be unjust not to rectify the register against him.

(4) Where a person is in possession of registered land in right of a minor interest, he shall, for the purposes of this section, be deemed to be in possession as agent for the proprietor.

(5) The registrar shall obey the order of any competent court in relation to any registered land or being served with the order or an official copy thereof.

(6) On every rectification of the register the land certificate and any charge certificate which may be affected shall be produced to the registrar unless an order to the contrary is made by him.

Rectification was ordered in several of the cases seen already in this chapter, for example *Chowood Ltd* v *Lyall* and *Peffer* v *Rigg* (above). It was also ordered in *Pollard* v *Jackson* (1994) 67 P&CR 327, above p. 73.

The operation of s. 82 and the discretion of the registrar is clearly demonstrated in cases of fraud:

Norwich and Peterborough Building Society v Steed (No 2) [1992] 1 All ER 330 (CA), Purchas, Butler-Sloss and Scott LJJ[38]

Mr Steed owned a house subject to a small loan; it was lived in by his mother and sister and brother-in-law, the Hammonds. He lived in California, and so he gave his mother power of attorney over the house. His mother, at the instigation of the Hammonds, transferred the house to them without knowing what she was signing and they immediately mortgaged it for £15,000. (The transfer of the house to them was voidable for fraud, but was valid until avoided; therefore the mortgage was valid when it was made.)

When the Hammonds failed to meet the repayments, the building society sued for possession. Mr Steed found out just in time and succeeded in halting the possession order (in *Argyle Building Society* v *Hammond* [1985] 50 P & CR 148). He then claimed that the register should be rectified showing him as registered proprietor, and this was conceded. He also claimed that the register should be rectified to delete the building society's charge.

Scott LJ:

If an order of rectification is to be made the case must be brought within at least one of paras (a) to (h) of s. 82(1). The dispute in the present case is as to the breadth of the power conferred by paras (a) and (b) and, to a lesser extent, paras (d) and (h). There is no doubt but that, if Mrs Steed's [the mother's] signature had been forged [and therefore void] ... the case would have fallen squarely within para (g) ... If however, as is the case, the transfer is only voidable, para (g) does not apply. It is plain that, if title to the property had been unregistered, Mr Steed would have had no remedy against the building society. He would have recovered the property from the Hammonds but the property would have remained subject to the charge. It is submitted, however, that paras (a), (b), (d) or (h) can, since title is registered, be prayed in aid. This submission is made on the footing that, under one or more of these paragraphs, the court is given a general discretion to order rectification in any case in which it may be thought just to do so. If the submission is right, then s.82 ... achieved a remarkable and unnoticed change in the substantive law...

There is a sense in which the power to rectify under s. 82 is undoubtedly discretionary. The words in subs.(1) are 'may be rectified'. Section 83(2) shows that rectification is not automatic. The power to rectify may, in a particular case, be present but, none the less, there is, in every case, a general discretion to grant rectification. The power to grant rectification is limited in subs.(1) to 'any of the following cases'. The power to order rectification must, therefore, be found within one or other of the subs.(1) paragraphs and cannot be spelt out of the words 'may be rectified'...

---

38 See also C. Davis (1992) Conv 293.

Scott LJ proceeded to explain each of the paragraphs in turn, and concluded:

In my opinion the scheme is reasonably clear. Paragraphs (a) and (b) give power to the court to make orders of rectification in order to give effect to property rights which have been established in an action or which are clear. Paragraph (c) enables orders to be made by consent. The remaining paragraphs, paras (d) to (h), are intended to enable errors to be corrected. Paragraphs (d), (e), (f) and (g) each deal with an error of a particular character. But, since these paragraphs might not cover comprehensively all errors, para (h) was added as a catch-all provision to cover any other errors. The breadth of the catch-all provision was, I imagine, the reason why it was thought appropriate to make the power exercisable 'where ... it may be deemed just to rectify the register'. There are no comparable words in any of the other paragraphs.

Paragraph (h) is relied on by Mr Lloyd [for Mr Steed]. But in order for the paragraph to be applicable some 'error or omission in the register' or 'some entry made under a mistake' must be shown. The entry in the charges register of the building society's charge was not an error and was not made under a mistake. The legal charge was executed by the Hammonds, who were at the time transferees under a transfer executed by Mrs Steed as attorney for the registered proprietor. The voidable transfer had not been set aside. The registration of the Hammonds as proprietors took place at the same time as the registration of the legal charge. Neither registration was an error. Neither entry was made under a mistake. So the case for rectification cannot be brought under para (h)...

The financial consequences to the parties of ordering or refusing rectification make it difficult to weigh the 'equities'. If rectification were ordered, the loss would fall not upon the building society but upon the public purse. If rectification were refused, the public purse would be saved the burden of paying an indemnity...

Since the court did not have the power to rectify under any of the provisions, the question of the discretion inherent in rectification did not arise. Mr Steed failed in his claim to have the charge deleted from the register.

As regards rectification against a registered proprietor in possession:

London Borough of Hounslow v Hare (1992) 25 HLR 9 (Ch D), Knox J[39]

A 125-year lease of a flat was mistakenly sold by the local authority to the sitting tenant under the 'right to buy' provisions in the Housing Act 1980 (now 1985). The authority had not realised that charitable land, as this was, was exempt from these sections and could not be sold. Knox J had to decide whether, where a void lease had been registered, the register should be rectified against the proprietor in possession.

Knox J:

It is common ground that if I order rectification Miss Hare [the registered proprietor] will be entitled to compensation under s. 83 and that the ceiling provided for by sub-s. (6)(b) of that section will be the value of the estate, interest or charge

---

39 See also J. Martin (1993) Conv 224.

immediately before the time of rectification. In practical terms, that is the present-day value of Miss Hare's lease. Equally it is accepted that if I do not order rectification under s. 83(6)(a), the ceiling will be the value of the estate, interest or charge at the time when the error or omission that caused the loss was made. It is clear that that time is when the registration took effect, i.e. in February 1988. There is, of course, a difference in point of time between those two dates, between February 1988 and the present day, but I am not satisfied, in the absence of any evidence on the subject at all, that there has been a significant shift in property values in relation to leases of this length of time for flats in that part of London...

There was no doubt in my mind that Miss Hare was not only an innocent party in the sense that there was no way which I can discern that she could have known that there was the problem that emerged, based on the existence of the charitable trusts in the testatrix's will, either personally or through her solicitor...

What I have primarily, as I see it, to look at is whether it is considered that it would be unjust not to rectify the register against Miss Hare and I cannot reach that conclusion. She has been in possession of this property for a very long time. She [originally] went in, on her evidence, in 1972 ... [I]t seems to me that when one is dealing with a person's home the change from the near equivalent of a freehold that a 125-year lease gives to somebody of the age of nearing 40 to that of a tenant, assured or not, is one of very considerable significance. That feature does, in my judgment, far outweigh any financial considerations that there may be the other way.[40]

For these reasons I come to the conclusion that this is a case where s. 82(3) applies so as to prevent me from ordering rectification and I do not propose to do so.

Indemnity

Land Registration Act 1925

Right to indemnity in certain cases

83 (1) Subject to any provisions of this Act to the contrary, any person suffering loss by reason of any rectification of the register under this Act shall be entitled to be indemnified.

(2) Where an error or omission has occurred in the register, but the register is not rectified, any person suffering loss by reason of such error or omission, shall, subject to the provisions of this Act, be entitled to be indemnified.

(3) Where any person suffers loss by reason of the loss or destruction of any document lodged at the registry for inspection or safe custody or by reason of an error in any official search, he shall be entitled to be indemnified under this Act.

(4) Subject as hereinafter provided, a proprietor of any registered land or charge

---

40 Compare the 'waywardness' of occupation referred to in *Flegg's* case (1988) above p. 296.

claiming in good faith under a forged disposition shall, where the register is rectified, be deemed to have suffered loss by reason of such rectification and shall be entitled to be indemnified under this Act.

(5) No indemnity shall be payable under this Act in any of the following cases –
(a) Where the applicant or a person from whom he derives title (otherwise than under a disposition for valuable consideration which is registered or protected on the register) has caused or substantially contributed to the loss by fraud or lack of proper care;
(b) On account of any mines or minerals or of the existence of any rights to work or get mines or minerals, unless a note is entered on the register that the mines or minerals are included in the registered title;
(c) On account of costs incurred in taking or defending any legal proceedings without the consent of the registrar.

(6) Where an indemnity is paid in respect of the loss of an estate or interest in or charge on land the amount so paid shall not exceed –
(a) Where the register is not rectified, the value of the estate, interest or charge at the time when the error or omission which caused the loss was made;
(b) Where the register is rectified, the value (if there had been no rectification) of the estate, interest or charge, immediately before the time of rectification.

(8) Subject to subsection (5)(c) of this section –
(a) an indemnity under any provision of this Act shall include such amount, if any, as may be reasonable in respect of any costs or expenses properly incurred by the applicant in relation to the matter; and
(b) an applicant for an indemnity under any such provisions shall be entitled to an indemnity thereunder of such amount, if any, as may be reasonable in respect of such costs or expenses, notwithstanding that no other indemnity money is payable thereunder.

(9) Where indemnity is paid for a loss, the registrar, on behalf of the Crown, shall be entitled to recover the amount paid from any person who has caused or substantially contributed to the loss by his fraud.

Decisions on indemnity are inevitably entangled with the rectification discretion, as shown in the cases extracted above. In fact, few claims for compensation are made. One reason may be, as an early case shows, that no indemnity is payable where there is an overriding interest. This case is the consequence of *Chowood* v *Lyall* (1930) (see p. 289) on adverse possession:

In Re Chowood's Registered Land [1933] 1 Ch 574

Clauson J:
The question has been referred to the Court by the Land Registrar, and I have now

to determine whether any loss has been suffered. The claim is opposed by the Attorney General, on behalf of the trustees of the statutory fund out of which the indemnity, if any, is to be provided.

Chowood's title was all along subject to the rights which Lyall has succeeded in establishing; and the loss, if it may be properly so-called, which Chowood has suffered is that they have not got, and since the Act of 1925 came into force (whatever may have been the position before) have never had title to the strip, except subject to an overriding right in Lyall. That loss was occasioned by Chowood failing to ascertain that, when they bought, Lyall was in possession, and in possession under such circumstances that Ralli [their transferor] could not make a title to the strip. The loss was occasioned by paying Ralli for a strip to which Ralli could not make title. The rectification of the register merely recognised the existing position, and put Chowood in no worse a position than they were before.

In these circumstances I must hold that Chowood have suffered no loss by reason of the rectification of the register.

Reform of rectification and indemnity

The Law Commission summarised their proposals as follows:

Law Commission Report (1987) No. 158 *Third Report on Land Registration* para. 3.34

(1) Where the register does not reflect, whether through error or omission, the title to the land according to the rules of land law which prevail apart from registration of title then, if it is just to do so, the register may be rectified on application either to the registrar or the court.

(2) For these purposes the rules of land law include land registration procedural requirements and the requirement to protect on the register or as a land charge (where relevant) where failure to protect leads to the defeat of the right.

(3) Any such rectification may affect estates and interests already registered or protected or any existing overriding interest.

(4) However, there is to be no rectification against a registered proprietor who has taken the care of a prudent purchaser and who is a bona fide purchaser in actual occupation of the land unless the rectification is in favour of a trustee in bankruptcy.

(5) Where the register is rectified, any person suffering loss by reason of or despite such rectification should, subject as follows, be entitled to be indemnified in full.[41]

(6) Where an error or omission has occurred in the register, but the register is *not* rectified, any person suffering loss by reason of such error or omission should, subject as follows, be entitled to be indemnified in full.

---

41 What difference might this make to the cases recently decided under s. 70(1) (g)?

(7) Where an overriding interest is asserted against a registered proprietor or chargee, then he may apply for indemnity alone but, as a condition precedent to payment, there may be rectification of the register.

(8) There should still be provisions for indemnity in respect of an error in an official search or loss of documents or inaccuracy of an office copy.

(9) No indemnity should be payable where there is rectification in respect of fraud, mines or minerals, or legal costs incurred without consent.

(10) Any indemnity payable should be reduced by such amount as may be just and equitable in respect of any lack of proper care by the applicant.

In the Law Commission Report (1988) No. 173 Fourth Report on Land Registration, the Commission produced a draft Land Registration Bill incorporating these recommendations.

Gray *Elements of Land Law* (Butterworths: 2nd edition 1993 at p. 241) concludes:

It remains to be seen whether the Law Commission's admirable proposals will be implemented in statutory form. Already the draft Land Registration Bill has lain dormant since 1988, and there are disquieting indications that there is no overwhelming political will to institute a sensible, but considerably more expensive, reconciliation of the mutual antagonisms inherent in this (as indeed in any) scheme of title registration.

11 The changing nature of property

INTRODUCTION

A new property

At the beginning of this book, the notion of property was briefly introduced as a means of allocating scarce resources, and of providing certainty, security and economic efficiency. In legal thought, 'property' was seen to involve essentially the rights to use (involving both security and exclusivity) and to transfer, by sale or will, and that these rights 'bind the whole world'. It is obvious that, as times change, the nature of property – the objects of property and limits on the rights to use and transfer – must also change, to take account of new technology and new needs. Every discourse has its marginal voices:

B. Edgeworth 'Post-Property?: A Postmodern Conception of Private Property' 11 *Univ of NS Wales L Jo* (1988) 87

[There is a] radical democratic tradition for which personal, moral and cultural aims are at least as important as distributional ones, where sexual and racial equality, the right to control one's body, the right to a safe and clean environment, rank alongside the question of who owns what. In this respect, the 'time-worn claims' of liberalism's and Marxism's property metanarratives[1] 'ring hollow to many modern ears'. The politics of *becoming* are precisely the postmodernist core: to create new vocabularies in order to create new selves, new identities, new communities in the face of economic orders controlled by multi-national corporations under the banner of private property or state-socialist systems extolling a bureaucratised public ownership.

In the optimistic 1960s, Charles Reich (below) wrote of 'the emergence of government as a major source of wealth', which was gradually replacing more orthodox forms of property. He argued that it was essential that the positive features of old property should be applied to government largesse, government franchises, contracts, services, benefits, licences, etc.

---

1 'Large-scale theoretical interpretations purportedly of univesal application.'

C.A. Reich 'The New Property' (1964) 73 *Yale LJ* 733

Property is a legal institution, the essence of which is the creation and protection of certain private rights in wealth of any kind. The institution performs many different functions. One of these functions is to draw a boundary between public and private power. Property draws a circle around the activities of each private individual or organisation. Within that circle, the owner has a greater degree of freedom than without. Outside, he must justify or explain his actions, or show his authority. Within, he is master, and the state must explain and justify any interference ... Thus, property performs the function of maintaining independence, dignity and pluralism in society by creating zones within which the majority has to yield to the owner. Whim, caprice, irrationality and 'antisocial' activities are given the protection of law; the owner may do what all or most of his neighbours decry...

If the individual is to survive in a collective society, he must have protection against its ruthless pressures. There must be sanctuaries or enclaves where no majority can reach. To shelter the solitary human spirit does not merely make possible the fulfilment of individuals; it also gives society the power to change, to grow, and to regenerate, and hence to endure. These were the objects which property sought to achieve, and can no longer achieve. The challenge of the future will be to construct, for the society that is coming, institutions and laws to carry on this work. Just as the Homestead Act[2] was a deliberate effort to foster individual values at an earlier time, so we must try to build an economic basis for liberty today – we need a Homestead Act for rootless twentieth century man. We must create a new property.

An alternative, post-liberal, vision of a new property is provided in the next, more recent, extract.[3]

S. Bowles and H. Gintis, *Democracy and Capitalism: Property, Community and the Contradictions of Modern Social Thought* (Basic Books: 1986)

We conceive of postliberal democracy as more than a new set of rules of the game. It ... encompasses a set of human purposes, embracing a broad vision of human development as its guiding principle. If for liberalism the archetypal human activity is choice, and for Marxism it is labor, postliberal democratic theory represents people as learners for whom both choice and labor are indispensable means toward personal development. We thus follow John Stuart Mill in celebrating Wilhelm von Humboldt's profession of Enlightenment:

> 'The grand, leading principle, towards which every argument unfolded in these pages directly converges, is the absolute and essential importance of human development in its richest diversity...'

This vision of a postliberal democracy is unmistakably the product of the

---

2 See also L. Ingalls Wilder, *The Little House on the Prairie* (Harper: 1953).
3 See also K.J. Vandervelde (1980) 29 Buffalo LR 325; P.D. Cameron, *Property Rights and Sovereign Rights: the Case of North Sea Oil* (Academic Press: 1983), especially Chapter 8.

aspirations of the liberal era itself, yet it breaks sharply with the liberal tradition in two respects. It represents the individual as an intrinsically social being actively engaged in the continual transformation of one's own and others' capacities, sentiments, and attachments; and it represents private control over productive property, not as a salutary barrier to the pretensions of the state, but as a bedrock of economic dependence and an obstacle to popular sovereignty.

A new interest in land

It might be thought that the nature of property rights in land are like the land itself, permanent and fixed. Nonetheless, rights in land do change with the changing conditions of human life. The triumph of nineteenth-century land lawyers was the invention of the restrictive covenant, a new property right in land born out of urban crisis. Twentieth-century academic lawyers ask themselves too, 'What have we created?' And their answer echoes faintly, 'Perhaps it is the licence?'

G.C. Cheshire 'A New Equitable Interest in Land' 16 (1953) *MLR 1*

In *Errington v Errington* [[1952] 1 KB 290][4] the Court of Appeal has recognized a new interest in land. This is what journalists call 'news', and is news moreover that is calculated to excite our admiration or our pity according to our individual views upon the underlying purpose of the law. To some this judicial adventure will represent normal evolution, to others it will smack of blasphemy. It concerns that Cinderella of the common law – the licence to enter land for a particular purpose.

Sir Robert Megarry and H.W.R. Wade *The Law of Real Property* (Stevens: 1984)

It has been truly said that the new principles have not yet been fully explored, and that they seem sometimes to be invoked simply because there would otherwise be hardship to a plaintiff... Nevertheless, the courts appear to be well on their way to creating a new and highly versatile interest in land which will rescue many informal and unbusinesslike transactions, particularly within families, from the penalties of disregarding legal forms. Old restraints are giving way to the demands of justice.

This chapter evaluates the different types of licence in land, and assesses whether they might amount to 'property', either by satisfying the conditions of 'property-ness' (an exclusive, secure and alienable right) or by forcing us to change the definition of 'property'. It concludes with questions as to what the role of 'property' should be at the beginning of the twenty-first century.

---

4 Compare the *Ashbum Anstalt* case below.

LICENCES IN LAND

A licence is simply a permission to be on land owned by another person. There are several kinds, from that of the casual visitor (a bare licence), to that 'coupled with an easement or profit' (that is, the right to go onto the land of another to do/collect the subject-matter of the right). There is also the 'mutual licence' – your foundations may encroach on my garden if I can use your drive (see *Ives ER Investment Ltd* v *High* [1967] 2 QB 379).[5] Another model is the contractual licence, familiar from Chapter 4 where it takes the form of a 'quasi-tenancy' arrangement. Closely linked to this is the licence by estoppel (see Chapter 2, p. 54).

It is these last two types of licence which seem sometimes, through equity's intervention, to be capable of achieving the status of 'property'. The security and alienability of a contractual licence depends to a large extent on the terms of the contract. The strength of the licence by estoppel depends on whatever is necessary in order to satisfy the equity. Every case is treated on its own merits so that the creative and persuasive powers of counsel are central. In such cases consistency and predictability have often appeared less important than 'justice between the parties'.

The modern story starts with two House of Lords decisions which maintained the traditional view that contractual licences cannot be 'property'.

King v *David Allen & Sons Billposting Ltd* [1916] 2 AC 54 (HL)
Lord Buckmaster LC, Earl Loreburn and Lord Atkinson

There was a contract giving the company a 'Licence' to advertise on the side of King's building for four years in exchange for an annual payment. The arrangement was determinable on six months' notice. King then leased the building to another, who refused to allow the billboard.

The House unanimously held that King was liable in damages for breach of contract. The personal (that is, 'non-property') right of the company was merely a licence and therefore not enforceable against a lessee or any other third party not privy to the contract:

Lord Buckmaster LC:
There is a contract between the appellant and the respondents which creates nothing but a personal obligation. It is a licence given for good and valuable consideration and to endure for a certain time... I find it difficult to see how it can be reasonably urged that anything beyond personal rights was ever contemplated by the parties.

---

5 See also *Rhone* v *Stephens*, Chapter 7, p. 194.

Winter Garden Theatre (London) Ltd v *Millennium Productions Ltd* [1948] AC 173 (HL), Viscount Simon, Lord Porter, Lord Uthwatt and Lord MacDermott

During the war, the theatre agreed a licence with the respondents that they could produce plays in the theatre, for a weekly money payment. The agreement was for two terms of six months and then from month to month; the licensee could give a month's notice, but there was no provision for the theatre to end the agreement. However, three years later, at the end of the war, the theatre gave the licensee one month's notice. The licensee argued that they could not be given notice unless they had breached a term of the agreement, or, alternatively, that one month was not reasonable, but they lost on both counts.

Lord Porter:

My Lords, there are very few, if any, contracts which can be construed without taking into consideration a long background of gradual development and the implication of customary provisions, and I do not think that the meaning of a licence can be reached by considering the matter, as it were, in the air: its incidents have a long history behind them. What is the effect of that history or indeed what it is may well be in dispute, but whatever it is I do not think it can be neglected. The general proposition as to the rights conferred by a licence is to be found as early as 1673 in the judgment of Vaughan CJ in *Thomas* v *Sorrel* [(1673) Vaugh. 330, 351] in the words 'a dispensation or licence properly passeth no interest nor alters or transfer property in anything, but only makes an action lawful, which without it had been unlawful'...

The rule of law applicable to the licence granted to the respondents in the present case, is, I think, that prima facie licences are revocable: the circumstances of the case are (1) that this was a licence to use a theatre and (2) are to be found in the terms of the document itself ... If it were a tenancy I should interpret it as requiring no more than reasonable notice, and indeed, as rent is payable weekly, it might require only a week's notice. I cannot think that the rights acquired by means of a licence exceed those which a tenancy might give...[6]

The House, however, agreed that, since the respondent licensees claimed that the written agreement should be rectified, the case should be remitted back to the Chancery Division for final decision.

This then was the position as regards licences: they could not be 'interests in land' ('property'), but contractual licences were subject to the ordinary rules of contract law which could provide some protection to the licensee.

LICENCES AND EQUITY

With Lord Denning in the Court of Appeal, this wider protection grew out of equity.

---

6 Compare *Verrall* v *Great Yarmouth Borough Council* [1981] 1 QB 202.

Errington v *Errington and Woods* [1952] 1 KB 290 (CA) Somervell, Denning and Hodson LJJ

A father bought a house partly on a mortgage for his son and daughter-in-law, and handed her the building society paying-in book, saying that the property would be hers, so she paid the mortgage from that time onwards. When he died, he left all his property to his widow. The son left his wife and moved in with the widow (his mother), and they tried to evict the daughter-in-law.

Lord Denning:

The father's promise was a unilateral contract – a promise of the house in return for their act of paying the instalments. It could not be revoked by him once the couple entered on performance of the act, but it would cease to bind him if they left it incomplete and unperformed, which they have not done. If that was the position during the father's lifetime, so it must be after his death...

[T]he couple were licensees, having a permissive occupation short of a tenancy, but with a contractual right, or at any rate, an equitable right to remain so long as they paid the instalments, which would grow into a good equitable title to the house itself as soon as the mortgage was repaid.

This decision was followed by a succession of cases in the High Court and Court of Appeal in which a number of licensees were protected from *any* revocation, by one (largely, equitable) means or another. These mechanisms included settled land's tenancy for life (*Binions* v *Evans* [1974] Ch 359), estoppel and constructive trusts (for example, *Inwards* v *Baker* [1965] 2 QB 29 and *Crabb* v *Arun District Council* [1976] Ch 179), and the principle of mutuality (for example, *Hopgood* v *Brown* [1955] 1 WLR 213 and *Ives* v *High* (above)).

By 1980 at least one judge was ready to express confusion and polite exasperation.

In Re Sharpe [1980] 1 WLR 219

An aged aunt provided money towards her nephew's home and business, and lived with him and his family. Unfortunately, he went bankrupt and the trustee in bankruptcy needed vacant possession of the property in order to repay the creditors. There was no intention that she should have an equitable interest in the property under a constructive or resulting trust, but:

Browne-Wilkinson J:

I turn then to the alternative claim that Mrs Johnson is entitled to something less than an aliquot share of the equity in the premises, namely the right to stay on the premises until the money she provided indirectly to acquire them has been repaid. This right is based upon the line of recent Court of Appeal decisions which has spelt out irrevocable licences from informal family arrangements, and in some cases characterised such licences as conferring some equity or equitable interest under a constructive trust. I do not think that the principles lying behind these decisions have yet been fully explored and on occasion it seems that such rights are found to exist simply on the ground that to hold otherwise would be a hardship to the plaintiff. It appears that the principle is one akin to or an extension of a proprietary estoppel... Recent authorities have extended the doctrine and, in my judgment, it is now established that, if the parties have proceeded on a common assumption that the plaintiff is to enjoy a right to reside in a particular property and in reliance on that assumption the plaintiff has expended money or otherwise acted to his detriment, the defendant will not be allowed to go back on that common assumption and the court will imply an irrevocable licence or trust which will give effect to that common assumption...

Applying those principles to the present case, I have little doubt that as between the debtor on the one hand and Mrs Johnson on the other, the circumstances in which she provided the money by way of loan in order to enable the premises to be bought do give rise to some right in Mrs Johnson. It is clear that she only loaned the money as part of a wider scheme, an essential feature of which was that she was to make her home in the property ... there is no reason why one should not imply an intention that she should have the right to live there until her loan is repaid...

Are rights of the kind spelt out in the cases I have referred to merely contractual licences or do they fetter the property and create some right over it? On the authorities as they stand, I think I am bound to hold that the rights under such an irrevocable licence bind the property itself in the hands of the trustee in bankruptcy ... Accordingly, in my judgment, it follows that the trustee in bankruptcy takes the property subject to Mrs Johnson's right to live there until she is repaid the moneys she provided to acquire it...

I reach this conclusion with some hesitation since I find the present state of the law very confused and difficult to fit in with established principles. I express the hope that in the near future the whole question can receive full consideration in the Court of Appeal so that, in order to do justice to the many thousands of people who never come into court at all but who wish to know with certainty what their proprietary rights are, the extent to which these irrevocable licences bind third parties may be defined with certainty. Doing justice to the litigant who actually appears in the court by the invention of new principles of law ought not to involve injustice to the other persons who are not litigants before the court but whose rights are fundamentally affected by the new principles.

Finally, I must reiterate that I am in no way deciding what are the rights of a purchaser from the trustee as against Mrs Johnson...

These questions were addressed by the Court of Appeal.

Ashburn Anstalt v WJ Arnold & Co [1988] 2 WLR 706 (CA) Fox, Neill and Bingham LJJ

Arnold had been sublessee of a shop, and when the then landlord wished to redevelop the site, they agreed a 'Licence' of the premises without any payment but subject to three months' notice by the licensor when he was ready to proceed with the rebuilding. When the redevelopment was completed, Arnold was to be offered a 21-year lease in the new premises. Later, Ashburn Anstalt bought the freehold and, although their purchase had been expressly subject to Arnold's rights, they sought to evict them.

The court held that this was in fact a lease rather than a licence[7] because the occupier was entitled to exclusive possession. Therefore, under s. 70(1)g), Land Registration Act 1925, Arnold had an overriding interest which bound Ashburn Anstalt. Nonetheless, the Court considered what the position would be if this were a contractual licence only. Would it, together with actual notice, be sufficient to bind a purchaser?

Fox LJ:

[There are no cases] in which a contractual licence is held to bind a third party in the absence of a finding that the third party took the land as a constructive trustee ... The constructive trust principle ... has been long established and has proved to be highly flexible in practice. It covers a wide variety of cases, from that of a trustee who makes a profit out of his trust or a stranger who knowingly deals with trust properties, to the many cases where the courts have held that a person who directly or indirectly contributes to the acquisition of a dwelling house purchased in the name of and conveyed to another has some beneficial interest in the property. The test, for present purposes, is whether the owner of the property has so conducted himself that it would be inequitable to allow him to deny the claimant an interest in the property... It is, we think, in every case a question of what is the reasonable inference from the known facts ... It is said that when a person sells land and stipulates that the sale should be 'subject to' a contractual licence, the court will impose a constructive trust on the purchaser to give effect to the licence... We do not feel able to accept that as a general proposition... The court will not impose a constructive trust unless it is satisfied that the conscience of the estate owner is affected... In matters relating to the title to land, certainty is of prime importance. We do not think it desirable that constructive trusts of land should be imposed in reliance on inferences from slender material. In our opinion the available evidence in the present case is insufficient.

Fox LJ's concluding statements, about certainty and the need for strong evidence prior to the imposition of a constructive trust, are supported by Court of Appeal judgments in the following case. The court is loathe to provide too strong a protection to the licensee:

Matharu v *Matharu* (1994) *The Independent,* May 18 (CA), Dillon, Hirst, Roch LJJ

Mr Matharu bought a property with a mortgage. His son lived in the house for many years with his wife, Mrs Matharu. The son made improvements and alterations to the property and paid the mortgage instalments. The marriage broke

---

7 Note that *Ashburn Anstalt* has since been overruled by *Prudential Assurance Co Ltd* v *London Residuary Body* (see Chapter 4, p. 81).

down in 1990 and the son died in 1991. One year later Mr Matharu demanded possession of the property from Mrs Matharu. The trial judge dismissed Mr Matharu's claim and held that the defendant had a beneficial interest in the property as a result of her husband's expenditure upon it. The plaintiff appealed:

Lord Justice Roch said that the judge found that there was a proprietary estoppel of which the defendant was entitled to take advantage. The basis of proprietary estoppel was the interposition of equity to mitigate the rigours of strict law. It would prevent a person from insisting on his strict legal rights where it would be inequitable for him to do so having regard to the dealing which had taken place between the parties...

The defendant was able to satisfy each of [the requirements for estoppel][8] ... The defendant had an equity which defeated the plaintiff's claim for possession. The plaintiff created and encouraged the defendant's mistaken understanding of the basis on which she and her husband occupied the property and her belief that it was her husband's property.

However, his lordship disagreed with the judge's finding that the defendant had a beneficial interest in the property owing to the proprietary estoppel. What had been created was a licence for the defendant to remain in the house for her life or such shorter period as she might decide. To give effect to the equity the claim for possession would be refused on the terms that the defendant be responsible for outgoings on the property and keep the premises in good decorative repair...

Lord Justice Dillon, dissenting, said that the mere fact that no steps were taken to evict the defendant until 1992 did not give rise to any equity or right or legitimate expectation in the defendant that she would be allowed to live in the property for the rest of her life. His lordship found it repugnant that the plaintiff should be seeking to evict his widowed daughter-in-law and grandchildren but that was not enough *per se* to render the plaintiff's conduct so unconscionable in the eyes of equity as to entitle the court to refuse him possession. A possession order should be made.

Similar caution is shown by the courts when it is compensation by way of proprietary estoppel, rather than any interest in land itself, which is sought:

Baker v *Baker and Baker* (1993) 25 HLR 408 (CA), Dillon, Beldam, Roch LJJ

Mr Edward Baker, an elderly man, made an arrangement with his son and daughter-in-law – Mr and Mrs Baker – to enable them to purchase a home for their family. Mr Edward Baker paid £33,950 towards the purchase price (the balance being raised on a mortgage by Mr and Mrs Baker) and in return he was promised a bedsitting room rent-free in the house for the rest of his life. The purchase was duly made but the arrangement came to an abrupt end when Mr Baker made the unfounded accusation that his father had sexually molested his

---

8 See *Walton* v *Walton*, Chapter 2, p. 54.

grandchild. Mr Edward Baker left the property and was eventually housed in council accommodation by Plymouth City Council. The trial judge found for Mr Edward Baker on grounds of estoppel and awarded him £33,950 with interest. Mr and Mrs Baker appealed against the level of compensation:

Dillon LJ:

...The general rule is stated in *Snell's Equity*, 29th Edition, at p. 576 as follows:

> 'The extent of the equity is to have made good, so far as may fairly be done between the parties, the expectations of A which O has encouraged. A's expectation or belief is the maximum extent of the equity.'

...In the present case the greatest interest in the property that the parties envisaged Mr Edward Baker having was the right, living as part of the family, to occupy the granny room rent-free for the rest of his life...

What he was deprived of was that right – and no more – as from 13 June 1988, when owing to a false accusation he had to leave 32, Rowley Road. Therefore, what he is entitled to in satisfaction of that equity should not, in my judgment, be more than the value of that right as at 13 June 1988, with interest from that date.

That approach ... is consistent, in my judgment, with a telling phrase used by Scarman LJ in *Crabb* v *Arun District Council* [1976] 1 Ch 179 ... where, referring to the extent of the equity, he said it should be 'the minimum to do justice to the plaintiff'.

Dodsworth v *Dodsworth* [(1973) 227 EG 1117] also shows that in deciding how such an equity should be satisfied so as to do justice to the plaintiffs the court must take into account the circumstances of the defendant, so as not to produce an order which would be oppressive to the defendant...

...the gift in the present case was directed to achieving two aims – the provision of a family home for Mr and Mrs Peter Baker and their children, as well as the rent-free occupation of the granny room for life by Mr Edward Baker ... the correct appreciation is, in my judgment, that what Mr Edward Baker has lost is not the whole £33,950 but merely the right to rent-free occupation of the granny room in a family home from 13 June 1988, for the rest of his life ... The judge's award was therefore excessive and wrong in principle and I would set it aside ... We do not, in my judgment, have the necessary material to make an informed assessment of the amount that should be paid; any figure I put forward would be a mere guess, based on a feeling that the amount should not be large because of the rent-free accommodation Mr Edward Baker now has.

Roch LJ:

The questions which should be asked and answered are those set out by Scarman LJ ... in *Crabb* v *Arun District Council* ... 'What is the extent of the equity?' And when that has been determined, 'What is the relief appropriate to satisfy the equity in the circumstances which have arisen?' On this last question, the courts adopt an approach which is flexible but at the same time cautious in the giving of relief...

...what is the extent of the equity? ... the plaintiff intended that part of the money was to be the first defendant's 'inheritance' and he intended that the defendants were to be the owners of the house and to enjoy the whole of the property without encumbrance in favour of his estate on his death. None of the parties to the arrangement contemplated that the plaintiff's enjoyment of the property would be commensurate with his contribution to the purchase price of the house...

...what is the relief appropriate to satisfy the equity...? The starting point, in my judgment, must be an assessment of the value of the occupation of the room and the other incidents of the plaintiff's equity, in the light of the plaintiff's life expectancy. The fact that the plaintiff now has suitable accommodation where he has good neighbours and is very happy should not deprive him of relief, but is a factor which should be taken into account by the court in seeking the minimum equity to do justice in this case...

There is then the question whether the court should take into account the fact that the plaintiff's present accommodation is paid for by the local authority under a housing benefit scheme and is therefore 'rent-free' as far as the plaintiff is concerned ... this could become a factor when answering the last of the ... questions posed by Scarman LJ because the task of the court here is not to assess loss as though it were awarding damages, but to maintain a more flexible approach designed to achieve justice between the parties ... In that exercise the court must bear in mind the needs of the plaintiff and the capacity of the defendants to pay compensation ... I too would order that the case goes back to the judge.

THE FUTURE

J.F. Garner 'Land Law 1900–1992' (1992) *NLJ* 785

Fundamentally ... the law of real property remains as it has been known for centuries. Although the Englishman's home may on occasion be assaulted by the compulsory acquisition powers of the local and central authorities, it remains his castle, provided he owns the fee simple, still guaranteed by s.1 of the 1925 Act.

Political governments come and go but, minor patchings to the legislation apart, the main principles of our old common law are strong enough to survive into the 21st century and, hopefully, beyond.[9]

J. Dewar 'Licences and Land Law: An Alternative View' 49 *MLR* (1986) 741

Licences in relation to land have been a fruitful source of academic debate for over 30 years, and recent events have caused the debate to take on a new and vigorous lease of life. Successive protagonists each claim to have discovered a more convincing rationalisation of the existing law, and although differences of viewpoint exist within the framework of this discussion, they share one crucial feature in common – an assumption of the importance of the quest for conceptual answers to conceptual questions. Amongst these, two questions stand out as the

---

9 Compare J.A. Greed (1993) NLJ 628.

most controversial: first, do licences bind third parties, and secondly, can licences be accommodated within existing concepts, or are new ones needed?...

I shall argue that in attempting to reduce the complexity of the law to a level acceptable for judicial consumption, the way in which the courts have developed the licence as a technique of dispute-settlement has been obscured while the significance of the licence has been systematically underplayed and discussed in the light of only a limited range of 'policy' issues. In short, the debate is characterised by what Robert Gordon has termed 'Cartesianism' – that is, 'the intellectual strategy of constructing highly simplified models of social reality for the sake of analytic rigour and elegance' ['Historicism in Legal Scholarship' 90 *Yale L J* (1981) 1017, 1026]...

Dewar uses the term 'conceptual formalism' to describe the way in which the debate has progressed amongst academic writers: 'the view that either judges *do* or *ought to*, decide cases according to a limited range of pre-ordained conceptual categories; that the categories have distinguishable features and consequences, and that it is the task of the judge to determine whether the differing conceptual requirements are satisfied, and to allow the result to be dictated accordingly.'

The comparative novelty of the licence does not of itself explain why it is so hotly debated. I will argue that the licence poses a threat of considerable proportions not only to the conceptual orderliness of land law, but to the very values of the enterprise of academic land law as traditionally understood. Conceptual formalism is part of an attempt to stave off that threat...

He identifies two features of the modern cases which are overlooked by other writers. The first is the value judgments which 'seem to be inevitable concomitants of an increasingly discretionary law of licences'. The second is that 'licences cannot be regarded as merely subverting formal requirements'. He concludes therefore that licences are resulting in:

... a different form of property right, ie, the personal right of access to property. This represents a shift away from the notion of property as a freely assignable right of exclusion in relation to the use or benefit of something which MacPherson has argued was associated with the rise in the seventeenth and eighteenth centuries of industrial capitalism, and which is the form to which the vast majority of interests in land correspond...

I would suggest that licences, far from being orthodox categories of interest in land, are consistent with this evolutionary notion of property, and constitute a unique (and controversial) category of rights over land...

[T]he case for conceptual formalism has been ... on the ... basis of the need for certainty in land transactions. The best example of this comes from Browne-Wilkinson J in *Re Sharpe* ... This is an important point and bears examination. In essence, it is the argument that certainty in law is a virtue since it enables people to plan ahead on the basis of legally protected expectations, and that by exercising what looks like an *ad hoc* remedial jurisdiction, the courts are making this impossible. Yet it is worth pointing out that the uncertainty that has arisen has been in a particular context, the 'family' context... Indeed, it seems to have been precisely because family members do not hammer out their position in advance that the 'remedial' nature of the law arose in the first place. Further, the rules concerning licences and estoppels are no more and no less certain than, for example, the guidelines to divorce courts concerning the distribution of family property on divorce, or the use and occupation of the matrimonial home during marriage, yet the fact of uncertainty *itself* has rarely been advanced as a criticism of this legislation; and there remains a range of legal devices geared to planning in a family context which continues unaffected.

The only remaining argument, then, in favour of the certainty provided by conceptual formalism is that it clarifies the position of 'third parties', ie, purchasers, mortgagors, creditors and so on. If indeed this is the case, and the primacy attached by conceptual formalists to the importance of ascertaining beyond doubt the impact of licences on third parties suggests that it is, then we may regard it as open to challenge. The reason for this is that the stress on the importance of 'third parties' suggests a view of land law, and of the academic land law enterprise, that is primarily geared towards promoting the exchange of land (whether on conveyance, mortgage or bankruptcy) since it is only in the context of such exchanges that the third party issues become relevant. The view that land is an important resource in the satisfaction of basic human needs, and that the law plays an important role in the distribution and protection of that resource (only partly through exchange) is not considered to be a part of this enterprise – and yet it is an equally valid way of describing what land law is 'about'...

The 'third party' point deserves closer attention, however, and it is worth revealing at this point a further crucial premise of conceptual formalism. This is that 'free alienability of land' (the assumed aim) requires, both as a necessary and sufficient condition, a *substantive* land law structure of impeccable orderliness. This explains the quest to accommodate the licence within conventional land law concepts...

[U]nless 'co-owners' (ie, including licensees) are in disagreement over whether or not to sell, the most 'vulnerable' category of 'third party' is the institutional lender, particularly those lending on second mortgage; yet, even here, it now seems possible to adopt the simple expedient of ensuring that such rights never take priority over the interests of a mortgagee. In other words, the assumption that conceptual tidiness is essential to promote the free transfer of land may be largely false; and to the extent that it may be true, the effect of its implementation would be to preserve the security of the interest of a selection of financial institutions. The degree of protection accorded to such interest should be openly discussed rather than covertly advanced through a particular form of conceptual debate.

Dewar's plea for an explicit debate on the conflicting interests of licensees (and other equitable claimants) as against third parties in the form of institutional lenders seems even more pressing since the cases of *Abbey National Building Society* v *Cann* and *City of London Building Society* v *Flegg*. It may be that we need not a 'new property' but a new way of deciding property questions, arising out of an overt recognition of all the functions of land law in society today.

Judicial recognition of the wider context as demonstrated in *Baker's* case perhaps marks the beginnings of such a new approach.

M.A. Glendon *The New Family and the New Property* (Butterworths: 1981)

In the past ... notions of property, families and law that bound people together over time as well as space not only existed in the world of ideas, but also animated long-lasting social orders. In art and literature for centuries, this sense of connection was expressed through the image of Homer's invisible golden chain linking the heavens and all the creatures of the earth together. Some believe that in today's world this continuity has come to an end ... This line of thought can seem especially convincing when one reflects on the heterogeneity and conflict within the global community and within certain countries.

Nonetheless, the cross-lighting we receive from the history of families, property and law afford some reassurance. It suggests that the world's reserves of values may indeed be greater than its supplies of fossil fuels, as well as more essential to survival... Furthermore, the older modes of behaviour and attitudes about families, property and law ... have not been merely latent; they have survived here and there. It is probable that this pattern of dormancy and random survival is more characteristic of the processes of social change than utter eclipse, for no mode of social organisation ... is complete...

Current changes in family behaviour, property and law, and ways of thinking about them, contain bewildering possibilities for good and ill, for renewal or deterioration.

B. Lopez *The Rediscovery of North America* (University Press of Kentucky: 1990)

How, then do we come to know the land, to discover what more may be there than merchantable timber, grazeable prairies, recoverable ores, damable water, netable fish? It is by looking at the land not as its possessor but as a companion. To achieve this, one must cultivate intimacy as with a human being...

It has been my privilege to travel, to see a lot of country, and in those travels I have learned of several ways to become intimate with the land, ways I try to practise. I remember a Nunamiut man at Anaktuvuk Pass in the Brooks Range in Alaska named Justus Mekiana. I was there working on a book and I asked him what he did when he went into a foreign landscape. He said, 'I listen'...

When we enter the landscape to learn something we are obligated, I think, to pay attention rather than constantly to pose questions. To approach the land as we would a person, by opening an intelligent conversation.

Appendix 1
Unregistered land

INTRODUCTION

As explained in Chapter 10, the unregistered land system is due to wither away as all land is now in an area of compulsory registration, and all titles must henceforth be registered on sale. Back in the 1920s, it may not have been envisaged that it would take so long to extend the title registration system, but:

[Lawyers] love and revere the mysteries which they have spent so much time in learning, and cannot bear the rude hand which would wipe away the cobwebs, in spinning which they have spent their zeal and their days for perhaps half a century. (Lord Brougham, quoted by S.R. Simpson in *Land Law and Registration* (Cambridge University Press: 1976), Book 1, p. 70.)

However, the unregistered land system is still important because:

1. when land is first registered, whether or not an interest is binding on the buyer may depend on the Land Charges Act 1972;
2. the old rules will still apply to other transactions in unregistered land, such as mortgages, where there is no sale.

In the simplest terms, the rule is that a legal purchaser, for value and in good faith, of unregistered land is bound by:

1. any legal interest (except a puisne mortgage); and
2. any interest which is registrable under the Land Charges Act, and is properly registered; and
3. any other interest which has not been overreached, and of which the purchaser has notice.

THE LAND CHARGES ACT

Registrable charges

Land Charges Act 1972

The register of land charges

2 (1) If a charge on or obligation affecting land falls into one of the classes described in this section, it may be registered in the register of land charges as a land charge of that class.

(a) A rent or annuity or principal money payable by instalments or otherwise, with or without interest, which is not a charge created by deed but is a charge upon land (other than a rate) created pursuant to the application of some person under the provisions of any Act of Parliament, for securing to any person either the money spent by him or the costs, charges and expenses incurred by him under the authority of an Act of Parliament; or

(b) a rent or annuity or principal money payable as mentioned in paragraph (a) above which is not a charge created by deed but is a charge upon land (other than a rate) created pursuant to the application of some person under any of the enactments mentioned in Schedule 2 to this Act.

(3) A class B land charge is a charge on land (not being a local land charge) of any of the kinds described in paragraph (a) of subsection (2) above, created otherwise than pursuant to the application of any person.

(4) A class C land charge is any of the following (not being a local land charge), namely –

(i)   a puisne mortgage;
(ii)   a limited owner's charge;
(iii) a general equitable charge;
(iv) an estate contract;

and for this purpose –

(i)   a puisne mortgage is a legal mortgage which is not protected by a deposit of documents relating to the legal estate affected;
(ii)   a limited owner's charge is an equitable charge acquired by a tenant for life or statutory owner under the Inheritance Tax Act 1984 or under any other statute by reason of the discharge by him of any inheritance tax or other liabilities and to which special priority is given by the statute;
(iii) a general equitable charge is any equitable charge which –
(a) is not secured by a deposit of documents relating to the legal estate affected; and
(b) does not arise or affect an interest arising under a trust for sale or a settlement; and
(c) is not a charge given by way of indemnity against rents equitably apportioned or charged exclusively on land in exoneration of other land and against the breach or non-observance of covenants or conditions; and
(d) is not included in any other class of land charge.

(iv) An estate contract is a contract by an estate owner or by a person entitled at the date of the contract to have a legal estate conveyed to him to convey or create a legal estate, including a contract conferring either expressly or by statutory implication a valid option to purchase, a right of pre-emption or other like right.

(5) A class D land charge is any of the following (not being a local land charge), namely –
  (i)   an inland revenue charge;
  (ii) a restrictive covenant;
  (iii) an equitable easement;[1]
and for this purpose –
  (i)   an inland revenue charge is a charge on land, being a charge acquired by the board under the Inheritance Act 1984;
  (ii) a restrictive covenant is a covenant or agreement (other than a covenant or agreement between a lessor and a lessee) restrictive of the user of land and entered into on or after 1st January 1926;
  (iii) an equitable easement is an easement, right or privilege over or affecting land created or arising on or after 1st January 1926, and being merely an equitable interest.

(6) A class E land charge is an annuity created before 1st January 1926 and not registered in the register of annuities.

(7) A class F land charge is a charge affecting any land by virtue of the Matrimonial Homes Act 1983.

(8) A charge or obligation created before 1st January 1926 can only be registered as a class B or a class C land charge if it is acquired under a conveyance made on or after that date...

Registration of land charges

3 (1) A land charge shall be registered in the name of the estate owner whose estate is intended to be affected.[2]

The definition of 'estate contract' (class C (iv)) has arisen in two cases recently:

Phillips v Mobil Oil Co Ltd [1989] 1 WLR 888 (CA) May, Parker and Nicholls LJJ

The oil company had a 25-year lease (from 1961) which included an option to renew for a further 25 years. The reversion was eventually sold to Phillips (who was also a sublessee of Mobil). When Mobil tried to renew the lease, Phillips claimed the option to renew was void for non-registration.

---

1 See, for example, *Huckvale* v *Aegean Hotels Ltd* (1989) 58 P&CR 163, p. 190 above.
2 See also p. 343.

Nicholls LJ:

From the ... wording[3] three points at least are clear. First, an agreement whereby A confers on B an option to buy A's land is within the statutory definition. This is so whether A owns the freehold or only a lease. In each event he is the owner of a legal estate in the land, and as such is an 'estate owner'. Second, if A and B enter into a contract whereby A agrees to grant and B agrees to take a lease, the contract is within the definition as 'a contract ... by an estate owner ... to ... create a legal estate'. Third, if A and B enter into an agreement whereby A confers on B an option to acquire a lease, that also falls within the definition as 'a contract conferring ... a valid option of purchase ... or any other like right', that do fall within the definition ... given that an option to buy a freehold or leasehold is within the definition and given that an agreement to grant a lease is also within the definition, a construction of the definition which would exclude the grant of an option to acquire a lease would be without rhyme or reason'.

None of the points I have so far mentioned was in dispute before us. Mr Poulton's erudite argument was that the position so far described does not obtain in one particular case, namely a renewal option contained in a lease. He accepted that if L grants to T a lease containing an option to buy the reversion, that option does fall within the statutory definition and is registrable even though it is contained in a lease. He submitted that the position is otherwise where L grants to T a lease containing an option to call for a further term...[4] In that case the option is not within the definition of an estate contract and is not registrable...

I do not find this line of argument furnishes a compelling reason for construing the statutory definition ... in the manner contended ... I look to the definition in vain for the words which achieve the result that the definition (a) embraces an option to buy the reversion even when contained in a lease and (b) embraces an agreement conferring an option to call for a lease but (c) does not embrace an option of the latter type when contained in a lease...

In the result, therefore, Mr Poulton's argument is based on the twin supports of context and legislative antecedents. The context relied on is the distinction already mentioned between covenants which run with the reversion and those which do not. I do not find in this a sufficiently clear indication of what Parliament must have intended...

[Regarding the legislative antecedents] I do not consider that what is revealed sheds any clear light, either way, on the point...

The court held therefore that the renewal option was registrable, and was consequently void for non-registration. (Since the new freeholder would inevitably have seen the lease, including the covenant in question, the fairness of this decision is questionable.)

---

3 Of s. 10, Land Charges Act 1925, which was identical to the present s. 2.
4 Because this is a covenant which touches and concerns the land and runs with the lease and the reversion.

Armstrong and Holmes Ltd v *Holmes* [1994] 1 All ER 827 (Ch D)

Judge Paul Baker QC:

The point is whether the contract for the sale of land which results from the exercise of an option has to be registered as an estate contract under the Land Charges Act 1972 to preserve priority, notwithstanding that the grant of the option itself had already been so registered as an estate contract...

The purpose of the Land Charges Act 1972 is to give notice of contracts creating interests in land. The original option created an equitable interest in land ... I do not see that interest being altered or superseded by some other and different interest on the exercise of the option, although no doubt the respective rights and obligations of the grantor and option-holder change.[5] If we look at the matter more practically, the exercise of the option does not add to the burden on the land. Indeed, it may diminish it, as the option-holder may exercise the option well within the option period but subsequently fail to complete so that rescission follows. In other words, a later potential purchaser from the grantor is sufficiently warned by the registration of the option and does not require the further registration of the contract of sale envisaged by the option.

The consequences of registration or non-registration

Law of Property Act 1925

Registration under the Land Charges Act 1925 to be notice

198   (1) The registration of any instrument or matter in any register kept under the Land Charges Act 1972 or any local land charges register shall be deemed to constitute actual notice of such instrument or matter, and of the fact of such registration, to all persons and for all purposes connected with the land affected, as from the date of registration or other prescribed date and so long as the registration continues in force.

Land Charges Act 1972

Effect of land charges and protection of purchasers

4   (5) A land charge of class B and a land charge of class C (other than an estate contract) created or arising on or after 1st January 1926 shall be void as against a purchaser of the land charged with it, or of any interest in such land, unless the land charge is registered in the appropriate register before the completion of the purchase.

(6) An estate contract and a land charge of class C created or entered into on or after 1st January 1926 shall be void as against a purchaser for money or money's worth (or, in the case of an inland revenue charge, a purchaser

---

5 Compare the ruling on formality in Chapter 2 at p. 47.

within the meaning of the Inheritance Tax Act 1984) of a legal estate in the land charged with it, unless the land charge is registered in the appropriate register before the completion of the purchase...

(8) A land charge of class F shall be void as against a purchaser of the land charged with it, or of any interest in such land, unless the land charge is registered in the appropriate register before the completion of the purchase.

Law of Property Act 1925

Restrictions on constructive notice

199   (1) A purchaser shall not be prejudicially affected by notice of –
        (i) an instrument or matter capable of registration under the provisions of the Land Charges Act 1925, or any enactment which it replaces, which is void or not enforceable as against him under that Act or enactment, by reason of the non-registration thereof...

The case which follows demonstrates the rigid interpretation which the House of Lords chose to adopt as the model for this Act:

Midland Bank Trust Co Ltd v *Green* [1981] AC 513 (HL)
Lord Wilberforce, Lord Edmund-Davies, Lord Fraser of Tullybelton, Lord Russell of Killowen, Lord Bridge of Harwich[6]

A son had an estate contract – a right to buy the farm he lived and worked on – from his father, but it was not registered. In the course of family life, the father decided to go back on his promise, and he sold the farm cheaply to his wife (the mother), intending to destroy the registered charge. The court of first instance held that the estate contract was void for non-registration, but the Court of Appeal reversed this. In the House of Lords:

Lord Wilberforce:

Thus the case appears to be a plain one. The 'estate contract', which by definition ... includes an option of purchase, was entered into after January 1, 1926; Evelyne [the mother] took an interest (in fee simple) in the land 'for valuable consideration' – so was a 'purchaser': she was a purchaser for money – namely £500: the option was not registered before the completion of the purchase. It is therefore void as against her.

In my opinion this appearance is also the reality. The case is plain: the Act is clear and definite. Intended as it was to provide a simple and understandable system for the protection of title to land, it should not be read down or glossed: to do so would destroy the usefulness of the Act. Any temptation to remould the Act

---

6 See also B. Green 97 LQR (1981) 518; C. Harpum (1981) CLJ 213.

to meet the facts of the present case, on the supposition that it is a hard one and that justice requires it, is, for me at least, removed by the consideration that the Act itself provides a simple and effective protection for persons in Geoffrey's position – viz. – by registration.

The respondents submitted two arguments as to the interpretation of section 13(2):[7] the one sought to introduce into it a requirement that the purchaser should be 'in good faith'; the other related to the words 'in money or money's worth'.

The argument as to good faith fell into three parts: first, that 'good faith' was something required of a 'purchaser' before 1926; secondly, that this requirement was preserved by the 1925 legislation and in particular by section 13(2). If these points could be made good, it would then have to be decided whether the purchaser (Evelyne) was in 'good faith' on the facts of the case...

My Lords, I recognise that the inquiring mind may put the question: why should there be an omission of the requirement of good faith in this particular context? I do not think there should be much doubt about the answer. Addition of a requirement that the purchaser should be in good faith would bring with it the necessity of inquiring into the purchaser's motives and state of mind. The present case is a good example of the difficulties which would exist. If the position was simply that the purchaser had notice of the option, and decided nevertheless to buy the land, relying on the absence of notification, nobody could contend that she would be lacking in good faith. She would merely be taking advantage of a situation, which the law has provided, and the addition of a profit motive could not create an absence of good faith. But suppose, and this is the respondent's argument, the purchaser's motive is to defeat the option, does this make any difference? Any advantage to oneself seems necessarily to involve a disadvantage for another: to make the validity of the purchase depend upon which aspect of the transaction was prevalent in the purchaser's mind seems to create distinctions equally difficult to analyse in law as to establish in fact: avarice and malice may be distinct sins, but in human conduct they are liable to be intertwined. The problem becomes even more acute if one supposes a mixture of motives. Suppose – and this may not be far from the truth – that the purchaser's motives were in part to take the farm from Geoffrey, and in part to distribute it between Geoffrey and his brothers and sister, but not at all to obtain any benefit for herself, is this acting in 'good faith' or not? Should family feeling be denied a protection afforded to simple greed? To eliminate the necessity for inquiries of this kind may well have been part of the legislative intention. Certainly there is here no argument for departing – violently – from the wording of the Act ...

It is not fraud to rely on legal rights conveyed by Act of Parliament.[8]

My Lords, I can deal more shortly with the respondent's second argument. It relates to the consideration for the purchase. The argument is that the protection of ... the Act does not extend to a purchaser who has provided only a nominal consideration and that £500 is nominal. A variation of this was the argument accepted in the Court of Appeal that the consideration must be 'adequate' – an expression of transparent difficulty. The answer to both contentions lies in the language of the subsection. The word 'purchaser' by definition ... means one who

---

7 Now s. 4(6) of the 1972 Act.
8 Compare the *Lyus* and *Peffer* cases in Chapter 10, pp. 312 and 313.

provides valuable consideration – a term of art which precludes any inquiry as to adequacy... There is nothing here [in the Act] which suggests, or admits of, the introduction of a further requirement that the money must not be nominal...

This conclusion makes it unnecessary to determine whether £500 is a nominal sum of money or not. But I must say that for my part I should have great difficulty in so holding. 'Nominal consideration' and a 'nominal sum' in the law appear to me, as terms of art, to refer to a sum or consideration which can be mentioned as consideration but is not necessarily paid. To equate 'nominal' with 'inadequate' or even 'grossly inadequate' would embark the law upon inquiries which I cannot think were contemplated by Parliament.

The son's unregistered estate contract was therefore destroyed by the sale to his mother. (However, the father's representative was liable for breach of contract, and the son's estate also sued his parents' estates for conspiracy and his lawyer for negligence in failing to register the land charge.)

Comment

H.W.R. Wade 'Land Charge Registration Reviewed' *Camb LJ* (1956) 216

Certain other criticisms of the scheme of 1925 may be ventured at this point... One important question is whether it is right to exempt a purchaser from a registrable but unregistered charge when he takes with actual notice of it. The policy of 1925 was to abandon the equitable principle of notice in favour of the mechanical principle of registration. This was a shift from a moral to an amoral basis. Its justification was that the doctrines of constructive and imputed notice had been overrefined, 'to such an extent that it had become dangerous to employ in the purchase a solicitor of good practice and reputation' [Jessel MR in *Greaves* v *Tofield* [1880] 14 Ch D 563, 565]. But those difficulties could be avoided without the defiance of ethics which occurs when a purchaser with *actual* notice is allowed to disregard a third party's rights. This is putting an unreasonable penalty on the venial fault of non-registration. Under earlier Registration Acts the courts always struggled to reconcile them with the spirit of equity, even to the extent of holding a deed made 'void against a subsequent purchaser' to be valid against a purchaser with *constructive* notice... A similar interpretation was given to the father of all registration acts, the Statute of Enrolments, 1535. Between the two extremes of making all notice relevant, or all notice irrelevant, lies the middle road of making actual notice relevant, but not constructive notice. The benefits of registration can be obtained, and unconscionable results also avoided, by providing that an unregistered charge shall be void against a purchaser provided that he or his agent (acting as such and in the same transaction) had not actual notice of it.

But there is one case where even constructive notice ought to be respected: where the owner of the charge is in possession of the land. The 1925 legislation has destroyed much of the protection which used to be given, and rightly, to equitable owners in possession. They can, it is true, protect themselves by registration. But in practice they will often fail to register, quite excusably, and it is unrealistic to maintain that their position has not been gravely weakened. Take the case of a tenant who is let into possession under an agreement for a lease. Under the old law he was safe, for no later purchaser could secure the legal estate from the landlord without at least constructive notice of the tenant's interest. But today, unless he registers an estate contract, the tenant will be defeated by any later purchaser of the legal estate. [*Hollington Brothers Ltd* v *Rhodes* [1951] 2 All ER 578.] It is safe to guess that very few people in such a position register their interests, bearing in mind, as already noted, that solicitors commonly do not register estate contracts. The anomaly is all the more glaring when compared with the rules for land with registered title. Under the Land Registration Act, 1925, all purchasers are bound by overriding interests, and overriding interests include 'the rights of every person in actual occupation of the land or in receipt of the rents and profits thereof, save where inquiry is made of such person and the rights are not disclosed' [s. 70(1)(g)]... The rule for registered land is much more reasonable, for possession is the strongest possible title to security. Unfortunately, section 14 of the Law of Property Act, 1925,[9] which is a saving for interests of persons in possession is too restricted in its effect to be of help[10] ... A learned Lord Justice of Appeal has indeed expressed the opinion that it will avail against non-registration [Denning LJ in *Bendall* v *Mcwhirter* [1952] 2 QB 466, 483; criticised by R.E. Megarry in 68 *LQR* (1952) 385], but in the face of the express terms of the legislation he would be a bold spirit indeed who would rely upon it. For more timorous souls the law must be taken as it appears to stand in the Acts.

OVERREACHING

If an interest is capable of being overreached, it will not bind a purchaser who conforms to the requirements of s. 2, Law of Property Act 1925. If a purchaser does not so conform, however, that person will be bound only if he or she had notice of the equitable interest.

THE DOCTRINE OF NOTICE

As shown earlier (Chapter 10) a bona fide purchaser of the legal estate for value in unregistered land is only bound by an equitable interest of which she has notice, actual, imputed or constructive (see *Hunt* v *Luck* [1901] on p. 290). The following case demonstrates this rule, and also illustrates some of the problems that can arise generally concerning whether or not a person is 'occupying land'.

---

9 See *Flegg*, Chapter 10, for an interpretation of s. 14, p. 293.
10 Because s. 14 applies only to Part 1 of the Law of Property Act 1925 which is not material to the Land Charges Act.

Kingsnorth Trust Ltd v *Tizard* [1986] 2 All ER 54[11]

Mr Tizard was the sole legal owner of the family home, and he and his wife shared the beneficial ownership. The marriage broke down so Mrs Tizard moved out to a nearby house, but looked after the children daily at the family home, and slept there when he was away. He mortgaged the house and left for America. The bank therefore tried to repossess the house in order to get its money back but Mrs Tizard argued that, since she was in occupation, the mortgagee had (through its agent) constructive notice of her equitable interest.

John Finlay QC:

Mrs Tizard was, in my judgment, in occupation of Willowdown notwithstanding that Mr Tizard was living there also; and notwithstanding the fact that on numerous occasions she slept elsewhere. The 'physical presence' to which Lord Wilberforce refers [in *Williams & Glyn's Bank Ltd* v *Boland* [1981]] does not connote continuous and uninterrupted presence; such a notion would be absurd. Nor, indeed, do I consider that the requisite 'presence' is negatived by regular and repeated absence. I find that Mrs Tizard was in Willowdown virtually every day for some part of the day, her life and activities were based on her presence, interrupted though it was, in Willowdown.

The agent for the mortgagee had known that Mr Tizard was married, but had failed to make reasonable inquiries about his wife. Therefore, it was held that the mortgagee had constructive notice of, and was bound by, her interest in the land.

The Prudent Purchaser

---

11 See also M.P. Thompson 50 Conv (1986) 283.

Appendix 2
A conveyance of land

Below is an example of a deed or a conveyance used to transfer legal title to unregistered land. This document also illustrates many of the issues with which land law deals.

THIS CONVEYANCE is made the first day of January One thousand nine hundred and ninety two BETWEEN PATRICIA BERWICK of Frog Hollow near Barking in the County of Essex (hereinafter called 'the Vendor') of the one part and SHARON ANN SENNER of Longbridge House Barking in the County of Essex (hereinafter called 'the Purchaser') of the other part

1. The Vendor is seised of the property hereby conveyed subject to the covenants and stipulations hereinafter mentioned but otherwise free from encumbrances.

2. By a contract dated 19th September 1991 the Vendor has agreed with the Purchaser for the sale to her for TWO HUNDRED AND FIFTY THOUSAND POUNDS (£250,000.00) of the fee simple of the property hereby conveyed free from encumbrances.

3. NOW THIS DEED in consideration of the sum of TWO HUNDRED AND FIFTY THOUSAND POUNDS (£250,000.00) paid by the Purchaser to the Vendor (the receipt of which sum the Vendor hereby acknowledges) WITNESSETH as follows:–

1. The Vendor as Beneficial Owner hereby conveys unto the Purchaser ALL the several pieces or parcels of land at Frog Hollow in the County of Essex as the same is more particularly shown on Plan No. 1 annexed hereto and thereon coloured blue TO HOLD the same unto the Purchaser in fee simple SUBJECT TO the covenants and stipulations referred to in a conveyance of 7th October 1960 and made between Phillip Smith of the one part and Jane Agu of the other part and the agreements declarations exceptions and reservations hereinafter contained.

2. The Purchaser hereby covenants with the Vendor that she shall at all times hereafter duly perform and observe the said covenants and stipulations and shall keep the Vendor and her personal representatives effectually indemnified against all actions proceedings costs claims and demands whatsoever in respect of the said covenants and stipulations or any of them so far as they relate to the property hereby conveyed.

3.   (i) IT IS HEREBY MUTUALLY AGREED AND DECLARED that
(a) the Purchaser shall not by virtue of this conveyance become entitled to any easement or right of light or air which would in any way restrict the free user by the Vendor or the persons deriving title under her of any adjoining or neighbouring land for building or other purposes

(b) where the boundary is along the line of an external wall of a building upon the adjoining land retained by the Vendor such wall and any overhanging gutter attached thereto shall remain the property of the Vendor and the Purchasers shall have no rights in respect thereof

(c) the expressions 'Vendor' and 'Purchaser' shall where the context permits or requires mean and include their respective successors in title

(d) the liability under any covenant given by the Vendor and the Purchaser by this conveyance shall cease upon parting with all interest in the property thereby affected provided that the successor of the Vendor and the Purchaser shall in every case give a covenant to comply with such covenant

(ii) The Purchaser hereby covenants with the Vendor for the benefit of the Vendors adjoining property that the Purchaser shall not make any additions to the drainage to the property hereby conveyed which connects to the cesspool referred to in the next subclause.

(iii) There is excepted and reserved out of the Conveyance unto the Vendor right in common with the Purchaser for the passage and running of water and soil through the drains or pipes leading from the Vendors adjoining property into the cesspool situate on the land hereby conveyed the approximate position of which is marked by the letter X on the Plan No. 2 attached hereto subject to the Vendor observing and performing the following covenant:–

The Vendor for herself and her successors in title HEREBY COVENANTS with the Purchaser for the benefit of the Yellow Land

(a) not to permit any parts of the property known as Frog Hollow to be drained into the cesspool at the point marked X on the said plan which are not at the date hereof drained into such cesspool

(b) to pay on demand one-half of the cost and expense incurred by the Purchaser and her successors in title as aforesaid in inspecting repairing maintaining renewing the said cesspool Provided that there shall be no liability upon the Vendor after she shall have parted with all her interest in the property known as Frog Hollow Provided that the said right for the passage and running of water and soil as aforesaid shall cease upon the Vendor or her successors in title failing to make payment after demand for 30 days.

(iv) For the benefit and protection of the Vendors adjoining property the Purchaser hereby covenants with the owner and occupier for the time being of such property not to carry on upon the property hereby conveyed or any part thereof the trade business or activity which involves any or all of the following: namely Pig Farming Poultry Farming Dog Kennels Cattery Metal Scrapyards Caravan Sites the Storage or Repair of Vehicles of any description for any Commercial Trade or Business except as ancillary to any business carried on at the property not in contravention to the foregoing.

(v) For the benefit of the property hereby conveyed the Vendor hereby covenants with the Purchaser owner or occupier for the time being of the property hereby conveyed not to carry on upon the property known as Frog Hollow shown coloured pink on the said Plan No. 1 or any part thereof the trade or business or activity which involves any or all of the following namely Pig Farming Poultry Farming Dog Kennels Cattery Metal Scrapyards Caravan Sites the Storage or Repair of Vehicles of any description for any Commercial Trade or Business except as ancillary to any business carried on at the property not in contravention to the foregoing.

4.   The Vendor hereby acknowledges the right of the Purchaser to the production of the documents mentioned in the Schedule hereto (possession of which is retained by the Vendor) and to delivery of copies thereof and hereby undertakes to the Purchaser the safe custody of the same.

IN WITNESS whereof the parties hereto have hereunto set their hands the day and year first above written.

THE SCHEDULE ABOVE REFERRED TO

7th October 1960   Conveyance.

Phillip Smith (1)

Jane Agu (2)

Appendix 3
A lease

Below follows an example of the standard form of long lease of a flat in a small building divided into two flats.

THIS LEASE is made on 2nd day of February 1992.

1. IN THIS LEASE:

(a) 'The Lessor' (which expression shall include the successors in title of the Lessor) is James Roy

(b) 'The Lessee' (which expression shall include the successors in title of the Lease) is Susanna Owen

(c) 'The Purchase Price' is £49,500

(d) 'The Property' is the lower flat known as 27B Cursley Avenue, Stanstead, Essex, edged red and the land edged blue on the attached plan

(e) 'The Reserved Rent' is:
 £50 for the first 25 years
 £50 for the next 25 years
 £50 for the next 25 years
 £50 for the last 24 years
payable in advance on 25 March every year (a proportionate part up to the next 25 March payable on the date of this Lease)

(f) 'The Other Flat' is the flat above/below the Property

2. THE RIGHTS included in this Lease are:

(a) The right to use existing and future drains and sewers gas and electricity and other wires and pipes serving the Property which pass through or beneath the Other Flat

(b) The right to enter upon any part of the Other Flat in order to connect into and subsequently inspect test repair renew any existing or future drains sewers electricity cables gas or other pipes or wires provided that the Lessee shall except in emergency give reasonable notice to the occupiers of the Other Flat and make good any damage resulting from his exercising this right

(c) All rights of protection and support now enjoyed by the Property

(d) The benefit of the stipulations and restrictions affecting the Property imposed or to be imposed by the Lease of the Other Flat

(e) The right in common with the owner or occupier of the Other Flat to pass to and from the Property over the area hatched black on the plan subject to the payment of one half of the cost of keeping the area clean and in good condition and repair and to maintain and have access to and from a dustbin in the position marked 'D' on the plan

3. THE RIGHTS in favour of the Lessor and the owner or occupier of the Other Flat and excepted from this Lease are:

(a) The right to use existing and future drains and sewers gas and electricity and other wires and pipes serving the Other Flat which pass through or beneath the Property

(b) The right to enter upon the Property in order to connect into and subsequently inspect test repair or renew any existing or future drains sewers electricity cables gas or other pipes or wires provided that the person exercising this right shall except in emergency give reasonable notice to the occupiers of the property and make good any damage resulting from his exercising this right

(c) All rights of protection and support now enjoyed by the Other Flat

(d) The burden of the stipulations and restrictions affecting the Property imposed or to be imposed by the lease of the Other Flat

(e) The right of the owner or occupier of the Other Flat or other person having similar right to pass to and from the other Flat over the area hatched black on the plan subject to the payment of one half of the cost of keeping the area clean and in good condition and to maintain and have access to and from a dustbin in the position marked 'D' on the plan

4. THE LESSOR acknowledges receipt of the Purchase Price from the Lessee and demises the Property to the Lessee for 99 years from the 2nd day of February 1992.

5. THE LESSEE covenants with the Lessor as follows:

(a) to pay the Reserved Rent out of the Property

(b) to pay and indemnify the Lessor against all outgoings payable in respect of the Property

(c) subject to clause 5(h) to keep the interior and the exterior of the Property in repair (and so yield it up to the Lessor on the determination of this Lease) and if necessary to rebuild any parts that require to be rebuilt and to paint the exterior parts normally painted every three years in a colour determined by the Lessor after discussion with the Lessee and the lessee of the other Flat and to carry out all this work in a proper manner. If the Lessee fails to comply with this covenant the Lessor may (but is not bound to) enter the Property and repair at the expense of the Lessee who shall repay such expenditure

(d) to allow the Lessor after giving reasonable notice to enter the Property twice a year in order to inspect its condition

(e) to maintain the fences indicated on the attached plan and marked within the area edged blue with the letter 'T'

(f) to register with the Lessor within 30 days of the event particulars of any change in the person liable for payment of the Reserved Rent

(g) to use the property exclusively as a private dwelling

(h) in common with the Lessee of the Other Flat or the Lessor (if possession of the Other Flat is retained by the Lessor) to keep in good repair and (as a separate covenant) to pay one half of the cost of repairing anything (including the roof, foundations, dividing joists amd beams, pipes, drains, walls and easements) used in common with the occupier of the Other Flat all which shall be party matters to be repaired at the equally shared expense of the Lessee and the Lessee of the Other Flat and also to pay a proportionate part of the cost of repairing anything used in common with adjoining occupiers other than the occupier of the Other Flat

(i) not to carry out alterations or additions to the Property nor erect any other buildings whether temporary or permanent

(j) to perform and observe such restrictions and covenants affecting the freehold as are still effective and relate to the Property and to indemnify the Lessor against any liability resulting from their breach or non-observance

(k) to ensure that nothing shall at any time be done on the Property that shall be a nuisance annoyance or injury to owners or occupiers of neighbouring property or that may invalidate any insurance on the Property

(l) to keep the Property comprehensively insured to the full current insurable value with an Insurance Company and through an agency nominated by the Lessor and if required by the Lessor to produce evidence that this covenant is being performed

(m) to use all insurance money received to make good the damage or destruction for which the money has been received and if that money shall not be sufficient to make up the deficiency from his own money

(n) to pay all expenses (including solicitor's and surveyor's fees) incurred by the Lessor incidental to the preparation and service of a notice under Section 146 of the Law of Property Act 1925 notwithstanding forfeiture is avoided otherwise than by relief granted by the Court

6.   THE LESSEE shall not be entitled to any rights of access of light or air to the Property which would interfere with the free use of any neighbouring land for building or any other purpose.

7.   IF AT ANY TIME the whole or any part of the Reserved Rent shall be unpaid for one month after becoming due or if there shall be a breach of any of the Lessee's covenants the Lessor shall be entitled (in addition to any other right) to repossess the whole or any part of the Property and this Lease shall then

immediately terminate but without affecting the Lessor's right to sue the Lessee for any breach of covenant

8.   THE LESSOR COVENANTS with the Lessee as follows:

(a) The Lessee shall have quiet enjoyment of the Property against the Lessor and all persons claiming title through the Lessor

(b) To impose in every lease to be granted of the Other Flat covenants and conditions similar to those imposed on the Lessee in this lease with such variations and additions as the Lessor considers necessary

(c) To perform in relation to the Other Flat so far as appropriate and until the Other Flat is transferred or let covenants similar to the Lessee's covenants contained in this lease

(d) To take such action (if so requested in writing by the Lessee and upon prior payment to the Lessor of a sum as security for costs which the Lessor considers reasonably adequate) as the Lessor's Surveyor considers necessary and practicable to enforce any covenant on the part of the Lessee of the Other Flat to repair or contribute to the cost of repair if the Surveyor considers that a breach of such covenant adversely affects the Property

9.   IF DURING THIS LEASE any dispute arises between the Lessee and the Lessee or occupier of the Other Flat relating to the Property or the Other Flat or any joint or party matter relating to either property or any repairs or contributions towards repairs or any alleged nuisance or annoyance then such dispute shall be referred (at the joint expense of the Lessee and the Lessee of the Other Flat) to the Lessor's Surveyor whose decision on the matter in question shall be final and binding on the Lessee

10.   WHERE THE LESSEE consists of more than one person then all Lessee's covenants expressed or implied in this Lease shall be deemed to be joint and several

Index